Walvoord: A Tribute

Walvoord: A Tribute

edited by

Donald K. Campbell

MOODY PRESS

CHICAGO

The assistance of others in preparing this volume is
gratefully acknowledged. Special thanks, however,
must go to Charles H. Dyer, assistant to the academic
dean of Dallas Theological Seminary, who gave me
excellent help in the work of editing the articles.

Library of Congress Cataloging in Publication Data
Main entry under title:

Walvoord, a tribute.

Includes bibliographical references.
1. Theology—Addresses, essays, lectures.
2. Walvoord, John F.—Addresses, essays, lectures.
I. Walvoord, John F.   II. Campbell, Donald K.
BR50.W33   230'.044   81-16888
ISBN 0-8024-9227-4   AACR2

Printed in the United States of America

Contents

Part I
BIBLICAL

Part II
THEOLOGICAL

Part III
MINISTRY AND COMMUNICATION

Biographical Introduction

Donald K. Campbell

Few men teach in one institution for more than forty years. Fewer still serve as a school's president for thirty years. The man in whose honor these essays are published, John F. Walvoord, has served the Lord at Dallas Theological Seminary for these significant spans of time. This *Festschrift* volume commemorates the thirtieth anniversary of his inauguration as the Seminary's second president.

The majority of the contributors to this volume are former students of Dr. Walvoord; most are also his colleagues on the faculty of Dallas Seminary. One indication of the high esteem in which Dr. Walvoord is held was the enthusiastic response of those who were asked to contribute articles. That others were not invited to participate is due only to the necessary space limitations imposed on any collection of essays published in a single volume.

Many factors have shaped Dr. Walvoord's life and ministry. Certainly his home was one. Prior to his birth his mother had

DONALD K. CAMPBELL (A.B., Wheaton College; Th.M., Th.D., Dallas Theological Seminary) is academic dean and professor of Bible exposition at Dallas Theological Seminary, Dallas, Texas.

been ill. The doctor felt it would be dangerous for her to bear a child, and he strongly recommended an abortion. However, she was convinced that the Lord wanted her to have the child, and her faith was rewarded. Not only did she give birth to a boy named John, but she regained her health and lived past the century mark.

John grew up in a Christ-centered home. Scripture reading and prayer were daily practices, and his parents actively served Christ in the church. His father, a public school teacher and administrator, was an elder in their church and served as superintendent of the Sunday school. At the age of nine John joined the First Presbyterian Church of Sheboygan, Wisconsin, and was awarded a Bible for having memorized the Shorter Catechism. When he was twelve he committed himself to daily Bible reading. But it was not until he was in high school that he realized he was attempting to earn his salvation by pleasing God with good works. Dr. William McCarrell, pastor of the Cicero Bible Church of Cicero, Illinois, presented the gospel in a Bible class young Walvoord attended; for the first time John understood the gospel message and trusted Christ alone for his salvation.

Patterns of discipline were deeply established in John Walvoord's life in high school, and he excelled in both athletics and academics. His college years at Wheaton College afforded further challenges. He applied himself wholeheartedly to his studies, to collegiate debate, and to track and football.

Having committed his life to the Lord for Christian service, John faced the important question of where to attend seminary. Princeton, his denominational school, seemed the logical preference; but as he prayed earnestly about the matter the Lord seemed to say, "Go to Dallas." When asked for advice, Wheaton's president, Dr. J. Oliver Buswell, recommended Dallas Theological Seminary. And so the crucial choice was made.

Arriving in Dallas in the fall of 1931, John Walvoord determined to gain the maximum benefit from his association with the eighty students and eight resident professors. Though he earned two degrees (Th.B. and Th.M.) in three years, he did not spend all of his time in the books. His seminary years were enriched by preaching in surrounding areas on weekends and by conducting vacation Bible schools (some forty in all) in many of the rural communities of Nebraska. During one school year he ministered in the small Texas town of Sublet. The grateful Sunday school superintendent presented John with a love offering for the year's ministry—three dollars and a few cents, raised by the sale of eggs at the Depression price of nine cents a dozen.

John's long range goal was to become a missionary. Feeling God's further direction during his final year in the master's program, he wrote to various mission boards for applications. His desire was to serve in either China or India, but he could not proceed—the Lord had different plans. As he launched into his doctoral studies at Dallas in 1934, the young graduate was called to the Rosen Heights Presbyterian Church in nearby Fort Worth, where he served as pastor for sixteen years. Then in 1936 more responsibility came. He was asked to fill temporarily the position of registrar at the Seminary, and in a short time he did much to organize and structure the office. President Lewis Sperry Chafer, in fact, asked him to stay on permanently; but John immediately declined saying his interests lay elsewhere. He candidated at churches, but offers were few and the peace of God was hard to find.

John was puzzled. He had tried to be a missionary. He had explored the possibility of a full-time pastorate. What did the Lord want him to do? Then he remembered. He had not really sought God's will about the registrar's job, and so he prayed that if the Lord wanted him to serve at the Seminary Dr. Chafer would be moved to offer him the position a second time. Ten days later it happened. Not only did Chafer offer him the position again, but he suggested that John be his assistant in theology, sharing teaching responsibilities in that department. The two men then prayed, and John was solemnly set apart to his new and important work. As Chafer shook young Walvoord's hand at the door he said, "Oh yes, your salary will be $100 a month." Reflecting on that moment years later in a chapel message, Dr. Walvoord said, "I really didn't pay any attention, because I knew that they couldn't afford $100 a month and I'd never get it. And I was right. Nevertheless, that was the beginning of my service on the faculty, something I certainly didn't seek, but a position in which I have been greatly blessed of God."

In 1945, after nine years of faculty service, Dr. Walvoord was asked to assume the role of assistant to the president, a position he held until the death of Dr. Chafer seven years later. On February 6, 1953, John F. Walvoord was inaugurated as the second president of Dallas Theological Seminary.

The many years of Dr. Walvoord's leadership have seen the Seminary rise from a small, struggling school to become one of the largest theological institutions in the country. The decade of the fifties witnessed the completion of Mosher Library and the introduction of the Department of Christian Education. The sixties saw the development of the Department of World Missions with an increased determination to reach the world for Christ. Accreditation of all degree programs by the Southern Association of Colleges and Schools, the regional accrediting agency, was achieved in 1969.

In the 1970s major campus expansion was undertaken to cope with the large tide of student applications. Two new, fully-equipped academic buildings were constructed, summer school was begun, and new degree programs were launched. With the completion of the Student Center in 1981 the main campus was finished. Central to all this achievement has been the man at the helm of the Seminary — a man who has been an indefatigable worker, a dynamic leader and, more than anything else, a faithful servant of Christ.

Dr. Walvoord's gifts and ministry have not been limited solely to the sphere of administration. He also has excelled as a teacher. When I came to Dallas in 1947, I was told by older students prior to the start of my first semester, "Be sure and take everything you can under Professor Walvoord." It was good advice. Some of my finest academic experiences were in his courses. His assignments were demanding and his tests were hard, but his careful scholarship and analytical skill made our studies in theology profitable indeed. Those of us who were privileged to spend so much time under the tutelage of Dr. Walvoord find it regrettable that his pressing tasks of administration have deprived later generations of Dallas students of more exposure to him in the classroom.

Dr. Walvoord's ministry has extended far beyond the Seminary campus. He is in constant demand as a Bible conference speaker in churches and conference centers both in this country and around the world. In fact, he maintains a travel schedule that many of his younger colleagues would not even attempt. Often his subject is biblical eschatology, his field of specialization and expertise.

Dr. Walvoord's classroom and pulpit ministries have been supplemented and expanded by means of the printed page. Serving as editor of *Bibliotheca Sacra*, the theological quarterly published by Dallas Seminary, he has worked to increase its circulation and has himself contributed 121 articles to that publication through 1981. He also has been a contributor to numerous published symposia and reference works, has written many articles in Christian magazines, and has served as a member of the revision committee for the *New Scofield Reference Bible*.

Several books written by Dr. Walvoord are widely used as textbooks. These include *The Holy Spirit, Jesus Christ Our Lord*, and *The Millennial Kingdom*. His other books are *The Return of the Lord; The Thessalonian Epistles; The Rapture Question; Israel in Prophecy; The Church in Prophecy; The Nations in Prophecy; The Revelation of Jesus Christ; Daniel; Philippians; The Holy Spirit at Work Today; Major Bible Themes; Armageddon, Oil, and the Middle East Crisis* (coauthor), *Matthew: Thy Kingdom Come; The Blessed Hope and the Tribulation; Inspiration and Interpretation* (editor); and *Truth for Today* (editor).

The titles of the writings indicate the emphasis of Dr. Walvoord's thought and teaching. He has been an ardent exponent of the premillennial and dispensational system of theology, but he has written with an irenic spirit so that those who disagree cannot charge him with a divisive bitterness. As a college debater he deplored the practice of trying to win a debate through deception or trickery, and he has refused to try to win theological arguments by misrepresentation or by overriding the real issue.

During Dr. Walvoord's years of service his most faithful supporter has been and continues to be his wife, Geraldine. In her special way she gives strength and assistance to her husband. Her support can be seen in the leadership she gives to Wives' Fellowship, a ministry to Dallas Seminary student wives. As adviser to this large and significant group she helps the leaders plan their weekly meetings and other special activities. She also finds time to assist other student wives personally as they adjust to life in Dallas as "book widows." From her own rich background as a pastor's wife she is able to help prepare the wives for a lifetime of effective ministry alongside their husbands.

Dr. Walvoord's love for and devotion to God, his family, and the Seminary are best reflected in his own words to students assembled in chapel. "What I covet for you is the same experience that I had — of discovering God's perfect will for your life. Nothing less, nothing more, nothing else. This is the place of supreme fulfillment, regardless of what it is. . . . May God grant that each one of us, as he spends his life, spend it exactly as God wants."

To President John F. Walvoord, a man who found God's will and performed it, this volume is presented as a tribute of esteem and deep gratitude.

Part I
Biblical

1

Application in Biblical Hermeneutics and Exposition

Roy B. Zuck

Is Bible Knowledge Enough?

Several years ago I passed by a partially constructed apartment building twice daily on my way to and from my place of employment. For some reason the construction work, once begun, had been discontinued. Many months later, however, the project was finally resumed and the building was completed.

Similarly many people, having begun the process of Bible study, fail to finish the task. Neglecting to *apply* the Scriptures to their lives makes their study of God's Word incomplete and deficient.

This short-circuited approach to the Bible reduces God's Word to a mere object or antique museum piece[1] to be examined by scientific inquiry, relegates Bible study to an academic exercise, and restricts the Scriptures to being only a sourcebook of information with little regard for its life-changing relevance.

Roy B. Zuck (A.B., Biola College; Th.M., Th.D., Dallas Theological Seminary; graduate study, Northern Illinois University and North Texas State University) is associate academic dean and associate professor of Bible exposition at Dallas Theological Seminary, Dallas, Texas.

15

Theoretical knowledge of the content of the Bible, while absolutely indispensable, does not in itself automatically guarantee spiritual development. More is needed—a responsive heart with a willingness to appropriate the truths of the Scriptures into one's own experience. As Sterrett has well stated, "The Bible has spiritual dimensions that can be grasped only when the will responds to what God says, not simply when the mind analyzes the language."[2]

This deficiency is one of the greatest problems in Christianity today. The popular home Bible class movement reveals that many people desire to acquire more Bible facts and to amass more scriptural knowledge. And yet many Christians with extensive comprehension of the truth of God are not putting that truth into action. They know more than they live, and that borders on hypocrisy.

Furthermore, when believers possess the truth without letting the truth possess them, non-Christians question the authenticity and value of Christianity. Elwell urges churches to "find ways to help people turn their religious beliefs into action," for, as he concludes, "the world needs to see life in action."[3] Without such a personal appropriation of the truth, the Christian life remains sterile and fruitless.

WHY DOES THIS PROBLEM EXIST?

Several factors may account for this problem of Christians' mastering the Book without the Book mastering them.

"APPLICATION WILL FOLLOW AUTOMATICALLY"

Failure to apply the truth is often caused by assuming that if one knows the meaning of the Scriptures, correct application will follow. Christian leaders often feel that their responsibility in expounding the Bible ends when the text is explained. They apparently believe that somehow their people, by knowing the content, will thereby act in accord with its standards and precepts. Consequently, application is missing from many Bible messages and from many lessons in Bible teaching.

This is a dangerous assumption, for the meaning of the Scriptures to its original audience may or may not be the same for today's audiences. The expositor must therefore determine how to transfer the meaning to current life. This involves answering several questions: Are the experiences and precepts that are explicated in a given Bible passage repeatable today? If not, why not? How does one determine whether they are universally applicable or limited to ancient cultures and conditions? To what extent is the Old Testament relevant for contemporary times? Do all biblical commands, promises, and examples have present-day relevance? How does one bridge the gaps that exist between the Bible and today, including the geographical, chronological, cultural, linguistic, and literary gaps?

Application, then, in Bible preaching and teaching and in personal Bible study involves determining how the relevance of a passage for hearers/readers today may or may not differ from its relevance for its original hearers/readers. Unless this is done, some rather unwarranted points of relevance may be taught. For example, should Christians today be stoned if they pick up sticks on the Sabbath (Num. 15:32-36)? Should Christians in church gatherings today give each other a holy kiss (Rom. 16:16; 1 Cor. 16:20; 2 Cor. 13:12; 1 Thess. 5:26; 1 Pet. 5:14)? Obviously the first of these has been abrogated by a dispensational change, and the second has been altered by a cultural difference.

"ONLY THE HEARER AND THE HOLY SPIRIT CAN APPLY THE BIBLE"

Some assume that because the Holy Spirit applies the truth a Bible teacher is incapable of applying it. Clines argues that "the aim of the expositor should be to lay bare the text so that it can apply itself to the listeners"[4] and that "to apply is the task of the hearer and of the Holy Spirit and not of the preacher-expositor."[5] He seeks to support this view in several ways.

First, "the expositor does not usually know how the text applies to each of his hearers, except perhaps in the most general way."[6] But would not at least a general kind of application help one's hearers sense the Scriptures' relevance? And should not an expositor seek to know his audience's needs?

Second, Clines suggests, "There is no such thing as the application of the text; each text is capable of manifold applications."[7] This is granted, but why should that mean the expositor can therefore eliminate application entirely?

Third, according to Clines, the expositor's "application and not the text is the message, for the application is the point at which the hearer is personally addressed."[8] This is an unfortunate confusing of terms. The *purpose* of the message—to "change lives in some specific way"[9]—differs from the message (the explication of the text) itself. Application does not replace the message of the text; it builds on it.

Fourth, Clines writes that if an expositor gives an application he should explain that it is not binding ("prescriptive," to use his term) on the individuals since that limits the ways the text can be used.[10] It is agreed that the specific applications made by an expositor do not carry divine authority as do the biblical texts. However, citing examples of spiritual relevance hardly limits that relevance. To say, "These are examples of how a text touches on today's living" is not the same as saying, "This is the only way this text touches on today's living."

Fifth, it is argued by Clines that application to contemporary issues should be avoided by the expositor because he probably does not know enough about those issues to make such a judgment.[11] Is this not like saying that if one does not know how to preach, he should not try or seek to find out how?

The notion that the Holy Spirit and not the Bible teacher applies the truth overlooks the several ways in which the Word *apply* may be used. *The expositor or teacher applies* in the sense that he points out ways (some, if not all) in which the passages may be applied. *The hearer applies* in the sense that he selects from those possible applications or others he thinks of and decides how and when to carry out that application and follows that with the actual doing of it. And *the Holy Spirit applies* because He prompts and enables the hearer to live out that truth in the area of his conduct where the truth is needed.[12]

"THE BIBLE IS ALREADY RELEVANT"

Several Christian leaders and laypersons deliberately avoid pointing out applications of the Scriptures because, they reason, the Bible is already relevant in itself. "The Word need not be *made* relevant because it *is* relevant," Greidanus asserts.[13] According to Veenhof, since "Scripture *is* applied" it is only necessary "to pass on its message in its 'applicatory' character."[14] Veenhof affirms that "the only application which the minister of the Word must make is the *choice of the text.*"[15]

Two observations may be made in response to this view. 1. It is agreed that the Bible is life-relevant. It confronts man in his areas of deepest need and meets his greatest problems. This will be discussed more later. 2. Seeing the relevance of the biblical text is not the same as pointing out how that passage may be applied or carried out specifically in one's life. Thus, if Greidanus, Veenhof, and others mean that one need not "apply" the Bible in the sense that he need not add a relevancy to the Scriptures that is already there, their view is acceptable. However, if they mean that no attempt should be made to suggest specific courses of action one may take in order to appropriate a biblical text to one's experience, then that, to me, is unacceptable. The latter view seems to be what Greidanus is suggesting for he says that the preacher "should not add a subjective application."[16]

WHAT THEN IS APPLICATION?

Application in Bible exposition (preaching or teaching) may be defined as the process of communicating the present-day relevance of a biblical text, specifying how that relevance may be translated into action, and inviting and urging the hearers to make that transference. Stated in another way, the application process involves communicating the Bible's relevance in both a general way and in a specific way, and then calling for a response.

In personal Bible study the application process is similar, but the difference is twofold: 1. Instead of a preacher or teacher stating the general and specific aspects of relevance, the student himself observes those points of relatedness. 2. Instead of a preacher or teacher inviting and urging his congregation or class to put into action the biblical truths, the student himself makes the decision to respond and actually carries out the truths in his experience.

In a congregation or class, application involves the communicator and the hearers. A preacher or teacher is thus a channel for motivating his people to respond, and it is their responsibility to transfer the truth to their experience as needed. On the other hand, in personal Bible study the student is responsible both for observing the life-relatedness of the scriptural material and for deciding how to apply it to his needs.

Many times the applicational relevance of a Bible passage is explicitly evident in the text itself. This is especially true in the New Testament epistles, in which commands are clearly relevant to all Christians. Other times, however (e.g., in Old Testament narratives), the relevance may be implicit, not explicit, and the relevance may need to be spelled out. (How this can be done will be discussed later.)

Greidanus suggests, however, that the latter is undesirable, that preaching is not to be dualistic in the sense that it contains explication *and* application.[17] Following Van Dijk, he prefers not to think of application as separate from exposition, and thus he calls preaching "the applicatory explication of God's Word."[18]

If Greidanus means by this that the exposition of a text is to include both meaning and relevance, then that is acceptable. However, if Greidanus means that implicit relevance is not to be made explicit, then that is unacceptable. And if he means to exclude stating how the audience can respond to the truth and if he means to exclude appealing for response, then that too is undesirable.

To exclude any of these aspects — general life-relevance, specific relevance, and action response — means that application is missing. Application in this essay may be thought of as *relevance* (both general and specific) *plus response*. This concept may be summarized by the equation, $R+R=A$.

WHY IS RELEVANCE-AND-RESPONSE APPLICATION ESSENTIAL?

Applying the Bible to life is an essential step in Bible study and exposition for five reasons.

THE NATURE OF THE SPIRITUAL LIFE

Growth in the spiritual life comes not merely from hearing but from hearing and doing. This is why James wrote, "But prove yourselves doers of the word, and not merely hearers who delude themselves" (James 1:22). If a person hears (or reads) the Bible and does nothing about its implications for his attitudes and conduct, he deceives himself into thinking he has fulfilled his obligations when actually he has not.

Whereas deception comes from not heeding the Word, blessing stems from obeying it. The "effectual doer . . . shall be blessed in what he does" (James 1:25). "If you know these things, you are blessed if you do them" (John 13:17).

The Bible emphasizes that head knowledge, although crucial to the spiritual life, is not enough. Continually, obedience is enjoined, development of the inner quality of life is encouraged, and outward conduct consistent with God's standards is commanded. The New Testament, for example, frequently encourages Christians to "walk" (conduct themselves) in a manner that is pleasing to God (Rom. 13:13; Gal. 5:16-25; Eph. 4:1; 5:2, 8; Phil. 3:16; Col. 1:10; 2:6; 4:5; 1 Thess. 2:12; 1 John 1:7; 2:6; 2 John 6; 3 John 4).

Those who "profess to know God" but who "by their deeds . . . deny Him" (Titus 1:16) are strongly condemned. Scriptural depth is measured by a demonstration of "good behavior . . . in the gentleness of wisdom" (James 3:13), not by the extent of one's knowledge of the Scriptures. That is why Ezra was determined (he "set his heart") not only "to study the law of the LORD," but also "to practice it" (Ezra 7:10).

The Christian is to grow, not merely to know (1 Pet. 2:2). Since he is God's "workmanship, created in Christ Jesus for good works" (Eph. 2:10), he is to be "zealous for good deeds" (Titus 2:14) and to "be careful to engage in good deeds" (Titus 3:8).

Those "good deeds" in the life of the Christian stem from an inner quality of life. "Spirituality," as Ramm explains, "is striving toward correct attitudes, spiritual graces, the fruit of the Spirit (Gal. 5:22-23)."[19]

Luther wrote that the Bible "is not merely to be repeated or known, but to be lived and felt."[20]

THE PURPOSE OF THE SCRIPTURES

The reason God has given the Scriptures is to change man's

basic nature, including His attitudes and actions, thus making him more Christ-like.

This purpose is spelled out in Paul's classic statement on the inspiration of the Scriptures. "All Scripture is inspired by God and profitable for teaching, for reproof, for correction, for training in righteousness; that the man of God may be adequate, equipped for every good work" (2 Tim. 3:16-17). The inspired Word teaches man the ways of God, rebukes him when he fails to heed those ways, restores him back to those ways, and gives him training (*paideia*, "child nurture") in righteous living. The ultimate result of these immediate purposes is that the believer (the "man of God") may be "adequate" and "equipped." Interestingly, these two words (*artios*, an adjective, and *exērtis-menos*, a participial adjective) are related and thus are close in meaning. Lenski suggests that the first word means "in fit shape or condition" and the second word means "altogether fit."[21] Each word occurs only here in the New Testament. In the Greek papyri the second word refers to a boat "supplied" with two oars and an oil-press in working order and "completely finished."[22]

The practical nature of the Bible is seen in that it convicts (Heb. 4:12-13), regenerates (2 Tim. 3:15; 1 Pet. 1:23), nurtures (1 Pet. 2:2), cleanses (Psalm 119:9; John 15:3; 17:17; Eph. 5:25-26), counsels and guides (Psalm 119:24, 105), prevents sin (Psalm 119:11), revives (Psalm 119:50, 88, 93, 107, 149, 154, 156), strengthens (Psalm 119:28, 116), gives wisdom (Psalm 119:98, 130, 169), delivers (Psalm 119:170), and helps (Psalm 119:175).

The Scriptures are called a fire, to consume false teaching, and a hammer, to shatter man's hard heart (Jer. 23:29); food, to nourish man's soul (Psalm 119:103; Jer. 15:16; 1 Cor. 3:2; Heb. 5:13-14; 1 Pet. 2:2); and a sword, for offense against Satan (Eph. 6:17; cf. Luke 4:4, 8, 12).

The psalmist, recognizing the life-related value of the Scriptures, used many words in Psalm 119 to describe his attitude toward them. Often those words are verbs, given variously in the indicative past, present, or future ("I delighted," "I delight," "I will delight") or in the imperative (e.g., "teach me Thy statutes," v. 12). Other times they are nouns (e.g., "Thy Law is my delight," v. 174). Sometimes those affirmations are given as a result of God's working in the psalmist's life; other times they are stated as means for obtaining God's blessing. These verbs include the following: *walk in* (v. 1); *observe* (vv. 2, 22, 33, 34, 56, 69, 100, 115, 129, 145); *keep* (vv. 4, 5, 8, 17, 34, 55, 57, 60, 63, 67, 88, 101, 106, 134, 146, 158, 167, 168); *do* (v. 166); *trust in* (v. 42); *seek* (vv. 45, 94, 155); *delight* (vv. 16, 24, 35, 47, 70, 77, 92, 143, 174); *meditate* (vv. 15, 23, 48, 78, 97, 99, 148); *rejoice* (vv. 14, 111, 162); *behold* (v. 18); *understand* (vv. 27, 100, 104, 130, 169); *wait for* (vv. 74, 81, 114, 147); *teach* (and desire to *learn*) (vv. 7, 12, 64, 68, 71, 73, 108, 124, 135, 171); *hope* (v. 49); *speak of* (v. 46); *remember* (and *not forget*) (vv. 16, 52, 61, 83, 93, 109, 141, 153, 176); *did not forsake* (or *turn aside, gone astray*) (vv. 87, 102, 110, 157); *believe* (v. 66); *consider* (v. 95); *esteem* (v. 128); *long for* (v. 40, 131); *love* (vv. 47, 48, 97, 113, 119, 127, 140, 159, 163, 165, 167); *incline* (v. 112); *stand in awe* (and *afraid*) (vv. 120, 161); *sing* (v. 172); and *choose* (v. 173). Those verses make it abundantly clear that the instructions in the Scriptures (variously called in Psalm 119 God's commandments, judgments, law, precepts, statutes, testimonies, ways, and word) are given to man so that he may respond to them with commitment, delight, and obedience.

The New Testament makes it clear that the Old Testament has relevance for the present church age. In Matthew 15:7 Christ applied Isaiah 29:13 to the Pharisees when He said, "You hypocrites, rightly did Isaiah prophesy of you." And to the Sadducees Jesus said that the words of Exodus 3:6 were "spoken to you" (Matt. 22:31). Paul argues that the words, "He reckoned it to him [Abraham] as righteousness" (Gen. 15:6) were written not only for Abraham's sake "but for our sake also" (Rom. 4:23-24). And in Romans 15:4 Paul wrote, "For whatever was written in earlier times was written for our instruction [*didaskalia*, "teaching"], that . . . we might have hope." Certain events in Israel's wilderness wanderings "happened as examples [*tupoi*] for us" (1 Cor. 10:6), and "these things happened to them as an example [*tupikōs*, "in an examplary way"], and they were written for our instruction [*nouthesia*, "nurture"] . . . ." (10:11).

It is evident that the purpose of the Bible is more than to give facts to satisfy one's curiosity. Its purpose is to change lives.

THE EFFICACY OF THE SCRIPTURES

Another reason for including application in Bible study and exposition is that the Bible—and the Bible alone—realistically and sufficiently meets man's deepest problems, longings, needs, and inadequacies. As Marshall puts it, "The Bible presents a picture of man and the human situation which rings true in the modern world and offers a diagnosis of our maladies which is profoundly true and relevant. Prescription for our maladies deserves equal respect."[23]

No other book provides the answers to man's need for deliverance from the penalty of sin, for spiritual progress, for daily victory over the power of sin, for guidance in personal relationships and conduct. "Scripture contains all the information which a man needs in order to set forth the way of salvation. Further, the Bible contains all the guidance which is needed for the continuous living of the Christian life."[24]

And the Bible speaks to people in all cultures, in all ages, and in all circumstances. As Schonkel wrote, "Holy Scripture is at once ancient and contemporary; incarnate in a particular time, it claims to speak to all generations; circumscribed in language and cultural perspective, it lays claim to universality."[25]

In all its pages the Bible shouts its relevance to man. How then can the Bible student or expositor neglect to relate the Scriptures and all their practicality to man's needs?

THE NATURE OF LEARNING

Application is necessary because without it true learning has not taken place. This writer has discussed this point elsewhere.

> Pupils have not necessarily learned if there is only a mental apprehension of truth without an actual experiencing of the truth, appropriated to their lives by the Holy Spirit. Facts not perceived, skills taught in isolation, and verbalisms presented to passive, unmotivated pupils fall short of effecting genuine spiritual growth. Learning is the process in which a pupil modifies his behavior, through the Spirit's enabling, to conform more to the will of God and the image of Christ.[26]

THE OBJECTIVE OF PREACHING AND TEACHING

Effective preaching and teaching has as its objective the

changing of lives and the alteration of undesirable attitudes and behavior into desirable ones. This calls for proper attention to application.

Football teams do not play merely for the sake of throwing and catching the ball. They play in order to reach the goal line, to make touchdowns, to win the game. Likewise, effective Bible communicators drive toward a goal. Each message moves toward a climax, builds toward a verdict, calls for a "signing on the dotted line."

Educators commonly refer to three kinds of desirable behavioral changes: cognitive (knowledge), affective (feeling and attitude), and psychomotor (doing). Stated generally, teachers want three things to happen in their students: 1. that they will increase in what they know; 2. that they will improve in how they feel toward God, others, and themselves; and 3. that they will develop helpful skills, practices, and habits. Ford has divided the first of these three learning outcomes into two parts — "knowledge" and "understanding" (or "insight") — and calls the others "attitudes" and "skills."[27]

To enable the preacher or teacher to move toward a specific goal or learning outcome for his hearers or students, his sermon or lesson should state a purpose, written in terms of "what one expects to happen in the hearer."[28] That goal or purpose may be that the hearers/students will: 1. increase in knowledge (indicated by their ability to list, state, recite, write, identify, recall, describe, define, recognize, etc.); 2. gain insight (indicated by their ability to discuss, differentiate, analyze, compare, contrast, select, choose, examine, evaluate, think, discern, clarify, etc.); 3. improve in attitude (indicated by their desiring, determining, developing, planning, appreciating, being enthusiastic about, enjoying, committing, sympathizing, etc.); or 4. develop in skill or action (indicated by their ability to interpret, produce, make, use, solve, explain, assist, integrate, communicate, engage in, assist, etc.).

Because the ultimate objective of Bible exposition is to change lives by gaining an action/response from the hearers, preachers and teachers should state specific purposes for each sermon or lesson, and should focus their sermons or lessons toward those accomplishments, the climaxes of their messages.

WHAT ARE SOME GUIDELINES FOR
PROPER RELEVANCE-AND-RESPONSE APPLICATION?

APPLICATION MUST STEM FROM THE PROPER UNDERSTANDING OF THE PASSAGE

Correct interpretation of a passage is basic to proper application. If a text is interpreted inaccurately, then the application will be faulty as well. Unfortunately many people go to the Bible for a "blessing" or for guidance for the day, and therefore they either build an application on an invalid interpretation or ignore the interpretive process altogether. In their intense desire to find something devotional or practical, many Christians distort the original meaning of some passages of Scripture. "The first question of Bible study is not: 'What is devotional here?' nor 'What is of practical importance here?' nor 'What is inspirational here?' but '*What does this passage mean?*' "[29]

The personal response to a passage should be based, as suggested earlier, on that passage's relevance, which in turn stems from the meaning of the text to its original audience in light of the purpose of the book. Sound exegesis, which may be defined as determining the meaning of a biblical text in its historical and literary contexts, is the only adequate basis for relevant application.

In exegesis one examines the *meaning* of a passage in its original setting, and in application he looks at the *significance* of that meaning for current situations. Using proper procedures of interpretation, exegesis seeks to answer the question, What did this text mean to its original audience? Application seeks to answer the question, How does that original meaning relate to present audiences? Only after the Bible student has accurately determined the meaning of the passage for the initial hearers in the "then and there" can he accurately apply that meaning to himself and others "now and here."

APPLICATION MUST BE BASED ON PRINCIPLES

Principles, often stated in single sentences, serve as bridges between interpretation and application. Latent in the text, they summarize the essence of a Bible passage in terms that are applicable to a broad spectrum of readers and situations. Without such a bridge, a passage would simply remain as a recording of what God had done or said in the past. The principlizing bridge spans the gulf between the past and the present, with a truth that is relevant to both.

"To *principlize* is to discover in any narrative the basic spiritual, moral, or theological principles. These principles are latent in the text and it is the process of deduction which brings them to the surface. It is not an imposition on the text."[30]

A "principlizing bridge" is the same as the "relevance" of a passage discussed earlier. The relationship of this bridge to interpretation and application may be illustrated in this way:

Determine the *meaning* of the passage to its original audience.	Write out the *principle*.	Decide on a specific *action/response*.
Interpretation (Meaning)		*Application* (Significance)

The principle stems directly from the meaning and thus is inherent in the meaning. The principle also expresses the meaning's present relevance and thus is part of the application.

The principle is a generalized statement deduced from the specific original situation then and applicable to different though specific, similar situations now.

Principles are necessary because the emphasis of the Bible is on principles for moral and spiritual conduct more than it is a catalog of specific directions.[31] Sometimes the general principle underlies a concrete instruction. As Fisher illustrates, "When Jesus said, 'If anyone forces you to go one mile, go with him two miles' (Matt. 5:41), He was putting a general principle into concrete terms. The application goes far beyond the particular situation."[32]

Ramm gives several examples of principles drawn from biblical narratives:

> When David repeatedly refused to slay Saul we see the principle of obedience to powers that be. When Saul was not patient with God's prophet we see the principle of disobedience. When

Isaiah prays for the shadow to retreat on the sundial we see the principle of great spiritual courage. In truth, Hebrews 11 is a magnificent example of principlizing. The great faith of a multitude of men is set before us as the true principle of their lives.[33]

The principle or general truth pertaining to Ramm's example of Saul and Samuel may be stated in this way: "Believers should be obedient to the Lord, for impatient disobedience results in punishment." Audiences or individuals may be challenged to respond to that principle in various specific ways, depending on their needs.

The words, "in everything give thanks" (1 Thess. 5:18), were addressed originally to the Thessalonian believers. The meaning of the passage in reference to that original audience could be stated this way: "Thessalonian believers should be thankful in every circumstance of life." The principle for *all* believers would be very similar in wording, because many commands in the epistolary literature of the Bible are obviously intended, by the inspiration of the Holy Spirit, for all believers. The principle may be worded, "All Christians should be thankful in every one of their circumstances." It can be seen that this is a universal statement that relates the truth of that verse to both the Thessalonian culture of Paul's day and to every generation of Christians in all cultures everywhere.

Numbers 15:32-36 instructs Israelites that if they gather wood on the Sabbath they will be stoned. The meaning may be stated, "If an Israelite does not follow God's commands explicitly, God will punish him." Since this is part of the Mosaic law and the Mosaic law has been abolished, that command is not directly relevant to Christians. But the underlying principle is relevant. Deduced from the passage and confirmed by other Scripture is the principle that "God punishes disobedience."

Mickelsen cites Paul's words to Euodia and Synteche to live in harmony in the Lord (Phil. 4:2), and adds these comments:

> Certainly, two Christians who are quarreling today . . . might well apply this statement about living in harmony to themselves. The principle, then, is that of believers living in harmony with one another. This is true even though today's Christians cannot—like those to whom Paul's statement first came—claim that they helped Paul the apostle in his ministry in Philippi.

This obvious fact helps to make clear the confined or limited meaning in the passage as well as the universal possibilities of application in the principle of harmonious living.[34]

APPLICATION MUST BE BASED ON ELEMENTS THE READER SHARES WITH THE ORIGINAL AUDIENCE

Sometimes the audience to which a passage of Scripture was initially addressed, such as the believers at Philippi, is similar to audiences today. For this reason the principle is similar in wording to the meaning of the text (meaning: "Euodia and Synteche should stop quarreling and should live harmoniously"; principle: "Christians who are quarreling should stop doing so and should live harmoniously").

Other times the audience to which a passage of Scripture was initially addressed, such as Israel in the wilderness, is rather dissimilar to present-day audiences. In this case the wording of the principle differs substantially from the summarized interpretation.

Applying to today the scriptural admonitions, commands, counsel, instructions, and truths given to those audiences requires finding a point in common between the original and the current audiences. The point in common between the Corinthians, for example, who were commanded to do all things to the glory of God (1 Cor. 10:31), and Christians today is that both groups are members of the church, the Body of Christ. The instruction to the Corinthians is immediately relevant to today. The point in common, however, between Israel under the Law and believers today is that both are God's people. The first example of a point in common involves direct application and the second indirect application.

Situations between original and subsequent audiences are often diverse. For example, God's instruction to Noah to build an ark is hardly a directive for the twentieth century. And Paul's injunction to the Corinthians to refrain from eating meat sacrificed to idols in order to avoid causing other Christians difficulty (1 Cor. 8:7-13) is a situation that is not current now. Therefore application requires determining what aspects of those situations may be parallel to present circumstances. In the case of Noah and the ark, the parallel idea is not to build an ark, but to obey God when there is no visible evidence for doing so. In the case of the Corinthians, the parallel is to avoid involvement in any practice, innocent in itself, which may cause others to sin.[35]

This raises the hypothetical question of cultural relativity, that is, how to ascertain what in the Bible pertains only to those cultural situations and therefore has little direct relevance to the present, and what in the Bible pertains to present as well as past cultural environments. This involves ascertaining which Bible passages are "culturally conditioned" and which ones are "transcultural." It is evident that some commands in the Scriptures are a reflection of local custom. Jesus said, "Carry no purse, no bag, no shoes; and greet no one on the way" (Luke 10:4). As Sproul has observed, if this is transcultural, then evangelists should preach in their bare feet![36] He adds, "Obviously, the point of this text is not to set down a perennial requirement of barefooted evangelism."[37]

Space does not permit a full discussion of this involved issue,[38] but it may be helpful to point out four kinds of situations, with varying degrees of cultural transference.

1. Some situations, commands, or principles are repeatable, continuous, or not revoked, and/or pertain to more theological subjects, and/or are repeated elsewhere in Scripture, and therefore are transferable. Examples of those are Genesis 9:6; Proverbs 3:5-6; John 3:3; Romans 12:1-2; 1 Corinthians 12:13; Ephesians 6:10-19; Colossians 3:12-13; and 1 Peter 5:6.

2. Some situations, commands, or principles pertain to an individual's specific nonrepeatable circumstances, and/or nonmoral or nontheological subjects, and/or have been revoked, and are therefore not transferable. Examples of this are Leviticus 20:11 (cf. 1 Cor. 5:1-8); Matthew 21:2-3; 2 Timothy 4:11, 13; and Hebrews 7:12; 10:1.

3. Some situations or commands pertain to cultural settings that are only partially similar and in which only the principles are transferable. Examples are Deuteronomy 6:4-6; Romans 16:16; and 1 Corinthians 8.

4. Some situations or commands pertain to cultural settings with no similarities but in which the principles are transferable. Examples are Exodus 3:5 and Matthew 26:7.

The first category may be called "direct application" because the application is directly related without change to subsequent cultures.[39] Categories 3 and 4 may be called "indirect application" because the application does not arise in the immediate biblical context.[40]

In order for an expositor to determine the common elements shared by an original and a present audience, he must know something of the needs and characteristics of that present audience. Expositors often spend much time studying the biblical text and its historical background in order to know that original audience, to the neglect of studying their own contemporary hearers. Without knowledge of both audiences, the expositor may distort the shared part(s) and thus misconstrue the application.[41]

How do examples of Bible personalities relate to application? How does the Bible student determine which examples to follow and which ones not to follow? Several suggestions may be given.[42]

Learn from poor examples what not to do. "Certainly the rebellion of Saul, the immorality of David, the pride of Absalom, the treachery of Judas, the denials of Peter, and the lying of Ananias and Sapphira stand as examples of what not to do."[43] Studying examples such as these helps the Bible student see the serious consequences of wrongdoing.

Learn from good examples what to do. "The faith of Abraham, the obedience of Moses, the loyalty of Elijah, and the love of John the Apostle stand out as great examples to follow."[44] But are these and other worthy examples to be imitated today? Abraham is certainly to be commended for offering up his son Isaac in obedience to God, Solomon's building of the Temple is a praiseworthy accomplishment, and Paul's trip to Arabia is commendable. But are these to be heeded by all Christians today? No, for these were instructions to specific individuals, and thus are not universally applicable. This suggests another guideline.

Follow the example if a transcultural biblical command or principle is related to it.[45] Christian fathers are not to offer their sons as literal sacrifices as Abraham did because no such universal command is given to them. On the other hand, Elijah's fervency in prayer is an example for Christians to follow (James 5:17-18) for it illustrates the effectiveness of praying (5:16).[46]

Fee discusses this guideline. "For a biblical precedent to justify present action, the principle of the action must be taught elsewhere, where it is the primary intent so to teach."[47] He then develops this point further.

> Where there is ambiguity of models, or when a practice is reported but once, it is repeatable only if it appears to have divine approbation or is in harmony with what is taught elsewhere in Scripture. To illustrate: It would seem that some in what is often called the Jesus movement could justify their communal life and their having all things common on these grounds, since such life appears to have divine approval in Acts, and since there is no teaching elsewhere that would seem to prohibit such a practice. But one may well question the economic viability of the practice, since Paul eventually was raising money for the poor in Jerusalem.[48]

Wilson stresses the importance of determining the theological intent of the narrative passage (the principles) and its correlation to a current audience. "If we fail to discover the theological intent, we may make a good application from the wrong text. On the other hand, if we fail to ask the question of audience correlation, we may make a valid application, grounded in the theology of the text, but to the wrong audience."[49]

APPLICATION MUST INCLUDE SPECIFIC ACTION/RESPONSE

The goal toward which exposition and principlizing moves is a desired response on the part of the individuals in the congregation or class. As pointed out earlier, the communicator and the learner each has separate responsibilities.

The expositor's responsibilities. To encourage and motivate toward a proper response to the Word, the preacher or teacher may choose from several approaches.

1. State during or at the end of the message or lesson one or more specific ways in which the truth can be implemented. Sometimes an illustration may be included on how others have applied the Word in one of those specific ways.

2. In a class ask the students to list ways the truth can be carried out.

3. Have students individually write out ways they plan to put

the truth into practice. This may be done at the end of one session (e.g., "How can I work out this scriptural principle in my life?") or at the conclusion of a series (e.g., "I plan to do these three things as a result of our study in the book of James").

4. Have the students share how they applied a biblical principle the previous week.

5. Lead the group in singing a hymn that expresses a practical response to the truth studied.

6. Encourage the students to keep a spiritual diary in which they (a) write out how they plan to personalize a verse or passage that week, and (b) write a report on how they succeeded or did not succeed in living out that biblical principle and what, if anything, remains to be done.

7. Suggest that the students ask themselves these six questions:

- Is there any *example* for me to follow?
- Is there any *command* for me to obey?
- Is there any *error* for me to avoid?
- Is there any *sin* for me to forsake?
- Is there any *promise* for me to claim?
- Is there any *new thought about God Himself?*[50]

8. Suggest that the hearers/students think of *one* response they can put into action in the coming week. (It is helpful to have a date for fulfilling the response.)

9. Distribute cards with the following formula, and ask the students to complete it: "Knowing that _____ (Scripture truth), I desire to _____ (overall objective), by _____ (specific attitude or action) by the date of _____." This formula puts together the intellectual, emotional, and volitional aspects of a learning response, and includes a time element.

10. Point out that some responses pertain to the improvement of one's actions whereas others pertain to attitudes or motives. Improper attitudes may take longer to correct than the carrying out of certain actions, and are often more difficult to deal with.

The hearers'/students' responsibilities. Application may be pointed out by a preacher or teacher (or counselor), but it must be carried out by the individual himself. Without this final step, application is aborted. An individual in personal study may see truths to apply, but it still remains his responsibility to carry them out. The following suggestions are offered to help individuals appropriate the Word in this crowning step in Bible study.

1. Have a receptive attitude toward the preaching and teaching of the Word. Ask the Lord to give an openness to the Scriptures (cf. Acts 16:14, "The Lord opened [Lydia's] heart to respond to the things spoken by Paul," and Eph. 1:18, "I pray that the eyes of your heart may be enlightened").

2. During a message, lesson, or personal Bible study, be thinking of (and/or write down) one or more ways to apply the truth.

3. List areas of one's life where spiritual improvement is needed. Ask others to suggest (lovingly!) areas where one's life may be improved. Then as the Word is heard and studied, see if and how those passages relate to the area(s) of need.

4. Think of application in terms of relationships: one's relationship to God, to Satan, to others (at home, church, work, school), and to oneself.[51]

5. Choose one course of action or attitudinal response from the several possibilities.

6. Make a firm decision to carry out the response. Make this decision a firm commitment between the individual and the Lord. This will help motivate one toward the "doing."

7. Be personal. Use the first person singular pronouns ("I," "me," "my," "mine"), not plural pronouns ("we," "us," "our").[52] Application that remains in the "we" category is too general and impersonal.

8. Be specific. Application that is stated in general terms (such as "I should be more like Jesus" or "I should love my wife more") is inadequate and difficult to carry out. Complete the formula suggested in point 9 given earlier under *The expositor's responsibilities*. Or write a sentence beginning with the words "I will . . ." followed by one of the ninety action verbs (or others) from the accompanying list.

Accept	Ask	Be sensitive
Admit	Ask myself	Be willing
Analyze	Avoid	Build

Buy	Help	Schedule
Choose	Invite	Select
Claim	Isolate	Send
Collect	Keep	Share
Commit	List	Show
Compliment	Listen	Sing
Comply	Look for	Spend time
Confess	Look up	Stay away
Control	Love	Stop
Count	Meet with	Study
Create	Memorize	Substitute
Decide	Organize	Take
Develop	Plan out	Talk with
Direct	Praise	Teach
Discourse	Pray about	Telephone
Do	Pray to	Thank
Eliminate	Pray with	Think about
Encourage	Prefer	Value
Enjoy	Pursue	Visit
Evaluate	Read	Wait
Exemplify	Realize	Wake up
Experiment	Record	Walk
Find	Rejoice	Watch
Follow	Repair	Witness
Give	Respond	Work on
Go	Sacrifice	Write down
Guard	Save	Write to

Henrichsen illustrates this kind of specific action for applying meekness from the life of Moses:

> I will memorize Numbers 12:3 and review it daily throughout the year.
>
> I will write meek on a card and tape it to the mirror in the bathroom, so that daily I will be reminded of my need to work on this. Each morning I will review Numbers 12:3 and pray about its application in my life for that day.
>
> I will share this need with my spouse and with [a friend], who knows me well. Once a month I will talk over my progress with them and ask for a frank evaluation.[53]

9. Have a deadline for completing the application, and work toward it.

10. Review the progress. The day after the deadline for completing an action/response, evaluate the progress made and if necessary write the same, a revised, or an entirely different course of action for another date.

11. Pray for the enabling of the Holy Spirit to incarnate God's truth in one's life.

CONCLUSION

A common reaction to many sermons and Bible lessons is the question, "So what?" People long to know how the Bible, written in ancient times, relates to them.

Indifference to the Bible often sets in after a prolonged exposure to applicationless preaching and teaching. But enjoyment of the Word comes as one not only observes its marvels (Psalm 119:18) and understands (interprets) what it says (cf. Acts 8:30-31), but also as he personalizes the Bible to himself. For after all, God has given His Word so that believers may "grow thereby" (1 Pet. 2:2, KJV).*

"If you know these things, you are blessed if you do them" (John 13:17).

NOTES

1. John R. W. Stott, *Understanding the Bible* (Glendale, Calif.: Gospel Light, Regal, 1972), p. 242.
2. T. Norton Sterrett, *How to Understand Your Bible*, rev. ed. (Downers Grove, Ill.: Inter-Varsity, 1974), p. 171.
3. Walter A. Elwell, "Belief and the Bible: A Crisis of Authority?" *Christianity Today*, 21 March 1980, p. 23.
4. David J. A. Clines, "Notes for an Old Testament Hermeneutic," *Theology, News and Notes*, March 1975, p. 10.
5. Ibid.
6. Ibid.
7. Ibid. (italics Clines').
8. Ibid.
9. Haddon W. Robinson, *Biblical Preaching* (Grand Rapids: Baker, 1980), p. 108.
10. Clines, "Old Testament Hermeneutic," p. 10 (italics Clines').
11. Ibid.

*King James Version.

12. Roy B. Zuck, *Spiritual Power in Your Teaching* (Chicago: Moody, 1963), pp. 83-84.
13. Sidney Greidanus, *Sola Scriptura: Problems and Principles in Preaching Historical Texts* (Toronto: Wedge, 1970), p. 230.
14. C. Veenhof, cited by Greidanus, *Sola Scriptura*, p. 157.
15. Veenhof, cited by Greidanus, *Sola Scriptura*, p. 168 (italics Veenhof's).
16. Greidanus, *Sola Scriptura*, p. 172.
17. Ibid., pp. 93, 157.
18. Ibid.
19. Bernard Ramm, *Protestant Biblical Interpretation*, 3d ed. (Grand Rapids: Baker, 1970), p. 188.
20. Martin Luther, cited by A. Skevington Wood, *The Principles of Biblical Interpretation* (Grand Rapids: Zondervan, 1967), p. 80.
21. R. C. H. Lenski, *The Interpretation of St. Paul's Epistles to the Colossians, to the Thessalonians, to Timothy, to Titus and to Philemon* (Minneapolis: Augsburg, 1961), p. 847.
22. James Hope Moulton and George Milligan, *The Vocabulary of the Greek Testament Illustrated from the Papyri and Other Non-Literary Sources* (Grand Rapids: Eerdmans, 1930), p. 222.
23. I. Howard Marshall, "How Do We Interpret the Bible?" *Themelios* 5 (1980):10.
24. Paul Woolley, "The Relevancy of Scripture," in *The Infallible Word* (Philadelphia: Presbyterian and Reformed, 1946), p. 199.
25. Luis Alonzo Schonkel, "Hermeneutics in the Light of Language and Literature," *Catholic Biblical Quarterly* 25 (1963):382.
26. Zuck, *Spiritual Power*, pp. 122-23.
27. LeRoy Ford, "Developing Performance-Oriented Learning Purposes," *Search* 4 (Winter 1974):31-40.
28. Robinson, *Biblical Preaching*, p. 108.
29. Bernard Ramm, "But It Isn't Bible Study," *Eternity*, February 1960, p. 22.
30. Ramm, *Protestant Biblical Interpretation*, pp. 199-200.
31. Ibid., p. 186.
32. Fred L. Fisher, *How to Interpret the New Testament* (Philadelphia: Westminster, 1966), pp. 167-68.
33. Ramm, *Protestant Biblical Interpretation*, p. 200.
34. A. Berkeley Mickelsen, *Interpreting the Bible* (Grand Rapids: Eerdmans, 1963), pp. 357-58.
35. Fee suggests a distinction between what he calls "comparable contexts" and "extended application," illustrating this with 2 Corinthians 6:14—7:1, which prohibits Christians from being "unequally yoked" with unbelievers (v. 14, KJV). He says that, because no situation today is an exact equivalent of going with pagan friends to an idolatrous temple, using this passage against Christians' marrying non-Christians may be called "extended application" (Gordon D. Fee, "Hermeneutics and Common Sense: An Exploratory Essay on the Hermeneutics of the Epistles," in *Iner-*

rancy and Common Sense, ed. Roger R. Nicole and J. Ramsey Michaels [Grand Rapids: Baker, 1980], pp. 176-78).

36. R. C. Sproul, *Knowing Scripture* (Downers Grove, Ill.: Inter-Varsity, 1977), p. 106.

37. Ibid.

38. For more on the question of cultural relativity, see Alan Johnson, "History and Culture in New Testament Interpretation," in *Interpreting the Word of God,* ed. Samuel J. Schultz and Morris A. Inch (Chicago: Moody, 1976), pp. 128-61; Charles H. Kraft, "Interpreting the Cultural Context," *Journal of the Evangelical Theological Society* 21 (December 1978):357-67; Robert C. Sproul, "Controversy at Culture Gap," *Eternity,* May 1976, pp. 12-15, 40; and Henry A. Virkler, *Hermeneutics: Principles and Practices of Biblical Interpretation* (Grand Rapids: Baker, 1981), pp. 211-32.

39. The Scriptures are full of imperatives that are direct applications for Christians. Mickelsen refers to the many imperatives in 1 Thessalonians 5:13-22 (*Interpreting the Bible,* pp. 361-62).

40. Elliott E. Johnson, "Application," class lecture notes in advanced hermeneutics, Dallas Theological Seminary, 1980, p. 4.

41. For more on the necessity of knowing the audience as an important step in applying Scripture, see Gregg Purviance, "An Application of Amos to Modern Society" (Th.M. thesis, Dallas Theological Seminary, 1980), pp. 14-16, 19-20.

42. For further discussion on the application of Old Testament historical narratives, see Dan R. Johnson, "Guidelines for the Application of Old Testament Narrative," *Trinity Journal* 7 (Spring 1978):78-84; and Eugene A. Wilson, "The Homiletical Application of Old Testament Narrative Passages," *Trinity Journal* 7 (Spring 1980):85-91.

43. Ramm, *Protestant Biblical Interpretation,* p. 191.

44. Ibid.

45. Walter A. Henrichsen, *A Layman's Guide to Interpreting the Bible,* rev. ed. (Grand Rapids: Zondervan, 1978), p. 31.

46. Related to the problem of applying examples is the applying of commands and promises. Helpful principles are given by Henrichsen (*A Layman's Guide,* pp. 42-48), Ramm (*Protestant Biblical Interpretation,* pp. 189-90, 192-95), and Sterrett (*How to Understand Your Bible,* pp. 172-76).

47. Wilson, "Homiletical Application," p. 87.

48. Gordon D. Fee, "The Genre of New Testament Literature and Biblical Hermeneutics," in *Interpreting the Word of God,* p. 118.

49. Ibid.

50. *Quiet Time* (Downers Grove, Ill.: Inter-Varsity, 1945), p. 20 (italics by the author).

51. Irving L. Jensen, *Enjoy Your Bible* (Chicago: Moody, 1969), pp. 120-21.

52. Henrichsen, *A Layman's Guide,* p. 218.

53. Ibid., p. 219.

2

Psalm 8 and Hebrews 2: A Case Study in Biblical Hermeneutics and Biblical Theology

Donald R. Glenn

As the title implies, the purpose of this article is twofold: 1. to show one of the ways in which a New Testament writer used the Old Testament Scriptures, and 2. to show how that New Testament use modified or expanded the Old Testament doctrine or motif. Psalm 8 and Hebrews 2 have been chosen for this study because the quotation of Psalm 8:4-6 in Hebrews 2:5-9 raises several interesting hermeneutical questions and because both passages make significant contributions to the biblical doctrines of anthropology and Christology. The study of Psalm 8 is also of further hermeneutical and theological interest because of its relationship to Genesis 1:26-28, a passage to which it alludes in verses 5-8.

In order to surface and solve some of the hermeneutical questions and to state clearly the contribution of Psalm 8 and He-

DONALD R. GLENN (B.S., Wheaton College; Th.M., Dallas Theological Seminary; M.A., Brandeis University; graduate study, Brandeis University) is professor of semitics and Old Testament studies at Dallas Theological Seminary, Dallas, Texas.

brews 2 to the biblical doctrines of anthropology and Christology, the specific argument of those passages will be given
against the background of their Old and New Testament contexts.

THE OLD TESTAMENT CONTEXT

THE ARGUMENT OF PSALM 8

Psalm 8 is generally classified as a creation hymn.[1] According to Westermann the normal motifs in this kind of Psalm are:
1. an imperative call to praise, 2. a reason for praise, and often 3.
a renewed call to praise. He notes that the reason for praise is
frequently given in an introductory summary statement that
praises God for His majesty in creation and for His condescension toward man. Westermann further notes that this introductory summary statement is often expanded in the verses that
follow.[2] Though the schemas from form critical categories
should not be foisted on the Scriptures, form criticism, if not
too rigidly applied, does help to explain the structure of this
psalm. Thus the first two lines of verse 1 may be seen as an
exclamation of praise to the Lord for His extraordinary display
of His name or character in creation and condescension.[3] This
exclamation is then reiterated in verse 9 at the end of the psalm.
The last line of verse 1 together with verse 2 may be seen as an
introductory summary statement praising the Lord for His
glory, which was manifested in the heavenly creation, and for
His condescension to weak and frail humanity. This theme is
somewhat modified and expanded in verse 3 (His glory in the
heavenly creation) and in verses 4-8 (His glory in condescension to frail and seemingly insignificant man).

Expanding somewhat briefly on this basic outline, it may be
seen in the last line of verse 1 that David praises the Lord for
His glory that is spread across the heavens.[4] He then praises the
Lord in verse 2 for His condescension in using the weakest and
frailest of humans (i.e., children and nursing babies) to silence
the arguments of His enemies by giving to these weak, frail
beings the capacity for rational expression.[5] That capacity may
find expression in praising Him (cf. Matt. 21:16).

This theme of praise for creation and condescension is expanded in verses 4-8. In verse 4 David acknowledges with grateful awe that the existence and marvelous order of the heavens and their starry host are the products of the personal handiwork of the Lord. Then in verses 6-8 he marvels that the author of such a vast creation should so condescend to elevate such a relatively puny and insignificant creature as man over all the rest of earthly creation. God has conferred such honor and dignity on man that he ranks in significance only slightly below God Himself (v. 5).

Me'lōhîm, THE EXEGETICAL AND HERMENEUTICAL CRUX

The phrase in verse 5, "Yet Thou hast made him a little lower than God," forms the basic crux of the interpretation of this psalm and raises a basic hermeneutical problem. It is true that the term 'ĕlōhîm ("God") in this phrase can refer to beings other than God Himself, such as heathen gods or idols (e.g., Psalm 96:5; Exod. 18:11), or representatives of God (e.g., Exod. 4:16; 7:1; Psalm 82:1, 6). It is also true that the term bᵉnê 'ĕlōhîm ("sons of God") may refer to angels (e.g., Job 1:6; 38:7). However, it is a matter of considerable debate whether the term 'ĕlōhîm by itself ever refers to angels.[6] Consequently, it is somewhat surprising to find that the Septuagint translation, supported by the Jewish Targums, the Syriac Peshitta, and the Latin Vulgate, renders the phrase mē'lōhîm, "than the angels." It is even more surprising that the author of the book of Hebrews appears to validate this interpretation when he follows his normal practice of quoting from the Septuagint.[7]

It is this latter point that raises a very crucial hermeneutical question, Does a New Testament writer's quotation of an Old Testament text establish the details of the interpretation of the Old Testament text? That is, Can the New Testament citation be used to determine the original text, the meaning of terms, and the exegetical and theological significance of the text for the original hearers or readers? Though a negative answer to this question may raise theological difficulties regarding verbal plenary inspiration for some—difficulties that will be dealt with later—it appears to me to be the only answer consistent with a literal, grammatical, historical, cultural hermeneutic. Thus, the Old Testament usage and context are more crucial for determining the meaning of *'ĕlōhîm* than is the acceptance of the Septuagint translation by the writer of Hebrews. The Septuagint translation may, by the way, have been influenced by the translator's theological sensitivity to the transcendence of God.[8]

'Ĕlōhîm IN GENESIS 1:26-28

While almost all commentators agree that Psalm 8:5-8 is a poetical allusion to Genesis 1:26-28, they do not all agree on the significance of the term *'ĕlōhîm* in the phrase "in the image of *'ĕlōhîm* He created him" (Gen. 1:27). Thus Delitzsch argues from 1. the plural verb "let Us make," 2. the plural possessive pronouns "in Our image, according to Our likeness," and 3. the Septuagint translation of Psalm 8:5 (verse 6 in the Hebrew and Greek) that God made man in the likeness of angels, beings with which He shares a family likeness.[9] However, as Kidner notes, the implication that others had a hand in creation is foreign to the context of Genesis 1 and to the challenge of Isaiah 40:14.[10] This would also conflict with the parallel account in Genesis 2:7, where man is the product of the creative activity of the Lord God alone. Also, one is prohibited by both the immediate and broader contexts from allowing the plurals in Genesis 1:26 to influence the interpretation of the term *'ĕlōhîm* in Genesis 1:27. Thus it would seem obvious to take the term in the same sense that it has been used throughout the chapter — as a reference to God the Creator of all.

THE THEOLOGICAL SIGNIFICANCE OF PSALM 8

If the term *'ĕlōhîm* in Genesis 1:27 refers to God and if Psalm 8:5-8 is a poetic allusion to Genesis 1:26-28 as is generally affirmed, then *'ĕlōhîm* in Psalm 8:5 must refer to God and not to angels. Psalm 8:5 is stating the fact that man is only a little lower than the sovereign Lord of creation Himself. Since the two passages are so closely related, the distinctive theological contributions of Psalm 8 are slight. Therefore both passages relate primarily to the status of man, not his nature.[11] They express the truth that man, though merely one of God's creatures — and a comparatively insignificant one at that, according to David's reflection on the rest of creation (vv. 3-

4)—has been given dominion over the rest of created beings. However, Psalm 8 does make a distinctive theological contribution. That which Genesis 1:26-28 views as a divine directive is pictured as a divine grant in Psalm 8:6-8.[12] Moreover, David sees this divine grant as being effective in his own time. Calvin denies the present dominion of man and affirms that the Fall led to a divestiture of this prerogative.[13] However, at least three elements within the psalm itself argue for the continuing existence of this prerogative bestowed on man at creation: 1. the term 'ĕnôsh, which David uses for man in verse 4, refers to man in general, not man in particular (i.e., Adam);[14] 2. the tense of the verbs in verse 4 is imperfect rather than perfect; and 3. the mood of the psalm is that of praise for condescending to exalt puny and insignificant man, not a lament for a lost prerogative. In addition, Genesis 9:1-7 makes clear that man continues in the divine image and retains the right to rule even though that rule may be dominated by fear and challenged by violence.

In conclusion, it may be said that Psalm 8 refers to the regal dignity and prerogative that man has over the rest of creation by reason of divine decree and divine constitution. This regal dignity and prerogative is retained despite the Fall of Adam.

THE NEW TESTAMENT CONTEXT

As Longenecker has shown, the argument of the book of Hebrews is inextricably bound up with the author's use of the Old Testament, particularly with the concept of anticipation and consummation. Thus the theme of the book is the consummation of God's program of salvation in the Person and work of Jesus, God's Son.[15] That program was anticipated in the promises, events, and institutions of the Old Testament. Longenecker has further shown that that theme is built around five portions or collections of Old Testament passages. The passage containing the quotation of Psalm 8:4-6 is the second of those collections.[16] The writer begins the first series of passages by setting forth the excellencies of the Son as God's vehicle of revelation and redemption in this final stage of redemption (Heb. 1:13).[17] The author then demonstrates the superiority of Christ over the angels, whom his readers evidently believed were agents of

God's former revelation (cf. 2:2),[18] and warns them not to ignore the Son's revelation and their consequent opportunity for salvation (2:1-4). In the process of this demonstration the author shows that Christ is God's Son and heir (1:5), who has been given dominion over all things, including angels (1:6-9). Christ is currently waiting for God to inaugurate this dominion through the defeat of His foes (1:13). Christ's coming was announced by the Word of the Lord and confirmed by signs and wonders from the Spirit (2:3-4).

THE ARGUMENT OF HEBREWS 2:5-9

In Hebrews 2:5-9 the author is looking toward the Messianic age or "world to come" (2:5; cf. 6:5; 13:14), in which salvation is to be fully realized (1:14; 2:3, and note 2:10; 5:9; 9:28).[19] The writer argues that this new age is not to be subjected to angels (as his readers and their Jewish contemporaries may have believed),[20] because in Psalm 8:4-6[21] God promised dominion over the works of His hands to man (2:6-8a). However, it is also obvious from experience that the divinely ordained prerogative of dominion has not been fulfilled in the case of man in general (2:8b). The writer then states that the promised dominion has been fulfilled in Jesus, who as man suffered death and was as a consequence crowned with glory and honor (2:9). This is the glory and honor that Psalm 8 had promised to mankind (2:7b). Thus the writer is arguing that what was true of man in general has proved true only in the case of one man in particular—the man Jesus. This application of Psalm 8 is consistent with the apostle Paul's use of the psalm in 1 Corinthians 15:27 and Ephesians 1:22.

THE USE OF PSALM 8:6 IN 1 CORINTHIANS 15:27 AND EPHESIANS 1:22

Paul quotes part of Psalm 8:6 in 1 Corinthians 15:27 in the context of his argument on the historicity of the resurrection of Jesus Christ (1 Cor. 15:1-11) and the significance of His resurrection for the life of Christian believers (1 Cor. 15:12-58). In this passage Paul is answering several objections against the doctrine of resurrection. In 15:12-19 he argues that a denial of the doctrine of resurrection would result also in the denial of Christ's resurrection (15:13, 16). Such a denial would controvert the testimony of proved witnesses (15:14, 15; cf. 15:5-8), invalidate their faith (15:14, 17), and leave them in their sin (15:17).

In 15:20-28 Paul argues that Christ's resurrection abrogates the power of death (cf. 15:26) that has held man since the sin of Adam (15:21-22). This abrogated power, however, will only be realized progressively. The power of death was initially abolished through Christ's resurrection (15:20). It will be abolished further through the resurrection of believers at Christ's second coming (15:23) when He has destroyed all the enemies of God's rule according to the Messianic promise of Psalm 110:1 (15:23). In 15:26-28 Paul argues that death is one of the enemies that will be abolished because God promised in Psalm 8:6 that all things were to be put in subjection to Him. Paul sees Psalm 8:6 as a promise of absolute and universal dominion which is fulfilled in Christ. The only exception to Christ's dominion is, obviously, God the Father who subjected all things to Christ. This fulfillment will come to complete fruition only when every enemy, including death, is defeated (15:26), and when the Son delivers up the kingdom to God the Father (15:24, 28).

The application of Psalm 8:6 to absolute and universal dominion is also emphasized in Paul's allusion to this passage in his prayer in Ephesians 1:15-23. Paul begins his epistle by setting forth the work of the Father, Son, and Holy Spirit in redemption (1:3-14). He then prays that the Ephesian believers may come to realize what a gracious calling they have, what a glorious inheritance they have waiting for them, and what power they have available to them (1:18-19a). These are all guaranteed by the power of God that was manifested in Christ's resurrection (1:19b-20). At His resurrection, Christ was exalted to the right hand of the Father (an allusion to Psalm 110:1) and granted a position of absolute and universal dominion over everything imaginable (an allusion to Psalm 8:6a). This dominion includes the present age and the age to come (1:21) and applies especially to the church that is His body (1:22b-23). Psalm 8 is thus seen to have its fulfillment in the Person of the resurrected Christ, who has been given dominion over the church, this age, and the age to come. This dominion is absolute and universal in its scope (1:21).

THE THEOLOGICAL SIGNIFICANCE OF PSALM 8 IN THE NEW TESTAMENT

In its Old Testament context Psalm 8 refers to the prerogative of man's dominion over all other created beings. This prerogative was conferred on man by God at creation (Gen. 1:26-28); and though perhaps modified and challenged (Gen. 9:1-7), man still retains his dominion despite his fallen, sinful condition (Psalm 8:4-8).

In the New Testament Psalm 8 finds its fulfillment in the man Jesus (Heb. 2:9). He is the resurrected Christ, or Messiah (Eph. 1:20; cf. 1 Cor. 15:20), who is seated at the right hand of God the Father (Eph. 1:20; cf. Heb. 1:13). He has been given dominion not only over the church (Eph. 1:22b-23), but also over this age (Eph. 1:21) and over the age to come (Eph. 1:21; cf. Heb. 2:5). According to Paul, this dominion was absolute. It involved dominion over spiritual beings (Eph. 1:21; cf. Col. 1:16)[22] and death (1 Cor. 15:26; cf. Heb. 2:9, 14, 15). This dominion also includes the second coming of the resurrected Christ (1 Cor. 15:23), the defeating of all His foes (1 Cor. 15:24-26), and the deliverance of the kingdom to God the Father (1 Cor. 15:28).

In conclusion, what appeared to the writers of the New Testament as unfulfilled in man in general (Heb. 2:8b) was considered as fulfilled in Jesus Christ. His resurrection and ascension to God's right hand inaugurated a new age. That which was decreed in Genesis 1:26-28 and gratefully acknowledged as the prerogative of man in general in Psalm 8:4-8 will be fulfilled through Christ in that new age.

HERMENEUTICAL CONSIDERATIONS

MESSIANIC FULFILLMENT

The fact that Psalm 8 is Messianic cannot be denied. However, a word must be said about the exact nature of the Messianic character of Psalm 8. As Louis has noted, few believe that Psalm 8 is a direct Messianic prophecy of Christ.[23] Most writers see Christ as the fulfillment of the psalm in that He embodies and fulfills all that was true of Adam, the first and representative man.[24] That this may be true is evident from the context of 1 Corinthians 15 where the universal and continuing effects of the acts of the two men, Christ and Adam, are so contrasted (cf. 1 Cor. 15:20-22, 45-49) that Christ is called the second man (1 Cor. 15:47) or the last Adam (1 Cor. 15:45). Though Hebrews 2 does not specifically use these terms, the context clearly emphasizes the fact that the psalm finds its fulfillment in the one who identified himself with man as man (cf. the argument of 2:10-15 and note especially 2:14).

The psalm is, then, in some sense typically Messianic. What was true of Adam in particular (Gen. 1:26-28) and of man in general (Psalm 8:4-8) finds its fulfillment in Christ. This method of application is characteristic of the author of Hebrews. For example, he argues for the Sonship of Messiah (1:5) from the words of Psalm 2, which was probably a liturgy recited at the coronation of the Davidic kings.[25] The parallels between these two uses are similar since both are based on a prior promise to a specific person (Gen. 1:26-28; 2 Sam. 7:14) and involve continuing expectations (Psalms 2; 8). These expectations will only be fulfilled in the Messianic age inaugurated by Jesus Christ. In the most literal sense both psalms involve an absolute and universal dominion that probably goes beyond the original hearer's expectations. David undoubtedly understood the promise of "the ends of the earth" in Psalm 2:8 to apply to the land promised to Israel between the Euphrates and the River of Egypt, and he understood the "all things" in Psalm 8:6 to apply to physical, earthly creatures—not to angels or death. Therefore both psalms should probably be classified in Delitzsch's categories as typico-prophetically Messianic.[26]

DISCREPANCIES IN DETAILS

If some New Testament quotations of Old Testament passages are not accurate in every detail, does this undermine the doctrine of verbal plenary inspiration? S. Lewis Johnson has dealt with this in some detail in a little book entitled *The Old Testament in the New*. Johnson sides with Calvin in arguing that the authors of the New Testament never misrepresent the Old Testament in any point on which they base their argument, but they appear to have been somewhat unconcerned about accuracy regarding details that were not germane to their argument.[27] This point certainly appears applicable to the matter of the New Testament quoting the Septuagint translation "a little lower than the angels" rather than "a little lower than God" which is the more accurate rendering of mē'lōhîm in Psalm 8:5.

The argument of Hebrews 2:5-9 deals with God's intention to subordinate the world to man, an intention that is only realized in Christ. For the writer the important part of the psalm is the last verse of his quotation (i.e., Psalm 8:6b). He has left part of the verse out because he wishes to emphasize the subjection of "all things" to man.[28] He sees this subjection as being manifestly unrealized by man in general but fulfilled in the glorification of Jesus. The author says absolutely nothing about the comparative status of man and angels and, as Hawthorne has noted, probably only uses the phrase about Jesus being "made for a little while lower than the angels" (2:9) to refer to the incarnation because it is the only description of man's nature readily available in the context.[29]

It is true that some writers wish to use the interpretation of the phrase "a little while lower than the angels" in Hebrews 2:9 to emphasize further the discrepancies between its function there and its function in Psalm 8:5. Thus Childs points out that the phrase refers to man's exalted dignity in Psalm 8:5 but in Hebrews 2 emphasizes Christ's temporary humiliation before His exaltation to become the representative for every man.[30] That the phrase refers to the incarnation may be admitted, but that it refers to a temporary humiliation must be questioned. In the context no emphasis is put on Jesus' having abandoned any former state. In fact, no former state is even referred to. Also, the Greek phrase brachu ti ("for a little while") that Childs refers to as a temporal indicator may refer to quality (cf. 2 Sam. 16:1 in the Septuagint and John 6:7) instead of time (cf. Isa. 57:17 in the Septuagint and Acts 5:24). It is taken by many as qualitative just like the Hebrew phrase me'at ("a little lower") in Psalm 8:5.[31] Thus in response to Childs it should be noted that the author of Hebrews did not intend to say anything about the temporary or permanent inferiority of Christ to the angels. His sole purpose in using Psalm 8 was to show that Jesus was the one through whom God brought to fulfillment everything that He had intended for man. As the verses that follow point out, the writer desired to identify Jesus with man (cf. the argument of 2:10-15, especially verse 14).

Too much should not be made of the "discrepancies" between the Old Testament interpretation of Psalm 8 and the New Testament writer's use of the passage. The one difference that does exist, the interpretation of mē'lōhîm as "angels" rather than "God," should be minimized because it forms no essential part of the argument in Hebrews and was not of sufficient importance for the writer to vary from his standard practice of quoting from the Septuagint.[32]

CONCLUSION

In summary, Psalm 8 has been taken as a poetic allusion to Genesis 1:26-28. Psalm 8 is a hymn of praise to the Creator of the vast universe for His gracious condescension in subordinating all the rest of creation to such a seemingly insignificant creature as man. The New Testament sees the dominion that was conferred on Adam at creation and claimed for man in general in Psalm 8 as being fulfilled in Jesus Christ. The basis for this fulfillment has been shown to be the typological connection between Jesus Christ and Adam as representatives of man. Bruce feels that this association is consistent with the Old Testament concept of God raising up a man to accomplish His original purpose in place of one who has failed in that purpose.[33]

The quotation in Hebrews does not agree in every detail with a proper interpretation of Psalm 8 in its Old Testament context. The Hebrew word mē'lōhîm in Psalm 8:5 should properly be translated "God" rather than "angel." This is consistent with the psalmist's allusion to Genesis 1:26-28. However, the difference does not bear on the essential argument of the author of Hebrews. Johnson has shown that this practice is typical of the New Testament writers and is not at all inconsistent with the doctrine of verbal plenary inspiration.[34]

NOTES

1. Bernhard W. Anderson, *Out of the Depths* (Philadelphia: Westminster, 1970), p. 102.

2. Claus Westermann, *The Praise of God in the Psalms*, trans. Keith R. Crim (Richmond: John Knox, 1965), pp. 122-30.
3. This interpretation of "name" in Psalm 8:1 was already suggested before the application of form critical criteria. See A. F. Kirkpatrick, ed., *The Book of Psalms*, The Cambridge Bible for Schools and Colleges (Cambridge: Cambridge U., 1891), p. 37.
4. This is based on reading the textually and morphologically debated form *t^enâ* as a Qal infinitive construct. See Franz Delitzsch, *Biblical Commentary on the Psalms*, trans. Francis Bolton, 3 vols., 2d ed., 1871 reprint ed. (Grand Rapids: Eerdmans, n.d.), 1:150.
5. For this interpretation of the enigmatic expression in 8:2a and for its application to the Lord's quotation of it in Matthew 21:16, see Carl Bernhard Moll, *The Psalms*, trans. Charles A. Briggs, John Forsyth, James B. Hammond, J. Fred McCurdy, *Lange's Commentary on The Holy Scriptures*, 12 vols., 1872 reprint ed. (Grand Rapids: Zondervan, 1960), 5:89-90.
6. J. J. Stewart Perowne, *The Book of Psalms*, 2 vols., 4th ed., 1878 reprint ed. (Grand Rapids: Zondervan, 1966), 2:155. See also Francis Brown, S. R. Driver, and C. A. Briggs, eds., *A Hebrew and English Lexicon of the Old Testament*, s.v. "'elōhîm," p. 43.
7. That this is the writer's normal practice is demonstrated by Brooke Foss Westcott, *The Epistle to the Hebrews*, 2d ed., 1892, reprint (Grand Rapids: Eerdmans, 1950), pp. 476-79.
8. A point made by W. E. Barnes, *The Psalms*, 2 vols., Westminster Commentaries (London: Methuen, 1931), 1:36.
9. Franz Delitzsch, *A New Commentary on Genesis*, trans. Sophia Taylor, 2 vols., 1888, reprint (Minneapolis: Klock & Klock, 1978), 1:98-99.
10. Derek Kidner, *Genesis* (Chicago: Inter-Varsity, 1967), p. 51.
11. For this point in Genesis 1 see Gerhard von Rad, *Genesis*, trans. John H. Marks, The Old Testament Library (Philadelphia: Westminster, 1961), pp. 57-58.
12. The verb in Genesis 1:26 is a jussive and those in Genesis 1:28 are imperatives. The verbs in Psalm 8:6-8 are preterites, preterites with *waw*-consecutive, or perfects, and refer to a definite past act. For the aspectual value of the preterite, see Ronald J. Williams, *Hebrew Syntax, An Outline*, 2d ed. (Toronto: U. of Toronto, 1976), pp. 32-33.
13. John Calvin, *Commentary on the Book of Psalms*, trans. James Anderson, 5 vols., 1843, reprint (Grand Rapids: Eerdmans, 1963), 1:104.
14. Brown, Driver, Briggs, *Lexicon*, s.v. "'ādām," p. 9, and "'enôsh," p. 60. Also compare Job 25:6.
15. Richard Longenecker, *Biblical Exegesis in the Apostolic Period* (Grand Rapids: Eerdmans, 1975), p. 175.
16. Ibid.

17. Gerald F. Hawthorne, "Hebrews," in *The New Layman's Bible Commentary*, ed. G. C. D. Howley, F. F. Bruce, and H. L. Ellison (Grand Rapids: Zondervan, 1979), p. 1585.

18. Acts 7:38, 53; Galatians 3:19. Also see Westcott, *Hebrews*, pp. 37-38 for further references.

19. James Moffatt, *A Critical and Exegetical Commentary on the Epistle to the Hebrews*, The International Critical Commentary, 1924, reprint (Edinburgh, T. & T. Clark, 1963), p. 21.

20. See Hawthorne, "Hebrews," p. 1588, for possible Old Testament and Apocryphal references to the authority of angels. For the possibility that his readers may have believed that angels would rule over the coming world order, see Philip Edgcumbe Hughes, *A Commentary on the Epistle to the Hebrews* (Grand Rapids: Eerdmans, 1977), p. 14.

21. For the method of citing Scriptures here, see Moffatt, *Epistle to the Hebrews*, p. 22.

22. J. Armitage Robinson, *St. Paul's Epistle to the Ephesians*, 2d ed. (London: James Clarke, n.d.), p. 41.

23. Conrad Louis, *The Theology of Psalm VIII*, The Catholic University of America Studies in Sacred Theology 99 (Washington, D.C.: Catholic U., 1946), p. 147. For an exception, see F. W. Grosheide, *Commentary on the First Epistle to the Corinthians*, The New International Commentary on the New Testament (Grand Rapids: Eerdmans, 1953), pp. 368-69.

24. For the clearest and fullest expression of this, see F. F. Bruce, *The Epistle to the Hebrews*, The New International Commentary on the New Testament (Grand Rapids: Eerdmans, 1964), pp. 35-36.

25. Ibid., pp. 11-12. See the literature cited there.

26. Delitzsch, *Psalms*, 1:69.

27. S. Lewis Johnson, Jr., *The Old Testament in the New* (Grand Rapids: Zondervan, 1980). Reference is made to Calvin's point on pages 11 and 64.

28. For a discussion of the textual problem here, see F. F. Bruce, *Hebrews*, pp. 31-32.

29. Hawthorne, "Hebrews," p. 1588.

30. Brevard S. Childs, "Psalm 8 in the Context of the Christian Canon," *Interpretation* 23 (1969):25-26.

31. Westcott, *Hebrews*, p. 44.

32. James Anderson, the translator of Calvin's *Commentary on the Book of Psalms*, compares the practice to an author today quoting from the English text; cf. Calvin, *Psalms*, 1:103.

33. Bruce, *Hebrews*, p. 35.

34. Johnson, *The Old Testament in the New*.

3

The Purpose of Tongues in 1 Corinthians 14:20-25

Harold W. Hoehner

First Corinthians 14:22 states that tongues constitute a sign not for believers but for unbelievers and that prophecy is not for unbelievers but believers. However, in the next verse Paul states that if unbelievers come into a church and hear the believers speaking in tongues they will think that the believers are mad. He goes on to add that when unbelievers hear believers prophesying they are convicted and possibly even converted. Although some might claim that there is a contradiction here, it seems rather incredible that Paul would make a statement only to contradict himself in the next sentence. It is better to think that there is something here that is not readily apparent. Therefore it is necessary to examine the passage more closely in order to grasp Paul's thinking.

CONTEXT

The Corinthian church had many difficulties. It seems that

HAROLD W. HOEHNER (A.B., Barrington College; Th.M., Th.D., Dallas Theological Seminary; Ph.D., Cambridge University; graduate study, Tübingen University) is professor of New Testament literature and exegesis and director of Th.D. studies at Dallas Theological Seminary, Dallas, Texas.

specific questions were asked of Paul in chapters 7-16. Paul repeatedly uses the phrase *peri de* ("now concerning") to introduce a new topic on which he had been asked to comment. The problems related to spiritual gifts are discussed in chapters 12-14. Paul states in 12:1-11 that diverse spiritual gifts are all given by the same Spirit for the purpose of building up the body of believers. Paul continues in 12:12-31a by using the human body to illustrate the unity and diversity of the spiritual gifts in the church. Then in 12:31b—13:13 Paul shows that love is more important than all the gifts because it will endure forever whereas the gifts are only for the development and edification of the church while it is on earth. Paul's application of chapter 13 is obvious for the discussion at hand. If love is most important, then it should also be demonstrated by the Corinthians in their use of the gifts. Gifts are to be used for the building up of the body rather than for any selfish purpose.

In 14:1-25 Paul returns to the subject of gifts and argues that prophecy is to be preferred over tongues. In 14:1-19 he shows that prophecy is preferred to uninterpreted tongues. The former is understood by all members of the church and, consequently, everyone is edified. In contrast, uninterpreted tongues are useless to believers because they are unintelligible to those who hear them.

The next section in Paul's discussion of spiritual gifts is the passage that will be discussed in this article, namely 14:20-25. Paul concludes his explanation of gifts in 14:26-40. There he states that the use of gifts should be done in an orderly manner in a church meeting in order to bring edification to the whole body of believers.

DEFINITIONS

Before one can go into the interpretation of the problem passage, there is a need to define briefly the terms that are used throughout the context.

TONGUES

The term *glōssa* ("tongue") was used in classical Greek in three ways. First, it was used to refer to the physical organ itself.[1] Second, the term was employed to describe something that was shaped like a tongue, such as the reed of an instrument or a shoe-latchet.[2] Third, *glōssa* was used in a broader sense to refer to a language or dialect.[3] These same three characteristics are seen in the Septuagint translation of the Bible[4] and in the Koine ("common") Greek spoken during the first century.[5] Again in the New Testament the same characteristics are seen. The term is used with reference to the physical organ (Mark 7:33; Luke 16:24), a shape like a tongue (Acts 2:3), and a language (Acts 2:4). The term is used forty-eight times in the New Testament: twenty-five times outside of Paul, twenty times in 1 Corinthians 12-14, and three times in the other books of Paul (Rom. 3:13; 14:11; Phil. 2:11).

The twenty times *glōssa* is used in 1 Corinthians 12-14 it is used of a language or speech. Because *glōssa* was unintelligible even to the speaker (14:15, 19), some feel that it refers to an ecstatic utterance.[6] However, it seems far better to take *glōssa* as a language in the normal sense. First, *glōssa* is normally used to refer to an actual language. When it occurs in the plural form (*glōssai*) it is an abbreviation of "different tongues" (*genē glōssōn*) and refers to "different languages" (cf. 12:10, 28, 30).[7] Second, Paul states that tongues need to be interpreted (*hermēneia*). This word has the primary sense of "translation" and suggests that there is to be a translation of a foreign language.[8] Third, Paul's quotation of Isaiah 28:11-12 in 14:21 uses the word *heteroglōssois*, which is translated "strange tongues." This word is a counterpart of *glōssai*,[9] and when one looks in the context of Isaiah, the "strange tongues" refer to the actual language of the Assyrians. Fourth, in Acts 2:4 Luke states that the apostles "began to speak with other tongues" (*glōssais*). Then in the next two verses Luke states that the Jews from various parts of the Roman Empire heard the apostles speaking in their own dialects, which indicates that the "tongues" were known foreign languages. Fifth, Paul and Luke were companions and Paul does not say that the gift of tongues being experienced in Corinth was different from that experienced on the day of Pentecost. Likewise, Luke (who wrote after Paul) did not make any qualifications to indicate that the Pentecost situation was different from the Corinthian situation. Sixth, the fact that Paul instructed the Corinthians to control the tongues by forbidding anyone to speak when there was no interpreter and by not allowing more than three to speak seems to indicate that the gift of tongues was not an uncontrollable ecstatic utterance (14:27-28). Thus it seems best to see tongues as a genuine human language that needs to be translated into another human language in order to be understood.[10]

PROPHECY

Three key Greek words focus on the content and activity of prophecy: *prophēteuō*, *prophēteia*, and *prophētēs*. Both *prophēteuō* ("to prophesy") and *prophēteia* ("prophecy") are used in 1 Corinthians 12-14. Kramer shows that Plato used *prophētēs* ("prophet") in two different ways.[11] First, a prophet is controlled by the gods and becomes the instrument of the oracles of the gods.[12] Second, a prophet is an interpreter and explains enigmatic statements of the gods.[13] The point of difference is that the first is overcome by ecstacy and reveals the inspired message of the gods, whereas the second is in control of himself and uses his skills of interpretation in order to discern the oracles of the gods. When one sees the usage in the Old Testament it is immediately apparent that the prophet is to be God's mouthpiece. His message is a revelation from God that could not be known through man's skill or learning (e.g., Num. 11:25; Jer. 1:4-9). That is true even of the false prophets, for they claimed that their message did not rest in themselves but came from God (e.g., Hananiah in Jer. 28 claimed his message was from God).

The use of the verb *prophēteuō* ("to prophesy") in classical literature primarily refers to interpreting the gods.[14] The noun *prophēteia* ("prophecy") is not used in classical literature. In the New Testament the verb form is used twenty-eight times and it always has (with the possible exception of John 11:51) the idea of revelation flowing from God. Paul uses it eleven times. He uses it nine times in 1 Corinthians 12-14 and two times in 1 Corinthians 11:45. The noun *prophēteia* is used nineteen times in the New Testament. Paul uses it once in Romans 12:6 and five times in 1 Corinthians 12-14. The consistent New Testament idea is that a prophecy is an actual message or oracle from God. The word is not used in the New Testament to refer to the interpretation of an oracle by a skilled interpreter. "In short, *prophecy in Paul cannot denote anything other than inspired speech. And prophecy as charisma is neither skill nor aptitude nor talent; the charisma is the actual speaking forth of words given by the Spirit in a particular situation and ceases when the words cease.*"[15]

UNGIFTED (*'Idiōtēs*)

In classical usage the word *'idiōtēs* has three distinct shades of meaning. First, it bears the sense of a private individual as distinct from one holding a public office like a ruler or king.[16] Second, it refers to a layman as opposed to a professional person like a trained soldier,[17] doctor,[18] or philosopher.[19] Third, it is used to describe one who is an outsider or alien as distinct from one who is a member.[20] In the Septuagint it is used only as a textual variant of Proverbs 6:8 to refer to one who is a private individual distinct from a king.

In the New Testament this word is used only five times. In Acts 4:13 Peter and John were considered by the religious leaders to be "uneducated" since they had not been trained in the proper theological schools. In 2 Corinthians 11:6 Paul claims that he is "unskilled" in his speech, meaning that he was not a trained rhetorician or professional orator. The other three times the word is used are in 1 Corinthians 14:16, 23, 24 where it has the idea of one who is not initiated into the membership of believers. They were outsiders who apparently had joined in the Christian gatherings but were not yet a part of them. The *New American Standard Bible* refers to those individuals as "ungifted."

INTERPRETATION

Having briefly discussed the problem, the context, and the terminology, it is now time to discuss the interpretation of the passage. The passage itself can be divided into four parts.

EXHORTATION TO MATURITY, 14:20

Although some commentators think verse 20 is the concluding sentence of verses 1-19,[21] it is best to see verse 20 as the introduction to a new paragraph.[22] There are two reasons for this. First, the introductory expression, "brothers," has already been used by Paul to introduce a new thought. He used the same expression in 10:1 to begin a new paragraph in order to soften his command.[23] Second, in verse 21 Paul quotes from Isaiah 28:11-12. Verse 20 has overtones of the context of Isaiah 28:1-10, so it fits better with verse 21 than with verses 1-19.

Paul has stated that prophecy is preferred over tongues because it is understandable, but the Corinthians seemed to prefer tongues. He states that they should not become children in understanding. Rather they should be mature in their understanding. This is similar to Isaiah 28:1-10 where the Israelites were infants in their understanding of the intent of Isaiah's message and consequently would face God's judgment. Paul is telling the Corinthians to "grow up" and prefer prophecy because it will be helpful to the community of believers.

QUOTATION FROM ISAIAH, 14:21

Paul begins his quotation of Isaiah with the introductory formula "in the Law it is written." "The Law" has reference to the whole of the Old Testament. Ellis states that there are nine quotations—four of them in Paul's letters—that have the phrase *legei kurios* ("says the Lord"). All of these quotations vary, to some extent, from both the Septuagint and the Masoretic text. In all four of Paul's quotations the phrase is neither a part of the Old Testament passage nor an introductory formula.[24]

Within Paul's quotation of Isaiah 28:11 three variations need to be discussed. First, Paul changes the third person plural of the Masoretic text and the Septuagint to the first person singular. This changes the wording of the text from "they shall speak" to "I shall speak." Second, Paul changes the word order in the first phrase of Isaiah 28:11. In the Old Testament "stammering lips" was followed by "a foreign tongue." However, in the New Testament "men of strange tongues" was followed by "lips of strangers." It seems that Paul reversed the order because he was dealing with the use of foreign languages. Third, Paul changed the last part of the clause, in which he added

The Purpose of Tongues

oud' houtōs. In Isaiah 28:12 the Masoretic text reads, "But they would not listen," and the Septuagint reads, "And they did not want to listen." However, 1 Corinthians 14:21 reads, "And even so they will not listen to Me." Paul is applying that quotation to the Corinthian situation.

The context of Isaiah must be examined. In Isaiah 28-33 the prophet is pronouncing woes against Israel. Isaiah 28:1-8 pictures God judging an Israel drunk with pride and power. In 28:9-13 Israel mocks the prophet for repeating the same simple message and asks if he thinks the people are little children who require statements to be continually repeated. Isaiah then says God will speak to them with stammering lips and a foreign tongue. When the foreign nation (i.e. the Assyrians) comes upon Israel it will be a sign authenticating Isaiah's message of judgment. That word from God through Isaiah came true a short time later when Sennacherib invaded Judah in 701 B.C., and it was ultimately fulfilled when the people were carried off into the Babylonian captivity in 586 B.C.

APPLICATION OF ISAIAH, 14:22

The Greek word *hōste* ("so then") that begins verse 22 acts as a result or conclusion of the quote from Isaiah. Paul is making an application of the quotation to his day. One notices that he mentions both tongues and prophecies, both of which were discussed in the context of 1 Corinthians 14. He first deals with tongues and states that they are for a sign. Robertson and Plummer correctly point out that Paul does not say that tongues are a sign. However, the *eis* plus the accusative indicates purpose, and hence tongues are intended to serve as a sign.[25] Paul does not indicate what kind of sign was to be given. Some think it was to be a sign of judgment,[26] but that view has some problems. When tongues are used in the book of Acts they are employed as an aid to faith rather than as a sign of judgment.[27] Also, tongues did not bring judgment on unbelievers in Corinth. It seems better to see tongues serving as a sign of authentication for God's message and activity. "Paul's usage of *sēmeion* is especially instructive. It stands for a miraculous authenticating pointer (Rom. 15:19; 1 Cor. 1:22; 2 Cor. 12:12; 2 Thess. 2:9), and is an authenticating sign elsewhere (Rom.

4:11; 2 Thess. 3:17). Usage throughout the New Testament substantiates this (cf. Acts 2:22; 14:3)."[28]

The use of tongues as an authenticating sign matches the Isaiah passage well. The sign in Isaiah 28 did not produce judgment. Isaiah had already spoken God's judgment in simple words. It was after the people had mocked Isaiah that he provided the sign of a foreign tongue to authenticate or confirm his message of judgment.

Burdick has shown that tongues were used among unbelievers in Acts 2; 10; and 19. In Acts 2, tongues were used by the messengers for the purpose of convincing the unsaved of the authenticity of the outpouring of the Holy Spirit. In Acts 10 and 19 tongues were used by the recipients of the gospel message—after they were converted—to confirm what had occurred.[29] It is interesting to notice that in each occurrence no interpreter acted as an intermediary between the one who was speaking in tongues and the listener. The point is that tongues were used to serve as a sign to authenticate God's activity among unbelievers in an evangelistic setting.

The next item to be discussed concerning 14:22 is the composition of the unbelievers. Did Paul have in mind Jewish unbelievers, Gentile unbelievers, or both? One view is that Paul had in mind only Jewish unbelievers because tongues as a sign are to be restricted to the Jewish nation. The expression "this people" in the quotation from Isaiah can have reference to no one else but the Jews.[30] Furthermore, Paul states in 1 Corinthians 1:22 that the Jews seek a sign. However, there are problems in trying to restrict tongues as a sign to unbelieving Jews only. This view has difficulty in trying to make a distinction between the Jewish unbelievers in verse 22 and the Gentile unbelievers in verses 23-25. There is nothing in the text to make that distinction. It would seem that if Paul had intended to make that distinction he would have done so more clearly.

The other view is that tongues can be valid as a sign to any unbeliever whether Jew or Gentile. This seems to fit best in the context. The same term is used for the unbelieving in verses 22-24, and to make a distinction between the Jewish and Gentile unbelievers seems to be forced. It may be that because the Jews did want a sign the primary application of the gift of tongues could be for the Jews, but certainly the context would seem to include Gentiles as well. One sees that tongues were used for a sign in Acts 10 and 19 among Gentiles as well as Jews. It seems that to have the sign as applicable only to the Jewish unbelievers is too restrictive and cannot be borne out in the passage at hand.

How long will the tongues serve as a sign? That question is not answered here, but Hebrews 2:3-4 seems to indicate that signs ceased with the apostles.

The second part of verse 22 states that prophecy is not for unbelievers but for believers. To think, as Dunn does,[31] that prophecy was also a sign is unwarranted and confusing.[32] Prophecy did not serve as a sign, but it was useful for building up of the believers.

In conclusion then, tongues served as a sign to authenticate God's message and activity to the unbelievers. Paul applies this principle from the passage in Isaiah 28.

INFERENCE TO BE MADE IN THE CORINTHIAN SITUATION, 14:23-25

One needs to note Paul's structure in verses 23-25.[33] First, he begins with the inferential particle oùn ("therefore"). This conjunction introduces an inference from what he had just discussed in verse 22. Paul is applying the tongues and prophecy to the Corinthian situation. Second, in making the inference Paul is very careful to describe the group to whom he is making the application. His statement, "the whole church should assemble together," in verse 23 is pleonastic. It seems that Paul deliberately included this to indicate that he is making the application to the church situation. He did not want anyone to miss this. Third, in verses 23-24 Paul has two third-class conditional sentences that denote a more probable future. These two conditional sentences are contrasted by the use of the conjunction de ("but"). Here one sees two opposite hypothetical situations. The first situation is where tongues are used, and the second situation is where prophecy is used. Fourth, the uninitiated ones or unbelievers who come in to the church service are in the plural in the first hypothetical situation ("ungifted men or unbelievers") but in the singular and in reversed order in the second hypothetical situation ("an unbeliever or an un-gifted man").

Having made some observations on the structure, one now needs to interpret the passage. First, Paul is introducing an inference regarding tongues and prophecy in a church situation. In the broader context he has been talking about these two gifts and demonstrating the superiority of prophecy. He then quotes Isaiah 28:11-12 and concludes in verse 22 that tongues are a sign to unbelievers while prophecy is for believers. Now he proceeds to apply that truth to the church situation, and he illustrates it through the use of two hypothetical circumstances. The first is one in which uninitiated ones or unbelievers enter and hear all the church speaking in tongues and think the believers are mad. The uninitiated ones were those who were outsiders. They were attending the gatherings of believers but had not yet become members of the church because they judged the members as being mad. The unbelievers, it seems, had not partaken in the meetings at all. Some think the Corinthians were judged as being mad because "all" (pantes) were speaking in tongues at one time.[34] But "pantes cannot mean that in v. 24 and therefore does not mean it here."[35] Rather it meant that they all spoke in tongues one after another. The use of the plural for those who came into the church situation only indicates that not just one person would make this judgment that the Corinthians are mad, but that no matter how many witnessed the event they would all make the same criticism.

Why were the unbelievers at Corinth judging the believers to be mad if the gift of tongues was a sign to unbelievers? It is because the gift of tongues was a sign to unbelievers in a non-church situation in which its use without interpretation was designed to authenticate God's message and activity, as seen in the book of Acts. But in a church situation the gift of tongues was to be used for the building up of the saints, and this could happen only when the tongues were interpreted. The Corinthians were incorrectly using uninterpreted tongues in a church situation. When the unbelievers entered the assembly, saw the people using uninterpreted tongues, and realized that no one was communicating with anyone, they could only conclude that the believers were all mad.

The second hypothetical situation is given in verses 24-25 where a certain unbeliever or uninitiated one enters a church service and all the congregation (in order) prophesy. Because of this action "he is convicted by all, he is called to account by all; the secrets of his heart are disclosed; and so he will fall on his face and worship God, declaring that God is certainly among you." The conjunction *de* sets this hypothetical circumstance in contrast to the one given in verse 23. The unbeliever is mentioned before the uninitiated (which is the reverse order of verse 23) possibly because Paul's topic in verses 24-25 is conversion.[36]

The one who entered the service is singular as opposed to the use of the plural in verse 23. Since it is hypothetical, Paul is showing what would possibly happen to someone who came and heard the gift of prophecy used in a church situation for the purpose of building each other up. That person would be convicted that God is in the midst of these believers because they have concern for each other's edification. The plural was not used because that would imply that all who came in would be converted. But the singular eliminates the idea of an automatic conversion.

Prophecy was not to be used outside the church for unbelievers. It was to be limited to believers within the church context for the purpose of building one another up, as all the gifts should function. Prophecy was chosen here only because it was compared and contrasted with tongues in the whole of 1 Corinthians 14.

CONCLUSION

There is no contradiction between 1 Corinthians 14:22 and 23. Paul had been dealing with tongues and prophecy in chapter 14. In verse 20 he asks the Corinthians to be mature in their use of gifts. Paul quotes Isaiah 28:11-12, which mentions the use of strange or foreign tongues. In verse 22 the *hōste* ("so then") indicates that Paul is concluding from the quote that tongues serve as a sign not for believers but for unbelievers. In contrast, prophecy is not for unbelievers but for believers. From this statement Paul draws a conclusion for the church situation, and in verses 23-25 he illustrates it by two hypothetical circumstances. He is demonstrating that the Corinthians were using the sign gift in a wrong context. The sign gift was to be used uninterpreted in a nonchurch context to authenticate the message and the activity of God and to aid in evangelism. But the gift of tongues in a church situation was always to be interpreted (1 Cor. 14:5, 13, 26, 27) and was for the edification of believers. The Corinthians used the sign gift without the interpretation in a church situation and this caused problems.

Paul on the one hand is arguing that prophecy is superior because it communicates well. But on the other hand, Paul argues throughout the context that tongues should not be used unless they are interpreted. The next verses (vv. 26-27) state that there should be an interpretation of tongues. Paul is not arguing against the gift of tongues per se in the Corinthian church (cf. v. 29), but he is arguing against the misuse of tongues. Tongues are misused in the church when they are not interpreted. Therefore Paul is saying that all things are to be done in decency and order.[37] He exhorts them in verse 20 to be mature and to use the gifts properly and not with selfish motives.

NOTES

1. Homer *Odyssea* 3. 332.
2. Aristotle *Historia Animalium* 6. 10 (565a. 24).
3. Herodotus 1. 57.
4. See Genesis 11:7; Isaiah 11:15; and Zechariah 14:12.
5. Oxyrhynchus Papyri 1. 138; Appian *Punic Wars* 8. 18 (*Libuke* 121); *Griechische Papyri zu Giessen*, 1, 99[9] cited in James Hope Moulton and George Milligan, *The Vocabulary of the Greek Testament Illustrated from the Papyri and Other Non-Literary Sources* (London: Hodder & Stoughton, 1930), p. 128.
6. Johannes Behm, "Glōssa," in *Theological Dictionary of the New Testament*, ed. Gerhard Kittel and Gerhard Friedrich, 10 vols. (Grand Rapids: Eerdmans, 1964), 1:722; James Moffatt, *The First Epistle of Paul to the Corinthians* (London: Hodder & Stoughton, 1938), pp. 207-17; Charles R. Smith, *Tongues in Biblical Perspective* (Winona Lake, Ind.: B. M. H., 1972), pp. 25-40.
7. Jean Hering, *The First Epistle of Saint Paul to the Corinthians*, trans. A. W. Heathcote and P. J. Allcock (London: Epworth, 1962), p. 128.

8. J. G. Davies, "Pentecost and Glossolalia," *Journal of Theological Studies* 3 (October 1952):229-30.

9. James D. G. Dunn, *Jesus and the Spirit* (Philadelphia: Westminster, 1975), p. 244.

10. For further study, see Robert H. Gundry, " 'Ecstatic Utterance' (N.E.B.)?" *Journal of Theological Studies* 17 (October 1966):299-307.

11. Helmut Kramer, "Prophētēs," in *Theological Dictionary of the New Testament*, 6:787-89.

12. Plato *Timaeus* 71e-72b.

13. Ibid., 72b. This view is emphasized by Eduard Schweizer, "The Service of Worship," *Interpretation* 13 (October 1959):406-7.

14. E.g., Pindar *Fragments* 150.

15. Dunn, *Jesus and the Spirit*, p. 229.

16. Herodotus 1. 59, 123.

17. Xenophon *De Equitum Magistro* 8. 1.

18. Thucydides 2. 48. 3.

19. Aristotle *Politica* 2. 4. 1 (1266a. 32).

20. Heinrich Schlier, "Idiōtes," in *Theological Dictionary of the New Testament*, 3:216.

21. Thomas Charles Edwards, *A Commentary on the First Epistle to the Corinthians*, 3d ed. (London: Hodder & Stoughton, 1897), p. 371; F. Godet, *Commentary on the First Epistle of St. Paul to the Corinthians*, trans. A. Cusin, 2 vols. (Edinburgh: T. & T. Clark, n.d.), 2:287-88.

22. Charles J. Ellicott, *St. Paul's First Epistle to the Corinthians* (London: Longmans, 1887), pp. 271-72; H. L. Goudge, *The First Epistle to the Corinthians* (London: Methuen, 1903), p. 127; Moffatt, *First Corinthians*, p. 222; C. K. Barrett, *A Commentary on the First Epistle to the Corinthians* (New York: Harper & Row, 1968), p. 322; Hans Conzelmann, *A Commentary on the First Epistle to the Corinthians*, trans. James W. Leitch (Philadelphia: Fortress, 1975), p. 241.

23. Barrett, *First Epistle to the Corinthians*, p. 322.

24. E. Earle Ellis, *Paul's Use of the Old Testament* (Edinburgh: Oliver and Boyd, 1957), pp. 107, 111.

25. Archibald T. Robertson and Alfred Plummer, *A Critical and Exegetical Commentary on the First Epistle of St. Paul to the Corinthians*, 2d ed. (Edinburgh: T. & T. Clark, 1914), p. 317. Some may argue that under the Semitic influence, *eis* followed by an accusative with the verb "to be" is really only replacing a predicate nominative and would be translated "tongues are a sign." Paul's use of such a construction is seen in 1 Corinthians 6:16; 15:45; 2 Corinthians 6:18; Ephesians 5:31; and Colossians 2:22. However, in all these cases, except the last passage, Paul is quoting the Septuagint and in Colossians 2:22 it seems that the final sense is clear. This view is supported by A. T. Robertson, *A Grammar of*

the Greek *New Testament in the Light of Historical Research,* 4th ed. (Nashville: Broadman, 1923), p. 458; C. F. D. Moule, *An Idiom Book of New Testament Greek,* 2d ed. (Cambridge: Cambridge U., 1959), p. 70; F. Blass and A. Debrunner, *A Grammar of the New Testament and Other Early Christian Literature,* trans. Robert W. Funk (Chicago: U. of Chicago, 1961), § 145(1); and Bruce C. Johanson, "Tongues, a Sign for Unbelievers?: A Structural and Exegetical Study of 1 Corinthians XIV. 20-25," *New Testament Studies* 25 (January 1979):190-91, n. 5. The last article was most helpful.

26. Ibid.; Edwards, *First Epistle to the Corinthians,* p. 375; Barrett, *First Epistle to the Corinthians,* p. 323; Dunn, *Jesus and the Spirit,* p. 231. Cf. O. Palmer Robertson, "Tongues: Sign of Covenantal Curse and Blessing," *Westminster Theological Journal* 38 (Fall 1975):48-49. Robertson would also argue that the sign was a blessing for the new era.

27. Robert L. Thomas, *Understanding Spiritual Gifts* (Chicago: Moody, 1978), p. 222, n. 22.

28. Ibid., p. 224, n. 22.

29. Donald W. Burdick, *Tongues: To Speak or Not to Speak* (Chicago: Moody, 1969), pp. 29-31; cf. Robertson, "Tongues: Sign of Covenantal Curse and Blessing," p. 50; Bastian Van Eldern, "Glossolalia in the New Testament," *Bulletin of the Evangelical Theological Society* 7 (Spring 1964):57-58.

30. Zane C. Hodges, "The Purpose of Tongues," *Bibliotheca Sacra* 120 (July-September 1963):229-30.

31. Dunn, *Jesus and the Spirit,* pp. 231-32; cf. Barrett, *First Epistle to the Corinthians,* pp. 323-24; and J. P. M. Sweet, "A Sign for Unbelievers: Paul's Attitude to Glossolalia," *New Testament Studies* 13 (April 1967):244.

32. Johannes Weiss, *Der erste Korintherbrief,* 9th ed. (Gottingen: Vandenhoeck & Ruprecht, 1910), pp. 332-33.

33. Recently a structural study of this passage has been made with different conclusions (Johanson, "Tongues, a Sign for Unbelievers?: A Structural and Exegetical Study of 1 Corinthians XIV. 20-25," pp. 180-203). I had already finished the article and had it ready to be sent to the editor, hence was not able to interact with it except for a minor point (see above, n. 25). Johanson agrees with me that little has been written on this passage up to this time.

34. Edwards, *First Epistle to the Corinthians,* pp. 375-76.

35. Robertson and Plummer, *First Epistle of St. Paul to the Corinthians,* p. 317.

36. Conzelmann, *First Epistle to the Corinthians,* p. 243, n. 28.

37. Sweet, "A Sign for Unbelievers: Paul's Attitude to Glossolalia," pp. 254, 256-57.

4

The Rapture in
1 Thessalonians 5:1-11

Zane C. Hodges

The concept that the church will be removed from the earth before the Tribulation is sometimes said to be based on no direct teaching in the New Testament. Even those who defend the doctrine of the pretribulational rapture of the church have often alleged that it is largely a product of inferences drawn from various texts or have been satisfied to base it on a few isolated proof texts. Unfortunately, few attempt to justify this belief by appealing to a close exegesis of an extended passage of Scripture.

Although it would be pointless to deny the validity of comparing Scripture with Scripture (to draw the necessary inferences for doctrine) or to deny the validity of proof texts carefully weighed in their context, it is obvious that there is a special force and value to arguments derived from the connected exegetical analysis of an entire unit of biblical material. For the truth that the church is destined for rescue from the woes of the Tribulation, no passage has more to offer to exegeti-

ZANE C. HODGES (A.B., Wheaton College; Th.M., Dallas Theological Seminary) is professor of New Testament literature and exegesis at Dallas Theological Seminary, Dallas, Texas.

cal scrutiny than does 1 Thessalonians 5:1-11. It is the purpose of this article to focus on Paul's teaching in this crucial text.

GENERAL STRUCTURE OF THE EPISTLE

THE KEY PASSAGE

In the opening chapter of his epistle to the Thessalonians, the apostle informs those believers that the story of their conversion meets him everywhere. It is well known "how you turned to God from idols to serve a living and true God, and to wait for His Son from heaven, whom He raised from the dead, that is Jesus, who delivers us from the wrath to come" (1 Thess. 1:9b-10).

The last phrase of this statement has been poorly handled in the King James Version.[1] The Greek construction involves an inherently timeless form of expression. To assign it a past connotation as does the King James Version ("which delivered us from the wrath to come") is therefore not genuinely supported by the original text. Clearly Paul is thinking primarily of the future as his reference to waiting for God's Son from heaven makes plain, and the phrase about "the wrath to come" is redolent with eschatological overtones. If, therefore, the context assigns any time to the expression at all, the most natural temporal referent would be future. Thus the rendering "who will deliver us" would be in every way entirely appropriate. The practice of more modern versions in which the construction is handled by a present tense ("who delivers us") is also perfectly acceptable since the English context makes the reader think quite naturally of some deliverance that lies ahead. Perhaps there is nothing to be gained by going beyond the translation offered by the *New International Version*: "who rescues us from the coming wrath."

THE OVERALL DEVELOPMENT

In the statement quoted above from 1:9b-10, there appears clearly to be a succinct summation of the topics the apostle will discuss in the remainder of his letter. Hence the reference to "how you turned to God from idols" points to the *past* days of their conversion, and it is those early days that are particularly before the apostle's mind in chapters 2 and 3. In those chapters Paul explores in a most intimate way his personal relationship to the Thessalonians during the period when he had proclaimed the gospel to them and explains why he has been unable to return to them since then. Questions about the integrity of his love for them seem to lurk in the background, and he tries diligently to lay those questions to rest. To question the messenger's integrity was the first step to questioning the message and hence the validity of their conversion experience. Not surprisingly, Paul devotes much space to this concern. Under persecution, such as the Thessalonian converts were experiencing, the temptation to "give it all up" must have been quite real.

In like manner, the phrase "to serve a living and true God" points to their *present* attitude and conduct. This phrase anticipates the brief section in 4:1-12 where the apostle discusses the life-style that these believers must presently pursue in order to please the Lord. It is this section that focuses on "sanctification," "the love of the brethren," and proper behavior "toward outsiders."

If 1 Thessalonians 1:9b-10 offers an informal outline of the contents of the epistle, it might therefore be said that "to wait for His Son from heaven, whom He raised from the dead, that is Jesus, who delivers us from the wrath to come" points toward the *future* and outlines the eschatological portion of the epistle in 4:13 — 5:11. That is so because 4:13 — 5:11 is transparently divided into two subunits. As is well known, 4:13-18 reaffirms the validity of their belief in the coming of the Lord. Though dismayed by the unanticipated death of some of their number, they ought not, Paul affirms, be concerned either for those who have already died, or for themselves. At the coming of the Lord the dead, in fact, will come with Him, and the living will be caught up. Thus there is no cause for alarm. Rather they are to use this truth for their mutual comfort (4:18). Clearly, this initial section is anticipated in the phrase "to wait for His Son from heaven, whom He raised from the dead." Even the reference to Christ's own resurrection is pertinent to the resurrection of sleeping saints (cf. 4:14).

The unit found in 5:1-11 is equally well capsulized by the phrase "Jesus, who delivers us from the wrath to come." Attention will now be directed to a detailed consideration of this portion of the letter.

DETAILED ANALYSIS OF 5:1-11

THE THESSALONIANS' KNOWLEDGE (5:1-3)

The apostle opens this segment of the discussion with the assertion that the Thessalonians were well informed on the subject of "the times and epochs" (5:1). Whatever doubts about their eschatological information may have been aroused by the death of some of their fellow Christians, Paul feels that those doubts ought to be laid to rest. Their understanding of the prophetic foreview need not be called into question. This assertion is clearly intended to reassure them.

What then do the Thessalonians know about the program of prophecy? Paul affirms that, "For you yourselves know full well [akribōs, "accurately"] that the day of the Lord will come just like a thief in the night. While they are saying 'Peace and safety!' then destruction will come upon them suddenly" (5:2-3a). There can be no mistaking the formal allusions to well-known eschatological ideas in these verses. Just as the phrase "times and epochs" in verse 1 was no doubt known as a piece of prophetic terminology, so also was the expression "the day of the Lord." The former had been used by the Lord Jesus Himself when, in Acts 1:7, He declined to declare whether the time had arrived for restoring the kingdom to Israel. It may well have been a set phrase that He did not use for the first time on that occasion. The term "day of the Lord" is, of course, used frequently in the Old Testament (cf. Isa. 2:12; Amos 5:18, 20; Zeph. 1:7, 14; etc.). In the same way, the expression at the end of verse 3, "like birth pangs upon a woman with child," employs a well-known metaphor for the eschatological woes. Indeed, the Greek for "birth pangs" (ōdin) is precisely the one used by the Lord in the expression "beginning of birth pangs" (Matt. 24:8), where the word for "birth pangs" (ōdinōn) likewise means "labor pains."[2]

Here, then, the reader meets unmistakably the "wrath to come" to which Paul makes reference in 1:10. That wrath is nothing less than the "birth pangs" of the day of the Lord about which the Thessalonians already knew much.[3] To make the term *wrath* in 1:10 a reference to hell would be wholly gratuitous and without any meaningful support from the epistle itself. But since Jesus "delivers us from the wrath to come," that affirmation becomes an assertion that the Thessalonians are to be delivered from the calamities of the day of the Lord. The remainder of 5:1-11 makes plain how that is to be.

THE THESSALONIANS' POSITION (5:4-5)

It should be carefully observed that among the data that the Thessalonians knew "accurately" was that the day of the Lord came unexpectedly, that is "just like a thief in the night." Just exactly what this meant for Paul is made plain in verses 4-7 where the apostle describes the general stupor of the unsaved world in language suggesting sleep and drunkenness. This must also be combined with the assertion of verse 3 that "while they are saying, 'Peace and safety!' then destruction will come upon them suddenly."

The portrait the apostle thus draws of the world's condition at the time of the advent of the day of the Lord could hardly be clearer. There is a general feeling of peace and security (v. 3) during which the moral state of men is one of lethargic and sottish unwatchfulness (vv. 6-8). Suddenly, like a thief breaking in without warning, a reign of destruction begins. The scene the apostle describes is a familiar one in the prophetic materials. One need only think of the famous analogies with the days of Noah and with those of Lot (cf. Luke 17:26-30). The same effect is portrayed by Peter in another passage that speaks of the day of the Lord coming as a thief (2 Pet. 3:3-10).[4]

Clearly what is involved here is a well-known motif in New Testament prophecy: the era of eschatological climax has its advent in a situation where all seems well and where normal life proceeds as usual (Luke 17:27-28 — "they were eating, they were drinking, they were marrying, they were being given in marriage . . . they were buying, they were selling, they were planting, they were building"). The attitude of many who hear of the promised coming of Christ is one of supreme unconcern because nothing out of the ordinary has as yet transpired ("all continues just as it was from the beginning of creation" [2 Pet. 3:4]).

The failure to recognize that in 1 Thessalonians 5 Paul speaks in terms of a familiar eschatological scene has produced some very strange exegesis. In order to place this portrait immediately prior to the manifestation of Christ in glory at the end of the Tribulation, some posttribulational expositors have postulated a brief period of tranquility just after the major judgments of that era have run their course and just before Christ appears.[5] But New Testament prophecy knows nothing of such an interlude. In fact, such an interlude is unthinkable. According to the Lord Jesus Himself, that period of time is so severe that the very extinction of the human race is threatened (Matt. 24:22). Furthermore, at the end of the Tribulation, the armies of the world are being mobilized for the final battle of Armageddon (Rev. 16:13-16). The belief that somewhere at the climax of such a period room could be found to describe the world situation as Paul describes it is a concept that ought not to be taken seriously.

It is not, of course, by any means simply the reference to the day coming as a thief that leads to this conclusion, but rather the whole picture of a world both unconcerned and undisturbed. It should be clear, then, that the time frame to which Paul's words apply can be nothing less than a period before the eschatological woes begin — which is to say, prior to the Tribulation itself. If, as seems absolutely necessary, the two prophetic witnesses of Revelation 11 belong to the first half of Daniel's so-called seventieth week, then it may be further stated that the time frame is also prior to the final seven-year period.

With regard to these witnesses, it may be pointed out in passing that their period of ministry is specified as consuming one-half a prophetic "week" (Rev. 11:3), after which they are slain by the Beast and their bodies allowed to lie unburied for three and one-half days, during which time the world is engaged in joyous celebration over their demise. If their period of testimony belonged to the *last* half week, rather than the first, the anomaly would emerge that the world celebrates a satanic triumph *after* the completion of Daniel's seventieth week. That this is quite inconsistent with Daniel 9:24 is obvious. It should be plain, however, that this all fits well if the witnesses prophesy during the *first* half week, since then their death at the hands of the Beast is the beginning of his triumphant career, which also lasts for a half week (Rev. 13:5). In this light the apparent defeat of the witnesses (after which their resurrection occurs [Rev. 11:11]) becomes their final prophecy: the three and one-half days presage the three and one-half years during which the Beast will triumph over the saints (Rev. 13:7). Thereafter the victory of God's people is assured.

When the two witnesses are properly assigned to the first part of Daniel's seventieth week, it becomes clear that this period is a time of striking divine judgment, because these prophets exercise powers like those belonging both to Elijah and Moses in Old Testament days (Rev. 11:6). In their days, therefore, the eschatological woes will have already begun, even though the final half week escalates these woes to unprecedented proportions. But there is nothing unusual about this. The Lord's own reference to "the beginning of labor pains" followed by "great tribulation" (Matt. 24:8, 21) points in precisely the same direction.

In 1 Thessalonians 5, therefore, Paul is considering the advent of the woes of the day of the Lord. These come, he says in verse 3, at a time of seeming tranquility and security, a fact the Thessalonians already knew. What Paul particularly wishes to emphasize, however, is the issue of escape from those woes. With regard to the unsuspecting world there is no deliverance ("and they shall not escape" [v. 3]). The Greek expression used here involves a particularly emphatic assertion and might well be rendered, "they shall certainly not escape."[6] "They have absolutely no way out," the apostle insists.

But at once he turns to the contrasting lot of his readers. "But you, brethren, are not in darkness, that the day should overtake you like a thief; for you are all sons of light, and sons of day. We are not of night nor of darkness" (5:4-5). Of special interest here are the emphatic pronouns. The "you" of both verses is the personal pronoun (humeis), which is not strictly necessary to the sense of the Greek sentence. It is added for emphasis. In the same way the "you" of verse 4 is emphatically placed ahead of the verb "overtake." Nothing is plainer than that Paul regards his Christian readers as standing in a relationship to this eschatological outpouring that is markedly different from that of

the unregenerate world around them. This is because they belong intrinsically to the "light" rather than to the "darkness."

THE THESSALONIANS' RESPONSE (5:6-11)

From this consideration of the Thessalonians' position
emerges an exhortation. "So then let us not sleep as others do,
but let us be alert and sober. For those who sleep do their sleeping at night, and those who get drunk get drunk at night. But
since we are of the day, let us be sober . . ." (vv. 6-8a). Inasmuch
as you belong to the day and not to the night, Paul is saying,
your spiritual condition should reflect that fact and should contrast sharply with that of the denizens of night around you.

It would appear that, with these words, Paul communicates
his major concern. The Thessalonians were wearied under the
burden of their trials. The death of some of their number had
seemed to suggest the falsity of expecting the Lord's return — at
least in their own lifetime. Such concerns would furnish an
inducement to spiritual lethargy and unwatchfulness. "Be careful that you don't slip into that," Paul admonishes. The state of
somnolent, drunken indifference is one, the apostle affirms,
that can never be appropriate to his Thessalonian converts.
Sober alertness is their only proper demeanor.

They are therefore to arm themselves against the stupor and
unpreparedness of the surrounding world. How? "But since we
are of the day, let us be sober, having put on the breastplate of
faith and love, and as a helmet, the hope of salvation" (v. 8).
Two pieces of defensive equipment are here enjoined on the
readers: the breastplate and the helmet. The breastplate is composed of a spiritual "alloy" of "faith and love." Despite their
trials and the seeming delay of the second advent (a seeming
delay brought into focus by the death of fellow Christians), the
Thessalonians are not to waver in their faith, and neither are
they to neglect the mutual obligations that commitment to the
faith entails. They are also to maintain love.

It seems likely that in the back of Paul's mind lies the famous
parable of Jesus in which the unfaithful servant decides, "My
master will be a long time in coming," and then proceeds to act
uncharitably toward his fellowservants, whom he beats, as he

commences to "eat and drink and get drunk" (Luke 12:45).[7] The Thessalonians are not to behave like that. Continuing faith and love will constitute a bulwark, a breastplate, against the temptation to unwatchful self-indulgence.

In addition to the breastplate the Christian is also exhorted to arm himself with a "helmet," which is defined as "the hope of salvation." It might be clearer in this context to render this phrase as "the expectation of deliverance." Of the unregenerate world Paul has already affirmed, "They shall not escape" (v. 3). He then makes a contrast between those who have no way out and his readers who do. Thus the Greek word for "deliverance" (sōtērias) is the obvious nominal equivalent of the verbal expression in 1:10 ("Jesus . . . who delivers us"). The Thessalonians are, in fact, waiting for God's Son from heaven precisely because He will rescue them from "the wrath to come." This is the helmet of hope they are to wear constantly and not cast aside. Coupled with the breastplate of faith and love, it will serve as admirable protection against the attitudes of those round about them who "have no hope" (cf. 4:13).

But is that hope a valid one? Can the Thessalonians rely on it? They can. "For God has not destined us for wrath, but for obtaining salvation through our Lord Jesus Christ, who died for us, that whether we are awake or asleep, we may live together with Him" (5:9-10). In these two climactic verses Paul's concepts become explicit, and he fleshes out the allusive statement of 1:10 about rescue from the coming wrath.

Once again there is absolutely no exegetical basis for seeing the "wrath" as a reference to eternal damnation. The context is considering the advent of the eschatological woes, and these clearly constitute "the wrath to come" with which the apostle is occupied. Thus when he affirms that "God has not destined us for wrath" (v. 9), he means quite obviously that God has not appointed the Thessalonian believers to experience these end-time calamities.

But to what has God appointed believers? The answer, once again, is "salvation" (i.e. "deliverance"), the rescue referred to in 1:10. And through whom does this "deliverance" come? It comes through the One "who died for us, that whether we are awake or asleep, we may live together with Him" (5:10).

The true force of the phrase "whether we are awake or asleep" is crucial and has been widely overlooked by expositors, particularly those of a posttribulational persuasion. Frequently, the expression has been construed as a reference to Christians who are alive ("awake") and to those who are dead ("asleep") at the coming of Christ. But careful examination of the Greek text shows this to be impossible. In 4:14, the Greek word used to refer to "sleeping" believers (i.e. dead ones) is the Greek verb *koimaō*. However, in 5:10 the verb for sleep is quite different. Here it is the word *katheudō*. The context defines its meaning since it has been used in verses 5 and 6 to describe the state of unwatchfulness against which Paul is warning. In the same way, the verb in verse 10 for "awake" (*grēgoreō*) has been used in verse 6 to describe the state of alertness that Paul enjoins.[8]

Unless sound exegetical procedure is to be thrown to the winds, verse 10 cannot be seen as a description of living and dead Christians. Rather it refers to watchful and unwatchful believers. Hence Paul asserts that the Thessalonians have an inalienable hope that is theirs whether they watch for it or not. The believer's destiny, he insists, is not the wrath of the day of the Lord but rather deliverance from it to live "together with" Christ. This is true "whether we are awake or asleep."

If anyone is inclined to feel that such an assertion throws away the motivation to wakefulness that the apostle is trying to inculcate, such an opinion would be quite out of keeping with Paul's motivational techniques everywhere else. Paul did not feel, for example, that the assurance that a believer is justified by faith apart from works should lead to an indifference about good works. On the contrary, he believed his doctrine of justification was a powerful incentive to good works. In the same way, the apostle felt that the best way to stimulate a watchful spirit was to show that "the hope of deliverance" could not be forfeited even by the believer's failure to watch for it. A true perspective on the psychology of motivation will perceive that in this regard the inspired writer was correct. Those who believe that fear, rather than certitude about the grace of God, is the most powerful deterrent to immoral living need to reread the New Testament with greater care.

Once it is understood that the phrase "whether we are awake or asleep" refers to the contrasting states of watchfulness and unwatchfulness, it is plain that Paul is still thinking of the advent of the eschatological woes. That is, he is thinking of the advent of the day of the Lord, which brings an inescapable ruin to the unsaved and unwatching world (v. 3). But, as the high point of his contrast between the world and his readers, Paul affirms that they *will* escape, whether watching or not, and will live with their Lord. This, in fact, is what their rescue involves.

Special attention should be directed to the contrasting tenses employed in the last part of verse 10. Whereas the words for "awake" and for "asleep" are in the present tense, the word for "live" is in the aorist tense. This contrast imparts to "live" a touch of what the grammars call an "ingressive" force. That is, the Greek verb zēsōmen may be taken to imply "we shall commence to live." But this subtle nuance is not strictly necessary for gleaning the transparent force of Paul's declaration. "When the day of the Lord arrives," Paul means to say, "whether we are watching or sleeping, we will live with Him."

Paul's contrast between the unsaved world and his Christian readers is uncomplicated and straightforward. When the "sudden destruction" of the day of the Lord breaks out on mankind, the unregenerate "shall not escape" but the regenerate, whether awake or asleep, will "live together with [Christ]." Of course, the day of the Lord awakens *everybody,* saved and unsaved alike, and beyond the point of its initial catastrophes there would be no point in describing anyone as still "asleep." But Paul is not thinking beyond that point. The *arrival* of that eschatological era brings two contrasting experiences: ruin and rescue. The Thessalonians are destined for the latter.

That is why the Thessalonians are waiting "for His Son from heaven . . . who delivers us from the wrath to come" (1:10). It is Christ's coming that rescues them from the wrath. While the awful ruin of that climactic era sweeps over a world caught totally off guard, the Thessalonians will be living with the Lord Jesus, "who died for [them]" for that very end. "Therefore," in the light of this grand fact, Paul says, "encourage one another, and build up one another, just as you also are doing" (5:11). At the moment, the Thessalonians are properly attired with the breastplate of faith and love and with the helmet of "the hope of deliverance." "Keep the armor on," Paul exhorts.

CONCLUSION

In the exposition given above, it can be seen that 1 Thessalonians 5:1-11 is easily understood as a piece of direct teaching by the apostle Paul. Christ, at His coming, will deliver His people from the eschatological woes at their very outset so that those who have trusted Him might live with Him. Alternative explanations of this passage, while frequently offered, fail to grasp the smooth unity of the argument and the way in which it unfolds the programmatic statement of 1:10. In particular, the crucial force of "whether we are awake or asleep" is almost always overlooked. A correct analysis of this expression does much to invalidate the posttribulational approach. Thus the truth that the church will escape the Tribulation by means of the rapture has firm roots in the New Testament exegesis.

NOTES

1. The Greek construction is an articular present participle, *ton phuomenon.*
2. It should also be noted that the Greek word *thlipsis* could be associated with "birth pains," as it is in fact in John 16:21. This, however, is the word used for the "tribulation" in Matthew 24:21. Thus the "travail pains" of Matthew 24:8 and the "great tribulation" of 24:21 can both be understood of the agonies of the world's labor pains as a new age is brought forth. The "beginning of birth pangs" (v. 8) and the "great tribulation" (v. 21) do not differ in kind, but in intensity.
3. Leon Morris comments thus: "Paul speaks of 'the wrath to come,' which brings before us the eschatological wrath. The wrath of God is not only something which we see here and now. It will endure to the end of all things. It will be especially manifested in the end of all things" (*The First and Second Epistles to the Thessalonians: The English Text with Introduction and Notes,* The New International Commentary on the New Testament [Grand Rapids: Eerdmans, 1959], p. 65). This is essentially correct, but seems to soften somewhat the unparalleled distinctiveness of the eschatological woes.

4. According to the modern critical editions of the Greek New Testament, the phrase in 2 Peter 3:10 is *hōs kleptēs*, omitting the words *en nukti*, which are translated in the King James Version. The omission is supported by p[72], Aleph, A, B, and others. A vast majority of surviving Greek manuscripts, however, include the words *en nukti* in this Petrine passage. The omission is probably a simple scribal slip made in an early archetype of the Egyptian texts that support it. Peter is familiar with the Pauline letters (cf. 2 Pet. 3:15-16) and probably has the Pauline phrase of 1 Thessalonians 5:2 in mind. The addition of the words need not be thought of as a scribal conformation to the Pauline passage, since the original author no doubt knew this passage. Thus 2 Peter 3 and 1 Thessalonians 5 are very intimately related.

5. See Robert H. Gundry, *The Church and the Tribulation* (Grand Rapids: Zondervan, 1973), p. 92. Gundry also suggests that 5:2 expresses a "wish" and not the actual fact. But this completely overlooks the well-established prophetic motif, to which 5:2 belongs, that normal, undisturbed life prevails prior to the advent of the day of the Lord.

6. In the grammars this is the subjunctive of emphatic negation.

7. The parable is also found in Matthew 24:45-51, but Paul is most likely to have known it in its Lucan form, since he was well acquainted with Luke and once appears to quote from the gospel of Luke (1 Tim. 5:18*b*; cf. Luke 10:7).

8. That these observations can be made, and their force ignored, finds a typical illustration in Morris, *Thessalonian Epistles*, p. 162.

5

A Biblical Defense of Dispensationalism

Stanley D. Toussaint

In some respects the dispensational approach to the Scriptures has fallen on difficult times. It is commonly accused of being an innovation of comparatively recent derivation[1] and even has been denigrated as an *ism* along with the cults.[2] Other accusations have also been brought against dispensationalism. Some charge dispensationalism with teaching that God deals differently with men in different ages, even though God is immutable.[3] Others feel that the dispensational approach to the Scriptures makes a scrapbook of the Bible because it relegates passages like the Ten Commandments or the Sermon on the Mount to other ages or peoples.[4] Still others believe that dispensationalism makes Christians into heresy hunters because it teaches that the church age will culminate in apostasy.[5] Many feel that dispensationalism is too pessimistic in its outlook because it teaches that this age will not progressively become better.[6] Finally, some reject dispensationalism because they feel that it teaches different methods of salvation.[7] Ryrie, in his

STANLEY D. TOUSSAINT (A.B., Augsburg College; Th.M., Th.D., Dallas Theological Seminary) is professor of Bible exposition at Dallas Theological Seminary, Dallas, Texas.

classic defense of dispensationalism, presents a very able apologetic against such calumnies as these.[8]

It is the purpose of this article to defend dispensationalism by examining the Scriptures themselves. After all, the bedrock foundation for any doctrine or teaching must be the Bible. If the Scriptures uniformly and consistently set forth a dispensational viewpoint, it is incumbent on Bible students to approach God's Word from that standpoint and to defend that system from the Word of God itself.

A DEFINITION

It is imperative for any discussion of dispensationalism to begin with a mutual understanding of the subject. Perhaps the most famous definition is that given in the *Scofield Reference Bible*. It states, "A dispensation is a period of time during which man is tested in respect of obedience to some *specific* revelation of the will of God. Seven such dispensations are distinguished in Scripture."[9] The *New Scofield Reference Bible* uses essentially the same definition.[10]

There may be some objection to describing a dispensation as an age. However, a time element is always involved. It may be more accurate to say people live *in* an age but *under* an administration or dispensation. Chafer writes, "A dispensation is a specific, divine economy, a commitment from God to man of a responsibility to discharge that which God has appointed him."[11] The most recent workable definition has been given by Ryrie: "A dispensation is a distinguishable economy in the outworking of God's purpose."[12]

While the exact statements may vary, dispensationalists agree that a dispensation involves a responsibility or responsibilities placed on man during a particular stage of God's progressive revelation. Ryrie clearly points out three distinctives of dispensationalism on which all dispensationalists are agreed: 1. a distinction between the church and Israel, 2. a literal or "normal" hermeneutic for Scripture, and 3. the purpose of God for all dispensations being the glory of God.[13] Dispensationalism, then, simply results from an investigation into the progress of God's plan as revealed in the Scriptures. It recognizes various administrations or economies in this outworking of God's plan in history.

The noun *dispensation* comes from the Greek word *oikonomia*, which is derived from two Greek words: *oikos* ("house") and *nemō* ("to manage"). The word therefore looks at *the office of stewardship*, or is employed in reference to an *administration* or *dispensation*.[14]

The word occurs in Luke 16:24, where it is used of the office of stewardship. In the remaining six occurrences the noun is translated in the *New American Standard Bible* either as "stewardship" (1 Cor. 9:17; Eph. 3:2; Col. 1:25) or "administration" (Eph. 1:10; 3:9; 1 Tim. 1:4). In Ephesians 1:10 and 3:9 it is used of *God's* overall "arrangement" of history; in the other references it seems to refer to a stewardship given to *man*.

In Ephesians 3:2 and Colossians 1:25-26 the word *oikonomia* is used to refer to two distinct dispensations: the present age and the age to come. In both instances the basic concept of an arrangement or responsibility is evident. Regarding these two passages Ryrie asserts, "It is very important to notice that . . . *there can be no question that the Bible uses the word dispensation in exactly the same way the dispensationalist does.*"[15]

While Ephesians 3:2 and Colossians 1:25-26 do identify two dispensations as *oikonomia*, what about the other dispensations that are not specifically identified? The fact that other dispensations are not referred to by the term *oikonomia* in the Scriptures by no means implies they do not exist. Thus, while the Bible only specifically identifies two dispensations through the use of *oikonomia*, the existence of other dispensations can be determined through honest biblical deduction.

Before examining the relevant biblical material it is imperative to make some clarifications. The first clarification concerns the necessity of "tests" in each dispensation, as propounded by Scofield. It perhaps would be better to refer to a *responsibility* placed on individuals in a dispensation rather than a test. Nevertheless the various dispensations do render man accountable, and in that sense a test may be considered as a valid element of any dispensation.

A second clarification relates to the beginning of a new dispensation. The inauguration of a new stewardship or dispensation may or may not mark the conclusion of all elements of a preceding dispensation or dispensations. For instance, the age of law certainly did not render the promises made to Abraham void. On the other hand, the cross marked the conclusion of the dispensation of law. Each responsibility must be considered individually to determine if it continues into the next period or not.

A third clarification involves the ultimate goal of each dispensation. Each dispensation ends in man's failure; and yet, this ultimately contributes to God's glory. Thus while dispensationalists emphasize divine salvation, they see God's ultimate purpose to be His glory. The apostle Paul seems to agree in seeing God's glory as the overriding purpose in history. In his conclusion to the "dispensational section" of Romans 9-11 he writes, "For from Him and through Him and to Him are all things. To Him be the glory forever. Amen" (Rom. 11:36). Dispensationalism provides a philosophy of history in that it encompasses "all things." There is a unifying principle in that all is "to Him." The source is God and the process is His also in that the apostle writes "from Him" and "through Him" all transpires. According to dispensationalism, the final goal of all history is God's glory.

A fourth point of clarification concerns the dispensationalist's view of soteriology. The Scriptures clearly indicate that salvation has always been by grace through faith. Hebrews 11:1-7 contends that the saints of the Old Testament gained approval from God by faith. In the same vein Paul uses the examples of Abraham and David to argue for justification by faith in Romans 4:1-15 (cf. Gal. 3:6-9). All consistent dispensationalists believe that men of all ages are justified by faith alone.

DISPENSATIONAL DISTINCTIONS IN THE BIBLE

Any serious student of the Bible realizes that distinctions

need to be made within the Scriptures. Even the Bible itself makes a basic division between the Old Testament and the New Testament. As Ryrie has observed, "All interpreters feel the need for distinctions." He goes on to add that "every person who does not bring an animal sacrifice . . . recognizes the need for distinctions in the interpretation of the Bible."[16] Dispensationalism recognizes these distinctions and views them as differing administrations in God's management of His universe. It is the intent of this section to point out the biblical distinctions between these main dispensations.

THE DISPENSATIONS OF LAW AND GRACE

The most obvious distinction within the biblical record is the contrast between law and grace. John 1:17 says, "For the law was given through Moses; grace and truth were realized through Jesus Christ." This does not mean that there was no grace or truth before the ministry of Christ, but His coming brought such a revelation of God's grace and truth as had never been seen before. At the same time the cross of Christ brought the dispensation of law to an end. This is so evident it scarcely needs statement.

This passing of the law is declared in Hebrews 7:12. "For when the priesthood is changed, of necessity there takes place a change of law also." The very fact Christ is a priest after the order of Melchizedek makes essential the passing of the law with its Levitical order. The civil aspect of the law is also annulled. Even the Ten Commandments have been superseded by the grace system as indicated in Romans 7:4-7, which states that the believer has died to the law. In verse 7 the "law" is further explained as including the tenth commandment. The confirmation of this fact is found in 2 Corinthians 3:7-11. Here Paul asserts that what was written in stone (i.e., the Ten Commandments) came with glory but faded away. Other passages pointing to the abrogation of the law system are Acts 15:1-21; Galatians 3:19-29; Ephesians 2:15; Colossians 1:16-17; and 1 Timothy 1:6-11.

The failure of man under the law is seen a number of times. One clear passage is Romans 8:3a, "For what the Law could not do, weak as it was through the flesh." This statement is reinforced by Peter's statement at the Jerusalem Council. "Now therefore why do you put God to the test by placing upon the neck of the disciples a yoke which neither our fathers nor we have been able to bear?" (Acts 15:10).

The characteristics of the dispensation of law are not difficult to discern. It is far more difficult to recognize the distinctives of the dispensation of grace. Ryrie, however, points to two. "There are two aspects of the grace of God in this economy: (1) the blessing is entirely of grace and (2) that grace is for all."[17] These two aspects refer to the great blessings conferred on the church. A third may be added, namely, the enablement of the Holy Spirit. Such passages as Matthew 3:11; Mark 1:8; Luke 3:16; and John 1:33 show that the Messiah would identify His followers with Himself by the Holy Spirit. That this involved supernatural enablement is seen in such passages as Luke 24:49; John 14:16-18; Acts 1:8; 11:15-17; and Romans 8:9. The modus operandi of the law system was the flesh, that of the grace dispensation is the Spirit (Rom. 8:3-4; Gal. 5:16-23).

THE DISPENSATION OF PROMISE

The distinction between law and grace points to the existence of two dispensations. A third dispensation is found in the period of promise that preceded Sinai. That such an arrangement existed is seen in Galatians 3:15-19. Commenting on this section, Burton asserts, "Drawing his argument from the common knowledge of men that contracts once agreed to cannot be modified (except by mutual consent), the apostle applies this thought to the covenant with Abraham, contending that the law coming centuries afterwards cannot modify it."[18] Several observations may be made regarding this passage in Galatians. 1. God made a covenant with Abraham and thereby initiated a whole new dispensation of promise. Even a cursory reading of Genesis betrays this fact. The first eleven chapters of the book deal with the entire human race, but chapters 12-50 focus specifically on Israel. The cause for this change is found in God's promise to Abraham 12:1-3. 2. Galatians 3:15-17 states that the dispensation of law did not invalidate the promise. The law only was added. The verb that is used here is prosetethe, which "marks the law as supplementary. . . ."[19] In Romans 5:20 the verb *pareiselthen* implies that the law came in alongside. In other words, the law did not take the place of the promise; it only supplemented it. 3. The promise finds its ultimate fulfillment in the future in Christ; the law was only a temporary provision until He came.

THE DISPENSATION OF HUMAN GOVERNMENT

This dispensation begins with Noah in the post-Flood mandates from God. Skinner entitles Genesis 9:1-7 "The new world-order."[20] Several new responsibilities and privileges are given to Noah after the Flood. First, Noah was granted the freedom to eat all foods (Gen. 9:3). Up to this point man was a vegetarian (Gen. 1:29). Second, Noah was commanded to abstain from blood. That this law is still in effect is seen from Acts 15:20 where the Jerusalem Council recognized this as a pre-Mosaic imperative and therefore mandatory on the whole race. Third (and most important), Noah was granted the right of capital punishment. Genesis 9:5-6 asserts, "And surely I will require your lifeblood; from every beast I will require it. And from every man, from every man's brother I will require the life of man. Whoever sheds man's blood, by man his blood shall be shed, for in the image of God He made man." That right to take life was not granted indiscriminately. It had to be carried out by the proper authorities, and herein is the basis for human government (cf. Rom. 13:4). In discussing the institution of capital punishment Ryrie, with great insight, says: "It is this latter [revelation] that gives the distinctive basis to this dispensation as that of Human or Civil Government. God gave man the right to take the life of man, which in the very nature of the curse gave man the authority to govern others. Unless government has the right to the highest form of punishment, its basic authority is questionable and insufficient to protect properly those whom it governs."[21]

It is quite obvious this was a new stage in the progress of God's revelation to man.

THE DISPENSATION OF CONSCIENCE

There may be some discussion of the propriety of this title, but the term *conscience* has been used so much that it is difficult to displace it. At any rate, the existence of this dispensation can be deduced from a careful examination of the biblical evidence. First, it is clear the stewardship under which man lived after the Fall was different from before. No Bible student would contest this. Genesis 3:8-24 records this change in God's relationship to man. Second, Romans 5:13-14 makes a distinction between a pre-law age and the age of the law. "For *until the Law* sin was in the world; but sin is not imputed when there is no law. Nevertheless *death reigned from Adam until Moses,* even over those who had not sinned in the likeness of Adam's offense, who is a type of Him who was to come," (italics added). The pre-law age was marked by the entrance of death into the human race.[22]

Paul's point in Romans 5:13-14 is that from Adam to Moses men died even if they did not violate a specific command (as both Adam and the Israelites under the Mosaic law had done). He is saying that during the age from Adam to Moses men were held under the penalty of sin even if they would not commit specific acts of sin by directly violating God's expressed standards of righteousness. This does not mean, though, that men from Adam to Moses had no moral consciousness. They did. Romans 2:15 indicates people without a written revelation from God come to a sense of right and wrong by: an innate sense of morality, a conscience, and an intellect that comes to moral judgments through reasoning. This was the method employed by God to guide man before He gave a written ethical code as seen in the law of Sinai.

THE DISPENSATION OF INNOCENCE

As stated above, the realization that God began a new relationship with Adam and Eve *after* the Fall (Gen. 3:8-24) clearly indicates that He maintained a different relationship to them *before* the Fall. A question might arise once again as to the proper title for this age, but the fact remains that before the Fall Adam and Eve lived under an entirely different arrangement from what they did after. Certainly the Fall marked a change in dispensations.

THE DISPENSATION OF THE KINGDOM

It is in this dispensation that the whole premillennial system of doctrine comes to the fore. The key issue, of course, is the literal interpretation of the prophecies and promises of the Old Testament given to Israel. If these are to be taken at face value there must be a kingdom in the future. It should be noted that the prophecies of the New Testament also look toward a coming kingdom. A case in point is Matthew 19:28, "And Jesus said to them, 'Truly I say to you, that you who have followed Me, in the regeneration when the Son of Man will sit on His glorious throne, you also shall sit upon twelve thrones, judging the twelve tribes of Israel.' " If Matthew 19:28 is taken literally it says that there will be an earthly kingdom ruled by the Messiah. The prophecy concerns the "Son of Man," an expression that Bible students agree looks back to Daniel 7:13-14. This is obviously a prediction of the Messianic reign. In addition, Matthew 19:28 states that the promise will be fulfilled in the "regeneration." Every Jew would take this to be a reference to the promised Messianic age (cf. Acts 1:6; 3:19-21). Finally, there is the promise given to the Twelve that they will "sit on twelve thrones, judging the twelve tribes of Israel." It appears from the replacement of Judas by Matthias in Acts 1 that the early church took the prediction of Christ literally. Judas had vacated his position by betraying Christ, therefore another was assigned to fulfill it. The vacating of that position by Judas cannot simply refer to his death because no one was chosen to take the place of James when he was martyred (Acts 12:2). The early church filled the apostolic chair only once and that was to take the place of Judas in anticipation of the promised coming kingdom.

CONCLUSION

It is obvious from the Scriptures that God does have a successive series of dispensations or administrations through which He works out His eternal purpose in history. First, there is a distinction in His relationship to Adam before and after the

Fall. This results in two dispensations. A third change in God's administration of history is found after the Flood with the institution of human government and its authority to administer capital punishment (Gen. 9:1-17). A fourth dispensation began after the Tower of Babel when God stopped dealing directly with all mankind and instead began to mediate His blessing through the family of just one man, Abraham (Gen. 12:1-3). A fifth dispensation is found in the Mosaic law (John 1:17; Gal. 3:17). The dispensation of the church forms a sixth and is evidenced by such passages as John 1:17; Ephesians 3:4-6; and Colossians 1:25-27. The final dispensation preceding the eternal state is the millennial Kingdom (Rev. 20:2-4).

When a Christian begins to grasp the overall concept of God's glory as seen in the dispensations, he is bound to praise God with Paul as he also rejoices in God's sovereign rule. "Oh, the depth of the riches both of the wisdom and knowledge of God! How unsearchable are His judgments and unfathomable His ways! For WHO HAS KNOWN THE MIND OF THE LORD, OR WHO BECAME HIS COUNSELOR? OR WHO HAS FIRST GIVEN TO HIM THAT IT MIGHT BE PAID BACK TO HIM AGAIN? For from Him and through Him and to Him are all things. To Him be the glory forever. Amen" (Rom. 11:33-36).

NOTES

1. C. B. Bass, *Backgrounds to Dispensationalism* (Grand Rapids: Eerdmans, 1960), pp. 13-21, 26-27; E. J. Carnell, *The Case for Orthodox Theology* (Philadelphia: Westminster, 1959), pp. 117-18; C. Norman Kraus, *Dispensationalism in America* (Richmond: John Knox, 1958), p. 16.
2. Arnold B. Rhodes, ed., *The Church Faces the Isms* (New York: Abingdon, 1958). Cf. John Wick Bowman, "The Bible and Modern Religions: II. Dispensationalism," *Interpretation* 10 (April 1956): 170-72.
3. Bass, *Backgrounds to Dispensationalism*, pp. 19-21.
4. Ibid., pp. 37-38.
5. Ibid., pp. 46-47, 144-45; Kraus, *Dispensationalism in America*, p. 134; Carnell, *The Case for Orthodox Theology*, pp. 117-19.
6. Bass, *Backgrounds to Dispensationalism*, pp. 100-108, 127, 153-54; Kraus, *Dispensationalism in America*, p. 135.
7. Bass, *Backgrounds to Dispensationalism*, pp. 33-36; Kraus, *Dispensationalism in America*, pp. 117-18.

8. Charles Caldwell Ryrie, *Dispensationalism Today* (Chicago: Moody, 1965).
9. *The Scofield Reference Bible,* ed. C. I. Scofield (New York: Oxford U., 1945), p. 5.
10. *The New Scofield Reference Bible,* ed. E. Schuyler English (New York: Oxford U., 1967), p. 3.
11. Lewis Sperry Chafer, *Systematic Theology,* 8 vols. (Dallas: Dallas Seminary, 1947), 7:122.
12. Ryrie, *Dispensationalism Today,* p. 29.
13. Ibid., pp. 43-47, 211-12.
14. G. Abbott-Smith, *A Manual Greek Lexicon of the New Testament* (New York: Scribner's, 1956), p. 313.
15. Ryrie, *Dispensationalism Today,* p. 27.
16. Ibid., p. 16.
17. Ibid., p. 63.
18. Ernest DeWitt Burton, *A Critical and Exegetical Commentary on the Epistle to the Galatians* (Edinburgh: T. & T. Clark, 1959), p. 177.
19. Ibid., p. 188.
20. John Skinner, *A Critical and Exegetical Commentary on Genesis* (Edinburgh: T. & T. Clark, 1930), p. 169.
21. Ryrie, *Dispensationalism Today,* p. 60.
22. Note especially the "diary of death" in Genesis 5. This chapter is punctuated by the clause, "and he died."

Part II
Theological

6

God, Evil and Dispensations

Norman L. Geisler

One of the neglected values of the dispensational approach to Scripture is the light it casts on the problem of evil. Theodicy (a vindication of God's goodness and justice despite the presence of evil in the world) is both a fascinating and difficult topic in any theology, but a dispensational approach offers unexpected help for this old problem.

For the limited nature of this discussion it will be necessary for this writer to begin by assuming what he believes the Scriptures teach, namely, that there are seven dispensations.[1] That is to say, there are seven successive and different divine economies between creation and the new heaven and the new earth (Rev. 22). Granting this perspective one may ask, Why seven different dispensations? What is God's overall plan for these periods? and, Can one discern anything of the divine purposes throughout these ages?

NORMAN L. GEISLER (Th.B., Detroit Bible College; A.B., M.A., Wheaton College; Ph.D. Loyola University of Chicago) is professor of systematic theology at Dallas Theological Seminary, Dallas, Texas.

DISPENSATIONAL CHANGES ARE NOT SOTERIOLOGICAL

Most dispensationalists have been careful to point out that there are not several different plans of salvation corresponding to the various dispensations.[2] Despite the unfortunate wording of the footnote on John 1:17 in the old Scofield Bible,[3] dispensationalists consistently repudiate the charge that they accept the existence of many plans of salvation. There is only one way of salvation (Gal. 1:8), and it was preached to Abraham (Gal. 3:8) and is to be preached to the whole world (Matt. 28:18-20). That one gospel, which applies to every age, is simply this: Persons are saved "by grace through faith in the revealed will of God." To be sure, dispensationalists hold that the *content* of the revealed will of God has become progressively more explicit. Progressive revelation is a central tenet of dispensationalism. For instance, the *content* of the gospel preached by the apostle Paul (1 Cor. 15:1-8), that Christ died, was buried, rose and was seen of many, is surely more than the pagans on the streets of Nineveh heard from Jonah (Jonah 3:4). However, neither Ninevites nor first-century Corinthians (nor twentieth-century Americans) are saved apart from faith in a gracious God who acts in view of the atoning work of Christ (1 Tim. 2:5; Heb. 9:22). The point is that people were saved in every age through the work of Christ, even though they did not have the knowledge of that work which believers have today. So, in brief, dispensationalists do not believe that there are seven different dispensations because God had seven different plans of salvation. There is really only one common gospel that unites all dispensations soteriologically. What then is the purpose of seven different dispensations if it is not soteriological? It is my suggestion that there are at least three purposes of God in having seven different dispensations. One is doxological (having to do with God's glory), another is anthropological (having to do with God's goodness to man), and the last is theological or dispensational (having to do with the ultimate defeat of evil).

THREE REASONS FOR SEVEN DISPENSATIONS

Often dispensationalists have rested their case for justifying God in view of the problem of evil (called theodicy) almost completely on the glory of God. Although the overriding importance of the doxological answer cannot be disputed, it should be affirmed nonetheless that there are at least two correlative points that also should be stressed. Each of the three is essential in helping one formulate an adequate solution to the problem of evil.

DOXOLOGICAL REASON FOR EVIL

The glory of God is central to dispensationalism. Ryrie considers it the unifying theme for all of God's plan.[4] It alone is all-encompassing, spanning from eternity to eternity and covering both pre-Fall and pre-creation periods. In that sense it is important to point out that those covenantal schemes of theology that make redemption the unifying theme of God's eternal plan miss the mark "and fall short of the glory of God." The glory of God is eternal; redemption has a beginning point in time. Also, the glory of God applies to unredeemed beings as well as to redeemed ones. Thus glory is a far more inclusive and comprehensive theological theme than is redemption. Only a doxological theology, as dispensationalism truly is, can possibly be a *systematic* theology in the proper sense of the term. Systematic theology must be a *comprehensive* and consistent correlation of all revealed truth about God and His relation with His universe.

Before discussing God's glory as it relates to evil, a definition of *glory* is in order. An examination of the scriptural data will reveal that glory means "manifest excellence." Glory is the outward radiation of the inward perfections of God. No one can see God's essence (Exod. 33:20; John 1:18); and yet God's glory was often seen (Exod. 16:7, 10; Isa. 40:5). Indeed, the incarnate Christ is "the radiance of His [God's] glory . . ." (Heb. 1:3). So glory does for God what a magnifying glass does for a fine jewel; it does not change His nature, but it does enlarge it for His creature's view.

Granting that description and the centrality of the glory of God to dispensations, how does God's glory relate to the answer of the problem of evil?

Very simply put the answer often goes like this:

1. The glory of God is the ultimate good in the universe.

2. God is glorified by everything in the universe, including evil.

3. Therefore, even evil redounds to the glory of God.

Since most dispensationalists have Calvinistic leanings, the doxological purpose of evil is frequently justified in terms of an emphasis on the sovereignty of God. Verses such as the following are often used.

"For the wrath of man shall praise Thee" (Psalm 76:10).

"The Lord hath made everything for himself: yea even the wicked for the day of evil" (Prov. 16:4, KJV).

"I am the Lord and there is none else. . . . I make peace, and create evil" (Isa. 45:6-7, KJV).

"What if God . . . endured with much patience vessels of wrath prepared for destruction? And He did so in order that He might make known the riches of His glory . . ." (Rom. 9:22-23).

Those and like verses have been used by some to pronounce boldly that in the sovereign will of God even evil brings glory to God. It is that conclusion that must be rejected. To argue that God is glorified by evil is biblically unsound, dispensationally untrue, and theologically unfounded.

First, a comment needs to be made about the above verses, which are often used to "prove" that God is glorified by evil. As to the Lord creating evil (Isa. 45:6-7), the Hebrew word means "evil, distress, misery, injury, calamity."[5] Although the word sometimes means evil in a moral sense, it need not have any direct moral connotations at all. It may mean no more than that God sends a plague. There is certainly no support here for the idea that God can do anything that is morally evil, since the Scriptures are clear in their assertion that He is absolutely good (1 John 4:16; cf. 1:5) and cannot even look on evil (Hab. 1:13).

Regarding Proverbs 16:4, the *New American Standard Bible* translates it, "The Lord has made everything *for its own purpose,* even the wicked for the day of evil" (italics added). Delitzsch renders the first part of the verse "Jahve hath made everything for its contemplated end" and adds appropriately, "the wickedness of free agents is comprehended in this plan and made subordinate to it."[6] In Romans 9 it is noteworthy that the passage does not say that God is glorified by the vessels of wrath. What it actually says is that His *power* is manifested on the vessels of wrath (v. 22). Then in the next verse it says God's *glory* is made known through the vessels of honor. In point of fact, there is no passage of Scripture that teaches that God is praised or glorified by evil. God is good and only what is good brings glory to Him. What is evil is contrary to God and cannot possibly complement Him.[7]

If God is not glorified by evil, then in what sense is evil included in God's all-encompassing plan that brings glory to Him? The answer can be more readily understood once one understands God's purpose in allowing evil. Although God is not glorified by evil, He is glorified by His attribute of love in permitting the freedom that caused the evil. Further, God is glorified by His attribute of justice that punishes the evil. This is no doubt the meaning of the phrase, "the wrath of man shall praise Thee" (Psalm 76:10). Man's evil wrath does not bring glory to God directly but only indirectly in that it occasions His just wrath. God is actually glorified by His own attributes of goodness and justice in the face of (and in spite of) man's wrath. Yes, evil does have a doxological purpose; God does and will receive glory *through* the evil He has allowed. But God can never receive glory *from* evil. That is to say, God is not glorified *by* evil itself but only *by means of* using evil to manifest His own good attributes. This distinction is necessary to preserve one's theology (theodicy) from blasphemy. It is morally impossible for man's moral imperfections to reflect the glory of a morally perfect God.

THE ANTHROPOLOGICAL REASON FOR EVIL

There is another danger in a purely doxological theodicy. Not only do some, in their enthusiasm to capture the glory of God in all things, wrongly claim that evil brings glory to God, but they also separate the glory of God from the good He intended for man. In other words, by separating glory from good they are able to claim that God is glorified even when He does not produce all the good possible in the circumstances.

The Scriptures make it clear that God glorifies Himself (Isa. 44:23; Ezek. 39:13), that He is glorified in Christ (John 1:14; 2 Cor. 4:4), and that He is even glorified by natural creation (Psalm 19:1). In addition, God is glorified in His sanctuary

(Exod. 40:34), by man's redemption (Exod. 14:17; Psalm 96:2), in the cross and resurrection (Rom. 6:4), by believers (John 17:22; Eph. 1:18), by Christ's second coming (Matt. 24:30; Phil. 3:20) and in His righteous judgments (Exod. 14:4, 17; Ezek. 28:22; Rev. 15:4). Indeed, God is glorified in every realm: the natural world, the human world, and the angelic world.

God receives glory from virtually everything—everything, that is, except evil. God does, however, receive glory *through* evil. That is, by permitting evil (suffering, etc.) God is glorified. Peter wrote, "But to the degree that you share the sufferings of Christ, keep on rejoicing; so that also at the revelation of His glory, you may rejoice with exultation. If you are reviled for the name of Christ, you are blessed, because the Spirit of glory and of God rests upon you" (1 Pet. 4:13-14). A few verses later Peter adds, "But if anyone suffers as a Christian, let him not feel ashamed, but in that name let him glorify God" (v. 16).

Paul also claims that God is glorified through suffering, saying, ". . . but we also exult in our tribulations, knowing that tribulation brings about perseverence; and perseverence, proven character; and proven character, hope" (Rom. 5:3-4). Thus he can say, ". . . and we exult in hope of the glory of God" (Rom. 5:2). A few chapters later the apostle writes, ". . . if indeed we suffer with Him in order that we may also be glorified with Him. For I consider that the sufferings of this present time are not worthy to be compared with the glory that is to be revealed to us" (Rom. 8:17-18). Indeed, despite his own tremendous suffering (cf. 2 Cor. 11:23-28), Paul could confidently say, "For momentary, light affliction is producing for us an eternal weight of glory far beyond all comparison" (2 Cor. 4:17).

By building on those biblical truths one can see how God permits all suffering for His glory. Suffering is God's instrument for producing both God's *and* man's greater glory. But if that were all to be said one might inquire as to whether God were merely interested in His glory but not His creature's good. Surely it would be slander to the nature of God to suggest that He is not really interested in His creatures' welfare. No, there is more to biblical theodicy than God's glory; there is also *man's good*. It is true that God is glorified through suffering and evil, but it is also true that man is *perfected* through it. Job cried out,

"When He has tried me, I shall come forth as gold" (Job 23:10). James wrote, "You have heard of the endurance of Job and have seen the outcome of the Lord's dealings . . ." (James 5:11). What was the outcome of Job's suffering? It was that "the LORD restored the fortunes of Job. . . . And the LORD blessed the latter days of Job more than his beginning . . ." (Job 42:10, 12).

There are numerous indications in Scripture that the purpose for permitting suffering and evil is to produce a greater good. It is in the context of suffering that Paul uttered perhaps his most famous line in this regard. "And we know that God causes all things to work together *for good* to those who love God . . ." (Rom. 8:28; cf. vv. 17, 23). Indeed, only a few chapters earlier Paul made one of the boldest statements in Scripture on the role of evil in producing a greater good. He wrote, "But where sin increased, *grace* abounded all the more" (Rom. 5:20, italics added). It is undoubtedly true that, like discipline, all suffering "for the moment seems not to be joyful, but sorrowful: yet to those who have been trained by it, afterwards it yields the peaceful fruit of *righteousness*" (Heb. 12:11, italics added). That is why James could say, "Consider it all joy, my brethren, when you encounter various trials, knowing that the testing of your faith produces endurance. . . . that you may be perfect and complete, lacking in nothing" (James 1:2-4). In point of fact, even the sinless Son of God was made *perfect* "through sufferings" (Heb. 2:10). How much more can sinful creatures learn and be perfected through suffering!

There are two forceful illustrations in the book of Genesis of how and why God permits evil in order to achieve a greater good. The first is found in Joseph's gracious word to his brothers who had sold him as a slave to Egypt. "You meant evil against me but God meant if *for good* . . ." (Gen. 50:20, italics added). The fact that God was able to save Joseph and his family through the brothers' evil in no way made the evil good. But it does show how a sovereign God can bring good even out of evil. So it is with the universe as a whole. God allows men to sin, and when they do He is somehow able to bring about good results through their evil.

The other illustration is found in two seemingly contradictory commands of God to the chosen line of Abraham. First,

God said, "Do not go down to Egypt; stay in the land of which I shall tell you" (Gen. 26:2). Later God said, "Do not be afraid to go down to Egypt . . ." (Gen. 46:3). The full explanation for this later concession is found in the prophet Hosea who wrote, "Out of Egypt I called My son" (11:1). In brief, the first command was God's *prescriptive* will (do not go); the second was His *permissive* will (you may go), and the last verse reveals God's *providential* or overruling will (I will bring a greater good out of your suffering).

In accordance with this pattern a model for a biblical theodicy may be developed. First, God's prescriptive will is that sin and suffering should not occur at all. God is not a cosmic sadist; He takes no pleasure in suffering or death (Ezek. 18:32). Second, God's permissive will is that suffering occur. That is, He sovereignly wills to *permit* evil, even though He forbids that anyone commit evil. Finally, since God knows the end from the beginning (Isa. 46:10), He determinately foreknew (cf. Acts 2:23) that He would bring a greater good out of evil, namely, the redemption of all who will believe. In short, what brings glory to God also brings good to mankind. Good and glory cannot be separated. God is interested in bringing good to men—the greatest good possible.[8]

The truth is that God is concerned about man's greatest good, that "God so loved the world, that He gave His only begotten Son . . ." (John 3:16), that Christ "died for all" (2 Cor. 5:15) by giving Himself as "the propitiation for our sins; and . . . for those of the whole world" (1 John 2:2).[9] It is because of this that God "desires all men to be saved and to come to a knowledge of the truth" (1 Tim. 2:4).[10] Indeed, God would save all men if He could for the Lord is "not wishing for any to perish, but [wants] all to come to repentance" (2 Pet. 3:9). The fact that some do not choose to repent, and so will not make it to heaven, cannot veto the God-given right of others to be there. God will achieve the greatest number in heaven that He possibly can. He does not love just some men; He loves all and will do everything within His loving power to save all He can. If some are not saved it is because, to quote the Lord, "I wanted to gather your children together, the way a hen gathers her chicks under her wings, and *you were unwilling*" (Matt. 23:37, italics added).

When the statement is made that God will achieve the greatest good "possible" it does not mean the greatest number of people will be saved that is *logically possible* (that would be 100 percent). What is meant by that statement is that God will save the greatest number of people that is *actually achievable* without violating their free choice.[11] A loving God will not force anyone against their will to love Him or to worship Him. Forced love is not love; forced worship is not worship. Heaven will not be composed of robots. God is not a kind of "Cosmic B. F. Skinner" who believes in manipulating people into certain behavior patterns which are pleasing to Himself.[12] God does not, as Skinner wishes, go "beyond freedom and dignity." In short, God will not save people at all cost—not if it is at the cost of their freedom and dignity—for that would mean at the cost of their humanity. God will not dehumanize in order to save. To dehumanize is to de-create, since that is what God created—a human. In fact, to dehumanize man would be to strip man of the image of God (Gen. 1:26), which image even fallen man has (Gen. 9:6). If God did that He would in an indirect sense be de-deifying Himself! So just as surely as God will not attack His own image in man whom He created, even so God will not force a man against his will to go to heaven. God is love, and love works persuasively but not coercively. Those whom God can lovingly persuade have been foreordained to eternal life. Those whom He cannot, are destined in accordance with their own choice to eternal destruction (2 Thess. 1:7-9; Rev. 20:11-15). The net result will be the greatest good achievable for mankind and the greatest glory obtainable for God. Good and glory are inseparably related because God is not only sovereign and self-sufficient (which obligates men to glorify Him), but He is also loving and merciful (which obligates Him to do all the good He possibly can in the moral world that He has willed). While there is nothing in fallen man that demands that God redeem, there is something in God that demands that He do so, namely, His unmitigated goodness.

Now if God actually achieves the greatest good possible by allowing evil, then the theodicy is sufficient. All that is necessary in a theodicy is to show how, in spite of evil, God will (in the end) bring about the greatest possible good. And if good cannot be separated from glory, then the greatest good of glorifying God will be in concert with the greatest good of saving man.

Several loose ends to most theodicies are tightened up by a dispensational perspective. First, there is the problem of why God permitted so much suffering for so long (thousands of years of human history). Second, there is the problem of how men can be truly free in heaven while guaranteeing that evil will never break out again. A dispensational perspective casts new light on these age-old problems.

Many dispensationalists accept the following tenets: 1. there are seven dispensations that are commonly labeled the ages of *innocence, conscience, human government, promise, law, grace,* and the *kingdom*; 2. each age tests man under a new and specific condition; and 3. man proves to be a failure under all of these conditions. Now if all of that is true, what would be the point of it? The point may very well be that God is trying to accomplish several things through His plan for the ages. First, He wants to prove to the universe (of rational creatures) that creatures always fail and bring evil (not good) on themselves when they disobey God's commands. Second, and conversely, God wants to prove that it is always right to obey His commands, for when individuals do they bring good and blessing on themselves. In that way heaven can be full of free creatures and yet justly rule out any rebellion again.

The sevenfold test is given so that man can be tested concerning good and evil under every major condition. Seven is not an arbitrary number of dispensations for two reasons. First, seven is a number of completion or earthly perfection. God did appoint seven days in a complete earthly week (Gen. 1). Second, each dispensation provides a *different* condition under which man is tested. Indeed, one could speculate that these are *all* the necessary conditions for testing man. For example, man was tested when he did not know either good or evil by experience (the age of *innocence* in the Garden of Eden), but even here he chose to do evil. Then men, knowing good and evil, were tested as to whether they would now follow the good and shun the evil (the age of *conscience*). But here too men failed and did more evil than good, thus filling the world with violence (Gen. 6:13). After this men were given the more explicit commands of government to restrain evil and promote good (the age of *human government*, Gen. 9:6; Rom. 13:1-7). But here again men used even the intended good of governmental power to exalt themselves against God, which climaxed at the Tower of Babel (Gen. 11). After the failure at the Tower of Babel God gave to certain men a special promise (the age of *promise*) by which they could guide their nation in separation from the contamination that had come on the nations at large. God could then through that nation ultimately bless all nations and eventually pick out a people from all nations who could experience the good God intended for all men (Gen. 12:1-3). Here too, however, the patriarchs failed to stay in the land of promised blessing and ended in bondage in Egypt. Following that failure the people needed more explicit directions from God (called the age of *law*). The Bible records that even with all that explicit, divine direction men still rebelled against God and brought evil on themselves. That then would seem to call for a more gracious and less judicial approach (called the age of *grace*) under which man is tested as to whether he will respond purely and simply to the grace of God. But amazingly enough, even here men refuse the grace of God and bring condemnation on themselves. Thus ends the age of grace. But throughout all those six ages there has been one common and sinister figure who has sanctioned evil—Satan. Hence, there is always the possibility that men could blame him for their evil, saying, "The devil made me do it!" To ward off this possibility, God in His wisdom designed one dispensation wherein the devil would be bound and man would be freed from his temptation (called the *kingdom* age). But inconceivable as it seems, even after a thousand years of Christ's perfect reign without satanic intervention, man proves again that he is a failure when innumerable people turn against God at the end of the Millennium (Rev. 20:7-9).

Now if that is true, as the foregoing Scriptures would indicate, what does it prove? It seems to indicate exactly what every complete theodicy would like to show, namely, that God surely has just grounds before all His creatures to put away sin forever, because He has proved to all that it is never right to disobey His will. God has tried evil in every age and condition and has proved how evil it is. Or, to put it another way, the only way to defeat evil is to permit it. The only way to defeat it completely is to try it completely. One cannot defeat an opponent unless he is willing to get into the "ring" with him. Hence, God allowed evil into the ring of human history for a seven-round (seven-dispensation) championship bout, winner take all. It was in the sixth round that a knockout punch was given (by the cross and resurrection), and the staggered foe was floored forever at the end of the seventh round.

In this dispensational drama, God is the victor and all good men are the benefactors. Evil is defeated, God is justified, and the universe is secured forever from another outbreak of evil. What makes it justly secure? *God* makes it secure. He is omnipotent, and He will not allow another outburst.

What makes the universe *justly* secure from evil? The *redeemed* do—the redeemed of all ages who can stand to testify from every dispensation, no matter what the conditions, that it is always right to obey God's sovereign will, which they have willingly pledged to do for all eternity. How about those who do not will to do God's will? To them God will justly say, "Thy will be done!"[13] Thus according to the will of each, God has determined the eternal destiny of all. The only *just* way to bring about the greatest good in a free universe is first to assign each his destiny in accordance with his freedom (forced freedom is not freedom). And the only just way to bring in *permanent* good is to *separate* each according to his free choice. What really hinders good men is evil, and what really bothers evil men is good. So it is that God has a place where there will be no more evil to hinder good men (called heaven) and a place where there will be no more good influence to bother evil men (called hell).[14] The wheat and the tares must be separated; there will be a final harvest (Matt. 13:24-30, 36-43). And when the end comes God will have achieved: (1) His greatest glory, (2) His creatures' greatest good, and (3) the most just and lasting security of the universe against evil. Evil will have been completely tried and proven entirely wrong. It will have been permitted and defeated. William James once observed that the world is better for having the devil in it, if men have their foot on his neck. It is better yet that *God* has His foot on his head and has crushed the serpent's power (Gen. 3:15). What really happened, then, at the cross of Christ, by which both evil and the evil one were defeated, is that Satan was definitively conquered and ultimate victory over his kingdom was triumphantly assured (Col. 2:15). Praise God that evil is defeated and the universe is being forever secured. The fact that it will take seven dispensations and thousands of years to do it should offer no real problem. For the suffering caused by evil in this short span called *time* is, by comparison with the eternal good and glory, more than worth it. As Paul said, "For momentary, light affliction is producing for us an eternal weight of glory far beyond all comparison" (2 Cor. 4:17). That point was summed up beautifully by Patterson.

> The question is often asked, Why did God permit the fall. . . . It is enough for the believer to know it was the will of God. God's will needs no defense. It is the standard of righteousness. This is to be fully demonstrated before all the universe, but now we must believe it to be so by faith. We are not left wholly in the dark, however, as to the purposes of God, and he invites our inquiry that we may see and learn and believe. We say, and in a sense correctly, that God does all things for his own glory. But to think of this glory apart from the welfare of the beings of his creation, is not the Scriptural idea of the glory of God. . . . The purpose undoubtedly was to settle eternal problems. In some world, if not in this, in some time, if not at this time, the question was sure to arise whether the will of God was best and right. . . . God could have met it by a display of power and might and silenced all opposition, but that would not be an answer but a supression. It would not be worthy of the plan which God had before him as seen in the ages. To silence by authority is not to settle the question. . . . Better this issue fully and fairly met now, and the questions answered at once, than that it should be left open, a constant danger ever threatening the universe, hanging like an avalanche over the future, to break forth perhaps when the universe was filled with holy, happy beings. . . . There seems to have been but one way—to permit an actual experiment and demonstration of the whole question. To this end sin must be allowed to present itself in all its hideous nature and effects; suffering must follow, and sorrow deep and widespread must be felt and endured. When this great experiment is over, every ques-

tion will be forever settled. Every alternative opposed to the will of God will have been solved. It will be apparent as the noon-day sun to all intelligences that all has been passed through the crucible of actual demonstration. The verdict from this will be that there is but one standard of right, but one way of happiness, but one way of holiness, and that is the will of God. The participants in this struggle are to be rewarded for their part in this sad stage of suffering by correspondingly and vastly increased benefits hereafter. They are to have the highest state in that kingdom to come.[15]

SUMMARY AND CONCLUSION

Dispensationalists stress several things. Among them is that God has an eternal plan that He is working out for His glory and for the good of the universe. That plan includes the permission of evil. This article has suggested that God permits evil in order that He may produce a greater good that will redound to His great glory. That is, God does indeed have a good purpose for permitting evil. He has permitted it in order to defeat it.[16] But He has defeated evil without destroying the good He has created, namely, free creatures made in His image and likeness. Each creature is free to accept or reject the grace of God in salvation. Of course, God determinately knew from all eternity who would and who would not believe. Hence, God elected "according to [His] foreknowlege" (1 Pet. 1:2). And as many men as have been so ordained to eternal life will believe (Acts 13:48). Indeed, it is *necessary* that they believe.[17] It is necessary because God cannot be wrong about what He knowingly determines (or, determinately knows). However, that necessity is not *compulsive*. Divine love is never coercive; it is only persuasive. God knows with necessity who will and who will not respond to His overtures of love. Hence, God wills their salvation necessarily but He does it *through* their free choice. As many as will are sovereignly chosen by Him to eternal life. They are not chosen *on the basis of* their free choice (as Arminians believe); they are chosen on the basis of God's sovereign love but *in accordance with* their free choice.[18]

Redeemed men are given the grace to overcome sin. They can overcome sin in this life progressively (sanctification) and will overcome it by God's grace in the next life permanently (glorification). Likewise, God is overcoming evil in His universe both progressively (through seven dispensations) and permanently (in the new heaven and new earth, Rev. 22). God is doing that in order to secure the universe once and for all from all evil influence and to produce a permanent and greater good—all in accord with His eternal glory.

Like anything else, a tested and proved world is better than an untested and unproved one. But since suffering and evil are necessary conditions for producing a greater and permanent good, God permitted this brief "moment" of affliction (called human history) in order to produce an eternally secure universe. God, as it were, allowed the race to catch the disease (of evil) but sent His own Son to wound the virus fatally (through the cross) so that all who will to be innoculated can be forever immune from its contamination. And just as a broken bone is stronger after it heals than before it was broken, so too, a redeemed man is stronger than an innocent one. Likewise, a redeemed universe is better, for in it God can freely save and permanently cure those who come to Him. All who reject the cure will be forever quarantined (in hell), so that the contaminating influences of their disease can never spread. In that way the purposes of a *loving* God will have been achieved through the ages by overcoming evil and obtaining the greater good. And the plan of a *just* God to punish evil and to separate good and evil (so that one cannot unfairly hinder the other) will be accomplished. Justice demands "to each according to his due." And it is not just forever to inflict good on men who desire evil, or forever to inflict evil on men who choose good. Sooner or later there must be a final separation. It is fairer this way for all.

In this connection it is worth noting that the problem with universalism is that it turns out to be a dehumanizing form of determinism in which God forces a cure on patients without their informed consent. The permanently secure universe with its eternally redeemed people (and final quarantine of evil) will redound to the everlasting glory of God. The universalist's God treats free creatures like objects to be manipulated rather than as men in God's image to be respected.[19]

In brief, the scheme of dispensations provides a significant insight into the purposes of God in testing man in various ways through various days. These ages are all part of a complete (sevenfold) and progressive plan to defeat evil both fairly and finally without destroying the good but in the process to bring about a greater good.

NOTES

1. Ryrie is correct in stating that the *number* of dispensations is not crucial (Charles C. Ryrie, *Dispensationalism Today* [Chicago: Moody, 1965], p. 48). However, this writer personally believes there are seven dispensations (as divided by Scofield, Sauer, Ryrie et al.). This fits with the symbolic significance of the number seven in Scripture (as earthly completion or perfection); but one should not press this point, since the Bible does not explicitly say there are seven dispensations.
2. Ryrie, *Dispensationalism Today*, pp. 130-31.
3. Speaking of the age of grace in contrast to the age of law, Scofield wrote, "the point of testing is no longer legal obedience as the condition of salvation, but acceptance or rejection of Christ, with good works as a fruit of salvation" (C. I. Scofield, ed., *The Scofield Reference Bible* [New York: Oxford, 1917], p. 1115). This was an unfortunate wording which seemed to imply salvation by works in the Old Testament. Actually, Scofield did believe that Old Testament saints were saved by faith (as is plain from his notes on Gen 15:6 or Psalm 32:1, which he acknowledged are quoted in Rom. 4, as well as Gal. 3:8), as did Chafer (Lewis Sperry Chafer, "Inventing Heretics through Misunderstanding," *Bibliotheca Sacra* 102 [January-March 1945]:1) and Ryrie (*Dispensationalism Today*, pp. 110-31).
4. Ryrie, *Dispensationalism Today*, p. 46.
5. Francis Brown, S. R. Driver, and Charles A. Briggs, *Hebrew and English Lexicon of the Old Testament*, reprint (Oxford: Clarendon, 1974), p. 948.
6. Franz Delitzsch, *Biblical Commentary on the Proverbs of Solomon*, Biblical Commentary on the Old Testament, trans. M. G. Easton, reprint (Grand Rapids: Eerdmans. 1975), pp. 336-37.
7. It is a sad fact that many Christians have been urged to believe that the height of spirituality is the ability to praise God for evil (see Merlin R. Carothers, *Power in Praise* [Plainfield, N.J.: Logos, 1972], pp. 1, 5, 9, 130, 139). First Thessalonians 5:18 tells believers to praise God "in everything." No verse in the Bible exhorts anyone to praise God *for* evil. The "all things" for which believers are to give thanks does not state or imply that evil is to be included

(Eph. 5:20). It is to be done in fellowship with the light (Eph. 5:13), being filled with the Spirit (Eph. 5:18), and by renouncing evil (Eph. 5:11), not by approving evil in calling it good. Indeed, Scriptures pronounce condemnation on those who "call evil good, and good, evil" (Isa. 5:20).

8. For an elaboration of this "greater good" aspect of theodicy see my *Philosophy of Religion* (Grand Rapids: Zondervan, 1974), pp. 349-79, and *Roots of Evil* (Grand Rapids: Zondervan, 1978).

9. Contrary to the opinion of five-point Calvinists, this cannot mean Christian world or world of the elect, since v. 16 defines the world as the evil world of "lust of the flesh, lust of the eyes and pride of life."

10. It is instructive to see what abuse Augustine gave this verse as he became more deterministic in his later years. In *On the Spirit and the Letter* (413) he held that God desires all men to be saved but not at the cost of their freedom. By the time of the *Enchiridian* (421) Augustine interpreted the "all men" as all ranks and varieties of men. It is interesting to note that by this time he is claiming that infants are saved apart from their will by baptism and that heretics can be forced to believe *against* their free will (cf. *On the Correction of the Donatists* 3. 12).

11. Many years ago Warfield attacked the common myth that the Bible clearly teaches that only a few people will be saved in a perceptive article entitled, "Are They Few That Be Saved?" (Benjamin B. Warfield, *Biblical and Theological Studies*, ed. Samuel G. Craig [Philadelphia: Presbyterian & Reformed, 1952], pp. 334-50).

12. For a discussion of the determinism of Jonathan Edwards and B. F. Skinner see the article "Human Destiny: Free or Forced?" in *The Christian Scholar's Review* 9 (1979): 99-120.

13. C. S. Lewis makes this point in *The Great Divorce* (New York: Macmillan, 1946), p. 69.

14. Technically speaking there will in a sense still be good in hell since men in hell are still men, which means they still have the remnants of God's image. But the good that is there cannot *influence* evil men nor can it be salvaged. It is *unredeemable* good. Hell is the "dump" (Mark 9:45-48) of the universe, the cosmic scrapyard where all unsalvageable human wrecks eventually go. That is, even if they are dimly recognizable as men, nonetheless their lives are beyond repair.

15. Alexander Patterson, *The Greater Life and Work of Christ* (Chicago: Moody, n.d.), pp. 74-79.

16. In view of the greater good that God can produce by permitting evil (than by not permitting it), one can speculate that even *if* God could have made a world wherein Adam would *not* have fallen that He would not have done so. This may be supposed on the premises that: (1) God must do His *best* whenever He decides to undertake something and that (2) a world where sin is not de-

feated would not be as good as one where it is defeated (even if there are casualties in the process of victory).

17. This "necessity" for men to believe is the element of truth in "irresistable grace." There is no way for anyone not to do what God has ordained will be done. The "necessity," however, does not mean God *forces* them to do so. It means rather that He who is never mistaken determinately knows that they will receive salvation freely with the aid of His grace.

18. Dr. Walvoord's concept of the coextensive nature of election and foreknowledge is very helpful (*Major Bible Themes*, rev. ed. [Grand Rapids: Zondervan, 1974], p. 233).

19. See my comments on John Hick in "Human Destiny: Free or Forced," pp. 99-120.

7

The Inerrancy of the Bible

John A. Witmer

Sir Walter Scott, the great English novelist and poet, was on his deathbed. Feebly he whispered to his companion hovering nearby, "Bring me the book." "Which book, sir?" the companion asked solicitously. Gathering his strength, Scott raised himself in bed and asserted, "There is only one Book, man! Bring me the Bible!"

Scott stood in the centuries-old tradition established by the apostle Paul, who wrote to Timothy from a Roman prison asking him to bring his cloak, his books, and "especially the parchments" (2 Tim. 4:13). Christians have always been people of the Book, recognizing the Bible as God's Word.

Only in the last century has the equation between God's Word and the Bible been widely challenged. Of course, every century has had its Celsus, Marcion, Abelard, Voltaire, or Paine who denied the identity of the Bible as the Word of God. But only in the present century (and possibly during the last half of

JOHN A. WITMER (A.B., M.A., Wheaton College; M.S.L.S. East Texas State University; Th.M., Th.D., Dallas Theological Seminary) is assistant professor of systematic theology and director of the library at Dallas Theological Seminary, Dallas, Texas.

the preceding century) have the leaders of the churches taken the initiative in denying the inspiration and authority of the Bible. Orr, writing prophetically at the threshold of this century concerning the chief task of theology, declared, "The battle will have to be fought . . . round the fortress of the worth and authority of Holy Scripture."[1]

The battle was already joined when Orr wrote those words; the Fundamentalist-Modernist controversy had already begun. In 1893 Charles Augustus Briggs was tried, condemned, and dismissed from the Presbyterian Church in the USA as a heretic for affirming that the Bible contains errors. Yet by 1924 the Auburn Affirmation, which endorsed the same position, was signed by 1300 Presbyterian ministers and leaders. The liberals won control of the mainline Protestant denominations in the first quarter of the century, but in that conflict the theological conservatives stood as one man in affirming the full authority, inspiration, and inerrancy of the Bible.

Now in the last quarter of the century the "Battle for the Bible"[2] has broken out again. This time the conflict is a civil war among those who claim to be theological conservatives. On the one side stand those who still affirm the full inspiration and inerrancy of the Bible; and on the other side stand those who insist that the Bible contains errors in historical, geographical, and scientific details that do not affect its revelational and soteriological trustworthiness. Proponents of the latter position insist that they believe in the inspiration of the Bible as well as their opponents, but that the phenomena of Scripture require them to recognize incidental factual errors and to hold a view of limited inerrancy (or limited errancy).

In reality, adherents of the limited errancy view of the Bible actually hold to the partial inspiration of Scripture. That could also be described as a form of the "degrees of inspiration" theory. The point is that in so-called revelatory portions of Scripture the level of inspiration guarantees inerrancy, whereas in nonrevelatory portions inerrancy is not guaranteed. As a result, whether admitted or not, this position endorses two forms or degrees of inspiration in the Bible—one that insures inerrancy and a second that does not. The limited errancy view is held and promoted in spite of the straightforward statement in the Bible—"All Scripture is inspired by God [God-breathed]" (2 Tim. 3:16)[3]—which denies either partial inspiration or degrees of inspiration. The question arises whether exponents of limited errancy classify 2 Timothy 3:16 as revelatory Scripture or not. If it is considered revelatory, it condemns their position because as revelatory it is inerrant.

The crux of the argument by those today who deny the total inerrancy of the Bible is the phenomena of Scripture. By that phrase they mean primarily the facts of chronological, geographical, historical, mathematical and scientific detail embedded in the Bible. Also involved are the characteristics of Scripture reflected in parallel accounts, comparision of teaching, and the use of both scriptural and nonscriptural sources. Examination of that evidence demonstrates factual errors and contradictions in the Bible, they contend, which makes acceptance of the total inerrancy of the Scriptures untenable.

THE SCRIPTURAL ARGUMENT FOR INERRANCY

Any consideration of the evidence of Scripture must embrace the total body of material involved. That of necessity includes the teaching of the Bible concerning its own character. In fact, determining what the Bible teaches concerning itself is the logical starting point. The Bible's claims concerning its own nature form the first and highest level of scriptural evidence. Next, and closely related to the Bible's claims for itself, is the attitude toward and the use of previous Scripture such as the New Testament writers' use of the Old Testament. That also includes the attitude and use of the Old Testament by the Lord Jesus Christ, the incarnate Son of God. Only after those two factors do the facts and characteristics of Scripture come into consideration and, even then, they are not determinative of the biblical doctrine of the Scriptures. As Johnson states, "In cases of apparent conflict between the teaching of Scripture regarding its own inspiration and the phenomena of Scripture, it is the phenomena that must give way."[4]

Warfield faced the same problem in his day. He warned against those who appeal "to the so-called phenomena of the Scriptures" and set those in opposition "to the doctrine of the

Scriptures," seeking to justify "a modification of the doctrine taught by the Scriptures by the facts embedded in the Scriptures."[5] Later he wrote, "The effort to modify the teaching of Scripture as to its own inspiration by an appeal to the observed characteristics of Scripture, is an attempt not to obtain a clearer knowledge of what the Scriptures teach, but to correct that teaching. And to correct the teaching of Scripture is to proclaim Scripture untrustworthy as a witness to doctrine."[6]

THE BIBLE'S CLAIMS FOR ITSELF

When the claims of the Bible concerning its own character are considered, the classic passage is Paul's statement, "Every Scripture is [God-breathed]" (2 Tim. 3:16). That is a literal and accurate translation of the Greek words. The opening phrase is frequently translated "all Scripture" to emphasize that the totality of what is properly recognized as Scripture is involved. That emphasis is correct, but the fact remains that the singular number of the noun and the adjective is used. Therefore, without minimizing the fact that the totality of what is recognized as Scripture is involved, the stress falls on the fact that each unit of Scripture that makes up that totality is in view. That dual emphasis on the whole made up of its parts constitutes the "verbal, plenary" aspect of the biblical doctrine of inspiration.

The significant part of this statement is the description of Scripture as "God-breathed." That is a coined word found only here in the entire Bible. It is a compound word composed of the noun translated "God" and a form of the verb translated "to breathe." It affirms that everything that is recognized as Scripture originated with God and was breathed out by God as His expression, His Word. As a result, when the Bible is read or heard, it is as though God Himself spoke the words; they are "God-breathed."

THE NEW TESTAMENT USE OF THE OLD TESTAMENT

The affirmation of 2 Timothy 3:16 is the basis for the identification of the Bible in its totality as the Word of God. That identification has been made not only by Christians throughout the history of the church but also by the New Testament writers with reference to the Old Testament. Speaking of the New Testament writers, Warfield describes "their habitual appeal to the Old Testament text as to God Himself speaking" and "the absolute identification . . . of the Scriptures in their hands with the living voice of God."[7]

Two major types of passages illustrate the identification between God and Scripture. The first type focuses on those New Testament passages that identify the words of God recorded in the Old Testament as "Scripture." For example, in Galatians 3:8 Paul refers to God's promise to Abraham recorded in Genesis 12:1-3. Paul quotes the last clause, "All the nations shall be blessed in you," and attributes it to "the Scripture" even though the words were spoken by God Himself. Similarly, in Romans 9:17 Paul quotes a clause from God's message through Moses to Pharaoh found in Exodus 9:16 and attributes it to "the Scripture." Still another example is Romans 10:11, which attributes to "the Scripture" part of God's message in Isaiah 49:23.

The second type focuses on those passages where the New Testament attributes a statement to God even though God is not speaking in the Old Testament passage being quoted. Included among those passages are Matthew 19:4-5, where Jesus attributes to God the words of Adam in Genesis 2:24; Hebrews 3:7, where the words of the psalmist from Psalm 95:7 are attributed to the Holy Spirit; and Acts 13:34-35, where the words of David from Psalm 16:10 are attributed to God. Still another example of that identification is a comparison of Romans 11:32, which declares that "God has shut up all in disobedience," with Galatians 3:22, which states that "the Scripture has shut up all men under sin. . . ."

THE CHARACTER OF THE DIVINE AUTHOR

The character of the Scriptures in their totality as "God-breathed" carries with it the logical corollary of freedom from error—inerrancy. The Scriptures, being fully and verbally the written Word of God, partake of the characteristics and perfections of their ultimate author. God is absolute truth (Deut. 32:4; Psalm 31:5; 1 John 5:20), and so God's Word must also be true (John 17:17). One of the titles of the Holy Spirit, who produced the Scriptures through human authors, is "the Spirit of truth"

(John 14:17; 15:26; 16:13; 1 John 5:7). God is holy, pure, and free from any sin and error (Job 4:17; Isa. 5:16; Hab. 1:13; 1 John 1:5); and so is God's Word (Psalm 12:6; Prov. 30:5). God is perfect in His being and His ways (Deut. 32:4; 2 Sam. 22:31), and so is God's Word (Psalm 19:7; James 1:25). Psalm 19:7-11 is a description of the attributes of the Scriptures and their ministry to men. The Scriptures are pictured as perfect, sure, right, pure, clean, true, and righteous — all attributes of God Himself, whose Word the Scriptures are.

This logical equation of the inerrancy of the Bible with its character as God-breathed, however, is disputed by those who reject inerrancy. Patton, for example, considered it wrong "to substitute the word 'inerrancy' for 'inspiration' in our discussion of the Bible unless we are prepared to show from the teaching of the Bible that inspiration means inerrancy — and that, I think, would be a difficult thing to do."[8] The preceding discussion attempts to demonstrate that inherent in the declaration that "every Scripture is God-breathed" is the freedom of Scripture from error as God's Word, else the character of God, Scripture's ultimate author, is impugned.

Harrison acknowledges that inerrancy "is a natural corollary of full inspiration,"[9] and yet he insists, "One must grant that the Bible itself, in advancing its own claim of inspiration, says nothing precise about its inerrancy."[10] Apparently what he means by that statement — along with others who insist on the same position — is that the Bible nowhere uses the word *inerrancy* or directly states, "All Scripture is inerrant." But the mere absence of the word *inerrancy* is no argument against recognizing the fact of inerrancy as a necessary concomitant of the God-breathed character of Scripture. The Bible nowhere uses the word *trinity* either, and it does not directly state "The one God eternally exists in three persons." Yet orthodox Christians accept the doctrine of the Trinity as a biblical doctrine based on biblical evidence.

THE SUPERINTENDING OF THE HUMAN AUTHORS

The classic passage of 2 Timothy 3:16 affirms God as the ultimate and original author of "every Scripture," and yet human authors obviously were also involved. God did Himself originally inscribe the Ten Commandments on two tablets of stone (Exod 31:18), but God used human authors to produce most of the Scriptures. Some of the human authors are directly named (e.g., Hab. 1:1; James 1:1), some can almost positively be identified, and some still remain unknown (e.g., the author of the epistle to the Hebrews). That dual authorship of Scripture is recognized and affirmed in the Bible itself in 2 Peter 1:20-21.

Those who deny inerrancy focus on the reality of the human authorship of the Scriptures as the basis for their denial. Their argument is that the participation of human beings in the production of the Bible of necessity involves the existence of error. Barth presented the famous analogy that just as the light of the sun is discolored by passing through the stained glass of the cathedral window, so also the revelation of God is contaminated with error by passing through the human authors of the Bible. Jewett makes the same point when he writes, ". . . the Bible, which is God's holy word, is also a library of Jewish-Christian documents. And because it is the latter, it participates in the limitations of our finite humanity."[11]

According to Jewett the only way that an individual can hold to the inerrancy of the Bible while allowing for human authorship is by holding a dictation or mechanical theory of inspiration. The dictation view was held at various times in church history, particularly during the post-Reformation period, and is held by some groups today. Jewett rightly says, "Happily, as Conservatives, we have been delivered from such a one-sided view of Scripture. We know that the Bible was not dictated by the Holy Ghost."[12] He is not right, however, when he concludes, "If, then, we no longer believe that the Spirit of God dictated the Bible, we no longer need postulate an inerrant text as a theological a priori." Nor is he correct in saying, "To be sure, divine dictation requires inerrancy; but divine inspiration does not."[13] As has been seen, divine inspiration does require inerrancy, but inerrancy does not require the dictation theory of inspiration.

The Bible nowhere spells out in specific detail how the God-breathed Scriptures were produced—the process of inspiration or inscripturation. The Bible simply affirms the result of the process—"every Scripture is God-breathed." All that the Bible states concerning the process is found in 2 Peter 1:20-21.

That declares first of all that "no prophecy recorded in Scripture was ever thought up by the prophet himself" (TLB*). That is not a literal translation of the Greek text, but it is an accurate paraphrase of the idea, as Robertson confirms.[14] The passage continues to explain, "For not by the will of man was prophecy ever borne" (personal translation to bring out the force of the Greek word order). Finally, the passage concludes, "But, by the Holy Spirit being carried, men were speaking from God" (personal translation to bring out the force of the Greek word order and tenses). The point of the whole passage is "that no prophet starts a prophecy himself. He is not a self-starter. . . . Prophecy is of divine origin, not of own's [sic] private origination."[15]

Second Peter 1:20-21 simply confirms what 2 Timothy 3:16 declared—every Scripture originated in the mind of God, not in the mind of the human author; and the human author was motivated and carried by the Holy Spirit with the result that "every Scripture is God-breathed." But the passage does describe the human authors of Scripture as being "moved [or 'carried'] by the Holy Spirit," which is as far as the Bible goes in explaining the process of inspiration. No specific process of inspiration is disclosed, but an adequate explanation is stated—the carrying ministry of the Holy Spirit—which insures the validity of the result: "every Scripture is God-breathed."

Those who deny the inerrancy of the Bible because of human authorship are minimizing the ministry of the Holy Spirit and the infinite power of God. After discussing the evidence from Scripture why "God would not *intentionally* mislead or disceive us," Geisler and Feinberg ask, "Is it not possible . . . that God might be unable to communicate His knowledge without error. . . ?" They reply:

> Such might be the case were it not for the fact that Scripture teaches that God is also omnipotent or all-powerful (Matt. 28:18; Luke 1:37; 18:27). Therefore, if God does possess the truth, and if He has the will or motivation to communicate it (both points we have demonstrated above), then He cannot lack the power to communicate it to men. Hence, it seems clear that any conceivable reason for denying the indubitability or infallibility of God's revelation in the Bible is answered.[16]

*The Living Bible

The "limitations of our finite humanity" certainly cannot be so great that they thwart the limitlessness of God's infinite divinity.

THE PARALLELISM BETWEEN THE INCARNATE WORD
AND THE WRITTEN WORD

Another argument for the inerrancy of the Bible in addition to the claims of Scripture concerning its own character is the obvious parallelism that exists between the Lord Jesus Christ as the personal Word of God incarnate and the Bible as the written Word of God incarnate. Many Christians through the centuries have seen that parallelism, but its significance as support for the inerrancy of the Bible has seldom been noted. For orthodox Christians at least a forceful argument for the inerrancy of the Bible can be developed from that parallelism.

It is interesting to notice that those who deny the inerrancy of the Bible try to use the parallelism between Jesus Christ and the Bible to support their position. They warn that insisting on the inerrancy of Scripture is akin to docetism. Jewett writes:

> Hence, even as it is necessary by faith to hear the divine word in the human words of the Bible, so also it is necessary for faith that we should recognize these human words for what they are and not seek to obviate the obvious by so stressing the divinity of the Scriptures as to suppress their humanity. So to identify the human with the divine in the Bible that the former is swallowed up in the latter, is but an instance—to refer to our Christological model once more—of the ancient heresy of docetism.[17]

The obvious implication is that to insist on the inerrancy of the Bible is to suppress its humanness and to be guilty of a form of docetism.

That line of argumentation raises the question as to whether or not Jewett understands what docetism really is. For the record, "Docetism was the doctrine that Christ did not actually become flesh, but merely seemed to be a man."[18] Biblical inerrantists do not deny the human authors of the Scriptures nor the human words of the Scriptures. They simply affirm the freedom from error of those human authors and those human words under the superintendency of the Holy Spirit in producing the "God-breathed" Scriptures. If affirming freedom from error for the Scriptures is a form of docetism, then insisting on the sinlessness of Jesus Christ is docetism, too. Surely, "as Conservatives," Jewett and his associates affirm the sinlessness — the freedom from sin by nature and by act — of Jesus Christ. Conversely, if affirming the sinlessness of Jesus Christ is not docetism but orthodox biblical Christology, then affirming the errorlessness (inerrancy) of the Scriptures is not docetism either, but orthodox biblical bibliology. Charging biblical inerrantists with docetism is a non sequitur argument.

BOTH ARE THE ETERNAL WORD

Returning to the parallelism between Christ and the Scriptures as an argument for the inerrancy of the Bible it should be noted that the starting point for both sides of the parallelism is the eternal Word of God. On the one side is the eternal Word as the Son of God, the second Person of the triune Godhead (John 1:1-2); and on the other side is the eternal Word as the eternal decree and plan of God, which He is executing and has expressed in the Bible (Psalm 119:89, 152; Acts 15:18). God's nature and being have been manifested to men in the Lord Jesus Christ (John 1:18; 14:9; Col. 1:15; Heb. 1:3), and God's thoughts and plan have been manifested to men in the Bible as God's Word (Gen. 18:17; Deut. 29:29; John 16:12-15).

BOTH WERE MANIFESTED TO MEN

The next step in this parallelism is the process through which God's eternal Word was manifested to men. On the one side stands the process called "incarnation," involving the miraculous conception and the virgin birth; and on the other side stands the process called "inscripturation," involving revelation, inspiration, and illumination, although not necessarily all three at the same time. Inspiration ("being moved [or 'carried'] by the Holy Spirit") was coextensive with inscripturation, and from time to time either revelation or illumination or both were also involved.

BOTH INCORPORATED THE DIVINE AND THE HUMAN

Both processes of incarnation and inscripturation incorporated a divine factor and a human factor. In both processes the divine factor was the same, the Holy Spirit of God. In the process of incarnation the angel Gabriel explained to Mary how she as a virgin would conceive by saying, "The Holy Spirit will come upon you, and the power of the Most High will overshadow you" (Luke 1:35). The specific details of the process of incarnation remain a mystery, but an adequate explanation for the promised result is provided. Similarly, in the process of inscripturation, Peter explained that "men moved by the Holy Spirit spoke from God" (2 Pet. 1:21). Paul expressed the same idea when he wrote, "Which things we also speak, not in words taught by human wisdom, but in those taught by the [Holy] Spirit" (1 Cor. 2:13). Once again the specific details of the process of inscripturation remain a mystery, but an adequate explanation for the promised result is provided.

The human factor in the two processes is different. The virgin Mary is the human factor in the process of incarnation, and the authors of Scripture are the human factor in the process of inscripturation. And yet, there is a common element in both factors — sinful human nature. The Scriptures do not teach (and Protestant Christians do not accept) the dogma of the sinlessness of the virgin Mary. A godly and devout Jewish maiden, Mary still had a sinful human nature. Similarly, the human authors of Scripture were godly and devout individuals, but each one still had a sinful human nature.

BOTH RESULTED IN AN ERRORLESS PRODUCT

The final step in the parallelism is the product or result of the process. On the one side is the Lord Jesus Christ, the personal Word of God incarnate; and on the other side are the Scriptures, the written Word of God incarnate. Without denying the genuineness and completeness of the human nature of Jesus Christ, the angel Gabriel called Him "the holy offspring" (Luke 1:35). Similarly, without denying the genuineness and completeness of the humanness of the Bible, the apostle Paul called it "the holy Scriptures" (Rom. 1:2; 2 Tim. 3:15).

The significance of the designation "the holy offspring" concerning the Lord Jesus Christ was that by the miracle of the Holy Spirit He was conceived free from the sin nature and the contamination of Adam's fall, the only person since Adam and Eve of whom that will ever be true. Paul described Jesus as the one "who knew no sin" (2 Cor. 5:21). The writer to the Hebrews says that Jesus "has been tested according to all things according to likeness to us apart from sin" (Heb. 4:15, personal translation). The phrase *apart from sin* means more than that Jesus did not sin by responding; it means that He had no sin nature within Him. The Lord Jesus Christ was sinless, free from every taint of sin from inward nature, thought, or action. Entirely apart from the disputed issue of the impeccability of Christ (his inability to sin), orthodox theology through the centuries and today has unanimously proclaimed the sinlessness of Jesus Christ. That emphasis on the sinlessness of the Lord Jesus Christ is totally apart from any accusations of docetism.

The bottom line of this discussion on the parallelism between the Lord Jesus Christ and the Scriptures is obvious. If in the womb of the virgin Mary, a sinner by nature and action, the Holy Spirit produced the personal Word of God incarnate free from all taint of sin, is it not reasonable to conclude—yes, necessary to conclude—that in the minds and through the pens of human authors, sinners by nature and action, the same omnipotent Holy Spirit by the process of inscripturation produced the written Word of God incarnate free from all error? Why is insisting on the freedom from error (inerrancy) of the Bible "an instance . . . of the ancient heresy of docetism," when to insist on the freedom from sin (sinlessness) of Jesus Christ involves no hint of docetism?

CONCLUSION

In affirming the inerrancy of the Bible it is important to remember that the quality of inerrancy is ascribed only to the autographa—the original manuscripts—of the human authors of the Scriptures. Although God has providentially preserved the Scriptures from repeated Satanic attempts to utterly destroy them, He has not maintained them free from error through repeated copying and through translation into other languages. Transcriptional errors (copying mistakes) have crept into the text despite ingenious and assiduous efforts, especially among the Hebrew scribes, to avoid them.

That raises the very practical question, Why the insistence on the inerrancy of the Bible if the Hebrew and Greek texts available today are not inerrant? The first answer is that the transcriptional errors are few in number compared to the totality of the biblical text. They are incidental. The second answer is that they affect no major doctrine or teaching of the Bible. They are insignificant. The final answer is that it is of vital spiritual importance to know that there was an inerrant original text that the present text practically duplicates.

A second practical question is, Why did God not preserve the inerrant autographa of the Bible? Related to this is the question, What happened to the original manuscripts? To answer the second question first, No one knows what happened to the original manuscripts. They probably were handled and read so much that they finally disintegrated. No one except God really knows the answer to the first of those two questions either; but, recognizing the human proclivity to idolatry as seen in the adulation of the Shroud of Turin, God likely destroyed them or removed them to reduce man's temptation to sinful worship.

A final question is, How are the so-called errors and apparent discrepancies in the Bible to be handled? Almost without exception the same list of problem passages has been presented by every critic of the Bible since Celsus and has been answered by those who believe in the Bible's inerrancy; and yet they are still presented today. The first answer is harmonization. Clark writes, "Therefore an evangelical must of necessity try to harmonize all Scriptural statements with each other. He may sometimes fail, either because he sees no solution, or because his solution is a blunder. But he must try, unless he wishes to charge God's own words with falsehood."[19] The second answer is to suspend judgment for additional evidence or illumination. If no reasonable explanation is available, it is never wrong to say, "I don't know. We must continue to study the problem and wait for God to disclose additional evidence or to provide additional insight."

The Lord Jesus Christ, the personal Word of God incarnate, said concerning the written Word of God incarnate, ". . . the

Scripture cannot be broken" (John 10:35), and "until heaven and earth pass away, not the smallest letter or stroke shall pass away from the Law, until all is accomplished" (Matt. 5:18), and "Heaven and earth will pass away, but My words shall not pass away" (Matt. 24:35). Jesus affirmed the Scriptures as the inerrant Word of God. Can those who believe in Him as Savior and Lord do any less?

NOTES

1. James Orr, *The Progress of Dogma* (London: Hodder and Stoughton, 1901), p. 352.
2. Harold Lindsell, *The Battle for the Bible* (Grand Rapids: Zondervan, 1976).
3. J. B. Rotherham, *The Emphasized Bible* (Grand Rapids: Kregel, 1959).
4. S. Lewis Johnson, Jr., *The Old Testament in the New* (Grand Rapids: Zondervan, 1980), p. 10.
5. Benjamin Breckinridge Warfield, "The Real Problem of Inspiration," in *The Inspiration and Authority of the Bible* (Philadelphia: Presbyterian and Reformed, 1948), p. 201.
6. Ibid., p. 204.
7. Benjamin Breckinridge Warfield, " 'It Says:' 'Scripture Says:' 'God Says,' " in *The Inspiration and Authority of the Bible*, p. 299.
8. Francis L. Patton, *Fundamental Christianity* (New York: Macmillan, 1926), p. 164.
9. Everett F. Harrison, "The Phenomena of Scripture," in *Revelation and the Bible*, ed. Carl F. H. Henry (Grand Rapids: Baker, 1958), p. 250.
10. Ibid., p. 238.
11. Paul K. Jewett, "The Doctrine of Scripture: The Divine Word in Human Words" (class notes in Systematic Theology 1. Fuller Theological Seminary), p. 4.
12. Ibid., p. 5.
13. Ibid.
14. A. T. Robertson, *Word Pictures in the New Testament*, 6 vols. (Nashville: Broadman, 1930), 6:158-59.
15. Ibid., 6:159.
16. Norman L. Geisler and Paul D. Feinberg, *Introduction to Philosophy: A Christian Perspective* (Grand Rapids: Baker, 1980), p. 130.
17. Jewett, class notes, p. 4.
18. *Baker's Dictionary of Theology*, s.v. "Docetism," by Merrill C. Tenney, p. 171.
19. Gordon H. Clark, *The Concept of Biblical Authority* (Phillipsburg, N.J.: Presbyterian and Reformed, 1980), p. 19.

8

The Historical Development of the Doctrine of Christ

John D. Hannah

The answer that Peter gave in response to Christ's question, "But who do you say that I am?" (Matt. 16:15) appears remarkably forthright and clear; it stands in vivid contrast to the plethora of answers given within Christendom today. To some theologians today Christ is merely a god-intoxicated, and hence elevated, ideal of temporal and eschatological hope; He is an example of hope for a struggling humanity. To others He is a projection of the inquirer's inner confrontation with a demythologized, hence personalized, message of the church's witness.

In contrast to those evaluations of Christ by Barthian, Bultmannian and post-Bultmannian theologians, Walvoord wrote in 1969 a major text defending the person of Christ. Stone noted in his review of the volume that "his is an unswerving espousal of the orthodox position on the person of Christ. Eternal, pre-existent, self-existent, sovereign, unchangeable, true

JOHN D. HANNAH (B.S., Philadelphia College of Bible; M.A., Southern Methodist University; Th.M., Th.D., Dallas Theological Seminary; graduate study toward Ph.D., University of Texas at Dallas) is professor of historical theology at Dallas Theological Seminary. Dallas, Texas.

Son of God—this is our Lord Jesus."[1] Another reviewer described it as "a great new work on Christology."[2] A third review stated that the book is "comprehensive in scope," and suggested that "the work is clear in its presentation and will undoubtedly be a standard textbook in this area of doctrine."[3] The work is currently in its eleventh printing with thousands of copies in circulation and has indeed become a standard text in many Christian educational institutions.

In recognition of Walvoord's contribution to the defense of orthodox Christology, the following survey of the history of that doctrine is offered. A complete study of the doctrine of Christ's person is beyond the limited scope of a single chapter. But it is hoped that by concentrating on the logos-sarx relationship (the unity of His deity and humanity) the development of the doctrine of Christ might be perceived in general and that the significance of Walvoord's contribution to the subject might be better understood and appreciated.

THE CENTURIES OF FORMULATION

The testimony of the church Fathers, the immediate successors of the apostles, is both unsystematic and unspeculative. While they believed that Christ was both God and human (logos-sarx), they did not attempt to understand or unravel the implications or difficulties inherent in such a view. Clement of Rome (c. 100) wrote of Christ's real humanity, quoting from Isaiah 52-53,[4] and recognized His preexistence in a beautiful rehearsal of Hebrews 1.[5] Ignatius of Antioch (c. 110) explicitly denied a docetic Christ and alluded to a logos-sarx relationship. "We have also as a physician the Lord our God, Jesus the Christ, the only-begotten Son and Word, before time began, but who afterwards became also a man, of Mary the virgin."[6] With the possible exception of Ignatius, the Fathers did not venture into speculation. To them Christ was simply logos and sarx. Grillmeier concludes, "Despite this emphatic delineation of the God-manhood of Jesus Christ, there is still no doctrine of two natures in a technical sense."[7]

The attacks by heathen philosophers in the second and third centuries forced the church to carefully examine the doctrines it proclaimed. Origen (c. 185-254) quotes Celsus as charging, "God either really changes himself, these assert, into a mortal body and the impossibility of that has already been declared, or else he does not undergo a change but only causes the beholders to imagine so, and thus deceives them and is guilty of falsehood."[8] The church was forced to reckon with the implications of true humanity and true deity. Iraneaus, in battling Basilides and Valentinus, who were prominent Gnostics, and Marcion, argued forcibly that Christ was truly man and God ("the incomprehensible being made comprehensible, the impossible becoming capable of suffering, and the Word being made man").[9] Tertullian of Carthage (c. 160-220) laid the foundation for the resolution of the Christological debate in the West. Although his thought still needed refinement, his striking contribution was his stress on deity and humanity in one person.[10] The Alexandrian theologians, principally Clement and Origen, viewed the incarnation through the veil of Platonic thought. Origen saw in the incarnation the real arrival of the logos, but he appeared to subordinate the human Jesus. He was correct in asserting that the linking of the logos and humanity was real and permanent, but he erred in saying that the human soul of Christ became divinized and aglow as iron in a fire. The apologists of the third and fourth centuries saw that Christ was God incarnate, but they could not find a fitting arrangement of words to express that perception. Grillmeier notes, "It is clear from this survey that the rise of christological reflection was a very slow process."[11]

Until the fourth century the question, What is the relationship between the divine and human in Christ? was not the object of intensive research in the church, although Tertullian anticipated the answer by saying, "we see plainly the twofold state, which is not confounded, not intermixed but conjoined in One person, Jesus, God and Man."[12] Before the relationship between the divine and human in Christ could be resolved, the question of His preexistence had to be delineated. The resolution of that issue at the Council of Nicaea (A.D. 325) with the condemnation of any kind of subordinationism between the Father and Son, paved the way for a careful examination of the question of Christ's incarnate nature. Thus after the Council of

Nicaea (which argued that in Christ's preincarnate being He was co-equal, co-eternal, and one essence with the Father), the fourth-century church was able to debate the relationship between Christ's deity and humanity.

Apollinarius (c. 310-390), bishop of Laodicea, attempted to answer the question of the logos-sarx relationship by a synthesis of body and soul within substantial unity. His thought evidences the echoes of Origen with the concept of an emerging soul that combines the two natures into one. To Apollinarius the logos-sarx relationship arose from a trichotomist presupposition: deity occupied or supplanted the human spirit so that in the one person a human body and soul was joined to divine reason. Or, as Gonzalez writes, "Christ is human because his body and his soul—or vital principle—are human; but he is divine because his reason is the very Word of God."[13] Thus Apollinarius championed the unity of Christ's two natures and the full deity of Christ but deprecated His true, total humanity. Gregory of Nazianzus revealed the dangers of Apollinarius's position. "But if He has a soul, and yet is without a mind, how is He man, for man is not a mindless animal."[14] From the decade of the 370s onward the Cappadocians assailed Apollinarius and his disciple Vitalis. The dispute ended when the Council of Constantinople (A.D. 381) condemned his views, as well as those of Arius, thus bringing a final refutation of his views in the ancient church.

The condemnation of one position does not automatically guarantee that a proper alternative can be formulated. Gonzalez notes that that is clearly the case in the mystery of Christ's incarnate person. "The rejection of the theories of Apollinarius was in no way a solution of the Christological problem. The Cappadocians themselves, although they were convinced that it was necessary to condemn the elderly Laodicean theologian, did not have a clear alternative to offer."[15] An alternative was set forth in 428 by Nestorius who occupied the patriarchal see of Constantinople. He violently opposed any who spoke of Mary as "mother of God" (theotokos), accepting only that Mary was the mother of the human Christ because he felt that the former position intermingled the two natures. ("Mary has not borne the godhead, for that which is born of flesh is flesh. . . . A creature has not borne the creator.")[16] Because of his fear that the divine and human natures of Christ might be dissolved into one, Nestorius erred by denying the unity in one person of the two natures. He taught that the conjunction of the two natures in one person was moral, not organic. Nestorius's Christ was a God-bearing man, not the God-man; his Christ was not two natures unified in one person. His view was condemned at the third great council of the entire church held at Ephesus in A.D. 431.

A clear, holistic construction of the biblical data was still not in focus. The church appeared much more efficient at detecting error than at formulating the truth. Because of its conflict with the Gnostics, the church saw the truth of a truly human Christ. The error of Arius forced the church to perceive the absolute deity of Christ and to grapple with the paradox of the two natures present in the incarnation. In condemning Apollinarius the church perceived the seriousness of denigrating His humanity to perserve His deity, and from the Nestorian debates the church was warned that true deity and humanity had somehow to be articulated in a real unity. Yet how was the mystery to be explained? It finally took the heterodox formulation of Eutyches, a monk from Constantinople, to force the church to articulate the doctrine of the hypostatic union correctly.

Eutyches was condemned by the patriarch of Constantinople at a local synod for believing that at the incarnation the two natures of Christ ceased to exist. He taught that the incarnate Christ had a single, composite nature. The beleaguered monk conceded on investigation that "our Lord was of two natures before the union but after the union one nature."[17] The debate soon moved beyond the local synod. Dioscurus, bishop of Alexandria, defended Eutyches, and both appealed for support from Leo, the bishop of Rome. A gathering of the churches at Ephesus to arbitrate the issue ended in confusion in 449. Dioscurus shamefully mistreated Flavian, and Leo's letter was not read. Opponents of Dioscurus's actions dubbed it the "Robber's Council." Two years later at Chalcedon, near Constantinople, a gathering of 520 bishops not only condemned Dioscurus but affirmed Leo's letter (*Tome to Flavian*) as the proper statement of the hypostatic union. The resultant creed read in part, "two natures, unconfusedly, immutably, indivisibly, inseparably; the distinction of natures being preserved and concurring in one person and hypostasis, not separated or divided into two persons, but one and the same Son and only begotten."[18] Thus the church recognized that Christ was fully God and fully man in one person without confusion — the God-Man.

THE CENTURIES OF ACCEPTANCE

Although it is apparent that the findings of Chalcedon clearly articulated the doctrine of the logos-sarx issue and that advances in the understanding of the doctrine were not put forth for a time, it must be understood that theologians continued to debate Christology. In the medieval era there were three major controversies over this issue: Monophysitism, Monotheletism, and Adoptionism.

According to Orr, the Monophysite controversy was simply a continuation of the Eutychian controversy.[19] It involved a revolt of Eastern churchmen who believed that the Chalcedonian Creed repudiated the existence of a single nature in Christ. The largely Eastern controversy was ended in 553 when the fifth ecumenical council held in Constantinople condemned Monophysitism. That occasioned a split in the physical unity of the church as the rejected party established separate communions in Syria, Egypt, and Armenia.

In the early seventh century an attempt was made to conciliate the Monophysites (largely for political reasons) by arguing that Christ had one will (Monotheletism). But after the Islamic hordes conquered Syria and Egypt, the bastions of the Monophysite churches, there was no military advantage to be secured by courting their favor. Therefore at the sixth ecumenical council in Constantinople in 681 Monotheletism was condemned. "We likewise [teach] two natural operations indivisibly, unchangeably, inseparably, unconfusedly, according to the teaching of the holy Fathers. And these two natural wills are not contrary one to the other."[20]

The only major eruption of a Christological nature in the West (by major is meant one that precipitates a dissident movement) was the Adoptionistic controversy of the eighth and ninth centuries. This occurred within the context of both the Carolingian revival and the Arab expulsion from Europe. In attempting to refute Sabellianism, two Spanish theologians, Elipandus of Toledo and Felix of Urgel, appeared perilously close to Nestorianism.[21] They allowed Christ's humanity to fall into neglect in order to emphasize His deity (something of a quasi-Apollinarianism). They presented an altogether divine person who assumed human substance. Charlemagne had Adoptionism condemned at several provincial councils as did Bishop Hadrian I and Leo III of Rome.

Apart from those disruptions, Christological formulations did not advance during those centuries. Chalcedon was perceived as the sum of orthodoxy. Of the medieval scholastics Seiberg writes, "The great Scholastics present in their Christology merely a reproduction of the traditional dogma."[22] In the sixteenth century when the church was rent over theological (particularly soteriological) issues, Christology was not a dividing point. The Roman church agreed with her Protestant opponents on the nature of the preincarnate Christ. Accordingly, the Canons and decrees of Trent, as well as the Tridentine Profession of Faith, were silent on this issue; that is, they accepted the earlier statements of the ecumenical councils. The Protestant reformers likewise understood and recognized Chalcedon as the most adequate expression of the Lord's incarnate person. Althaus notes of Luther, "As we have pointed out, Luther adopts the traditional dogmatic doctrine of two natures."[23] Calvin argued, "We maintain, that the divinity was so cojoined and united with the humanity, that the entire properties of each nature remain entire, and yet the two natures constitute only one Christ."[24] It may accurately be stated that Chalcedon established a formulation of the doctrine of the incarnate Christ that went without significant challenge from the fifth century through the prominent reformers of the sixteenth century.

A harbinger of significant change, however, manifested itself in the Spaniard Servetus (1511-1553) and in the rise of the Socinian movement within the Reformed Church of Poland. Servetus attacked the traditional understanding of theology proper and that in turn impaired his Christology. Servetus retreated to the ancient heresy of Modalistic Monarchianism, which denied the preincarnate person of Christ as put forth by the ancient creeds.[25] He also adopted a quasi-Eutychianism to explain Christ's incarnate person.[26] As Calvin wrote, "He denies that Christ is the Son of God, for any other reason than because he was begotten in the womb of the Virgin by the Holy Spirit. The tendency of this crafty devise is to make out, by destroying the distinction of the two natures, that Christ is somewhat composed of God and man, and yet not to be deemed God and man."[27]

Socinianism (which McLachlan understands to be rooted in Italian rationalism) denied the pre-existence of Christ, denouncing the truth of His deity.[28] The Racovian Catechism of 1574 states concerning those who ascribe to a trinity of divine persons within a singularity of essence, "In this they lamentably err deducing their arguments from passages of Scripture ill understood."[29] Socinian opinions of Christ rapidly spread throughout Northern Europe, but particularly in Holland (where it gained a hearing among the Remonstrant Party) and in England. In England Socinian views became manifest in two distinct movements: English Unitarianism and English Deism.[30] Not all Unitarians were deists, but all deists had a unitarian Christ.

Evidence of the rejection of the traditional understanding of Christ became manifest during the Reformation era outside the Protestant and Catholic communities and was accordingly perceived by both as outside the pale of orthodoxy. In the aftermath of the Reformation the traditional interpretation of Christ was reevaluated by the theologians of the Reformation churches.

THE CENTURIES OF DISSENT

In order to understand the theological drift of the Modern Era, it is imperative to understand that a philosophic shift has occurred from a theistic world view to that of an anthropocentric world view. That shift was neither sudden nor tragically planned, but arose in opposition to theism. The error was not in the rise of secular epistemology, particularly in the brilliant synthesis of Kant, but in the application of Kantian epistemology to the question of religious truth. Theologians did not err in the adoption of scientific method to arrive at truth; but they did err when they applied that method to religion, thus questioning any truth that could not strictly submit to the strictures of empiricism. That is, moderate fideism increasingly fell into disuse in the nineteenth century as generations of scholars arose who were enamoured with Kant and historicism.[31] The influence of Kant's philosophy set the framework for the nineteenth century. Kant's elevation of both the mind and empiricism provided the taproot for theological quest.

Schleiermacher (1768-1834), the Reformed pastor and theologian, was a unique blend of three crosscurrents: Reformed Theology, Pietism, and Liberalism. His view reflects the ancient heresy of Dynamic Monarchianism. He asserted the "divinity of Christ" and stressed that He was the "ideal of humanity." However, to Schleiermacher Christ's "divinity" was in His human perception of god-consciousness, not within His nature. As Mackintosh says, "The Redeemer, then, is like all men in virtue of the identity of human nature, but distinguished from them all by the constant potency of His God-consciousness, which was a veritable existence of God in Him."[32] Thus the degree to which one is God-conscious is the degree to which one is sinless since sin is merely a lack of God-consciousness. It is in that nonconstitutional sense that Christ was both sinless and deity. The feeling of "godness" came on Christ at birth, and that feeling was His "godness."

Schleiermacher rejected the concept of two natures and instead opted for a human Jesus who had become overpowered and dominated by a feeling of "godness." That feeling made the person of Christ "supernatural," and that feeling is the virgin birth. The birth was natural, but it was "supernatural" in that it was sinless (not lacking in god-feeling). Thus Schleiermacher confessed, "the assumption of a Virgin Birth is superfluous."[33] Although Schleiermacher had a one-natured Christ, his position should not be confused with the ancient Eutychian error. In contrast to Eutyches's stress on the blending of the divine and human natures, Schleiermacher denied that Christ had any objective deity. His "godness" was not actual. It was implanted at His "supernatural" birth. In reality Schleiermacher's Christ is merely a god-intoxicated man, not the God-man of Chalcedonian orthodoxy.

The nineteenth century had a human Christ who witnessed to the power of God in His life. Christ, as a man, became mankind's "window into the ways of God." But His claim to deity was not constitutional or eternal, but was merely the result of a power that influenced His being.

Ritschl (1822-1889) and the entire Ritschlian School adopted the same rubric but emphasized Christ's uniqueness predicated on His vocation. To Ritschl, Christ's "godness" came from the fact that He most consistently aligned with God's purposes; that is, Christ's relationship to deity is functional, not ontological. "Since, now, as the founder of the Kingdom of God in the world, or as the bearer of God's moral authority over men, He is the unique one in comparison with all those who have received from him a similar purpose."[34] Swing's analysis of Ritschl's kingdom-Christ is helpful.

> In other words, the Ritschlian argument is this—and it is not often surpassed in apologetic literature: There is one kingdom of God for which God has made the world. Jesus Christ, as the conscious founder of this kingdom in the world, is the one person to whom God looks, and to whom the members of this community look as head of this kingdom. Thrown upon the cosmic background for physical forces, he becomes the revealer of the purpose and character of the supramundane spiritual God, for the one divine purpose of making men free and independent of the world. Between God's self-end and Christ's self-end, there is a solidaric unity, by which men are to discover their own true self-end, and be won into its accomplishment through fellowship.[35]

The origin of the Christ-man, which Ritschl perceives as a unity of purpose, not being, is uncertain and unknowable. The question of beginnings "is not a subject for theological inquiry" and "serves to obscure the recognition of Christ as the perfect revelation of God."[36] Of Christ's eternal relationship to the Father, Ritschl asserts that something is real but that scientific explanations are limited in such problems.[37] Thus the Christ of Ritschl, the Ritschlians, and the nineteenth century was a human who, by virtue of His piety and vocation, was elevated to receive the title "Son of God"—a title signifying unity in vocation, not essence.

An outgrowth of Ritschl's teachings on Christ and the kingdom was the History of Religions School under Gunkel (1862-1932) and von Harnack (1851-1930). This school of thought brought a Kantian scientism to religion and sought to find revelation history (actually, man gaining insight into himself). They sought to recover the "kernel" or essence of Christianity out of a Bible polluted with Hellenism and mythology. To Harnack Christ was not unique in His person. Rather, Christ was unique in that He exemplified the principles of the Kingdom; that is, "Son of God" meant the knowledge of God, and "deity" meant filial vocation. Harnack stressed the religion *of* Jesus (what He lived and taught), not the religion *about* Jesus. The religion of Jesus and His disciples was that of an ethical, moral kingdom. That same line of thought became clearly evident in Bultmann (1884-1976), who, like the History of Religions School, attempted to demythologize the Bible to discover the true Christ—a Christ who is the ultimate, triumphant aspiration of an otherwise failing age.

As World War I forced European scholars to adopt a more realistic evaluation of nineteenth century progressivism, Barth (1886-1968) actuated a similar shaking of the theological world. Although Barth's doctrine of the Scriptures is a remarkable improvement over the previous century, he was not able to escape the taint of an existentialist epistemology; that is, Barth conceived the Bible as inerrant only in a subjective sense. He held to verbal plenary inspiration, but he took inspiration out of the realm of objectivity by relegating it to the "self-authenticating Christ event."[38] In the realm of theology proper and Christology, Barth was quite orthodox, a radical turn from Schleiermacher and Ritschl. Yet he built his orthodox position on a foundation that could not perpetuate his lofty conclusions.

> . . . his failure to be clear on the role of history in revelation and his tendency to regard real communication as suprahistorical has tended to make the main facts concerning Christ experiential. Hence, the Christ of the Scriptures is to some extent supplanted by the Christ of experience, and the resulting doc-

trines become subjective in contemporary theology rather than historical and revelatory in absolute terms in the Scripture.[39]

Although he was deficient in his perception of the Scriptures, Barth elevated and respected the testimony of holy writ. Accordingly, his view of the preincarnate Christ is one of absolute deity as explained in the historic creeds and the Protestant Reformers.[40] As regards the incarnate Christ, Barth is clearly Chalcedonian when he argues "that Jesus Christ is very God and very man."[41] Barth is abundantly clear that Christ, the eternal one, became flesh and dwelt among men. "That the Word was made 'flesh' means first and generally that He became man, true and real man, participating in the same human essence and existence, the same human nature and form, the same historicity that we have."[42] This God-man was both virgin born[43] and impeccable,[44] but at the same time He was not "a sort of superhuman quality." Barth, then, conceives of Christ in the orthodox formulation of the Chalcedonian creed; He is at once God and man in the unity of a single person.

> If we paraphrase the statement "the Word became flesh" by "the Word assumed flesh," we guard against the misinterpretation already mentioned, that in the incarnation the Word ceased to be entirely Himself and equal to Himself, i.e., in the full sense of Word of God. God cannot cease to be God. The incarnation is inconceivable, but it is not absurd, and it must not be explained as an absurdity. The inconceivable fact in it is that without ceasing to be God the Word of God is among us in such a way that He takes over human being, which is His creature, into His own being and to that extent makes it His own being. As His own predicate along with His original predicate of divinity, He takes over human being into unity with Himself. And it is by the paraphrase, "the word assumed flesh" that the second misunderstanding is also guarded against, that in the incarnation, by means of a union of divine and human being and nature, a third is supposed to arise. Jesus Christ as the Mediator between God and man is not a third, midway between the two. In that case God has at once ceased to be God and likewise, He is not a man like us. But Jesus is the Mediator, the God-Man, in such a way that He is God and Man.[45]

Barth reveals himself to be remarkably orthodox concerning the person of Christ. Christ is not the man with feeling for God as Schleiermacher would denominate His uniqueness; nor does he admit, as would the Ritchlians, that His divinity is kingdom-oriented. Christ is not related to God by alignment of mere ideas and aspirations, but by constitution. He is the God-man. And bound in the uniqueness of His person is the marvel of His provision.

> This is the revelation of God in Christ. For where man admits his lost state and lives entirely by God's mercy—which no man did, but only the God-Man Jesus Christ has done—God Himself is manifest. And by that God reconciled the world to Himself. For where man claims no right for himself, but concedes all rights to God alone—which no man did, but only the God-Man Jesus Christ has done—the world is drawn out of its enmity towards God and reconciled to God.[46]

German theology of the nineteenth century has been reproduced in the United States in Classic Liberalism, which held sway in many American denominations from 1890-1940 and which has continued under the rubric of Neo-Liberalism. Fosdick, the great apostle of theological latitudinarianism, argued from the Riverside pulpit in New York City in 1935 that Liberalism had won its intended victory over religiously narrow, even bigoted, Christianity and that "the church must go beyond liberalism." In both expressions of Liberalism in America there is little, if any, change in Christology from either Schleiermacher or Ritschl. The corrective influence of Barth's Christology has had little impact on American theology, although his views on the authority and integrity of the Bible are having a negative effect on evangelicals in this country.

Bultmann was not influential in the United States during his lifetime. However, he has received posthumous popularity through several radical expressions of his critical, demythological approach to the Bible which he conceived in much the same way as the History of Religions School under Gunkel and Harnack.

One example of the radical use of Bultmann as applied to Christology is Tillich (1886-1965) and the "Theology of Being." Tillich referred to Jesus as "the Christ" but rejected the term "Jesus Christ;" he preferred to think of the anointed one who became Christ. He rejected the term "divine nature" when applied to Christ and simply redefined theological terms so as to create a God-adopted man. "God chooses to 'adopt' the man Jesus as the Christ, and Jesus chooses to accept his adoption through obedience."[47] The assertion that "Jesus is the God-man" is a nonsensical statement to Tillich because to him it cannot mean what it says ("a mythology of metamorphosis"). McKelway writes, "Tillich has not said, nor will he say with the 'incarnational' christologies of Nicaea and Chalcedon, that Jesus was 'truly God and truly Man.' No, it is the adoptionist position to which he holds with greater consistency. God chose Jesus, Jesus became the Christ."[48] Thus Tillich essentially rehearses the Christology of the Socinians, Schleiermacher, the Ritchlians and the History of Religions School.

Process Theology, which is another example of radical Christological expression, finds its philosophic roots in Whitehead's belief that reality is "creativity" or "becomingness." That ideology was carried into the theological sphere by Hartshorne. Process Theology places stress on Jesus' uniqueness, but it does so in a way that rejects historic orthodoxy. Christ was a mere man who was given a subjective aim, that is, to realize Himself. Christ's true uniqueness lies in His accomplishment of that aim. Christ's vocation was not so much to align with God's kingdom-purposes, but to understand for Himself the task of self-understanding. "The Union of God and man in Jesus is more like what we know of personal relationship than it is like anything else."[49] Thus questions about Christ's sinlessness and constitutional nature are irrelevant; the issue is that Christ teaches man how to understand himself in that He uniquely understood Himself and His relationship to God. As Pittenger writes in Neo-Ritchlian terms, "The greatest single factor in determining that speciality is the way in which, with a high degree of awareness of what was going on, the man Jesus as the centre of the event accepts his vocation, made his decision and his subsequent decision, and set about fulfulling the aim which was his own."[50]

CONCLUSION

The statement that "Jesus is God" is an absolute statement

and a test of historic orthodoxy. The church struggled to explain the doctrine in the Ancient Period and did so because churchmen rightly conceived that "Jesus is God" although a reasonable explanation of the unity of the God-Man proved difficult and, therefore, took centuries of diligent debate. In the Medieval and Reformation periods the church affirmed the one great cornerstone of the faith within the rubric of the Chalcedonian formula, "Jesus is God." It was only in the aftermath of the Reformation that some began to doubt what had been affirmed by Christ, the apostles, and the church.

The harbinger of reevaluation initially emerged outside the traditions of the Reformation in the Socinian movement which, as the ancient heresy of Dynamic Monarchianism, denied the eternal deity of Christ. A far more penetrating attack on the statement "Jesus is God" came from the German theologians who denied that affirmation and asserted instead that "Jesus became godness." Their "reinterpretation" of Christ's essential nature amounted to a rejection of constitutional deity for vocational or personal divinity. To Schleiermacher Christ's uniqueness was in His feeling of divine purpose; to Ritchl and the Ritchlians His uniqueness was in His vocational kingdom idealism; and to the radical theologies, particularly Process Theology, His uniqueness was only in His sense of self-understanding. The statement that "Jesus is God" thus came to be interpreted personally, not constitutionally.

Current Christology is described by Walvoord as "contemporary confusion."[51] The modern wave of theological opinion could lead one to assert that the affirmation "Jesus is God," is an existential statement rather than an objective constitutional statement. Walvoord's text, Jesus Christ Our Lord, is clearly an assertion of historic orthodoxy; that is, that "Jesus is God." That alone is the answer to the Lord's provocative inquiry, "But who do you say that I am?"

NOTES

1. Robert Stone, "Book Review," Westminster Theological Journal 33 (May 1971): 230.
2. Paul Nevin, ed., "Books," Moody Monthly, November 1969, p. 50.

3. Charles C. Ryrie, "Book Review," *Bibliotheca Sacra* 127 (January-March 1970): 69.
4. Clement *The Epistles to the Corinthians* 16., in Alexander Roberts and James Donaldson, eds., *The Ante-Nicene Fathers*, 10 vols. (Grand Rapids: Eerdmans, 1977), 1:9.
5. Clement *To the Corinthians* 36., in Roberts and Donaldson, 1:14-15.
6. Ignatius *The Epistle to the Ephesians* 7, in Roberts and Donaldson, 1:52.
7. Aloys Grillmeier, *Christ in Christian Tradition*, 3 vols., 2 ed., trans. John Bowden (Atlanta: John Knox, 1975), 1:105.
8. Origen *Against Celsus* 4.18, in Roberts and Donaldson, 1:504.
9. Iraneaus *Against Heresies* 3.16.6, in Roberts and Donaldson, 1:443.
10. Tertullian *Against Praxeas* 12.6, in Roberts and Donaldson, 3:606-7.
11. Grillmeier, p. 148.
12. Tertullian *Against Praxeas* 27, in Roberts and Donaldson, 3:624.
13. Justo L. Gonzalez, *A History of Christian Thought*, 3 vols. (Nashville: Abingdon, 1970), 1:358.
14. Gregory of Nazianzus *Epistle to Cledonius* 101, in Philip Schaff and Henry Wace, eds., *The Nicene and Post-Nicene Fathers*, 12 vols. (Grand Rapids: Eerdmans, 1974), 7:440.
15. Gonzalez, p. 363.
16. Nestorius *Fragments*, p. 252, cited in Joseph Cullen Ayer, Jr., *A Source Book for Ancient Church History* (New York: AMS, 1970), p. 501.
17. *Council of Constantinople, A.D. 448*, quoted in Ayer, pp. 513-14.
18. Leo the Great *Epistola Dogmatica*, quoted in Ayer, pp. 515-16.
19. James Orr, *The Progress of Dogma* (London: Hodder and Stoughton, 1907), p. 194.
20. *Sixth General Council, Constantinople, A.D. 681*, quoted in Ayer, p. 670.
21. E. H. Klotsche, *The History of Christian Doctrine* (Burlington, Ia.: Lutheran Literary Board, 1945), p. 122.
22. Reinhold Seebert, *Text-Book of the History of Doctrines*, 2 vols., trans. Charles E. Hay, reprint (Grand Rapids: Baker, 1977), 1:109.
23. Paul Althaus, *The Theology of Martin Luther* (Philadelphia: Fortress, 1966), p. 194.
24. John Calvin, *The Institutes of Christian Religion*, 2 vols., trans. Henry Beveridge (Grand Rapids: Eerdmans, 1962), 1:415.
25. Ibid., 1:129.
26. Ibid., 1:419.
27. Ibid.
28. H. John McLachlan, *Socinianism in Seventeenth-Century England* (London: Oxford U., 1951), pp. 5-6.

29. Thomas Rees, ed., *The Racovian Catechism* (Lexington, Ky.: The American Theological Library Assn., 1962), p. 34.
30. James Orr, *English Deism: Its Roots and Its Fruits* (Grand Rapids: Eerdmans, 1934), p. 34.
31. *The Encyclopedia of Philosophy*, s.v. "Fideism," by Richard H. Popkin, 3:201-2.
32. Friedrich Schleiermacher, *The Christian Faith*, 2d ed., trans. and ed. H. R. MacKintosh and J. S. Stewart (Edinburgh: T. & T. Clark, 1928), p. 385.
33. Ibid., p. 405.
34. Albrecht Ritschl, *The Christian Doctrine of Justification and Reconciliation* (Clifton, N.J.: Reference Book Publishers, 1966), p. 436.
35. Albert Temple Swing, *The Theology of Albrecht Ritschl* (New York: Longmans, Green and Co., 1901), p. 98.
36. Ibid., pp. 451-52.
37. Ibid., pp. 469-71.
38. Karl Barth, *The Doctrine of the Word of God*, trans. G. T. Thomson (Edinburgh: T. & T. Clark, 1934), p. 533.
39. John F. Walvoord, *Jesus Christ Our Lord* (Chicago: Moody, 1969), p. 14.
40. Karl Barth, *Church Dogmatics*, 5 vols., trans. G. W. Bromiley (Edinburgh: T. & T. Clark, 1957), 1:437-39.
41. Ibid., 2:132,202
42. Ibid., 2:147.
43. Ibid., 2:182.
44. Ibid., 2:156.
45. Ibid., 2:160-61.
46. Ibid., 2:158.
47. Alexander J. McKelway, *The Systematic Theology of Paul Tillich* (Richmond, Va.: John Knox, 1964), pp. 166.
48. Ibid., p. 168.
49. Norman Pittenger, *Christology Reconsidered* (London: SCM, 1970), p. 12.
50. Ibid., p. 124.
51. Walvoord, p. 17.

9

Creation and Evolution: The Continuing Confrontation

Frederic R. Howe

The last two decades have witnessed significant changes in the confrontation between proponents of creation and evolution. Space does not permit a detailed summary of the fascinating developments in this field. The clarification and sharpening of the creation model and the era of scholarly debates on college and university campuses throughout North America between advocates of creation and evolution highlight those recent changes. It would be safe to say that from the middle 1960s to the present the continuing debate between the advocates of creation and those who espouse evolution has produced a new dimension in the dialogue between religion and science. Lessons apparently have been well learned from the past, and those who advocate creation as a model for origins are now skilled in the art of articulating and communicating their position. There is a third position that continues to seek to bring the two models of origins, creation and evolution, into

FREDERIC R. HOWE (A.B., Wheaton College; B.D., Fuller Theological Seminary; M.A., University of Portland; Th.M., Th.D., Dallas Theological Seminary) is associate professor of systematic theology at Dallas Theological Seminary, Dallas, Texas.

145

harmony. Adherents of that view, called Theistic Evolution, seek to solve the clash between creation and evolution by blending the activity of the Creator God into the mechanism of organic evolution. Theistic evolutionists feel that some type of harmonization is the most viable option for ending the confrontation, or at least for shaping it into a more meaningful dimension. This essay will summarize the two models of origins and will examine the position of Theistic Evolution to see if it is a viable alternative or an ill-fated attempt to defend biblical theism.

THE CREATION MODEL

Although those who hold to the creation model might differ on particulars, they are unified in their assertion that Scripture alone provides the only accurate and detailed account of the origin of life. Basic to this pattern or model of creation is the understanding that the biblical documents are absolutely trustworthy and are accurate in specifying the truth about the origin of all life. The common core of ideas held by creationists includes some very specific concepts.

First, creationists believe that the sovereign, infinite, triune God of Scripture has always existed, exists now, and always will exist independently from any finite creation.

Second, creationists believe that God, in an orderly and distinctively supernatural manner, brought all things into existence by divine fiat. Often overlooked in this regard is Revelation 4:11. Schaeffer summarizes its distinctive contribution.

> Then the verse continues: "Worthy art thou, our Lord and our God, to receive the glory and the honor and the power: for thou didst create all things, and because of thy will they were, and were created" (ASV). The New English Bible correctly translates it in modern terms: "By thy will they were created, and have their being!" This is the Christian cosmogony.
>
> Here is an answer for modern man overwhelmed by the problem of being. . . . Everything which has being, except God himself, rests upon the fact that God willed and brought it into creation. . . . Once and for all, God did create the being of the external world and man's existence. They are not God and they are not an extension of God, but they exist because of an act of

the will of that which is personal and which existed prior to their being.[1]

Third, creationists believe that God has set limitations and boundaries in His work, as designated in Scripture. The biblical term *kind* very carefully differentiates the levels of created life and sets the pattern of reproduction or replication (see Gen. 1:11, 12, 21, 24, 25). That means that the pattern of descent has been established by the Creator God and will move within specific boundaries. Morris states the significance of this truth.

> The Creation Model, on the other hand, postulates that all the basic kinds* of plants and animals were specially created and did not evolve from other kinds at all. . . .
> *The term "kind" is used to denote the originally created entity, within which variation could take place. The entities of the Linnaean system (species, genera, families, orders, etc.), are, of course, arbitrary human taxonomic inventions and are often changed. Though it is impossible to precisely equate one of these with the "kind," it may be that the "family" is a good approximation.[2]

Fourth, creationists believe that God has accomplished His work of creation. As He has revealed in His Word, He has completed that orderly work and now is active in maintaining it. A major theological difference between *creation* and *providence* must be preserved, and is often overlooked in the current literature.

There are other key points in the creation model, but these serve as a ground for the present study.

THE EVOLUTION MODEL

As commonly understood, evolution involves the entire process of the rise and development of life. That process is traced through vast aeons of time as life progressed from its simple beginnings into higher and more complex forms. Man is the final product of that process. A carefully prepared booklet written by Rhodes is helpful in delineating this position. The author is careful to view the position of evolution as a theory, and he unfolds the overview of life as a pattern of interrelated complexity. The presuppositions are apparent and openly stated.

Evolution in its modern format is based on the assumption that both the continuity and the close interrelationships of life at all levels suggest a common origin and a common development from the simple to the complex.

> The process of evolution is a fact, Numerous lines of evidence indicate the descent of new species by modification of ancestral forms over extended periods. Although the mechanism is still theoretical, there is very strong evidence that natural selection, genetic variation, and isolation are the chief components. . . .
>
> Evolution, like any other natural process or scientific theory, is theologically neutral. It describes mechanisms, but not meaning. It is based upon the recognition of order but incorporates no conclusion concerning the origin of that order as either purposeful or purposeless.[3]

Having stated his position on the theological neutrality of evolution, Rhodes goes on to state his conclusions.

> Mankind, the product of organic evolution, is now technically equipped with power, if not the will, to control the future development of life on earth. Psychosocial evolution has now displaced the older processes of organic evolution in human communities. . . . It is ironic that the future of the age-long process of organic evolution may now depend on the conscious choice of man, a product of that process.[4]

The continuing differences between evolutionists and creationists revolve around each group's explanation of the origin, diversity, and meaning of life.

UNDERLYING PRESUPPOSITIONS OF EVOLUTION

Evolution, contrary to Rhodes's statements in the previous section, most assuredly does make "theological" statements and most certainly does involve a concept of reality that closes the door on the supernatural origin of the various kinds of life present in the universe today. For example, in the conclusion just cited from the evolutionary viewpoint, man is assumed to be a product of the entire process of evolution (termed *macroevolution* in the technical sense). In contrast, the creation model accepts the biblical statement of man's origin in the image of God by special creation. Scripture declares definitively that God created man through a direct, supernatural act (Gen. 1:26, 27; 2:7).

When an evolutionist flatly states that man is the product of organic evolution, he is making a statement that moves into the realm of ultimate meaning. Since it is the discipline of theology that deals with this realm of ultimate meaning, one could accuse an evolutionist of straying from the realm of empirical science into the realm of theology when he offers statements about the origin of man. There is no misunderstanding of the point. The evolutionist states that through macroevolution man has come into being. Thus the evolutionist cannot plead for neutrality on the grounds that he is not assuming an ultimate origination of life.

Although not always articulated, the undergirding philosophy of evolution is philosophical naturalism, or humanism. Within the theory of total evolution there is no ground for assuming any external or supernatural power even as a "factor" in guiding the process of evolution.

> There was a time when there was no life on the earth. In very different atmospheric conditions from those which prevail today, chemical changes were brought about in material molecules which started the long and complex evolutionary chain which led from the amoeba to man. The details of the way the various species of living organisms were diversified do not now concern us. . . . There is no need to look for some agency outside the physical world. . . . The variations which gave rise to a multiplicity of species are due to mutations in the genetic material.[5]

In summary, the first major presupposition underlying the evolutionary position is its world view. Total evolution, or macroevolution, as an interpretation of origins assumes a theological stance that would rule out God as Creator. The reason for that is that evolution simply does not postulate any kind of "creation" activity in which a "Creator" would be necessary.

The second underlying presupposition of evolution relates to the question of a method or mechanism that is able to explain evolution as a process. Evolutionists for the most part still insist that microevolution (a process of small, minute changes in organisms) is a workable hypothesis on which to build macroevolution (large-scale change from simple to complex forms of life). It is vital to note the current dilemma faced by evolutionists. In the fall of 1980, for example, approximately 150 scientists who are specialists in evolution studies met for four days in Chicago. Those scientists were seeking to integrate and correlate evolutionary theory in light of its failure to explain how transitions were made in evolutionary history across all levels of life from simple to complex varieties. Commenting on that meeting, Rensberger wrote:

> EXACTLY HOW EVOLUTION happened is now a matter of great controversy among biologists. . . . Darwin suggested that such major products of evolution were the results of very long periods of gradual natural selection, the mechanism that is widely accepted today as accounting for minor adaptations. . . . The fossil record of his day showed no gradual transitions between such groups but he suggested that further fossil discoveries would fill the missing links.
>
> "The pattern that we were told to find for the last 120 years does not exist," declared Niles Eldridge, a paleontologist from the American Museum of Natural History in New York. . . . Eldridge, along with Stephen Jay Gould, a Harvard University paleontologist, reiterated the hypothesis that new species arise not from gradual changes but in sudden bursts of evolution. As they see it, species remain largely stable for long periods and then suddenly change dramatically. The transition happens so fast, they suggest, that the chance of intermediate forms being fossilized and found is nil. . . . Eldridge and Gould represent a school of thought called "punctuated equilibrium," and although many paleontologists are adherents, many evolutionists from other backgrounds still consider themselves gradualists closer to the traditional Darwinian mold.[6]

From the continuing dialogue among evolutionists comes the growing realization on the part of many scientists that evolution is a massive system built largely on presuppositions. When there is no evidence to explain transitions in evolution from one form to another, evolutionists are content to acknowledge the problem and search for more viable solutions. However, creationists feel that they have a far more coherent and consistent position which can account for the sudden burst of life forms marking the fossil record at the beginning of the Cambrian period. A scientist who is a believer in creation notes,

". . . the creation of major types at the beginning of the Cambrian period, with subsequent diversification, fits the fossil evidence. This does not require the postulation of a common origin supported by missing fossils. . . ."[7]

THE THEISTIC EVOLUTION MODEL

In spite of the apparent philosophical disharmony between evolution and creation, some scholars are still postulating Theistic Evolution as a meaningful defense of Christian Theism against the philosophical naturalism undergirding macroevolution. It is that position which must be analyzed critically. A recent statement of this viewpoint was articulated by MacKay.

> To most scientists today (whether Christian or non-Christian) these clues seem to fit together to indicate a history of many millions of years, during which it looks as if many species of plants and animals changed or evolved into the forms we know today.
> This idea, that (as a Christian would put it) God's way of working has been slow and gradual (the bodies of higher animals coming into being through descent with modification from earlier species), is all that should be meant by the term "evolution" as used in science. In this technical, scientific sense the idea is theologically neutral, and is widely accepted by biologists who are also biblical Christians. Nothing in the Bible rules it out; in fact, despite superficial appearances and popular belief, on this question the Bible is silent.[8]

The adherents of Theistic Evolution feel that their system allows Christians to have a better response to total evolution than is possible with any form of special creation. The author just cited reiterates the idea that evolution (and by that he clearly means macroevolution) is theologically neutral. Theistic Evolution is presented as a serious attempt to give evolution a "theology" or theism all its own. That theology will be, among other things, involved in showing that "God is declared in the Bible to be creatively active and supreme in *every* twist and turn of this great Drama. . . ."[9]

The concept of Theistic Evolution calls for careful evaluation and response on the part of consistent theists and creationists.

As has already been stated, evolution itself takes a theological stance or interpretive framework whenever it postulates man as a product of the realm of macroevolution. Theistic Evolutionists should listen to what a philosophical humanist says about the attempt to *defend* Christian theism by blending evolution into its structure.

> It might be said of course that God is responsible for these mutations and created all living things in this extraordinarily roundabout way. It is a last ditch argument. The objection is that the majority of mutations are harmful. They result in some species, like the giant reptiles which failed to adapt and became extinct after a run of millions of years.[10]

Theistic Evolutionists might feel that the author of the previous quotation is biased and is not giving them a fair chance to build a model of origins. As previously noted, Theistic Evolutionists believe that the Bible does not rule out their view. In fact, they believe that the Bible is silent about any mechanism for creation. Attention must be focused on that alleged biblical silence regarding a mechanism for creation.

The Theistic Evolution model meets a stern test in the exact exegesis of Genesis 2:7. It will be helpful to set up the model of Theistic Evolution and then that of creation, based on this text in Scripture. Theistic Evolution, regardless of its format or appeal to legitimacy as a method of defending theism, postulates that macroevolution is God's mechanism for creation. Furthermore, Theistic Evolution postulates the concept that the process of evolution functioned to bring man into existence. The implication is that Genesis 2:7 is descriptive of some finalizing action of God, either in a process or a crisis, whereby man came into existence as a total being, a spiritual being.

> Secondly, what about the concept of the soul? The early passages in the Bible say that man "became a living soul" (AV). I think the word "became" is important. A living soul, or as the RSV puts it "a living being," is something we *become*. The Hebrew word for "soul" here is *nephesh*, which we are told could well be translated "organism," or perhaps "mind-body." It is also used of lower animals. . . . The Bible insists both that man is responsible and that he is "dust." As dust he has continuity with the natural physical order. As *nephesh*, organism, mind-body, he has continuity with the animal kingdom.[11]

According to this position, man's bodily form, described as dust, is his connection with the natural order of life. Since Theistic Evolution postulates macroevolution as the total work of God in creation, it seems logical to conclude that its proponents postulate man as being alive bodily *prior* to the action described in Genesis 2:7. Notice the stress in the previous citation on man *becoming* a total being, a mind-body entity, by the action described in that verse. A fair way to state Theistic Evolution as a model for man's origin is as follows:

1. God, as Creator, is active in controlling the process of macroevolution. This is the mechanism He chooses.

2. Man is a product of that process.

3. Man as man, homo sapiens, *became* a total being when God worked so that the animated being or organism identified as man's nearest evolutionary ancestor (prehominid) *became* a total being, a mind-body being. Theistic evolutionists differ as to the method involved in that final step; but they unite in their belief that God is the one who controls the action and that man as a total being is a result of the activity described in Genesis 2:7. This view can be summarized very concisely with a formula statement.

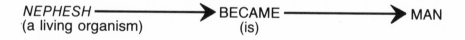

NEPHESH ⟶ BECAME ⟶ MAN
(a living organism)   (is)

The clear implication here is that in the process of macroevolution there is animal life or animation (described as *nephesh*) actually present and functioning *prior to* Genesis 2:7.

Does Genesis 2:7 support this concept of Theistic Evolution? A careful exegesis of the passage reveals that it does *not* allow for the Theistic Evolution model. The verse describes an entirely different pattern of activity. The contrast can be summarized with another formula statement.

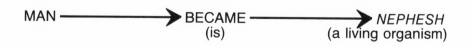

MAN ⟶ BECAME ⟶ NEPHESH
         (is)   (a living organism)

This verse presents the exact opposite of the Theistic Evolution model. In Theistic Evolution a living organism is said to be alive and functioning as nephesh prior to its becoming man. Strictly speaking, the Theistic Evolutionist must consistently hold that there was a living being or entity already present, classified as nephesh, and that that being or entity became man as a result of some unique or special work of God, either in process or in crisis.

The biblical text closes the door on that kind of speculation. Instead of allowing for animation prior to the activity resulting in man's origin, the text graphically states that God actively and dynamically formed man's body and breathed into his nostrils the breath of life. It is at that point that man came to life, and only then is the Hebrew word nephesh used to describe this new creation. Genesis 2:7 states, "Then the LORD God formed man of dust from the ground, and breathed into his nostrils the breath of life; and man became a living being [nephesh]." The term nephesh simply means living being. In fact, nephesh is used of animals in the creation narrative in Genesis 1 (see 1:20, 21, 24, 30). The force of this argument is that there is no living being, or animation, or functioning bodily mechanism whatsoever until the creative activity of God brings that organism to life. The importance of this biblical distinction must be stressed in refuting Theistic Evolution. Life for man (as indicated by the term nephesh) only began at the point of creation described in Genesis 2:7. This is in direct contrast to Theistic Evolution, which must hold to life being already present prior to God's action in Genesis 2:7. Therefore creationists are correct when they state that nephesh (animation), as far as man is concerned, began totally and completely at the point of God's action in Genesis 2:7.

There are other problems that Theistic Evolutionists face, but this one seems crucial in demonstrating the incompatibility of evolution and creation. In passing, it must be noted that only a special creation model can consistently stand on the ground of Genesis 2:7. All other positions (that hold to a prior existence of man) must force the text of Genesis 2:7 to say that man became something new or different. The Hebrew verb rendered became in Genesis 2:7 can just as accurately be rendered was. For example, in Genesis 1:3 the identical word is used in the phrase "and there *was* light." The point here is simply this: there is no ground for the inference that *became* in Genesis 2:7 implies a process of evolution whereby God forms man through successive stages into the final product of a total living being. That stress on time and process as concepts that are inherent in the word *became* simply cannot be borne out through a careful study of the Bible. The text does not allow that kind of theorizing and most assuredly does rule out the simplistic formula of Theistic Evolution: *Nephesh* became man.

CONCLUSION

The debate between evolution and creation will continue, but the attempt to salvage a meaningful Christian Theism by joining the two opposing positions in Theistic Evolution must be judged as faulty and ill-advised. Even those whom Theistic Evolutionists hope to influence to consider the claims of biblical theism seem to judge the effort as meaningless. Perhaps the theological difference between creation and providence has never been clearly grasped by Theistic Evolutionists. An attempt has been made in this study to test the Theistic Evolution model by propositions in Scripture. After all is said and done, Scripture alone must set the framework for all thinking concerning origins. Only God's Word can give the balance and perspective that is needed in this area. That balance is well expressed by Thurman. He notes crucial problems for Theistic Evolution, yet he also notes that the entire question of the creation/evolution confrontation must be seen in a proper balance. In pointing out some of the difficulties faced by proponents of Theistic Evolution, he states, ". . . how could God declare such a slow, wasteful, inefficient, cruel and mistake-ridden process to be good? How could a God of love use natural selection, in which the weak lose out, to create his perfect world?"[12] Then, while commenting on the need for balance and perspective, he writes, "It is important to know how to discuss the creation-evolution issue intelligently, but it is not the most important issue in a Christian's life."[13]

Perhaps the central passage cited at the beginning of this

discussion can serve as a fitting climax. In Revelation 4:11, the biblical concept of creation is beautifully enunciated in a context that shows worship and praise being offered to the Lord of glory. It is here where the believers' lives are to be focused, and the text reiterates this truth. "Worthy art Thou, our Lord and our God, to receive glory and honor and power; for Thou didst create all things, and because of Thy will they existed, and were created."

NOTES

1. Francis A. Schaeffer, *Genesis in Space and Time* (Downers Grove, Ill.: Inter-Varsity, 1972), pp. 25-26.
2. Henry M. Morris, *The Scientific Case for Creation* (San Diego: Creation-Life, 1977), p. 29.
3. Frank H. T. Rhodes, *Evolution* (New York: Western Pub., Golden Press, 1974), pp. 102, 152.
4. Ibid., pp. 153-54.
5. Hector Hawton, *Controversy: The Humanist/Christian Encounter* (Buffalo: Prometheus, 1971), p. 35.
6. Boyce Rensberger, "Evolution lacks the final solution," *Dallas Morning News,* 29 November 1980.
7. L. Duane Thurman, *How to Think about Evolution and Other Bible-Science Controversies* (Downers Grove, Ill.: Inter-Varsity, 1978), p. 114.
8. Donald M. MacKay, *The Clock Work Image* (Downers Grove, Ill.: Inter-Varsity, 1974), pp. 51-52.
9. Ibid., p. 55.
10. Hawton, p. 35.
11. MacKay, p. 70.
12. Thurman, p. 124.
13. Ibid., p. 137.

10

For Whom
Did Christ Die?

Robert P. Lightner

THE IMPORTANCE OF THE QUESTION

It is doubtful if a more important theological question could ever be asked than the one raised by the title of this article. The answer to this question will ultimately influence one's understanding of the other great truths of Scripture and will affect the way in which one lives out the Christian life. Christ's death is a vital part of the gospel message, and no individual has ever been (or will ever be) redeemed apart from a personal appropriation of Christ and what He did for him. Therefore it is imperative that one know for whom Christ died or one may be guilty of proclaiming a false hope to some believers when one declares the gospel message.

The question regarding the extent of the benefits provided through Christ's death is at the very heart of the gospel message and cannot be separated from it. To become a child of God one must believe that Christ died for one's sin. And if a person

ROBERT P. LIGHTNER (Th.B., Baptist Bible College; M.L.A., Southern Methodist University; Th.M., Th.D., Dallas Theological Seminary) is associate professor of systematic theology at Dallas Theological Seminary, Dallas, Texas.

must, in fact, believe that Christ died for him personally before he can become a member of God's family, then it is the Christian's responsibility to be sure such a work was indeed performed on behalf of an unbeliever before telling him so.

Virtually every major doctrine of the Christian faith is affected by the question of the extent of Christ's atoning death. Surely bibliology is, since it is the Scriptures alone that tell of those for whom Christ died. The answer to the question of the extent of the atonement depends on how one interprets specific words and passages of Scripture.

Theology proper is affected because God the Father is the one who sent His Son to be the Savior of the world. It was His love for mankind that prompted Him to give His Son. Christology is involved because the work of God the Son is inseparably linked to the extent of His death. Also the extent of Christ's death influences the doctrine of pneumatology because the work of God the Holy Spirit is based on the finished work of Christ. The Savior said the Spirit would come to continue the work He had begun. Surely the blessed Spirit of God, therefore, maintains a special relationship with those for whom Christ died.

The whole doctrine of anthropology is affected by the answer to the question of the extent of the atonement. It is the entire race of mankind that is under the condemnation of God. The Son of God died only for humans; but the burning question is, for which humans?

Both ecclesiology and eschatology are also affected by this query. Christ is said to have given Himself for the church (Eph. 5:25), but did He give Himself for any others? How does His death relate to Israel, for example? All of Christ's future work will be done on the basis of what He already did on Calvary. The cross is foundational to all of eschatology. With whom will Christ deal in His future comings, the resurrections, the judgments, the tribulation, and the millennial kingdom? It is obvious from Scripture that Christ's future eschatological work will involve the righteous and the unrighteous, the elect and the nonelect. If the basis for Christ's future relationship to mankind proceeds from His past work on the cross, it seems clear that the extent of that work is also necessarily involved.

THE HISTORICAL PERSPECTIVE

The extent of the atonement did not become a serious issue until the Synod of Dort. When Calvinists from all over Europe convened at Dordrecht, Holland in 1618 to evaluate and judge the Arminian theses, they soon discovered some serious disagreements among themselves.[1]

Prior to 1618 a number of early church Fathers and theologians supported an unlimited atonement. Those early writers were not writing to oppose a limited view. Rather, in the course of their comments on the Bible they wrote of the death of Christ for all and not for the elect only. Douty has collected an impressive list of names and creedal statements that span the history of the church in support of what he calls "general atonement."[2]

Those who subscribe to a limited atonement generally argue that that is the position espoused by Calvin. But it is highly debatable that he did, in fact, hold that view. One searches his writings in vain to find a definitive statement on either side of the issue. Whereas some scholars have attempted to show that there is harmony between Calvin and later orthodox Calvinism,[3] others have argued that contemporary Calvinism has veered significantly from Calvin's teaching, including his teaching on the extent of the atonement.[4]

THE PURPOSE OF CHRIST'S DEATH

Before it can be determined for whom Christ died, the reason for His death must be established. Why did the Savior die? What was accomplished by His death? The whole issue of whether Christ died for all mankind or only for the elect centers on the divine purpose for Christ's death on the cross. Boettner states the issue clearly when he says, "The nature of the atonement settles its extent."[5] Both those who limit the extent of the atonement and those who do not agree with that fact.

There are basically three answers given to the question regarding the purpose of Christ's death. They are mutually exclusive, so all three cannot be correct. Two of them must be wrong. Each of the views must be examined by the yardstick of God's Word because only the Word of God provides the necessary standard for measuring each position and thereby determining its validity. The three positions that have been advanced to explain the purpose of Christ's death are those of Arminianism, Five-Point Calvinism, and Moderate Calvinism.

THE POSITION ADVOCATED BY ARMINIANISM

James Arminius (1560-1609) was a professor of theology at the University of Leiden in Holland. He was asked to respond to some of the attacks being made against the Calvinism of his day. As a result of his study he actually came to embrace a belief that was far less rigid than the one he originally sought to defend. He soon became a key man in the theological controversy that was swirling through the Dutch Reformed Church.

Shortly after Arminius died, his followers set forth five articles of faith that came to be called the Remonstrance, or Five Arminian Articles.[6] Those articles were opposed to portions of the Belgic Confession of Faith and the Heidelburg Catechism, which later developed into what is now known as the five points of Calvinism.[7]

The full statement concerning the atonement will help clarify the answer given by Arminian theology to the question "Why did Christ die?" Article 2 of the Remonstrance deals with the extent of the atonement.

> That . . . Jesus Christ, the Saviour of the world, died for all men and for every man, so that He *has obtained for them all, by His death on the cross, redemption and the forgiveness of sins*; yet that no one actually enjoys this forgiveness of sins except the believer, according to the word of the Gospel of John iii. 16:, "God so loved the world that he gave his only begotten Son, that whosoever believeth in him should not perish, but have everlasting life." And in the First Epistle of John ii. 2: "and he is the propitiation for our sins; and not for ours only, but also for the sins of the whole world."[8]

The word *obtained* is crucial in this statement. By it more is meant than that provision was made for all. Arminian theology advocates that every member of Adam's race has been given sufficient grace to believe and be saved if he wants to. The following statement from the Confession of the Arminian Remonstrance helps to clarify what is meant by the words *ob-tained* and *sufficient grace:*

> Although there is the greatest diversity in the degrees in which grace is bestowed in accordance with the Divine will, yet the Holy Spirit confers or at least is ready to confer upon all and each to whom the Word is ordinarily preached, as much grace as is sufficient for generating faith and carrying forward their conversion in successive stages. This sufficient grace for faith and conversion is allotted not only to those who actually believe and are converted, but also *to those who do not actually believe,* and are not in fact converted.[9]

The Arminian view places man in a position where he can, in fact, determine what will become of the sufficient grace he is said to possess. God is viewed as an interested but uninvolved bystander. Such a view does a great injustice to the biblical doctrine of total depravity. Arminians do speak of the lost condition of man, but their view of sufficient grace grants to the sinner the ability to move toward God through his own volition. Their confused and conflicting position soon becomes obvious.

> It is allowed, and all scriptural advocates of the universal redemption of mankind will join with the Calvinists in maintaining the doctrine, that every disposition and inclination to good which generally existed in the nature of man is lost by the Fall; that all men, in their simply *natural* state are 'dead in trespasses and sins,' and have neither the will nor the power to turn to God; and that no one is sufficient of himself to think or do anything of the saving tendency. But, as all men are required to do those things which have a tendency, we contend that the grace to do them has been bestowed upon all.[10]

Thus Arminianism stresses the universal purpose of Christ's death in obtaining salvation for man to such an extent that man is able to participate in his own salvation.

> In conclusion, the point to be made here is that these other ideas regarding man's natural condition and native ability to cooperate with God stem from the idea that Christ's death *obtained* salvation for all and made possible sufficient grace for all to cooperate with God in salvation. This means in reality that the decision to believe or not to believe is quite unrelated to the electing purposes of God or the effectual working of the Holy Spirit, but rests ultimately and entirely with the individual.[11]

THE POSITION ADVOCATED BY FIVE-POINT CALVINISM

At the Synod of Dort the articles of belief set forth in the Remonstrance of 1610 were rejected. As an alternative to those articles the five points of Calvinism were presented and adopted. Those articles included a specific statement on the purpose of Christ's death. "For this was ths sovereign counsel and most gracious will and purpose of God the Father, that the quickening and saving efficacy of the most precious death of his Son should extend to all the elect, for bestowing upon them alone the gift of justifying faith, thereby to bring them infallibly to salvation. . . ."[12]

That statement has been understood by many to teach limited atonement or particular redemption. Those Calvinists believe the design of the atonement, the purpose of Christ's death, was to *secure* the salvation of the elect only. They believe Christ's death automatically guarantees salvation to those for whom He died. That is in stark contrast to the teaching of the Arminians. Integral to the view that Christ died only for the elect is the belief that His death effectively secured salvation apart from any human response. Kuiper's statement given in opposition to Arminianism is representative of the five-point Calvinist view. He said, ". . . the Atonement saves all whom it was intended to save."[13]

In summary, then, of the view advocated by five-point Calvinists, it must be said they believe Christ died to secure the salvation of only the elect. They also believe that the work of Christ on the cross was efficacious in and of itself. The cross both secures salvation and applies that salvation to those who have been chosen by God.

THE POSITION ADVOCATED BY MODERATE CALVINISM

Moderate Calvinists reject the answer provided by both Arminians and five-point Calvinists to the question, "Why did Christ die?" They believe there is an answer between those two that is in perfect harmony with Scripture.

> Certainly Christ's death of itself forgives no sinner, nor does it render unnecessary the regenerating work of the Holy Spirit. Anyone of the elect whose salvation is predetermined, and for

whom Christ died, may live the major portion of his life in open rebellion against God and during that time manifest every feature of depravity and spiritual death. This alone should prove that men are not severally saved by the act of Christ in dying, but rather that they are saved by the divine *applicaton* of that value when they *believe*. The blood of the Passover lamb became efficacious only when applied to the doorpost.[14]

The view advocated by the moderate Calvinists distinguishes between the provisional benefits of Christ's death and the appropriation of those benefits by the elect.

Moderate Calvinists acknowledge and fully accept the vicarious substitutionary nature of the Atonement, but they insist that the Bible makes that full and complete sacrifice provisionary. They believe the cross does not apply its own benefits but that God has conditioned His full and free salvation upon personal faith in order to appropriate its accomplishments to the individual. This faith which men must exercise is not a work whereby man contributes his part to his salvation, nor does faith, in the moderate Calvinist view, improve in any way the final and complete sacrifice of Calvary. It is simply the method of applying Calvary's benefits which the sovereign God has deigned to use in His all-wise plan of salvation.[15]

THE EXTENT OF CHRIST'S DEATH

Ultimately, the answer to the question of the *extent* of Christ's death will depend on one's answer to the previous question concerning the *purpose* of Christ's death. To be sure, the questions are not the same; but the answer to the second hinges on the answer one gives to the first.

Another way to put the question now under discussion would be, "Did Christ die as a substitute for all people of all ages, or did He die only for the elect of all ages?" There are really only two possible answers to the question. One is to say Christ did die for all. The other is to say He died only for the elect. The former is the unlimited or general redemption position whereas the latter is the limited or particular redemption view. One cannot appeal to the consensus of believers to find an answer to this problem because equally sincere and godly men can be found on both sides of the controversy. The true position regarding the extent of Christ's death can only be determined by asking, "What saith the Scriptures?"

Some of the many passages that seem to broaden the extent of the atoning death of Christ include the following (italics added).[16]

Luke 19:10. "For the Son of Man has come to seek and to save *that which was lost.*"

John 1:29. "The next day he saw Jesus coming to him, and said, 'Behold, the Lamb of God who takes away *the sin of the world!*' "

John 3:16-17. "For God so loved *the world,* that He gave His only begotten Son, that whoever believes in Him should not perish, but have eternal life. For God did not send the Son into the world to judge the world; but that *the world should be saved through him.*"

Romans 5:6. "For while we were still helpless, at the right time Christ died for the *ungodly.*"

2 Corinthians 5:14-15, 19. ". . . that one died *for all,* therefore *all died;* and He died *for all,* that they who live should no longer live for themselves, but for Him who died and rose again on their behalf. . . . namely, that God was in Christ reconciling *the world* to Himself. . . ."

1 Timothy 2:6. "Who gave Himself as *a ransom for all,* the testimony borne at the proper time."

Hebrews 2:9. ". . . that by the grace of God He might taste *death for every one.*"

2 Peter 2:1. "But false prophets also arose among the people, just as there will also be *false teachers* among you, who will secretly *introduce destructive heresies, even denying the Master who bought them,* bringing swift destruction upon themselves."

1 John 2:2. "And He Himself is the propitiation for our sins; and not for ours only, but *also for those of the whole world.*"

Those who believe that Christ died only for the elect are aware of verses like those above. However, their usual response to passages that include words like *all, whoever,* and *world,* is to restrict the meaning of those words so that they apply only to the elect, or to say that those verses teach that Christ died for all kinds of people without *distinction* but not for all without *exception*.[17] Limited redemptionists are quick to defend their approach to those verses by citing scriptural examples where "world" and "all" do not mean 100 percent.[18]

It cannot be denied that such words as "all" and "world" are sometimes used in a restricted sense. But that is not the central issue. The central question, rather, is this: On what basis may those and similar words be restricted in passages dealing with the extent of Christ's atoning work? That is the crucial question. Those who always limit the meaning of those terms in contexts that deal with salvation do so on the basis of theological presuppositions, not on the basis of the texts themselves.

SCRIPTURES USED TO SUPPORT LIMITED REDEMPTION

Some of the major passages generally used to support the concept of limited redemption include the following (italics added).[19]

Isaiah 53:5. "But He was pierced through for *our* transgressions, He was crushed for *our* iniquities; the chastening for *our* well-being fell upon Him, and by His scourging *we* are healed."

Matthew 1:21. "And she will bear a Son; and you shall call His name Jesus, for it is He who will save *His people* from their sins."

Matthew 20:28. "Just as the Son of Man did not come to be served, but to serve, and to give His life *a ransom for many*."

Matthew 26:28. "For this is My blood of the covenant, which is to be shed *on behalf of many* for forgiveness of sins."

John 10:15. ". . . I lay down My life *for the sheep*."

Acts 20:28. "Be on guard for yourselves and for all the flock . . . to shepherd *the church of God which He purchased with His own blood*."

Galatians 3:13. "Christ redeemed *us* from the curse of the Law, having become a curse *for us*. . . ."

Ephesians 5:25. "Husbands, love your wives, just as Christ also loved the *church* and gave Himself up *for her*."

Hebrews 9:28. "So Christ also, having been offered once to bear the *sins of many*. . . ."

Those who embrace the view that Christ died as a substitute

for all have no difficulty reconciling verses like those just listed with their position. None of the passages just cited offers compelling evidence to prove the position that Christ died only for the elect. The task of harmonizing those various Scriptures poses a far greater problem for those who hold to a limited atonement than it does to those who hold to an unlimited position. Those who hold to an unlimited atonement recognize that some Scriptures emphasize the fact that Christ died for the elect, for the church, and for individual believers. However, they point out that when those verses single out a specific group they do not do so to the exclusion of any who are outside that group since dozens of other passages include them. The "limited" passages are just emphasizing one aspect of a larger truth. In contrast, those who hold to a limited atonement have a far more difficult time explaining away the "unlimited" passages.

Advocates of an unlimited atonement have presented many reasons for their position as they have interacted with those who hold to a limited atonement.[20] At least three of those arguments are worthy of mention here.

1. The clear statements of Scripture in such passages as 2 Corinthians 5:14-19, 2 Peter 2:1-2, and 1 John 2:1-2 argue for an unlimited atonement. An unbiased exegesis of those texts demonstrates that they teach Christ died for *all* (and not just for the elect). In fact, no Scripture states that Christ died *only* for the elect.

2. The universal offer of the gospel supports the position of an unlimited atonement. Clearly, the Scriptures present a universal offer of the good news of salvation in Christ. One would suspect that they do so because of the universal provision Christ made for that salvation. Surely a salvation *offered* to all implies a salvation *provided* for all.

Belief in limited atonement means that the good news of God's saving grace in Christ cannot be personalized. Those who hold to such a position cannot tell someone to whom they are witnessing that Christ died for him because that one may, in fact, not be one for whom Christ died. As Adams is forced to admit, "As a reformed Christian, the writer believes that counselors must not tell any unsaved counselee that Christ died for him, for they cannot say that. No man knows except Christ himself who are his elect for whom he died."[21] That group feels that the gospel must be presented in broad, general terms such as, "God loves sinners and Christ died for sinners." But can a person pass from death unto life because he believes God loves others and Christ died for others? Is that the gospel?

3. The love of God for all argues for an unlimited atonement. Love, like all the other attributes of God, is not simply an expression He makes. It is part of His very essence. He loves because He *is* love. To restrict and confine His love only to the elect is inconsistent with both His person and with the clear statements of His Word.

Does the Bible really teach that God loves "only the elect"?[22] Is the conscience of the Christ-rejector really cauterized if he is told that God loves him? Is the love of God "a truth for the saints only"?[23] None of the attributes of God can be confined to one segment of the human race. He is holy in His dealings with all. He is just toward all. He is omnipotent toward all. And He loves all and demonstrated it climactically at Calvary when He gave His Son to die for all.

For whom did Christ die? The last Adam was a substitute dying in the stead of every member of the first Adam's lost race. There on the accursed tree He became a curse for all the men of all the ages. In that way He reconciled the world unto Himself; however, only when the individual sinner accepts Christ as his substitute (in response to the Spirit's work in his heart) is he personally reconciled to God. Election does not save. The death of Christ does not save. The Holy Spirit's convicting work does not save. Faith does not save. Only Christ saves. And He does so in response to the sinner's childlike faith in Him as his own and only Savior.

NOTES

1. W. Robert Godfrey, "Reformed Thought on the Extent of the Atonement to 1618," *Westminster Theological Journal* 37 (Winter 1975):133.
2. Norman F. Douty, *The Death of Christ* (Swengel, Pa.: Reiner, 1972), pp. 95-110.
3. Roger Nicole, "Moyse Amyraut (1596-1664) and the Controversy

on Universal Grace, First Phase (1634-1637)" (Ph.D. diss., Harvard University, 1966).

4. Brian G. Armstrong, *Calvinism and the Amyraut Heresy* (Madison, Wisc.: U. of Wisconsin, 1969).

5. Loraine Boettner, *The Reformed Doctrine of Predestination* (Philadelphia: Presbyterian & Reformed, 1965), p. 152.

6. Nicole accurately summarized these five as follows: "I. God elects or reproves on the basis of foreseen faith or belief. II. Christ died for all men and for every man, although only believers are saved. III. Man is so depraved that divine grace is necessary unto faith or any good deed. IV. This grace may be resisted. V. Whether all who are totally regenerate will certainly persevere in the faith is a point which needs further investigation" (*Baker's Dictionary of Theology*, s.v. "Arminianism," by Roger Nicole, p. 64).

7. The five are frequently set forth with the "tulip" acrostic: Total depravity, Unconditional election, Limited atonement, Irresistable grace, Perseverence of the saints.

8. Philip Schaff, *The Creeds of Christendom*, 3 vols. (New York: Harper, 1919), 3:546. Italics added.

9. Confession, chap. xvii. Cited by William G. T. Shedd, *Calvinism: Pure and Mixed* (New York: Scribner's, 1893), p. 102. Italics added.

10. Richard Watson, *Theological Institutes*, 2 vols. (New York: Carlton & Phillips, 1855), 2:447.

11. Robert P. Lightner, *The Death Christ Died* (Schaumburg, Ill.: Regular Baptist, 1978), p. 40.

12. Schaff, 3:587.

13. R. B. Kuiper, *For Whom Did Christ Die?* (Grand Rapids: Eerdmans, 1959), p. 73. See also David N. Steele and Curtis C. Thomas, *The Five Points of Calvinism Defined, Defended, Documented* (Philadelphia: Presbyterian & Reformed, 1963), p. 17; John Owen, *The Works of John Owen*, ed. Thomas Cloutt (London: J. F. Dove, 1823), 5:290-91; John Murray, *Redemption—Accomplished and Applied* (Grand Rapids: Eerdmans, 1935), pp. 73-74.

14. Lewis Sperry Chafer, "For Whom Did Christ Die?" *Bibliotheca Sacra* 137 (October-December 1980):314.

15. Lightner, p. 56.

16. Italics added for emphasis.

17. Steele and Thomas, p. 46.

18. A. A. Hodge, *The Atonement* (Grand Rapids: Eerdmans, 1953), p. 424.

19. Italics added for emphasis.

20. Douty, *The Death of Christ*; Lightner, *The Death Christ Died*.

21. Jay E. Adams, *Competent to Counsel* (Grand Rapids: Baker, 1970), p. 70.

22. Kuiper, p. 68.

23. Arthur W. Pink, *The Sovereignty of God* (Cleveland: Cleveland Bible Truth Depot, 1930), p. 246.

11

Universalism

Emilio Antonio Núñez

Several years ago while traveling by air to South America, this writer found himself seated next to a young Latin American diplomat. After a lengthy conversation about religious matters the diplomat said, "What I don't like about the evangelical religion is its insistence in affirming that only Jesus Christ saves. This seems to me an extreme exclusiveness." His reply was typical of those who deny the "exclusive" claims of the Bible in favor of a broad approach that sees many different roads to heaven.

Although the concept of many different roads to heaven might at first sound appealing, it must be rejected because it is in conflict with God's Word. To abandon the exclusive claims of Christianity would mean to be left without the gospel, because Jesus said, "I am the way, and the truth, and the life; no one comes to the Father, but through Me" (John 14:6). To deny the exclusiveness of the gospel is to ignore the clear testimony of Christ and His apostles, and to open the door to universalism.

EMILIO ANTONIO NÚÑEZ (A.B., Southern Methodist University: ThM., TH.D., Dallas Theological Seminary) is professor of systematic theology at Central American Theological Seminary, Guatemala City, Guatemala.

The gospel is inclusive in that it embraces without exception all who receive it by faith, and it is *exclusive* because it omits from its blessings all who reject it.

Universalism is the doctrine that teaches that all human beings will ultimately be saved. Universalist teaching can be found outside Christianity; but in this article the focus is on the universalism that exists within so-called Christendom. There are two varieties of "Christian" universalism. Some universalists believe that an individual's restoration to God is effected at the moment of death whereas others feel that a period of purifying punishment is essential before that restoration can take place. The second type of universalism is the one that has been predominant in Christendom from very early times.[1] It will be studied in these pages from the historical, theological, biblical, and missiological points of view.

Universalism in Historical Perspective

Universalism in the Early Church

Church historians generally agree that universalism first appeared in the Alexandrian School, especially with Origen (A.D. 185-254). Based on his idea that the divine purpose is to restore the original unity in creation, Origen taught that the condemned and even the demons would be brought into voluntary subjection to Christ after a period of severe punishment that would purify them to enter heaven.[2] That is the doctrine of the *apokatastasis pantōn* ("restoration of all things"). According to Schaff, Origen taught this only as speculation, not as dogma, and in his later writings modified the theory to exclude Satan from repentance and salvation.[3]

Gregory of Nyssa, of the school of Origen, also taught salvation for all, including Satan.[4] Other theologians from the East as well as the West were influenced by Origen. However, as Gonzalez points out, none of those early theologians accepted the doctrine of Origen in its totality.[5] Universalism was condemned by the Synod of Constantinople in 543.

The Testimony of the Medieval Church

During the Middle Ages orthodoxy was championed through

great theologians such as Augustine and Aquinas. In his work *The City of God* Augustine defended the thesis of eternal punishment and refuted the idea that the wicked will be purified through punishment after death. Hell is the ultimate destiny of the earthly city.[6] Aquinas spoke in unequivocal terms about the eternal condemnation of the wicked in frank opposition to the doctrine of Origen. He stated that the suffering in hell would be privative (the condemned will not see God), physical, spiritual, and eternal.[7]

One of the most dramatic descriptions during medieval times of the eternal sufferings of the wicked is the famous work of Dante Alighieri (1265-1321), the *Divine Comedy*, in which hell is presented in terrifying terms. Dante appears to reflect with precision the mentality of his age regarding the world beyond.

THE ERA OF THE REFORMATION

It is evident that there can be no communion between Calvinism and universalism. Calvin based his soteriology on the sovereign decree that favors exclusively the elect.[8] But Reformed Theology is not alone in its opposition to universalism. In their Formula of Concord (1580) the Lutherans upheld a moderate form of the doctrine of predestination.[9] The Arminians also affirmed in the *Remonstrance* (1610) that salvation is for those who believe in Jesus Christ.[10]

THE AGE OF THE ENGLIGHTENMENT

Humanism, which had as its outstanding representative Erasmus (c. 1466-1536), continued to progress and develop with unusual energy in the eighteenth century. That humanist revolution found its theological expression in Deism. The deists denied the doctrine of the trinity as Socinius (1539-1604) had done before. Latourette points out that anti-trinitarianism, or unitarianism, finds its roots in humanism.[11]

In North America there have been organized Unitarian churches since the end of the eighteenth century. Theologically, unitarians and universalists have much in common.[12] Both groups belong to the liberal camp. In 1961 the Unitarian and Universalist churches in the United States and Canada merged into what is now called the Unitarian Universalist Association.[13]

Schleiermacher (1768-1834), known as "the father of Liberalism," is theologically a son of the eighteenth century. The rationalism, romanticism, and pietism of that period converge in him.[14] According to Schleiermacher, the doctrine of eternal condemnation does not harmonize with the doctrine of perpetual bliss. The saved would not be completely happy knowing of the sufferings in hell. Therefore it is preferable to believe that through the power of redemption a universal restoration will be brought about.[15] The incarnation of Christ can be considered as the beginning of the regeneration of the entire human race.[16] Furthermore, if the universality of redemption is accepted in its full extent, it is necessary to accept also a universal preordination for blessing.[17] Liberalism is a form of humanism that exalts human reason above the authority of the Word of God.

UNIVERSALISM IN THEOLOGICAL PERSPECTIVE

The universalist thesis does not belong only to the past. Packer is right when he says that universalism "has come to stay" as a guest of Christianity.[18] In fact, universalism has gained strength and grown during the present century. Its influence stretches into both Protestant and Roman Catholic circles of theology.

PROTESTANT UNIVERSALISM

Neoorthodoxy is, in a sense, a reaction against the theological liberalism of the nineteenth century. But Barth, with his dialectical language, has been accused of being a universalist. At the end of his brief study on "The Coming of Jesus Christ the Judge," Barth affirms that the judge who places some on the right and others on the left is the one who put Himself under the judgment of God on behalf of the sinner, freeing him in this way from the curse. He goes on to clarify that that does not lead to the *Apokatastasis* or "universal restoration." There is a decision and a division, but those belong to Him who intercedes for His own.[19]

Nevertheless, with his reconstruction of the doctrine of election, Barth has raised suspicions of universalism among many theologians. It is easy to perceive in his *Church Dogmatics* that the whole human race has been elected in Jesus Christ.[20] Reymond, an opponent of Barthianism, recognizes that Barth neither affirmed nor denied the theory of universal salvation. He quotes the concepts of Barth in his book *The Humanity of God* and concludes that Barth remained on the level of agnosticism regarding the final result of the election of grace in order to preserve divine sovereignty.[21] Ramm resists calling Barth a universalist.[22]

The Barthian doctrine of reconciliation has also led to the suspicion of universalism. Bromiley detects in that doctrine "the trend toward an ultimate universalism."[23] Barthianism can also give the impression that the world is already redeemed and that evangelism consists simply of making known this fact. Referring to the Barthian concept of election, Berkouwer says that the Christian message goes from those who know they are elect (the Christians) to those who do not yet know it, but who are nevertheless included in election.[24]

The least that can be said of Karl Barth is that in his teaching about election and reconciliation he opens himself dangerously to universalism.

The existential theologians Bultmann and Tillich are also important for the study of contemporary universalism. For Bultmann, the apocalyptic elements of the New Testament belong to the mythological sphere and should be interpreted anthropologically or, better yet, existentially. For example, in mythological thought the concept of hell is formulated to express "the transcendence of evil as a terrible power that afflicts humanity without ceasing."[25] Biblical eschatology should be demythologized and converted into a present experience. In this way it takes on its true significance. Tillich is of the opinion that heaven and hell must be taken seriously, but not literally. Since all creation is rooted in the ground of being (God Himself), eternal death is an impossibility.[26] Man is never cut off from the ground of being, "not even in the state of condemnation,"[27] which is, of course, existential.

In his book *Honest to God* Robinson confesses to having been influenced by Bultmann (demythologizing), Tillich (God as the ground of being), and Bonhoeffer (Christianity without religion).[28] For Robinson, hell signifies being alienated from God while at the same time being in union with Him, as the ground of being; heaven, on the other hand, is union in love with Him. It is clear that all this takes place on an existential plane.[29] Robinson's inclination toward universalism is evident in his writings. He emphasizes the fact that divine love will not allow some sinners to perish.[30] Robinson's concept of the final destiny of man is the logical outcome of his effort to demythologize and interpret existentially the Word of God.

In any evaluation of current universalism, it is imperative to mention Ferré and his emphasis on the *Agape*. According to that Swedish-American theologian, God cannot condemn a human being to hell because that would be a negation of the Agape, which never fails and cannot be reduced to the finite. Neither is it possible to limit the sovereignty and power of God.[31] Consequently, all will be saved.

An ecumenical theology has been in vogue that passes over the singularity of the gospel of Christ in order to dialogue freely with non-Christian religions and with secular movements or ideologies. At the fifth assembly of the World Council of Churches, held in Nairobi in 1975, Stott affirmed that the World Council of Churches must regain the conviction regarding the singularity of Jesus Christ. He felt that they must recognize that the knowledge men have of God, according to Romans 1, does not save them but only leaves them without excuse.[32] Cullmann warns against false ecumenism, which he calls syncretism, that results in a departure from the foundations of the Christian faith.[33] In the opinion of Grau, a Spanish evangelical writer, syncretism "constitutes probably the most serious threat for the Church of our time."[34]

ROMAN CATHOLIC UNIVERSALISM

The Second Vatican Council (1962-1965) declared that those who refuse to enter the Catholic Church or to remain in it, knowing that it was made necessary by God through Jesus Christ, cannot be saved.[35] But at the same time the council affirmed that the plan of salvation includes those who acknowledge the Creator (the Muslims, for example) and those who through no fault of their own are ignorant of the gospel but sincerely seek God and try to do the will of God, following the dictates of their conscience. Neither is the aid of providence denied to those who, without blame on their part, have not yet come to the knowledge of God but seek to live morally upright lives by virtue of His grace.[36]

In the *Declaration on Non-Christian Religions,* Vatican II reaffirmed its purpose of announcing the gospel. But when the declaration refers specifically to Muslims and Jews it does not indicate the need to evangelize them. The exhortation given is to strive for mutual understanding and to defend and promote social justice, moral values, peace, and liberty for all men.[37]

In light of the ambivalence of the conciliar documents, the least that can be said is that Vatican II is not universalist in the classical sense of the term, but it opens the door to an ecumenism that runs the risk of becoming syncretistic and universalistic. And some Roman Catholic theologians have already walked through that door.

Küng wrote his book *On Being a Christian* with one central question in mind: What is the difference between Christianity, the other universal religions, and modern humanism? Küng declares that there is salvation outside the church, and he opposes the "stupid particularism" that completely condemns other religions. Although he does reject the doctrinal indifference and syncretism that suffocates the truth, he leaves Christianity in the role of simply a "critical catalyzer and point of crystalization" of other religious values. What he proposes for Christianity is not "exclusiveness" but "particularness" in the search for truth alongside other religions. The goal is to find "a new critical and inclusive synthesis, without false antithetic exclusivisms."[38] Christianity needs to accompany other religions in the search for yet unknown truth.

Liberation theology has also come under serious suspicion of universalism. Gutiérrez has given some basis for this suspicion. In his book *A Theology of Liberation* he emphasizes the qualitative character of salvation, indicating that there is salvation outside the church and that the man who opens himself to God and to others, even if he is not conscious of doing so, is saved.

Gutiérrez believes that that is true for all men. There is grace present in all men, and it is therefore possible to evaluate all human action in Christian terms. It is no longer appropriate to speak of a secular world.[39]

Another important concept in Liberation theology is that of one history in which God acts in a saving way. That history has its final goal in Christ. There are not two histories, one profane and the other sacred. God created all men that they might be sons.[40] Liberation theologians therefore conclude that since men have been created, they are already included in the plan of salvation.

The next concept in the Liberation theology paradigm is that of the Exodus. The act of creation is linked with the act of redemption. The Exodus is a political liberation that leads to a re-creation and a complete fulfillment. Israel is liberated in order to become a holy nation, a new society.[41] In that whole process God acts and man acts in order to establish a new order of social justice. Through his work man prolongs the work of creation, becomes truly man, and forges the human community as he fights against injustice. That is also salvation. To build the earthly city is to insert oneself fully in the saving process which "includes all men and all human history."[42]

If salvation begins with creation, if salvation is the work of God and the work of man, if human history is inseparably united to the history of salvation, if the Kingdom of God is advancing through liberating movements on the social plain (although those movements may be imperfect and not the equivalent of the Kingdom), if there is no significant difference between human progress and the Kingdom of God, if man is the forger of the new society, and if this human task is also salvation, then salvation will be universal because all human beings are God's creation, all belong to the one history, and all are involved in some way in the task of history. That the consummation of that saving process, in which man has a part, lies still in the future awaiting "the new action of God"[43] does not negate the right which all have to be saved.

It is obvious that Küng and Gutiérrez display a definite openness to neo-universalism in the ranks of Roman Catholicism.

The examples cited in this historical and theological overview demonstrate that universalism is ancient and modern. It
shows up in the church of the first centuries and is present in
the world today. Its arguments may have changed, but it continues to be derived from a humanism that overlooks or rejects
the written revelation of God.

UNIVERSALISM IN BIBLICAL PERSPECTIVE

Those who defend the doctrine of universal salvation make
an effort to provide biblical support for their thesis, either by
presenting arguments that they try to deduce from the general
doctrines of Scripture, or by using texts that seem to teach
salvation for all human beings.

DEDUCTIVE ARGUMENTS

Deductive arguments are those that move from the general to
the specific, from the known to the unknown, or from a prem-
ise to a conclusion. That type of argument is important, because it claims to be based on the whole tenor of biblical testimony and not only on certain texts of Scripture. Two deductive arguments need to be examined — one based on divine love
and the other based on divine justice.

Divine love. The argument that emphasizes divine love is
probably the one most often mentioned by universalists. Both
the Old Testament and the New Testament speak of God's great
love. But nowhere in the Bible does it say that that attribute is
the one that controls God's character and activity to the detri-
ment of the other divine attributes. No one attribute is superior
to another in the divine essence. All the attributes function
harmoniously in the carrying out of the divine purpose. God
does not cease to be love when He condemns the wicked, nor
does He cease to be just when He saves believers. In fact, the
salvation of sinners is an expression of sublime love (Rom. 5:8)
and an act of strict justice (Rom. 3:21-26).

God has shown His saving love in Jesus Christ so that "whoever believes in Him should not perish, but have eternal life"
(John 3:16). In that same verse, which sums up the gospel message regarding God's love, the possibility of eternal perdition is

mentioned. During His earthly ministry Jesus showed His incomparable love in word and deed, but He also pronounced words of judgment against the unrepentant (Matt. 11:20-24; 12:31-32). The sacrifice on Calvary is an expression of the love of God, who does not shrink back from giving His Son as a ransom for many (Rom. 8:32); but the cross also puts in bold relief the demands of divine justice, because "without shedding of blood there is no forgiveness" (Heb. 9:22).

Love itself is not void of moral content. Divine love is not amoral, much less immoral. It makes demands of an ethical nature. "If you love Me," Jesus said, "you will keep My commandments" (John 14:15). "He who has My commandments, and keeps them, he it is who loves Me" (John 14:21a). True love manifests itself in obedience to God's will. Jesus Himself went to the cross in subjection to His heavenly Father (Luke 22:42; John 10:17; Heb. 10:9).

Divine love should not be measured by the standards of human love, be it the most noble that there is on earth. Neither should God's love be compared with the irrational and sometimes sentimental love that frequently takes possession of the human heart. These remarks do not pretend to go against the genuine compassion that Christians are called to feel for those who do not receive the gospel. No one with Christian sensitivity takes pleasure in the thought that a human being should suffer eternally in the lake of fire. It is in that sense that Motyer says that when faced with the problem of the destiny of unbelievers, any sensitive person would like to be a universalist.[44]

The Christian who is zealous for the glory of God cannot put aside what He says in His written revelation about the eternal punishment of the unsaved. He accepts the fact that in this, as in other doctrinal and ethical themes, the Word of God is final. Furthermore, it is undeniable that the theologian's idea of God enters into the picture here. There is a temptation to imagine a God who answers meekly to the thoughts, desires, and whims of His worshipers. That is not the just, merciful, and sovereign God revealed in the Bible. God's love cannot be isolated from the rest of His nature. That nature can only be discovered as God chose to reveal it in the Bible, and the Bible states that God will condemn the wicked.

Divine justice. In regard to divine justice it is necessary to ask what concept of justice the defender of universalism has. When someone says that God would not be just if He sent sinners to eternal suffering, to what justice does that person refer—to the justice conceived by the human mind, or to the divine justice revealed in the Scriptures? Justice is normally defined as, "the maintenance or administration of what is just . . . the assignment of merited awards or punishments. . . ."[45] According to the Bible all that man merits from God is eternal condemnation. That is what belongs to him. He does not have merit in himself for salvation.

Divine justice is closely related to the holiness of God, and goes far beyond human justice in its demands. Before divine justice there is no one righteous, "not even one" (Rom. 3:10), among all men. None of those unrighteous beings has the right to accuse God of injustice. He has been just in declaring them guilty (Rom. 3:19). He is just in justifying those who have trusted in Christ (Rom. 3:21-26); and He is just in leaving in the state of condemnation those who reject the offer of His grace (John 3:36; 2 Thess. 1:5-10).

The anthropocentricity of universalism is evident. Man occupies the center and God the periphery in universalist thought. Man's importance is overestimated and God's is underestimated. Of course, man is of immense value in the eyes of God. He is His creature and bears His image; he is His representative in this world, and the supreme object of His providence and His love within creation. God made man for a glorious destiny. But man is also a sinner; he has become an enemy of his Creator (Rom. 5:10; Col. 1:21), taking up arms against Him. He is guilty before God and deserves divine punishment. But God loves him and has manifested His grace to him. He can be saved through faith in Him who died on the cross (John 1:12; 3:16; 5:24; 1 Tim. 1:15).

INDUCTIVE OR EXEGETICAL ARGUMENTS

In addition to the deductive arguments, one must also examine the inductive arguments presented in this debate. Inductive arguments are those that move from the part to the whole, from the specific to the general, or from the individual to the universal. The universalists use this type of argumentation when they resort to certain biblical texts in an attempt to prove their theory. Several of those texts need to be examined. They can be grouped into three major topics.

The saving desire of God. The apostle Paul says that God "desires all men to be saved" (1 Tim. 2:4). That biblical text, as any other, needs to be interpreted in the light of its context. Verses 5-6 clearly show the outworking of the saving desire of God—the provision of Christ "as a ransom for all." God's desire prompted Him to act on behalf of all men by providing Christ as a substitute for their sin. Christ is the universal provision of salvation available to all, but His death does not automatically guarantee salvation for all (as the universalists believe). Mankind must still respond to God's offer in faith. They must "believe in Him for eternal life" (1 Tim. 1:16). Because of His great desire to save the world, He sent His beloved Son to die on the cross. But only those who believe in Him are saved; the others remain in perdition.

The apostle Peter also expresses the saving desire of God. The Lord does not wish "for any to perish but for all to come to repentance" (2 Pet. 3:9). Yet in that text it is clear that the divine desire of salvation is only realized in those who repent. The rest have no hope. Instead, they face "the day of judgment and destruction of ungodly men" (2 Pet.3:7). In that case, the expression of the saving desire of God is found within the framework of a terrifying revelation of judgment.

The saving provision of God. Included under this topic are biblical passages that reveal the universal value of the work of Christ. Those include John 12:32; 2 Corinthians 5:19; Titus 2:11; Hebrews 2:9; 2 Peter 2:1; and 1 John 2:2. The universalists note that those passages speak of Christ dying for *all* mankind. Since Christ's death effectively paid for the sins of the world, they argue, then all the world will ultimately be saved.

The problem with the universalists' position is that they take each verse and examine it in isolation from its context. The text of John 12:32 should be interpreted in relation to the desire of certain Greeks to see Jesus (12:20-23). In response to the desire of those proselytes, Jesus reveals that He would die to draw all men to Himself—both Jews and Gentiles. Morris indicates that in the gospel of John the phrase "lifting up" refers to the cross.[46] Although the work of Christ thus became the basis for the salvation of the world (cf. 12:47), it did not automatically guarantee the salvation of all men. His provision can be rejected, and that rejection will result in judgment (12:48).

It is true that the apostle Paul states that "God was in Christ reconciling the world to Himself" (2 Cor. 5:19), but immediately he adds, "Be reconciled to God" (2 Cor. 5:20). The exhortation is not simply for the Corinthians to recognize that they are already reconciled, but for them to become reconciled to God. The apostle appeals not only to the intellect and emotions of his readers, but also to their will. They have to make a decision to respond to "the word of reconciliation."

The sacrifice of Christ has immense value. Yet the effectual application of that sacrifice is always limited to those who respond in faith to the free provision. It is one thing for the value of Christ's death to be sufficient for the salvation of the whole world (as Titus 2:11; Heb. 2:9; and 1 John 2:2 indicate). It is quite another for the individual to appropriate that great blessing. Salvation is by grace through faith (Eph. 2:8; cf. Acts 16:31; Rom. 1:16; 10:8-17). It demands an individual response. "He who believes in Him is not judged; he who does not believe has been judged already, because he has not believed in the name of the only begotten Son of God" (John 3:18). The death of Christ has value to redeem even the false prophets(2 Pet. 2:1). Yet they are on the road to their own destruction because they have rejected this provision and have denied "the Master who bought them" (2 Pet. 2:1).

The saving promise of God. The third group of biblical texts used by universalists deals with the consummation of God's plan of redemption in history. Those include Acts 3:21; 1 Corinthians 15:22-28; Ephesians 1:10; and Philippians 2:9-11. Again, each of those texts must be carefully examined in its context.

In Acts 3:21 is found the word that has become famous in relation to universalism: *apokatastasis* ("restoration"). It appears here in a definitely eschatological context, and the restoration it announces does not refer to the salvation of the whole human race. The restoration spoken of here is the restoration of the Kingdom of Israel (cf. Acts 1:6) under her Messiah. Those are the "times of refreshing" associated with the second coming of "Jesus, the Christ [i.e., Messiah] appointed for you" (Acts 3:19-20). Even in the midst of this announcement a note of judgment is heard in verse 23. Peter quotes Moses to warn his audience to accept Jesus as their Messiah because "EVERY SOUL THAT DOES NOT HEED THAT PROPHET SHALL BE UTTERLY DESTROYED FROM AMONG THE PEOPLE." That is hardly an announcement of universal reconciliation!

The central thesis of the apostle Paul in 1 Corinthians 15:1-58 is that there will be a resurrection of the dead. The emphasis falls on the resurrection of the *believers* in Christ. That passage has *nothing* to do with the salvation of all the world. Paul's focus is on "those who have fallen asleep in Christ" (v. 18), those who have "hoped in Christ" (v. 19), and "those who are Christ's at His coming" (v. 23). A universalistic interpretation of 1 Corinthians 15:22-28 finds no support within the context.

Ephesians 1:10 must be examined in its context. This verse speaks of "the fullness of the times, that is, the summing up of all things in Christ, things in the heavens and things upon the earth." Contrary to the statements of universalists, Ephesians 1:10 does not demand the salvation of all mankind; it is merely speaking of God's ultimate plan for the universe in relation to those who have trusted Christ. The sequence of events is clear in verse 13: "after listening to the message . . . having also believed, you were sealed. . . ." In 2:2-3 Paul states clearly that those who have not trusted Christ are "sons of disobedience" and "children of wrath." Salvation is not automatically bestowed on all. "For by grace you have been saved through faith" (Eph. 2:8).

Philippians 2:9-11 is another passage that must be examined in context. The verses state that "every knee should bow . . . and every tongue should confess that Jesus Christ is Lord. . . ." Although all individuals will one day be forced to admit that fact (cf. Rev. 20:11-15), such a statement does not guarantee universal salvation. Paul is clear in his distinction between believers and unbelievers. Unbelievers are "opponents" who have a "sign of destruction" (1:28). They are "a crooked and perverse generation" (2:15) and are "enemies of the cross of Christ, whose end is destruction" (3:18-19).

First Peter 3:19-20 is a very difficult text to interpret. But it cannot be concluded from this passage that Christ is going to preach to every soul that arrives in "hell." The apostle refers to a specific group of people, not to all who go to "hell." Christ's proclamation was to those "who once were disobedient, when the patience of God kept waiting in the days of Noah, during the construction of the ark" (1 Pet. 3:20). Also, the aorist tense of the verb kērussō ("to proclaim") within the context is better understood as a specific event that has already transpired.

The theory of "the second chance for salvation" in the world beyond has no support in the teaching of the Scriptures. The biblical emphasis is found in the determinative nature of human existence here in this world (Luke 16:19-31). Jesus declared, "I said therefore to you, that you shall die in your sins; for unless you believe that I am He, you shall die in your sins" (John 8:24).

UNIVERSALISM IN MISSIOLOGICAL PERSPECTIVE

The term *universalism* is sometimes used to indicate that the gospel should be announced to every human being. Berkouwer, for example, suggests that there is a universalism that consists of the universal offer of the gospel, although that offer is not received by every individual.[47] Stott also affirms, "The true universalism of the Bible is the call to universal evangelism in obedience to Christ's universal commission."[48] Both Berkouwer and Stott reject, of course, the universalism that teaches that in the end all will be saved. The great incompatibility between that universalism and the universal dimension of the missionary mandate is clearly evident.

If everyone will eventually attain salvation, or if the mission of the church is simply to inform people that they are already saved in Christ, then there is no great motivation to preach the gospel or to pray for the conversion of those who do not yet know Christ. Ryrie has well said that if all human beings will eventually end up in heaven, the task of making known that all are saved is not a matter of life or death, but simply "of life or life."[49]

The greatest danger today is found not in the organizations

that openly declare themselves to be universalist but in those theological systems and ecclesiastical movements which deny, overlook, or do not emphasize as they should the singularity of the gospel of Christ. Besides the traditional ecumenical movement that seeks to unite all professing Christians, there exists today an ecumenism that has syncretistic tendencies in both religious and secular areas. Its main objective seems to be to change economic and social structures.

The gospel is certainly more than a fire escape from hell; it is also more than just a passport to heaven, or an eternal insurance policy. The gospel produces a radical transformation in the individual believer; it imparts to him a new quality of life—it enables him to have fellowship with God. But that change also affects the final destiny of the redeemed man. He is now destined to be conformed to the very image of the Lord (Rom. 8:29; 1 John 3:1-3). God works in the believer for today and for eternity. He is forming the new race, which will enjoy a better world that He will establish.

The gospel is not just an ethical system for this earthly life. Whereas it does take into account personal, family, and social problems in today's world, it also projects itself into eternity and gives answers to the tremendous questions regarding death and the world beyond. When it comes to the eternal destiny of the unsaved, the Word of God is not ambiguous. Eternal condemnation awaits them.

There are ideologies and political systems that promise to change this world into a paradise, and there are religions that offer a heavenly Eden. But Jesus Christ said, "I am the way, and the truth, and the life; no one comes to the Father, but through Me" (John 14:6). That claim was affirmed by the apostle Peter. "And there is salvation in no one else; for there is no other name under heaven that has been given among men, by which we must be saved" (Acts 4:12). The testimony of the apostle Paul is the same when he states that there is no other gospel (Gal. 1:6-7) and that there is only "one mediator also between God and men, the man Christ Jesus" (1 Tim. 2:5).

According to those statements Jesus Christ is the only Savior. There is no room for neutrality or for substitutes of any kind. The church therefore has the unavoidable responsibility of proclaiming this message, and every human being has the obligation of accepting it.

It was certainly with reason that the participants in the Congress on the Church's Worldwide Mission, held in Wheaton, Illinois, in 1966, rejected universalism and reaffirmed their determination to preach the gospel of Jesus Christ to the whole world.[50] Those who signed the Lausanne Covenant in 1974 expressed themselves in similar terms.[51] There is no alternative for those who accept unconditionally the final authority of the written revelation of God.

CONCLUSION

Universalism is ancient and modern. Within Christianity there have been universalist tendencies since the third century. Today there are denominations that profess to be universalist, and there are Protestant and Catholic theologians who lean toward neo-universalism.

Any theology that denies or overlooks the including and excluding character of the gospel is very dangerous for the mission of the church. The naive openness to dialogue with other religions and the idea that Christianity depends on them to complement the truth can result in syncretism and universalism.

The antidote for universalism is the written revelation of God. When *all* that God says in His Word is accepted without reservation, universalism cannot be sustained. The biblical texts that speak of the saving desire of God and the universal offer of salvation need to be harmonized with those that reveal unequivocally the eternal punishment of the sinner. There is no contradiction between the justice and the love of God.

No one comes to the Father except by means of the Lord Jesus Christ. Because of that truth it is imperative to proclaim the gospel message with humility and love to all people, warning them of the terrible destiny that awaits them, and making known to them that "God so loved the world, that He gave His only begotten Son, that whoever believes in Him should not perish, but have eternal life" (John 3:16). God is glorified in the manifestation of His justice and His love.

NOTES

1. *Bakers's Dictionary of Theology*, ed. Everett F. Harrison (Grand Rapids: Baker, 1960), s.v. "Universalism," by John H. Gerstner, p. 539.
2. Origen *De Principiis* 1.6; 2.10, in *The Ante-Nicene Fathers*, 10 vols., ed. Alexander Roberts and James Donaldson (New York: Christian Literature, 1890), 4:260, 295-96.
3. Philip Schaff, *History of the Christian Church*, 8 vols. (New York: Scribner's, 1910), 2:611.
4. Ibid., 2:611-12.
5. Justo L. González, *Historia del Pensamiento Cristiano* (Buenos Aires: Methopress, 1965), 1:243-44.
6. *Obras de San Agustín. La Ciudad de Dios* (Madrid: Biblioteca de Autores Cristianos, 1965), 17:614-89.
7. *Suma Teológica* (Madrid: Biblioteca de Autores Cristianos, 1960), 16:575-79.
8. *Institución de la Religion Cristiana* (Rijswijk, Paises Bajos: Fundación Editorial de Literatura Reformada, 1968), 2:762-81.
9. Reinhold Seeberg, *Manual de Historia de las Doctrinas*, trans. José Míguez Bonino (El Paso, Tex.: Casa Bautista de Publicaciones, 1963), 2:377.
10. Ibid., p. 408; Albert H. Newman, *A Manual of Church History*, 2 vols. (Philadelphia: American Baptist Publication Society, 1957), 2:344-46.
11. Kenneth S. Latourette, *A History of Christianity* (New York: Harper, 1953), p. 795.
12. Karl M. Chworowsky and Christopher Gist Raible, "What is a Unitarian Universalist?" in *Religions of America*, ed. Leo Rosten (New York: Simon and Schuster, 1975), pp. 263-76.
13. Frank S. Mead, *Handbook of Denominations in the United States* (Nashville: Abingdon, 1975), p. 252.
14. José Ma. G. Gómez-Heras, *Teología Protestante. Sistema e Historia* (Madrid: Biblioteca de Autores Cristianos, 1972), p. 132.
15. Friedrick Schleiermacher, *The Christian Faith*, ed. H. R. Mckintosh and J. R. Stewart (Edinburgh: T. & T. Clark, 1976), p. 722.
16. Ibid., p. 535.
17. Ibid., p. 560.
18. James I. Packer, "The Way of Salvation," *Bibliotheca Sacra*, January-March 1973, p. 4.
19. Karl Barth, *Dogmatics in Outline*, trans. G. T. Thomson (London: SCM, 1966), p. 136.
20. Karl Barth, *Church Dogmatics*, 4 vols., ed. G. W. Bromiley (Edinburgh: T. & T. Clark, 1978), 2:94-506.
21. Robert L. Reymond, *Introductory Studies in Contemporary Theology* (Philadelphia: Presbyterian and Reformed, 1968), pp. 131-32.

22. Bernard Ramm, *Diccionario de Teología Contemporánea*, trans. Roger Velásquez V. (El Paso, Tex.: Casa Bautista de Publicaciones, n.d.), pp. 138-39.
23. G. W. Bromiley, "Karl Barth," in *Creative Minds in Contemporary Theology*, ed. Philip Hughes (Grand Rapids: Eerdmans, 1966), p. 54.
24. G. C. Berkouwer, *Divine Election, Studies in Dogmatics* (Grand Rapids: Eerdmans, 1960), p. 229.
25. Rudolf Bultmann, *Jesucristo y Mitología*, trans. Ramón Alaix and Eduardo Sierra (Barcelona, Spain: Ediciones Ariel, S.A., 1970), p. 24.
26. Paul Tillich, *Teología Sistemática*, trans. Damian Sánchez-Bustamante Páez (Barcelona, Spain: Ediciones Ariel S.A., 1973), 1:363-64; 2:109.
27. Ibid.
28. John A. T. Robinson, *Honest To God* (Philadelphia: Westminster, 1963), pp. 21-24.
29. Ibid., p. 80.
30. John A. T. Robinson, *In the End God* (New York: Harper & Row, 1968), p. 115.
31. Nels F. S. Ferré, *Evil and the Christian Faith* (New York: Harper, 1947); *The Christian Understanding of God* (New York: Harper, 1951); *The Sun and the Umbrella* (New York: Harper, 1953).
32. *Breaking Barriers: Nairobi 1975*, ed. David M. Paton (London: SPCK, 1976), pp. 18-19. Cf. Arthur Johnston, *The Battle for World Evangelism* (Wheaton, Ill.: Tyndale, 1978), pp. 352-53; *Bangkok Assembly 1973* (Geneva: World Council of Churches, n.d.), pp. 78-80.
33. Oscar Cullmann, *Verdadero y Falso Ecumenismo*, trans. Don Eloy Requena (Madrid: Studium, 1972), pp. 77-78.
34. José Grau, *El Ecumenismo y la Biblia* (Barcelona, Spain: Ediciones Evangélicas Europeas, 1969), p. 60.
35. "Dogmatic Constitution on the Church," in *The Documents of Vatican II*, ed. Walter M. Abbott (New York: Guild, 1966), pp. 32-33.
36. Ibid., p. 35.
37. "Declaration on the Relationship of the Church to Non-Christian Religions," in *The Documents of Vatican II*, pp. 663-68.
38. Hans Küng, *Ser Cristiano*, trans. J. Ma. Bravo Navalpotro (Madrid, Spain: Ediciones Cristiandad, 1977), pp. 105-41.
39. Gustavo Gutiérrez, *A Theology of Liberation* (Maryknoll, N.Y.: Orbis Books, 1973).
40. Ibid.
41. Ibid.
42. Ibid.
43. Ibid.

44. J. A. Motyer, "The Final State: Heaven and Hell," in *Basic Christian Doctrines,* ed. Carl F. H. Henry (New York: Holt, Rinehart and Winston, 1962), p. 290.

45. *Webster's Third New International Dictionary* (Springfield, Mass.: Merriam, 1976), s.v. "Justice," p. 1228.

46. Leon Morris, *The Gospel According to John* (Grand Rapids: Eerdmans, 1973), p. 598.

47. G. C. Berkouwer, p. 229.

48. As quoted by Harvey T. Hoekstra in *The World Council of Churches and the Demise of Evangelism* (Wheaton, Ill.: Tyndale, 1979), p. 138.

49. Charles C. Ryrie, "Otro Evangelio," in *La Fe* (Puebla, Mexico: Instituto y Seminario Bíblico, n.d.), p. 4.

50. "Wheaton Declaration," in *The Church's Worldwide Mission,* ed. Harold Lindsell (Waco, Tex.: Word, 1966), pp. 223-25.

51. "The Lausanne Covenant," in *Let the Earth Hear His Voice,* ed. J. D. Douglas (Minneapolis: World Wide Publications, 1975), pp. 3-4.

12

Contrasting Views on Sanctification

Charles C. Ryrie

Whereas definitions of sanctification tend to be similar, descriptions of the process of sanctification are quite dissimilar. Most would probably agree that the concept of sanctification "seems to be to set apart an object from ordinary usage for a special (religious) purpose of function, and in particular to set apart for God."[1] Also, most agree that sanctification consists of three aspects: positional, experiential, and ultimate.

Positional sanctification is that position every believer enjoys by virtue of being set apart in the family of God by faith in Christ. It is an actual, not theoretical, position and is not dependent on the state of one's spiritual growth. That is why Paul could reprimand the carnal Corinthian believers and yet address them as "those who have been sanctified in Christ Jesus, saints by calling" (1 Cor. 1:2; see also 6:11).

Experiential sanctification concerns the progressive development of holiness in the experience of the Christian. Every

---

CHARLES C. RYRIE (A.B., Haverford College; Th.M., Th.D., Dallas Theological Seminary; Ph.D., Edinburgh University) is professor of systematic theology at Dallas Theological Seminary, Dallas, Texas.

biblical exhortation to godly living underscores this aspect of sanctification (1 Pet. 1:16).

Ultimate sanctification awaits the believer's glorification in his resurrection body and the removal of the sin nature (1 John 3:1-3; Jude 24). Every believer is completely sanctified as far as position is concerned and will be completely sanctified ultimately. But each believer's progress in holiness is different at any given time.

Much disagreement, however, surfaces particularly in the theological discussion of the manner and relationships of progressive sanctification. Some of the areas of debate are: (1) the relationship between justification and sanctification, (2) the relationship between God's sovereignty and human activity in the work of sanctification, (3) the question of one or two natures in the believer, and (4) the means of victory in the Christian life. Although some of those areas overlap, the various answers given to those questions distinguish different schools of thought concerning progressive sanctification.

For the purpose of this investigation attention needs to be focused on the differences between three distinguishable viewpoints that have been advanced to answer those four questions. Although labels are never totally satisfactory, they do serve a useful purpose. Those viewpoints can be labeled the Reformed, the Chaferian, and the Victorious Life viewpoints.

In general, the Reformed view of sanctification may be summarized as teaching the gradual extirpation or extermination of depravity. Warfield said that "grace is progressively extirpating it [the old nature] now."[2] Perhaps Warfield learned the word *extirpate* from his predecessor, A. A. Hodge, who used it to describe his concept of sanctification.

> The orthodox doctrine is that the Holy Ghost, by his constant influences upon the whole soul in all its faculties, through the instrumentality of the truth, nourishes, exercises, and develops those holy principles and dispositions which he implanted in the new birth, until by a constant progress all sinful dispositions being mortified and extirpated, and all holy dispositions being fully matured, the subject of this grace is brought immediately upon death to the measure of the stature of perfect manhood in Christ.[3]

The Reformed view carefully distinguishes itself from the

idea of perfectionism or eradication of the sin nature in this life. Although it teaches that experiential sanctification is a gradual eradication of the old nature, that process is never completed in this life. The believer never arrives at a state of perfection until death.

> Sanctification is usually a lengthy process and never reaches perfection in this life. At the same time there may be cases in which it is completed in a very short time or even in a moment, as for instance, in cases in which regeneration and conversion are immediately followed by temporal death. . . .The sanctification of the believer must, it would seem, be completed either at the very moment of death, or immediately after death, as far as the soul is concerned, and at the resurrection in so far as it pertains to the body.[4]

The Chaferian view[5] of progressive sanctification may be summarized by the idea of counteraction of the new nature of the believer against the old, or of the Spirit against the flesh. It involves yieldedness to the will of God, confession of sins, and growing in grace.[6] This view agrees with the Reformed position in denying the eradication of the sin nature and in rejecting the idea that a believer can achieve perfection in this life. But there is more emphasis on human responsibility and activity in the process of sanctification than in the Reformed view. Also the existence and struggle between two natures and the possibility of carnality in the believer are affirmed in the Chaferian view but denied in the Reformed.

In the Chaferian view, the central doctrine concerns the filling of the Holy Spirit. A ministry that is both commanded and repeated, the filling of the Spirit is conditioned on (1) not quenching the Spirit (1 Thess. 5:19), (2) not grieving the Spirit (Eph. 4:30), and (3) walking in the Spirit (Gal. 5:16). Walvoord stresses the importance of this ministry.

> These three Scriptures provide a divinely-inspired outline of the conditions for the filling of the Holy Spirit. While there are many aspects to the spiritual life and experience, all will be found to be related to these simple commands. The importance of these Scriptures as the key to unlocking the truth of the conditions for the filling of the Holy Spirit cannot be overemphasized.[7]

Walvoord further explains that not quenching the Spirit is

equivalent to yieldedness of life, that not grieving the Spirit involves confession of sin, and that walking in the Spirit is the positive aspect of depending on the Spirit day by day. Progressive sanctification "is the main objective of the work of the Spirit and is accomplished by walking by the Spirit."[8] "Walking by the Spirit presumes activity; it is not a defensive stand against the enemy, but a positive approach to the problems of the spiritual life, endeavoring to be active in the will of God as well as resting in His sufficiency."[9]

The Victorious Life view (often associated with the Keswick movement) contains distinctives that mark it off from the other viewpoints. In England the Keswick movement originated not in a period of spiritual vacuum but in a time of fervent spiritual activity. It sought to promote a higher standard of personal holiness among God's people through conferences and writings. That "higher life" involved a life of entire surrender to the Lord and perfect trust in Him. The believer was urged to abandon himself to Christ in a crisis experience and to receive sanctification by faith as a gift of God's love, just as he received salvation by faith.

The five-part outline used in Keswick conventions summarizes well the Victorious Life viewpoint.

(1) Sin in man is seen as exceedingly sinful. It is a ruling principle, a spiritual disease, a moral defilement, an acquired habit, and an indwelling tendency. As directed to Christians, this teaching seeks to move believers from a carnal state that is not normal or God-honoring.

(2) God's provision for sin is not eradication, nor counteraction of the sin nature, but simply Christian growth. The provision of sanctification is a work of the Holy Spirit, which is ultimately based on the work of Christ at Calvary. The believer receives sanctification by faith through a crisis act of entire consecration to God.

(3) The consecration of the Christian is both a crisis and a process by which all the aspects of the offerer are put in the hands of God. Negatively it is dying to self; positively it is absolute surrender.

(4) The fullness of the Spirit is an experience that is not shared by all believers (though all have the Spirit, and there is

no "second blessing"). Receiving that fullness involves a definite act of faith that is separable from regeneration (though not necessarily separated from it in time). All believers may experience that fullness through faith and absolute surrender.

(5) Christian service is the outworking of the fullness of the Spirit.[10]

With that general background in mind, it is time to turn to the specific areas of discussion and debate among the three viewpoints.

THE RELATIONSHIP BETWEEN JUSTIFICATION AND SANCTIFICATION

Strictly speaking, there is little difference between the Reformed and Chaferian views of the relationship between justification and sanctification, though there are some distinctions in emphasis. In the Reformed position justification and sanctification occur simultaneously. A. A. Hodge explained this relationship. "The instant God regenerates a sinner he acts faith in Christ. The instant he acts faith in Christ he is justified, and sanctification, which is the work of carrying on and perfecting that which is begun in regeneration, is accomplished under the conditions of those new relations into which he is introduced by justification."[11]

More clearly, Berkhof wrote:

> Justification precedes and is basic to sanctification in the covenant of grace. . . . Justification is the judicial basis for sanctification. God has the right to demand of us holiness of life, but because we cannot work out this holiness for ourselves, He freely works it within us through the Holy Spirit on the basis of the righteousness of Jesus Christ, which is imputed to us in justification. The very fact that it is based on justification . . . excludes the idea that we can ever merit anything in sanctification.[12]

The Chaferian view basically agrees with those statements.

The Reformed and Chaferian views also distinguish between positional and progressive sanctification. Using the term *definitive sanctification* as an equivalent for positional sanctification, Murray states clearly, "The virtue accruing from the death and resurrection of Christ affects no phase of salvation more directly than that of insuring definitive sanctification. . . . It might appear that the emphasis placed upon definitive sanctification leaves no place for what is progressive. Any such inference would contradict an equally important aspect of biblical teaching."[13]

Similarly, Chafer wrote concerning positional sanctification that it "is a sanctification which comes to the believer by the operation of God through offering of the body and shed blood of the Lord Jesus Christ."[14] "Experimental sanctification," he continued, "instead may depend (1) on some degree of yieldedness to God, (2) on some degree of separation from sin, or (3) on some degree of Christian growth to which the believer has already attained."[15]

Thus both the Reformed and Chaferian views see justification and sanctification as inseparable, though the Chaferian view makes a great distinction between the two operations.

The Victorious Life view, on the other hand, sees justification and sanctification as two distinct gifts of God to be received by separate acts of faith. "Jesus, you know, makes two offers to everyone. He offers to set us free from the *penalty* of our sin. And He offers to set us free from the *power* of our sin. Both these offers are made on exactly the same terms: we can accept them only by letting Him do it all. Every Christian has accepted the first offer. Many Christians have not accepted the second offer."[16] In other words, just as one receives Christ by faith for justification, so also one receives Christ by faith for sanctification. Those are two distinct acts.

These three views on the relationship between justification and sanctification can be summarized rather succinctly. The Reformed view considers justification and sanctification inseparable yet distinct, whereas the Chaferian view sees justification and sanctification as distinct, yet inseparable. In contrast to both of those, the Victorious Life view understands justification and sanctification to be separate and distinct.

THE RELATIONSHIP BETWEEN GOD'S SOVEREIGNTY AND HUMAN ACTIVITY IN SANCTIFICATION

Again the Reformed and Chaferian views are not far apart in

what is taught concerning the relationship between human activity and divine sovereignty. The Victorious Life view is more distinct from the other two.

Warfield's expression of the Reformed view might be called an irresistible sovereignty view.

> It happens that the Scriptural doctrine on both matters [the doctrine of free will and the doctrine of Christ within the believer] may be suggested by a single Scriptural phrase, which may stand for us as their symbol: make the tree good that its fruit may be good also. Christ dwells within us not for the purpose of sinking our being into His being, nor of substituting Himself for us as the agent in our activities; much less of seizing our wills and operating them for us in contradiction to our own immanent mind [these phrases express Warfield's understanding of the Victorious Life teaching]; but to operate directly upon us, to make us good, that our works, freely done by us, may under His continual leading, be good also. Our wills, being the expression of our hearts, continually more and more dying to sin and more and more living to holiness, under the renewing action of the Christ dwelling within us by his Spirit, can never from the beginning of His gracious renewal of them resist Christ fatally, and will progressively resist Him less and less until, our hearts having been made through and through good, our wills will do only righteousness.[17]

Though Warfield's view includes human activity, it seems to slight human responsibility because of its emphasis on irresistibility and the almost automatic nature of sanctification. Although it is true that every true believer will give evidence of sanctification (1 Cor. 4:5), it is not true that that is automatic. The believer must act responsibly in obedience to God's commands.

In contrast to Warfield, Murray reflects a more biblical balance between sovereignty and responsibility.

> Out of deference to all the stress that falls upon God's agency in sanctification we must not fall into the error of quietism and fail to take account of the activity of the believer himself. The imperatives directed to the believer imply nothing less. Perhaps the most instructive text is Philippians 2:12, 13, a text frequently misapplied. The salvation spoken of is not initial salvation, but that to be attained at the revelation of Jesus Christ. It is salvation

as completed and consummated that we are to work out. And this means that our agency and activity are to be exercised to the fullest extent in promotion of this salvation. Hence, the implications: our working is not dispensed with or made superfluous because God works; God's working is not suspended because we work. There is the correlation and conjunction of both. The fact that God works in us is the encouragement and incentive to our working. Indeed, God's working is the energizing cause of our working; if we do not work, the working of God is absent. . . . Yet, the more assured we are that God works in us, the more diligent and persistent we are in our working. Our whole personality is not only drawn within the scope of but also enlisted in all its functions in that process that moves to the goal of being conformed to the image of God's son.[18]

The Chaferian view is very similar to Murray's. Even the Chaferian emphasis on an initial act of dedication in a believer's life is found in Murray. On "present yourselves to God" in Romans 6:13 Murray wrote, "The tense that is used in this instance indicates the once-for-allness of the dedication involved in the presentation of ourselves and of our members."[19] Chafer stated that the theme of Romans 6:1-23 "is sanctification in daily life and by the power of the Holy Spirit alone. . . . There follow two vitally essential responsibilities which rest directly and unceasingly upon the child of God: He is to *reckon* . . . and he is to *yield* himself unto God. . . ."[20] When commenting on dedication, Chafer said, "Dedication, if done at all as God would have it, hardly needs to be done over. In other words, dedication is an all determining act and not a process."[21]

Similarly, Walvoord wrote on Romans 6:13b: ". . . the exhortation is to present yourself unto God, *parastesate,* in the aorist tense, meaning, 'Present yourself to God once and for all.' A Christian is called upon to make a definite yielding of his life to God to make possible its full blessing and usefulness just as he was called upon to believe in order to be saved."[22]

The difference, then, between the Reformed view and the Chaferian view in this area is principally one of emphasis. Both incorporate the divine and human aspects, though some Reformed writers inject the idea that progressive sanctification is automatic. Both would agree that it is assured, but Chafer and his followers emphasize more the necessity of human responsibility and activity.

The Victorious Life view is quite distinct. Here the emphasis is almost entirely on God's activity in sanctification. The secret of victory is summed up in the phrase, "Let go and let God." Letting go is surrender and letting God is the faith to let Him live His life of victory in the believer. Those are two separate acts, so it is possible to have surrender without victory (though there can be no victory without surrender). This approach tends to promote quietism and passivism. Holiness is not something that needs to be attained. Rather, it is something already obtained by faith, which then is lived out in the life of the believer. Human activity is minimized, though it is necessary to keep on believing and reckoning.

The teachings of Trumbull, one of the early Victorious Life leaders in this country, present this position. "The victorious Christian is one who has gotten into the boat and is living in the rest of faith. He is not holding on to the boat, but letting the boat hold him."[23] "The secret of complete victory is faith: simply believing that *Jesus has done and is doing it all.* Victory is entered upon by a single act of faith, as is salvation. Victory is maintained by the attitude of faith."[24] "True, victory is by faith; but faith must be fed; and faith cannot be fed apart from daily nourishment from the Word of God, and daily time alone with God in prayer."[25] Trumbull advocates the position that sanctification is received as a separate act of faith. His emphasis on letting God "do it all" promotes the concept of quietism. Yet he still emphasizes the necessity of continual believing nourished by the Word and prayer.

THE QUESTION OF ONE OR TWO NATURES IN THE BELIEVER

On the question of one or two natures in the believer the Reformed view stands alone in teaching that the believer has only one nature. The Chaferian and Victorious Life views both hold that the believer has two natures.

Warfield's view is that the believer has a single, sinful nature and that grace is gradually extirpating that nature (though never totally eradicating it in this life). The two-nature concept is anathema to him. In rejecting Griffith Thomas's view of two natures, Warfield wrote that Thomas "errs when he says that 'grace does not improve the old nature, it overcomes it.' He errs when he teaches only that 'it promises hereafter to extirpate it,' but meanwhile, only 'counteracts its tendencies.' "[26]

Similarily, Charles Hodge says:

> Regeneration is the infusion of a new principle of life in this corrupt nature. It is leaven introduced to diffuse its influence gradually through the whole mass. Sanctification, therefore, consists in two things: first, the removing more and more the principles of evil still infecting our nature, and destroying their power; and secondly, the growth of the principle of spiritual life until it controls the thoughts, feelings, and acts, and brings the soul into conformity to the image of Christ.[27]

By contrast, both the Chaferian and Victorious Life views regard the believer as having two natures or capacities that are in conflict. "The presence of two opposing natures (not two personalities) in one individual results in conflict."[28]

THE MEANS OF VICTORY IN THE CHRISTIAN LIFE

At the risk of oversimplification, a summary of what each of these viewpoints says about the practical question of how to live the Christian life needs to be given.

The Reformed emphasis gives the impression that the sovereign God of the universe will bring the believer to maturity in His own time and that the believer has little to do with that process. Some within the Reformed position do emphasize the struggle and fight and the place of human responsibility in the process of sanctification. Overall, however, the words *sovereign*, *automatic*, and *extirpation* seem to characterize this view.

The Victorious Life teaching stresses surrender, faith (i.e. letting go and letting God), and the suppression of the old nature. One receives Christ by faith for sanctification just as one received Him by faith for justification. "We are to use our wills in all this. Mere passivity is fatal. We are to use our wills to *believe*. We are not to work *in order* to have victory, but we are to work *because* we have it. Then we can go out in the dynamite, the omnipotence, of God himself in victory, with sinful desires taken away. Not temptations taken away, but the sinful response in our heart taken away."[29]

Chafer and his followers emphasize the filling of the Spirit as the key to Christian living. To be spiritual requires the filling, and Chafer made famous three conditions for experiencing filling. The first he labelled "Grieve not the Holy Spirit of God," and it had to do with sin in the believer's life. Sin is what grieves the Spirit so it must be confessed. The second he placed under the heading "Quench not the Spirit," which concerned the yielded life. The third was "Walk in the Spirit," which referred to a believer's constant dependence on the Spirit.

Steering a careful course in relation to sovereignty and human responsibility, Chafer wrote, "Though the will be moved upon by the enabling power of God, spirituality, according to God's Word, is made to depend upon that divinely-enabled human choice; Romans 12:1, 2; Galatians 5:16; Ephesians 4:30; 1 Thessalonians 5:19 and 1 John 1:9 being sufficient evidence."[30]

That is the same viewpoint Walvoord has taught throughout his ministry, and it is, in this writer's judgment, correct both biblically and theologically.

NOTES

1. *Baker's Dictionary of Theology,* s.v. "Sanctify, Sanctification," by Philip E. Hughes, p. 470.
2. Benjamin B. Warfield, *Perfectionism,* 2 vols. (New York: Oxford U., 1931), 2:584.
3. A. A. Hodge, *Outlines of Theology* (Grand Rapids: Eerdmans, 1928), p. 521.
4. L. Berkhof, *Systematic Theology* (Grand Rapids: Eerdmans, 1941), p. 534.
5. This label serves to distinguish that position espoused by Lewis Sperry Chafer in his treatment of the doctrine of sanctification (see *Systematic Theology,* 8 vols. [Dallas: Dallas Theological Seminary, 1947], vol. 6; and *He That Is Spiritual,* rev. ed. [Grand Rapids: Zondervan, 1967]). This is also the official position of the Dallas Theological Seminary ("Doctrinal Statement," Article ix).
6. Chafer, *Theology,* 6:285.
7. John F. Walvoord, *The Doctrine of the Holy Spirit* (Dallas: Dallas Theological Seminary, 1943), p. 219.
8. Ibid., p. 238.

9. Ibid., p. 247.
10. See Steven Barabas, *So Great Salvation* (London: Revel, n.d.); and Herbert F. Stevenson, *Keswick's Authentic Voice* (Grand Rapids: Zondervan, 1959).
11. Hodge, p. 522.
12. Berkhof, p. 536.
13. John Murray, "Sanctification (the Law)," in *Basic Christian Doctrines*, ed. Carl F. H. Henry (New York: Holt, Reinhardt, & Winston, 1962), p. 229.
14. Chafer, *Theology*, 7:279.
15. Ibid., 7:280-81.
16. Charles G. Trumbull, "What is Your Kind of Christianity?" cited by Warfield, 2:567.
17. Warfield, 2:602.
18. Murray, "Sanctification," pp. 232-33.
19. John Murray, *The Epistle to the Romans*, 2 vols. (Grand Rapids: Eerdmans, 1965), 1:228.
20. Chafer, *Theology*, 6:253.
21. Ibid., 6:255.
22. Walvoord, p. 197.
23. Charles G. Trumbull, "Resting on the Facts," in *The Victorious Christ* (Philadelphia: Sunday School Times, 1923), p. 119.
24. Charles G. Trumbull, "The Period of Victory," Ibid., p. 126.
25. Ibid., p. 135.
26. Warfield, 2:584.
27. Charles Hodge, *Systematic Theology*, 3 vols. (Grand Rapids: Eerdmans, 1940), 3:221.
28. Chafer, *Theology*, 2:347.
29. Trumbull, "Resting on the Facts," p. 122.
30. Chafer, *He That Is Spiritual*, p. 67, n. 1.

13

The Gospel Message

Thomas L. Constable

Evangelism and theology must maintain close ties with one another in the church of Jesus Christ. They enjoy a symbiotic relationship; they need each other and profit from each other. Theology without evangelism can become dead orthodoxy, and evangelism without theology can degenerate into empty enthusiasm. Theology holds forth the light of truth that dispels the darkness of ignorance from men's minds. Evangelism provides the warmth of truth that drives the coldness from men's souls.

Unfortunately, theologians and evangelists have not always gotten along too well in the church. Some theologians have failed to appreciate the contribution of evangelism and have regarded evangelists as superficial. On the other hand, some evangelists have looked down on theologians, feeling that they are wasting their time studying while the world is going to hell. But evangelists and theologians are both needed in the Body of Christ and must learn to appreciate one another's gifts.

THOMAS L. CONSTABLE (Diploma, Moody Bible Institute; A.B., Wheaton College; Th.M., Th.D., Dallas Theological Seminary) is director of field education and director of D.Min. studies at Dallas Theological Seminary, Dallas, Texas.

A biblically accurate definition of the gospel message is essential to both theology and evangelism. The manner in which the gospel message is presented must be in harmony with Scripture. Since the gospel is the "power of God for salvation" (Rom. 1:16) its true dynamic must be understood and applied. The accuracy of the gospel message can be validated by the effects its proclamation produces. Those aspects of the study of the gospel message follow.

DEFINITION OF THE GOSPEL MESSAGE

THE MEANING OF "GOSPEL"

The New Testament word translated "gospel" is *euangelion*. It occurs many times and always means "good news." A contextual study of the passages in which *euangelion* is found in the New Testament yields five different gospels or messages of good news: the gospel preached to Abraham, the gospel of the kingdom, the Christian gospel, the false gospel, and the eternal gospel. Although each of those gospels is distinct in terms of the age in which it is proclaimed and the particular emphasis of that age, all of those gospels (with the exception of the "false gospel") are messages of good news based upon God's provision of salvation through Jesus Christ.[1]

The most important of those gospels in the present study is the so-called Christian gospel. Many texts clearly explain what the Christian gospel is (cf. John 1:12; 3:16, 36; 5:24; 6:47). Basically it is the good news that God loves man and has sent His Son, Jesus Christ, to pay the penalty for man's sins. Christ did that when He died on the cross of Calvary as man's substitute. God raised Him from the dead to demonstrate the acceptability of His sacrifice. The benefit of Christ's work must be appropriated individually by faith.

One of the texts that summarizes the gospel is 1 Corinthians 15:3-4. "For I delivered to you as of first importance what I also received, that Christ died for our sins according to the Scriptures, and that He was buried, and that He was raised on the third day according to the Scriptures. . . ." This is the essential message of good news that must be believed for salvation. It contains these facts: (1) man is a sinner, (2) Christ is the Savior,

(3) Christ died as man's substitute, and (4) Christ rose from the dead. Though the resurrection is part of the gospel message, it is not part of the saving work of Christ on the cross. The resurrection is stated as proof of the efficacy of Christ's death. Having accomplished redemption by His death, Jesus Christ was "raised because of our justification" (Rom. 4:25). The fact that Jesus Christ is alive is part of the Christian's good news, but individuals are saved by His death, not by His resurrection.

THE PRESUPPOSITIONS OF THE GOSPEL

The gospel message presupposes other truth set forth in Scripture which helps one to appreciate why the gospel is good news.

Human depravity. Mankind is in deep trouble. The Scriptures are clear that man can do nothing to commend himself to God (Gen. 6:5; Psalm 51:5; Eccles. 7:20; Isa. 64:6; Jer. 17:9; Mark 7:21-23; Luke 19:10; John 3:3; 8:44; Rom. 1:29-32; 3:10-18; 8:7; 10:1-2; 1 Cor. 2:14; 2 Cor. 4:3-4; Gal. 5:19-21; Eph. 2:1-3, 12; Col. 1:13; 1 John 5:19). Depravity does not mean that man is as bad as he could be or that he can do nothing that is good. But it does mean that man can do nothing to commend himself to God. That inability extends to every area of his life; depravity is total in that respect. Man needs some good news.

Divine love. The Bible is clear that the initiative in salvation is with God (Eph. 2:1-7). God's love for man does not spring from any inherent value in the character of man. It depends solely on the character of God. He first loved man (1 John 4:19). The love of God is one of the clearest revelations in the Bible (Deut. 4:37; 7:7-8; 10:15; 33:3; Psalm 63:3; 89:33; Jer. 31:3; John 3:16; 16:27; 17:23; Rom. 5:8; Eph. 2:4-5; 2 Thess. 2:16; Titus 3:4-5; 1 John 3:1, 16; 4:8-16). It was God's love that moved Him to send His Son to be the Savior of the world. And it was the Son's love that motivated Him to become "sin on our behalf, that we might become the righteousness of God in Him" (2 Cor. 5:21). The provision of salvation is traceable to the love of God for man.

Divine righteousness. Whereas love moved God to provide salvation, righteousness determined how it had to be provided. The righteousness of God is another foundational doctrine on which the gospel rests (Ezra 9:15; Job 36:3; Psalm 48:10; 71:15, 19; 97:2; 119:137; Isa. 56:1; Jer. 9:24; 12:1; Acts 17:31; Rom. 1:17; 3:4-6, 21-22; 9:14; 10:3-4; 1 Pet. 2:23; 2 Pet. 1:1). Because God is righteous, the penalty for sin had to be paid. It could not simply be pardoned. The gospel is good news because it explains how God remained just and still justified the ungodly. God's righteousness demanded the substitutionary death of a pure sacrifice on behalf of sinners. The gospel announces that such a sacrifice was provided and offered on man's behalf.[2]

PRESENTATIONS OF THE GOSPEL MESSAGE

Even though the gospel is simple enough for a child to understand and accept, it has been explained in such a variety of ways that its simplicity has been obscured. Many people have been led to believe that they have become Christians when they have not. Many earnest Christians cannot explain the gospel simply and clearly and cannot invite an unbeliever to make the proper response, even though their intentions are good. An accurate presentation of the gospel is absolutely crucial; the eternal destiny of men and women hangs in the balance (Gal. 1:8-9).

THE PROPER PRESENTATION

The Bible clearly reveals what the gospel is and what man's responsibility is in view of the gospel. The good news is that Jesus Christ is the Son of God and that He died as man's substitute on the cross of Calvary where He paid the entire debt of man's sin. There is nothing more for man to do but to trust in Christ's work as being sufficient for his salvation. In speaking of the finished work of Christ, the New Testament teaches that there is nothing a person needs to do to make his salvation secure except to trust in what Jesus Christ has done as being completely adequate in itself. "It cannot be too often emphasized that the gospel is not good advice to be obeyed; it is good news to be believed."[3] "The responsibility imposed on the sinner is that of *believing* the record God has given concerning this redemption which is in His Son."[4] "Salvation from the guilt and penalty of sin is wrought for us the *moment* we believe. It is conditioned on the *act* of faith."[5] "In the New Testament in about one hundred and fifty passages, the salvation of the sinner is declared to depend only upon *believing*, and in about thirty-five passages to depend on *faith*, which is a synonym of believing. . . . Believing is the opposite of doing anything: it is trusting another instead."[6] "To believe on Christ is to see and believe the all-sufficiency of His saving grace."[7]

IMPROPER PRESENTATIONS

In order to clarify the true gospel message it may be helpful to point out some of the more common perversions of it. Sometimes the message itself is distorted. Often the method by which it is presented militates against simple belief.

Many tormented souls have felt it necessary to plead with God to be merciful toward them. Painfully conscious of their own sin and their need of salvation, they have been encouraged to pray the publican's prayer: "God, be merciful to me, the sinner!" (Luke 18:13). But the gospel is the good news that God *has been* merciful to sinners and *has* provided salvation in Christ. Reconciliation with God has been provided at the cross; no one needs to ask God to provide it. Pleading for mercy evidences unbelief, either through ignorance or through lack of confidence, in the work of Christ. No one needs to plead with God for pardon because He has provided pardon already. One only needs to believe God's promise that pardon has been provided in Christ to be saved.

The old saying that "you don't get something for nothing" has led the unsaved man to conclude that the most precious of all possessions, eternal life, must certainly cost him something (and probably a great deal). That might seem right to a man, but its end is death (Prov. 14:12). Without the revelation of God's Word, man is unaware that eternal life has been paid for by someone else who offers it to him freely. Salvation is not cheap; it cost God His only Son. But it is freely offered to man as a gift. The congenital compulsion to do something for God to earn salvation has resulted in man's trying to add one or more works to the completed work of Christ. If anything needs to be added to Christ's work on the cross, then His death was not adequate in itself to affect salvation. The desire to add works to faith gives man a feeling that he has made a contribution to his own salvation. The Bible teaches that that is impossible. Adding works gives man a false sense of security and bolsters his pride by making him feel that God is in his debt to some extent and that he is equal to or even better than God (Eph. 2:8-9; Titus 3:5-6).

Other presentations of the gospel encourage the lost person to resolve to live as Christ lived and to follow His example. Books such as *The Imitation of Christ* by Thomas à Kempis have been understood to teach that one becomes a Christian by living as Christ did, obeying His teachings, and behaving as He would have behaved if He were in the professing Christian's place. Behind that idea lies the belief that anyone can become a Christian through self-discipline. Not only is that teaching un- scriptural, it is also impossible (as anyone who has attempted it can testify). A Christlike life depends on the indwelling Christ who manifests Himself through the believer. When a person trusts Christ for his eternal salvation God takes up residence in him (John 14:16-17, 23; Col. 1:27). He empowers the Christian to live a supernatural life of increasing freedom from the power of sin in his life. It is only the Holy Spirit of God who can imitate Christ in the life of a Christian (Gal. 5:16-23). To encourage anyone to try to imitate Christ is to frustrate that person and to pervert the gospel message.

Prayer has become so closely associated with becoming a Christian that some feel that a person must pray to be saved. Obviously many people who are not Christians pray. Apart from the prayer of the nonbeliever expressing trust in Christ for salvation, praying does not save anyone. Thus although prayer is useful in expressing one's faith in Christ to God, it is not prayer that saves. Only faith saves (Heb. 11:6). A person be- comes a Christian when he transfers his trust from whatever he may have been relying on for salvation to Jesus Christ and what He did on the cross. That is an act of the whole man: intellect, emotion, and will. A person may express that decision to God in prayer, but it is not necessary to do that to be saved. Prayer is certainly a worthwhile activity and should be practiced by every child of God. "Calling upon the name of the Lord" means praying to Him and expressing trust for salvation. Many people pray to God every day and trust in Him for their various needs. But it is only as a person trusts in God for eternal salvation from sin that God saves him eternally. The only prayer that God promises to hear from a nonbeliever is the prayer expressing trust in Christ for salvation (Acts 2:21).

Sometimes non-Christians are exhorted to "seek the Lord" (Isa. 55:6). That often leads to an agonizing period of prolonged praying until the "seeker" quits for one reason or another. That injunction was given to God's people, not unbelievers. The addressees needed to bring their lives into harmony with God's will and to walk with Him. The good news of the gospel is that "the Son of Man has come to seek and to save that which was lost" (Luke 19:10). When a lost person hears the gospel he does not need to seek God, he needs to believe the message of the gospel and he will be saved at that moment. It may be true that until a lost person hears the gospel he may be seeking salvation. In that case the Christian's responsibility is to explain the gospel to him, not to tell him to keep seeking God. The Christian's message to the unsaved is to "be reconciled to God." Reconciliation is possible through the work of Christ and only needs to be appropriated by faith (2 Cor. 5:18-20).

Repentance is seen by some as a separate activity that must precede believing. That idea is based on passages of Scripture that exhort people to repent and on passages that mention both repenting and believing within the same context. Repentance means to change one's mind; it does not mean to change one's life (though that should follow changing one's mind). Several times in the New Testament Israelites were called on to repent (Matt. 4:17, 10:5-6; Acts 2:38; 3:19). In those instances the Jews were being urged to change their minds with regard to their thinking concerning the Messiah and His kingdom. Jesus was the Messiah, yet many of the Jews refused to accept Him as such. His kingdom was approaching and they needed to change their minds regarding Him and their relation to Him. Only as they adopted a different attitude would it be possible for them to trust Christ and be saved. Other passages, addressed to unsaved Gentiles, call for repentance (Acts 11:18; 17:30; 20:21; 26:20; Rom. 2:4; 2 Pet. 3:9). In those passages repentance is viewed not as an act separate from believing but as the process involved in transfering one's trust to Christ. Whenever a person believes in Christ he repents, that is, he changes his mind about who Christ is and what He did. Placing confidence in Christ's death as sufficient for salvation involves changing one's mind. Repentance alone does not save, however. Saving faith involves repentance, but repentance does not necessarily involve saving faith.

Confession is also cited as a condition for salvation by some. Confession of sin is a prerequisite to salvation. If someone does not acknowledge that he is a sinner he will feel no need for salvation. The gospel is the message that Christ has paid the penalty for sin. By trusting Christ a person confesses that he is a sinner. This may be a separate act or part of the transfer of his trust. Public confession is not a condition for salvation; if it were, people who cannot speak could not be saved (Rom. 10:9-10). Public confession is the oral expression of faith in the heart. It is an important first step in bearing public testimony to one's faith, but it is not a prerequisite for salvation.

A similar condition that is often cited as a prerequisite to salvation is baptism. Like oral confession, water baptism has no part in salvation. Rather, it is a testimony to one's trust in Christ. Several texts have been understood by some to teach that belief must be accompanied by baptism to be efficacious. Acts 2:38 is one. "Repent, and let each of you be baptized in the name of Jesus Christ for the forgiveness of your sins. . . ." However, the word *for* (*eis*) may be taken as retrospective ("on the basis of") rather than prospective ("with a view to"). It is retrospective in Matthew 12:41 ("they repented *at* the preaching of Jonah"). Baptism, therefore, is commanded not as a condition of salvation but as a consequence of it.[8]

A second passage often used to teach that baptism is a necessary condition of salvation is Acts 22:16. This verse may be read in such a way that it seems to teach that baptism washes away sins. But a better translation would be "arising be baptized; wash away your sins by calling on His name" (author's translation). The washing away of sins comes as a result of calling on the name of Christ, not as a result of being baptized. Mark 16:16 has also led some to think baptism is essential to salvation. But it should be observed that baptism is not mentioned in the negative statement of the verse. Condemnation results from not believing rather than from failing to be baptized (cf. John 3:36). In that verse, as in many others, baptism is linked closely with belief because it is the God-ordained public testimony to belief that should immediately follow faith. But baptism is not a part of belief. That is clearly seen in Paul's statement that "Christ did not send me to baptize, but [strong negative, *alla*] to preach the gospel" (1 Cor. 1:17). If baptism were a part of belief Paul could not have made such a statement. The gospel and baptism are two different things.

Some today teach that in order to be saved a person must make Christ the Lord of his life. Those individuals teach that a person must surrender every area of his personality and life to the control of Jesus Christ in order to become a Christian. Although that surrender is certainly God's desire for every Christian, it is not a condition for salvation. If it were, it would be a work. Jesus is called Lord in two senses in the New Testament: Savior and Sovereign. Everyone who believes the gospel believes that Jesus is the Savior (1 Cor. 12:3). But not everyone who believes the gospel realizes that that Savior has the right to be Sovereign over his life. The child of God should also let Christ be sovereign over his life (Rom. 12:1-2), but obedience to that command is not a condition for salvation. Rather the command is addressed to Christians. All that is required for salvation is believing the gospel message.

In recent years some Christians have claimed that the gospel has not really been preached unless the needs of the whole man have been met. The Christian's responsibility is not just to preach the gospel but also to feed the hungry of the world. Often the impression is left that unless Christians feed the hungry and provide other forms of physical assistance they have not really preached the gospel to the whole man. Christians do have a responsibility to do good unto all men (Gal. 6:10), but their primary responsibility is to proclaim the good news of salvation in Christ to every creature (Matt. 28:19). Although ministering to the physical needs of people is an important ministry of the church, this is not part of the gospel message. The gospel message is that Christ died to save sinners.

Many times in Scripture men are said to be lost because they do not believe (Mark 16:16; John 3:18; 16:9; 20:30-31).

> This one work "believe" represents all a sinner can do and all a sinner must do to be saved. It is believing the record that God has given of His Son. In this record it is stated that He has entered into all the needs of our lost condition and is alive from the dead to be a living Savior to all who put their trust in Him. It is quite possible for any intelligent person to know whether he has placed such confidence in the Savior. Saving faith is a matter of personal consciousness. "I know whom I have believed." To have deposited one's eternal welfare in the hands of another is a decision of the mind so definite that it can hardly be confused with anything else. On this deposit of oneself into His saving grace depends one's eternal destiny. To add or subtract anything from this sole condition of salvation is most perilous.[9]

THE DYNAMIC OF THE GOSPEL MESSAGE

The gospel message has a power all its own. It can change the whole direction of a life and can transform character completely. It has power that no other message in all the world contains, and that power becomes effective through human instruments.

DIVINE CONVICTION

It does not take much time for the witnessing Christian to discover that he does not have the natural ability to bring others to faith in Christ. What is so clear and winsome to him is totally unappreciated by his unsaved friends (1 Cor. 2:14). He becomes convinced that Satan has blinded the minds of the unbelieving (2 Cor. 4:3-4), and he realizes his complete dependence on God to open blind eyes (Acts 26:18; Eph. 1:18) and to draw the sinner to Himself (John 6:44; 1 Cor. 12:3).

The Holy Spirit's ministry in drawing sinners to the Savior is threefold. He convicts the world of sin, righteousness, and judgment (John 16:8-11). He convicts or convinces unbelievers by illuminating their minds more than by creating a feeling of remorse. He enlightens unbelievers with respect to these three truths.

The Holy Spirit first "convinces" unbelievers that they are sinners. In particular, he brings conviction for the sin of not believing on Christ. Men face condemnation because they have rejected Christ (John 3:18; 1 John 5:10-12).

Second, the Holy Spirit convicts the unbeliever of righteousness. In convicting of righteousness the Holy Spirit enables the natural man to see that Jesus Christ is the Righteous One. The resurrection and ascension of Christ prove His righteousness, and His death is the ground of salvation. How man can be righteous before God is the great question of life. That question is answered in the gospel. Christ "who knew no sin [was made] to be sin on our behalf, that we might become the righteousness of God in Him" (2 Cor. 5:21). Christ took man's place and paid man's penalty. Now His righteousness is imputed to man.

Third, the Holy Spirit convicts the unbeliever of judgment. The Holy Spirit brings conviction of judgment to the natural man by enabling him to see that sin has been judged on the cross. Condemnation for sin has been removed. The prince of this world who controls sin has been defeated, his works have been ruined, and he has been dethroned (John 12:31; Col. 2:13-15).

The Holy Spirit seeks to clarify the significance of the finished work of Christ on the cross which Satan has obscured. The unregenerate man does not need to understand the atonement in all of its aspects to be saved. But he must understand enough of it to turn from his self-effort, to cling in intelligent faith to Christ, and to believe that what Christ has done is sufficient for his need.

The immediate instrument that the Holy Spirit uses to enlighten the blind soul is the Word of God. The written Word of God gives light (Psalm 119:130). It is the sword the Spirit uses to perform life-saving surgery on the soul (Heb. 4:12). As the Word of God is applied skillfully to the natural man, the Spirit brings conviction of the truth of the gospel.

HUMAN INTERCESSION

The sovereign Savior has subjected the convicting work of the Holy Spirit to the prayers of believer-priests. Every believer is a priest unto God and has the right and responsibility to intercede for man with God (Rom. 8:26-27; Heb. 10:19-20; 1 Pet. 2:5, 9; Rev. 1:6). God required purity of His priests under the

Mosaic Law, and He requires the same purity of His believer-priests in this dispensation. Only the ministry of pure priests can be acceptable to God. As Chafer has written, "All evangelism must begin with prayer. And no human service, or device, can take the place of the intercession of a priest who is cleansed, and 'acceptable to God.' "[10] Even though the gospel message is clearly and accurately presented, there may be no convicting by the Holy Spirit without prayer (John 14:14; cf. Luke 11:9; John 15:7; 16:23-24). Prayer is a cause and condition of God's working in the hearts of unbelievers. The Holy Spirit convicts and illuminates the unsaved in response to the intercession of believers who are functioning as priests. That aspect of evangelism is sadly lacking today. Believers are tempted to place too much confidence in what they say to men or in how they say it. There needs to be more emphasis on what believers say to God about men and how they say it.

HUMAN WITNESS

The importance of intercessory prayer should not obscure the responsibility of the believer to herald the gospel message to every creature (Matt. 28:19). But what has been pointed out should illustrate the importance of talking to God before witnessing to men. Though the leading of the Holy Spirit is very difficult to analyze (John 3:8), it is real. In sharing the gospel message with others, care must be taken to follow His leading. Unless the Spirit indicates otherwise, a believer can be certain that God would have him herald the gospel to every creature (Matt. 28:19). But this is not to say that one should force each individual to make a decision every time the gospel is presented. Such a practice can do great damage to the souls of men who have not yet been prepared by the Spirit to believe the gospel. One should press for a decision only when one is led to do so by the Holy Spirit. This requires sensitivity to the Spirit's leading and an attitude of complete dependence on Him since He is the one who effects salvation.

Whenever the gospel message is proclaimed, care must be taken to present the message as clearly and as simply as possible. The tendency of many earnest Christians is to say too much, to add conditions that do not apply, or to confuse the unbeliever with prolonged and complicated explanations.

There is no simple, painless method of evangelism. The rebirth of souls involves travail on the part of those who are laborers together with God. God is the initiator in evangelism, and believers need to work with Him by following His guidance in particular conversations and by desiring with Him that men might be saved (Matt. 10:25; John 7:7; 15:18-19; 17:18; Rom. 8:16-18; 2 Tim. 2:11-12; 1 Pet. 4:12-13).

EFFECTS OF THE GOSPEL MESSAGE

By its very nature the gospel demands a response. It is a message that one *must* either believe or disbelieve. A person cannot simply listen and remain neutral. When he goes on his way he has already made a decision. The decision to "think it over" is really a decision to continue in unbelief since every person is in the position of not trusting Christ until he believes the gospel (John 3:18). It is only when he hears the gospel that he has the opportunity to choose to believe and trust Christ. Consequently, whenever the gospel is presented to the unsaved predictable results follow.

EFFECT ON THOSE WHO DO NOT BELIEVE

To those who are perishing through unbelief the gospel is like the odor of a dead body (2 Cor. 2:14-16). Although it holds out the promise of deliverance, it reminds them of a terrible fate to come. Those who reject the gospel are "perishing." Unless they take the spiritual antidote they will die in their sins.

Every time an unbeliever hears the gospel one of two things happens. He is either moved toward belief or he is moved further from it. The reaction depends on his choice, and God holds him responsible (John 3:36; 5:40). The sun affects different substances in different ways: it melts wax, but it hardens clay. Such is the effect of the gospel on those who hear it.

EFFECT ON THOSE WHO BELIEVE

God brings about many changes in the life of one who believes the gospel. Unfortunately, those changes are generally unappreciated by believers. It is the lack of understanding the work of God in the believer that has resulted in many perversions of the gospel and has caused much uncertainty with regard to salvation. Some of those changes need to be examined in more detail.

Salvation. The word that encompasses all that happens when a person trusts Christ is *salvation.* Basically this term means that the believer has been delivered from condemnation unto righteousness. There are several aspects of salvation expounded in Scripture that explain its richness and depth.

The penalty of sin is set aside when one trusts Christ. The believer accepts Christ's payment on his behalf and is consequently no longer under the condemnation of the Law. Judicially he is a free man (Eph. 1:7; Heb. 2:9; 1 John 2:2).

The believer is also declared to be righteous by God. Not only is his guilt removed, but he also receives a positive standing before God that makes him acceptable. The righteousness of Christ is imputed to the believing sinner (Isa. 41:10; 42:6; Rom. 3:21-22; 4:1-6; 10:3-4; 2 Cor. 5:21; Phil. 3:8-9).

New life is given to the believer. This is more than eternal existence in the presence of God after death. It is the life of God Himself, which He imparts to the believer at the moment of salvation and which the believer possesses forever thereafter (John 5:24; 10:17-18; 1 John 5:11-13).

God Himself indwells the believer when he trusts Christ. The indwelling Christ enables the believer to experience deliverance from the power of sin as well as from the penalty of sin (2 Cor. 4:10; 13:5; Gal. 2:20; Col. 1:27). The indwelling Spirit is present to provide the power to overcome spiritual enemies (Rom. 8:9; 1 Cor. 6:19; Gal. 4:6).

A believer becomes part of the church (the Body of Christ) through the baptism of the Holy Spirit the moment he believes the gospel. Through that baptism the Christian is united to Christ and to all other believers in a union that is closer than any human relationship (1 Cor. 6:17; 12:13).

A believer becomes a priest before God when he is saved. This standing gives him access into the presence of God to offer sacrifices and to intercede on behalf of others (1 Pet. 2:5, 9). Christ as the great High Priest opened the way for believers to enter into the presence of God by offering His own blood as a sacrifice for sin.

A believer becomes the object of Christ's intercession and advocacy when he is saved. Christ prays constantly for the believer's safety and security (Rom. 8:33-34; Heb. 7:25; 9:24). When a Christian sins Christ acts as his advocate with the Father. As such He secures forgiveness for present sins on the basis of His atonement (1 John 2:1-12).[11]

Riches of grace. In addition to the major aspects of salvation mentioned above, God showers His children with boundless blessings the moment they turn to Him in faith. Chafer expounded thirty-three such blessings in his *Systematic Theology.* Believers are said to be in the eternal plan of God; redeemed; reconciled; related to God through propitiation; forgiven all trespasses; vitally cojoined to Christ for the judgment of the old man "unto a new walk;" free from the Law; children of God; adopted; acceptable to God by Jesus Christ; justified; made nigh; delivered from the power of darkness; translated into the kingdom of the Son of His love; on the Rock, Christ Jesus; a gift from God the Father to Christ; circumcised in Christ; partakers of the holy and royal priesthood; a chosen generation, a holy nation, and a peculiar people; heavenly citizens; of the family and household of God; in the fellowship of the saints; partners in heavenly association; having access to God; within the much more care of God; His inheritance; the inheritance of the saints; light in the Lord; vitally united to the Father, the Son, and the Holy Spirit; blessed with the earnest or first-fruits of the Spirit; glorified; complete in Him; and possessing every spiritual blessing.[12]

Assurance. Because salvation is based on believing that what God has said is true, every Christian can and should have the assurance that he is saved. Yet many professing Christians regard such assurance as an evidence of pride. Those individuals say they *hope* to be saved. Such an attitude may betray unbelief in the heart and may reveal a person who is trusting in his own good works rather than in the finished work of Christ. God has said that when one trusts in Christ alone he has eternal life (John 6:47). To doubt one's salvation, then, really means doubting the Word of God. That is not humility but unbelief. Christ said that "the one who comes to Me I will certainly not cast out" (John 6:37). The apostle John wrote his gospel that believers might know that they have eternal life (John 20:30-31). He gave extended attention to this subject in his first epistle (1 John 5:9-13). The believer's assurance of salvation is not based on his feelings or on his faithfulness; it is grounded on the promises of God. God wants all of His children to be sure of their salvation (Heb. 6:11; 10:22). Until a believer is able to trust God's promises regarding the security of his salvation, he will not be able to advance very far in Christian maturity. But when he realizes that his salvation is secure he can devote his energies to worshiping and serving Christ rather than to wondering and worrying about his eternal destiny.[13]

CONCLUSION

The importance of understanding what the Scriptures teach with regard to the Christian gospel cannot be overemphasized. The eternal destiny of millions of people depends, humanly speaking, on the church's correct understanding and accurate presentation of this message. Its dynamic will be observed and its effects realized only as believers herald the true gospel of the grace of God.

The purity of the gospel message was of great concern to the apostle Paul. He called down a curse on anyone who would distort it, and then repeated himself for added emphasis (Gal. 1:7-9). May the gospel of the grace of God ever be presented in its unadulterated simplicity to the glory of God who "so loved the world, that He gave His only begotten Son, that whoever believes in Him should not perish, but have eternal life" (John 3:16).

NOTES

1. *Theological Dictionary of the New Testament*, s.v. "euangelion," by Gerhard Friedrich, 2:721-37.
2. Lewis Sperry Chafer, *Salvation* (Philadelphia: Sunday School Times, 1926), pp. 15-30.
3. Henry A. Ironside, *In the Heavenlies* (New York: Loizeaux, n.d.), p. 76.
4. Lewis Sperry Chafer, *The Ephesian Letter* (Grand Rapids: Dunham, 1935), p. 47.

5. Lewis Sperry Chafer, *He That is Spiritual* (Findlay, O.: Dunham, 1918), p. 177.
6. Lewis Sperry Chafer, *Major Bible Themes* (Grand Rapids: Zondervan, 1926), pp. 157-58.
7. Chafer, *Salvation*, p. 50.
8. A. T. Robertson, *Word Pictures in the New Testament*, 6 vols. (Nashville: Broadman, 1930), 3:34-36.
9. Chafer, *Salvation*, p. 45.
10. Lewis Sperry Chafer, *True Evangelism* (Wheaton, Ill.: Van Kampen, 1919), p. 88.
11. Ibid., pp. 27-50.
12. Lewis Sperry Chafer, *Systematic Theology*, 8 vols. (Dallas: Dallas Theological Seminary, 1948), 3:235-65.
13. Chafer, *Salvation*, pp. 78-85.

14

Authority in the Church

Robert L. Saucy

R ecent interest in the nature and mission of the church has
spurred a renewed investigation of the New Testament in
an attempt to find a biblical pattern and norm for church life and
structure. One of the outgrowths of that desire to tie contemporary church experience to biblical moorings is the increasing
movement toward leadership in the local church by a plurality of
elders. Further impetus for that structure has come from the
breakdown of the clergy-laity dichotomy and the recognition
that the ministry of the church belongs to all members. Included
in that concept is the giftedness and functioning of some so-
called laity in the ministry of leadership.

The move toward leadership in the church by a plurality of
elders has given rise to the question of authority. Traditionally
this issue has been practically ignored. Church constitutions are
often vague as to the place of final authority. Functionally, the
issue depends more on the particular personality and effectiveness of the pastor and other leaders than on any formal church

ROBERT L. SAUCY, (A.B., Westmont College; Th.M., Th.D., Dallas Theological
Seminary) is professor of systematic theology at Talbot Theological Seminary,
La Mirada, California.

law. The search for a biblically based ecclesiology, however, has called for a more definitive explanation of the place of authority in the local church.

All agree that the only valid ultimate authority is Christ, the head of the church. However, the question of authority in the church concerns the functional application of Christ's authority as it is expressed in the local assembly. Although there are many facets to this question, the final issue is whether or not that authority rests with the elders or with the church body as a whole. The corollary question with either view is, What is the nature of the authority of the leaders?

THE TRANSMISSION OF CHRIST'S AUTHORITY

In a search for the solution to the problem of authority in the church it seems best not to begin with specific texts concerning the authority of leadership or of the church body. Instead one should begin by examining the broader concept of the ultimate nature and source of authority involved in the church. Since Christ is the Lord of His church, all agree that any valid human authority in the contemporary church can only be an expression of His authority. The solution to church authority thus lies in determining the means of communication and implementation of Christ's authority in the functioning of the church today.

THE APOSTLES

The first link in the chain of authority from Christ to the church is the apostles. The ministry of Jesus Himself was characterized by power and authority. On one occasion Mark records the amazement of the people who asked, "What is this? A new teaching with authority!" (1:27). Christ's authority was expressed both in "deed and word" (Luke 24:19). His actions paralleled His teaching. He acted with power and authority, demonstrating His lordship over evil spirits, diseases, and the forces of nature (Luke 4:32-36).

In commissioning His disciples and sending them forth later as apostles, Jesus communicated His same authority to them. That is already indicated in the historical mission of the disciples during the Lord's earthly ministry. Matthew records that

Jesus ". . . gave them authority over unclean spirits, to cast them out, and to heal every kind of disease and every kind of sickness" (Matt. 10:1; cf. Luke 9:1; 10:19). That authority enabled them to perform the same ministry as that of their Lord. They were to "preach, saying, 'The kingdom of heaven is at hand.' Heal the sick, raise the dead, cleanse the lepers, cast out demons . . .'" (Matt. 10:7-8; cf. 9:35).

As a result of that bestowal of authority, the disciples went out in the place of Jesus. "The one who listens to you listens to Me, and the one who rejects you rejects Me; and he who rejects Me rejects the One who sent Me" (Luke 10:16). According to that statement, a similar relationship existed between the disciples and Christ as existed between Christ and the One who sent Him. As He was given authority to represent His Father, so the disciples were commissioned with His authority to represent Him. The same transmission of authority lies behind the so-called Great Commission of the disciples by the resurrected Lord. Pointing to His universal authority in heaven and earth which was manifested in the resurrection, Jesus sent the disciples out with His authority to continue His ministry on earth (Matt. 28:18-20).

The book of Acts finds the apostles fulfilling their commission as they minister with the authority of Christ. They performed signs and wonders, healed the sick (3:1-10; 5:16), cast out evil spirits (5:16; 16:16-18), and raised the dead (9:36-43; 20:9-12). But above all they proclaimed the Word of God, witnessing to the mighty acts of God in Christ and interpreting their meaning with authority.

The authority of the apostles, however, rested solely on their commission from Christ. When asked, "By what power, or in what name, have you done this?" their answer was clear—"by the name of Jesus Christ the Nazarene" (Acts 4:7, 10). Their works were always performed in the name of Jesus (e.g. Acts 3:6). Likewise their word was authoritative only because it could be identified with the Word of God through the inspiration of the Spirit (cf. 1 Thess. 2:13; 2 Pet. 3:2).

The apostles thus stand as the first link in the transmission of the ministry and authority of Christ to His church. Because they were personally commissioned as apostles by Christ, they represent His authority in the church in a unique manner. Both personally and in their writings the apostles exercised Christ's authority over His people.[1] Because they are unique in their position as apostles, no person or persons in the church can be their successors. Thus in their particular position as authoritative representatives, they stand as foundational to the church (Eph. 2:20).

THE SCRIPTURES

Although the apostles have no personal successors who represent Christ in exactly the same way, Christ's authority over the church as exercised by the apostles does not cease. It continues in the written apostolic traditions preserved in the canonical writings of Scripture. The apostles were not only entrusted with the Old Testament Scriptures, which they imposed on the church as the authoritative Word of God, but their own teaching added to that tradition "whether by word of mouth or by letter" (2 Thess. 2:15). The portion of the apostolic tradition that the Lord deemed necessary as a norm for the church in succeeding history was inscripturated as a permanent deposit of apostolic authority.

The connection between the Scriptures and the authority of Christ is made all the more evident when it is recognized that the living Lord is the voice of Scripture. The Scriptures witness to Him (John 5:39), and He is the subject of their revelation. It is through the Bible that Christ makes Himself known as the Father's authoritative Word to the church. What the apostle John makes explicit in the letters of the exalted Lord to the seven churches of Asia Minor (Rev. 2 — 3) is also implicity true of the message of all Scripture. In them the living voice of God speaks to His church with full authority (cf. Heb. 1:1-2; 4:12).

THE HOLY SPIRIT

This living, authoritative voice of Christ in His Word is made real through the presence of the Spirit. Jesus foretold of the coming of the Spirit to continue His teaching through the apostles (John 16:12-15). The Spirit accomplished this as He revealed the message that the apostles spoke and passed down to the church (cf. 1 Cor. 2:12-13). However, the Holy Spirit's work did not cease when the Word was deposited in the church. He remains as the presence of the ascended Christ in the midst of His church, continually desirous of holding conversation with His church through the Word.

HUMAN LEADERS

The authority over the church that Christ gave to the apostles has continued through the Scriptures. Those remain as the continuing voice of that apostolic authority over the church. The Roman Catholic Church has retained a continuing authoritative human voice in addition to the Scriptures by holding to the concept of apostolic succession. But most Protestants and all evangelicals reject the concept of apostolic succession and instead insist on the supreme authority of the Word of God in the church. This does not yet, however, bring one to the actual functional authority within the church. The Scriptures exert their authority only as they are received, understood, and applied in the lives of people. The question of functional authority in God's plan, therefore, is the question of who has the final responsibility of interpreting and applying the Word with authority in the church.

CHRIST'S AUTHORITY IN THE LOCAL CHURCH

It is evident in the New Testament that God has placed in the church those with special responsibility to serve as leaders. He has also given to the church those with special ability to teach His Word. Moreover, the church is exhorted to obey those whom God has placed in positions of leadership. Such commands lead some to conclude that the responsibility of imposing the Word with final authority has been placed in the hands of the leadership of the church. Even the imagery of leaders as shepherds, it is sometimes argued, supports this conclusion since shepherds lead the flock and not vice versa.

Such biblical teaching concerning church leadership must be incorporated in any discussion on authority. However, there is much evidence concerning the nature and ministry of the church that argues for the conclusion that final authority rests not with the leadership but with the entire community of believers.

The Continuing Apostolic Ministry and Authority

As previously noted, the apostles were commissioned to continue Christ's ministry, and they were endowed with the authority to carry it out. Although their authoritative ministry in a unique sense continues in the deposit of Scripture, there is another sense in which it has been passed on to succeeding generations of the church. Those who continue to exercise leadership in the local church may be said to be successors of the apostolic authority. Of course, they do not exercise apostolic authority in an absolute sense since their authority is not based on the special commission of the risen Lord. Yet in a functional sense they are intrusted with communicating the authoritative commands of the Lord through teaching and modeling His Word in the church. The question of authority, then, relates to the identity of the apostolic successors. Are they a special group of leaders in the church or are they the church as a whole?

If the so-called Great Commission is accepted as the encapsulation of the apostolic ministry (i.e., to make disciples of all nations), then the New Testament makes it clear that that ministry is passed to the church at large. After acknowledging that the unique status of the apostles was not transmissible, Manson rightly argues that the continuation of the apostolic function does continue within the church.

> What is left? So far as I can see, three things: the need of the world, the call of Christ, and the tradition of His ministry in the flesh in Galilee and Judaea and in the Church which is His Body throughout the world. And, so far as I can see, it is the Church that succeeds to these things. The Church is apostolic because she is called by Christ and empowered and instructed by Christ to go and make disciples of the nations.[2]

Manson buttresses his conclusion by demonstrating that the ministry of the local church today is, in reality, the same twofold ministry of the apostles: "to proclaim the Kingdom to those who are still outside and to manifest the Kingdom in its own community life; to declare Christ to the world and to show the Lord's life and death and risen life within its own borders; to convert the non-Christian and to 'edify the Christian.' "[3]

The implementation of that twofold ministry in the early

church involved the exposition of the Word, the exhortation to service, and the establishment of the sacraments. Although some served as leaders in those functions, it is evident from the New Testament that those ministries belonged to the church as a whole. The assembly at Corinth, for example, is portrayed as one in which the Word could be ministered by a variety of individuals; in fact, each individual is a potential minister for the edification of the whole. "When you assemble, each one has a psalm, has a teaching, has a revelation, has a tongue, has an interpretation" (1 Cor. 14:26). The responsibility of the ministry of the Word both when the church is gathered as well as individually outside the actual congregation is seen further in the general exhortations to teach and admonish "one another" (e.g. Rom. 15:14; Col. 3:16; 1 Thess. 5:14).

The apostolic ministry also included the proclamation of the Word to those outside the church. Again the task was universal. All were called to "proclaim the excellencies of Him who has called you out of darkness into His marvelous light" (1 Pet. 2:9; cf. Matt. 5:13-16), and to be "ready to make a defense" to anyone who might ask them for an account of their hope (1 Pet. 3:15). The example of the early church gives clear expression to the belief that the ministry of preaching the Word to the world belonged not to a particular group but the whole church (Acts 8:4; 1 Thess. 1:8).

The ministry of service in helping and caring for one another likewise fell to the church body. There were those who were charged with leadership and administration (e.g. Acts 6:1-6), but the imperatives for such service were addressed to all (e.g. Gal. 6:2; 1 Thess. 5:14).

Finally, the ministry of baptism and the Lord's Supper is never exclusively linked to any office in the church. For the sake of order it was usually performed by those who were recognized as leaders. However, the right to perform those sacraments is never limited to those leaders. The New Testament pictures various individuals performing those ministries and makes it evident that the right to perform them belongs to the entire church (cf. Acts 8:12; 9:17-18; 1 Cor. 1:14-17). This is supported by the fact that the Great Commission (which included the command to baptize) was given to the entire church.[4]

The universal apostolic ministry of the church is also verified in the doctrine of the priesthood of all believers. All believers are priests because they all have equal access to God through Christ, the great High Priest, and because they are all endowed with the Holy Spirit. Based on that relationship to God, priests have various ministries to perform. Spiritual sacrifices of praise, good works, and personal devotion are incumbent on every church member (1 Pet. 2:5; Heb. 13:15-16; Rom. 12:1). The New Testament believer-priest (as his Old Testament counterpart) is also responsible for the ministry of the Word and for the administration of ceremonial rites that proclaim the Word in symbolic actions. In the New Testament those symbolic actions include baptism and the Lord's Supper. In short, any service that represents God before the outside world or that ministers to other believers is a function of the priesthood. There is no aspect of that ministry that rests on a special group; it belongs to the entire church.

When the apostles were charged with the responsibility of ministry, they were also given authority to carry it out. It seems difficult not to argue the same for the church. Where the Lord of the church commands and equips for ministry, He gives authority for ministry. Such is, in reality, the only authority that can be spoken of in the church. If the ministry belongs finally to the church, then in some ultimate sense Christ's authority must be communicated there as well.[5]

THE HOLY SPIRIT AND AUTHORITY

The rationale behind the ultimate authority in the church lies in the universal endowment of the Spirit. As Christ lives among His people through the presence of the Holy Spirit, so His authority is manifest through that same Spirit. At least two ramifications relative to church authority flow from the truth that all believers have the Spirit: (1) They are all taught by the Spirit, and (2) they are all equipped with a spiritual *charisma* (i.e. "gift") for ministry.

TEACHING ALL TRUTH

Against a background of apparently competing theologies

within the group to which he addressed his first epistle, the apostle John denounces the dependence on special leaders in the church for authoritative teaching. He writes, "But you have an anointing from the Holy One, and you all know. . . . and you have no need for anyone to teach you; but . . . His anointing teaches you about all things . . ." (1 John 2:20, 27). Although some commentators see a combination of the Word and the Spirit in the "anointing,"[6] it is preferable to see John focusing on the Spirit that Christ has given to His people to instruct them in the truth of God.[7] The Spirit of truth had brought the Word to them and had authenticated it in their experience (cf. 1 Cor. 2:4-5). He now continues that ministry by giving them inner witness to the truth, enabling them to accept it as such and to reject the false. That in no way negates the necessity of teachers for the church, but it does give the church the ability and authority to test all things, including teachers (1 John 4:1). Similarly, the Apostle Paul tells the Thessalonians that they are "taught by God" (1 Thess. 4:9), undoubtedly a reference to the ministry of the Spirit to whom reference had just been made (v. 8). Because of the Spirit's ministry, the church as a whole could be charged with the responsibility to "examine everything carefully" (1 Thess. 5:21).

The Holy Spirit is the final teacher of truth in the church. When this thought is combined with the reality that the Word is the expression of the risen Lord's will for His church, it becomes apparent that the application of authority belongs ultimately to those who are responsible for evaluating all things by the truth of the Word. That responsibility, then, belongs to the church by virtue of the universal teaching ministry of the Spirit.

EQUIPPING FOR MINISTRY

The second, and perhaps even more fundamental, relationship between the Spirit and authority in the church is seen in His universal equipping of each member of the church for ministry. To each is granted a *charisma* by the Spirit (1 Cor. 12:4, 11). As Küng notes, it was that reality that provided the primary authority in ministry.

It is from their charisms, not from the community and not

> from the apostle, not even from their own decision, that the individuals responsible for all these varied ministries derive their authority. . . . Submission is due to those who labour, not because of their appointment to a particular ministry, but because they are actually seen to perform that ministry. . . . Authority in the community is derived not from the holding of a certain rank, not from a special tradition, not from old age or long membership of the community but from the performance of a ministry in the Spirit. The obedience of all is due to God, Christ, the Spirit; only a limited, and never a unilateral obedience is due to other men in the community. The consequence of the obedience of all to God, Christ and the Spirit is voluntary and *mutual* submission, the voluntary ministry of all to all, voluntary obedience to the difference [sic] charisms of others.[8]

The truth that each member of the church is equipped for ministry by the Lord through the Spirit would point again to a certain diffusion of authority throughout the entire church. To be sure, certain gifts are given for leadership within the body; but these cannot possess final authority for they are dependent on the ministries of others who perform their services through the authoritative *charismata* of the Spirit. In an interesting discussion of authority in the church, McKenzie notes the interrelatedness between the authority of those with special functions of leadership and the authority of the church as a whole.

> If the Spirit is present and operative in the whole church, authority, as a work of the Spirit, must be the function of the whole Church. This does not mean that all the members of the Church have offices of authority, but that each member actively cooperates in the function of authority according to his own charisma. . . . Authority is one of the functions of the Spirit which needs the other functions in order that the function of authority itself may be fulfilled. . . . In the Church direction and motivation is from the Spirit to all the functions of the body; authority is not and cannot be absolute, for authority too, has its interdependence.[9]

In the truth of the *charismata* of the Spirit there is a dimension of authority in which each member of the community shares. This does not suggest the autonomous, authoritative operation of each of the spiritually gifted within the body. Rather, there is an interplay between the authority of the individual and the body as a whole. What Dunn says concerning leaders could be applicable to all expressions of spiritual gifts. He notes that the community is responsible "to recognize and acknowledge the manifest charismatic authority of those who do not spare themselves in the service of the church and to encourage them in these more regular ministries (1 Cor. 16:15-18; 1 Thess. 5:13-22; cf. Phil. 2:29-30)."[10] There was, according to Dunn, an "ongoing dialectic . . . between the individual with his word or act containing its authority within itself as charisma, and the community with its reponsibility to test and evaluate all charismata. . . ."[11]

It is sometimes argued that the nature of a "charismatic" ministry with its inherent authority based on the actual exercise of each *charisma* is contrary to the authority derived from the so-called institutional offices.[12] Although history does reveal a rapid decline in the various church offices to the place where the office itself endowed authority without concern for the genuine possession and ministry of spiritual gifts by the holder, there need not be any antithesis between charisma and office. Campenhausen aptly states:

> There is . . . no need to assume that office as such . . . must be set in diametric opposition to the Spirit. . . . It is not unspiritual just as long as it remains obedient to the Spirit of Christ, and performs that service of the Gospel of Christ for which it was appointed. Only where this original evangelical relation is inverted, and the authority of the official as such is made absolute, is the primitive Christian concept of the Church abandoned. . . .[13]

THE MINISTRY OF CHRIST AND AUTHORITY

The truth of the apostolic ministry continuing in the church through the presence of the indwelling Spirit leads finally to the recognition that Christ Himself is active in His church. The apostle Paul could ask the churches to follow his example not because of himself, but because Christ was displayed in his life. "Be imitators of me," he wrote to the Corinthians, "just as I also am of Christ" (1 Cor. 11:1). He commends the Thessalonians, declaring, "You also became imitators of us and of the Lord" (1 Thess. 1:6). Banks notes that this display of Christ in the

lives of the believers ". . . is why Christians are to submit to one
another in the community: each is the bearer to the other, in
some degree, of the Word and life of Christ. All, as Luther so
beautifully expressed it, are 'to be sort of Christ to one
another. . . .' "[14]

Relating the fact of Christ's ministry in the church to the
question of authority leads to the conclusion that the authority
of Christ is manifest through the church as a community. The
valid ministry of every believer is in reality an expression of
Christ's ministry with His authority. Thus the will of Christ for
the Body can only be expressed collectively.

The significance of the presence of Christ in the church with
regard to authority is illustrated in the instructions of the apostle concerning the discipline of the incestuous man in Corinth
(1 Cor. 5). The apostle cites the authority on which this action
is to be based in verse 4. "In the name of our Lord Jesus, when
you are assembled, and I with you in spirit, with the power of
our Lord Jesus. . . ." With reference to that statement, Goguel
explains the apostle's concept of authority.

> He [Paul] begins by censuring the Church for its slackness in
> taking measures to deal with it. This shows that in his eyes the
> Church, i.e. in fact the assembly of the faithful, possessed disci-
> plinary powers resembling those to which Paul himself laid
> claim as an apostle. Paul was not vacillating in his thought be-
> tween an aristocractic or even monarchial conception of author-
> ity in the Church and a democratic one. It was, if one may use the
> word, christocratic. The apostle based this authority on the
> charismatic gift of apostleship which Christ had conferred upon
> him, and from Christ also the assembly of the Church derived its
> power, whose name was invoked when it opened. Under the
> inspiration of the Spirit of Christ, which he himself possesses,
> Paul, absent in the body but present in the spirit, could know
> beforehand what decision the Corinthian assembly would make
> gathered together under the invocation of the name of the Lord.[15]

True authority in the church is indeed "christocratic" as
Goguel notes. Since Christ not only lives but also carries on His
ministry through all believers, it must be concluded that only
the church together, and not a particular group of leaders, can
finally express that authority.

THE CHURCH AND AUTHORITY

The church as a whole is the successor to the ministry of Christ and the apostles. It is universally equipped by the Lord of the church to carry on that ministry, which is nothing less than the revelation of Christ Himself. The final authority of Christ is communicated to the Body through all members. This is not to deny the ministry of authoritative leadership within the Body. It is to say, however, that such leadership is not the ultimate voice of the Lord over the Body, but is in the final sense responsible to the Body.

This conclusion can be supported by an examination of the actual experience of the early church. As noted at the beginning of this article, the New Testament evidence is not decisively explicit. It must be remembered that the church as it is described in the New Testament was in its foundational era. The apostles, as bearers of a unique authority, were still present. Care must be exercised to distinguish that which is normative and permanent from that which belongs peculiarly to the initiatory era. However, several instances where the church as a whole did exercise final authority are apparent in the New Testament record.

The exercise of authority by the Corinthian church in the matter of discipline has already been noted. All of the other references to discipline reveal the same authority residing in the church. Jesus explicitly views the church as the final court (Matt. 18:15-17). Likewise, the apostle Paul, although giving instruction on what should be done, calls on the churches to execute discipline (Rom. 16:17; 1 Cor. 5:5; 2 Thess. 2:6, 14-15). "In this," Schweizer notes, "Paul is obviously striving to establish the Church as the real bearer of responsibility."[16] Exceptions to that pattern appear only where the apostle or his delegated authorities are forced to take action themselves (1 Tim. 1:20; cf. Tit. 3:10).

The church as a whole also has final responsibility and authority in matters of doctrine and life. The church at large is to pass judgment on what is taught (cf. 1 John 4:1). It is to be on guard against false teachers (Col. 2:8) and must reject them regardless of their position (Gal. 1:8-9). Failure to do so leads to censure by the Lord of the church (Rev. 2:14-20). The right of judgment extends finally to "everything" (1 Thess. 5:18). The fact that all of the New Testament epistles, with the exception of the pastorals, are addressed to the churches is certainly to be understood in harmony with those exhortations. The writers view the communities of believers as ultimately responsible for carrying out their teachings.

An interesting instance of the interplay of responsibility between leaders and people is seen in the Jerusalem Council (Acts 15). The meeting is instigated by "the brethren" (vv. 1-2), a probable reference to the church at large. Paul and Barnabas are "sent on their way by the church" (v. 3). They are received in Jerusalem "by the church and the apostles and the elders" (v. 4). According to verse 6, "the apostles and the elders" take up the doctrinal matter. But apparently the congregation was also present, for "the multitude . . . were listening to Barnabas and Paul" (v. 12). They agreed with the apostles and elders to send representatives to Antioch with Paul and Barnabas (v. 22). There is also considerable textual evidence for including "the brethren" with the apostles and elders in the greeting of the letter (v. 23). Meyer suggests that the additional words are genuine and that they were omitted as a result of later hierarchical feeling.[17] Be that as it may, the church is again involved as the letter is delivered to the entire assembly at Antioch (v. 30).

In the Jerusalem Council the apostles and elders assumed their proper position of leadership in the discussion of the matter, and in all probability they initiated the concluding proposal. The final action, however, was not taken without the approval of "the whole church" (v. 22). Although it is impossible to determine from the incident the specific relationship between all parties (and even though the presence of the apostles adds a dimension not reproducible in contemporary churches), this instance can readily be harmonized with the concept of the ultimate authority of the church.

The predominant evidence in the New Testament also seems to indicate that the choice of those who served in official capacities was made by the congregation. Although the final decision was made by casting lots, the assembly put forward the two candidates to take the place of Judas (Acts 1:23). The seven chosen to oversee the care of widows were selected by the congregation (Acts 6:3-5). Similarly, the church sent out and received messengers (Acts 11:22; 14:27; 15:3-4; 1 Cor. 16:3; 2 Cor. 8:19). Although the churches did not assist in the appointment of elders by the apostles and their representatives (Acts 14:23; Tit. 1:5), that should not immediately be interpreted as indicating that elders were only selected by other elders. It must be noted that those instances pertain to the founding of new churches and, it might be argued, are not normative for established churches. Moreover, those passages can be interpreted as including the congregation in the process of appointment. The same Greek word (katastēsō) used with reference to Titus "appointing" elders is also used for the appointment of the seven in Acts 6 (cf. v. 3 "put in charge"). Since in the latter case the apostles' appointment meant commissioning those whom the church had chosen, such might also have been the procedure with Titus. The argument that leaders are more capable of recognizing the spiritual qualifications of potential candidates for ecclesiastical office (1 Tim. 3; Titus 1) flounders when one examines the requirements for the seven chosen in Acts 6. The church was entrusted with the responsibility of finding those "of good reputation, full of the Spirit and of wisdom" (v. 3). The qualifications for elders and deacons listed in the pastorals are surely no more difficult to apply.

It might be mentioned further that the *Didache,* a manual of the early church usually dated near the close of the first century, contains explicit instructions for the congregation to choose its leaders. "Appoint for yourselves therefore bishops and deacons worthy of the Lord. . . ."[18] Clement, in his first letter to the Corinthians, is the first individual to state clearly that the appointment of presbyters should be "by other eminent men" with only "the approval of the whole church."[19] It should be noted, however, that Clement had already moved away from the New Testament pattern of church leadership and had adopted a strong distinction between the laity and clergy. He felt that the clergy performed a cultic ministry in direct succession to the Old Testament priests.[20]

The thrust of the evidence from the New Testament church

experience thus portrays a church that bears final responsibility and authority for its life as a community. Although certain Scriptures are capable of other interpretations, none explicitly teach the contrary principle of the final authority of a person or group of persons.

Final authority in the church resides with the person or persons who have the ultimate responsibility to express the authoritative ministry of the Lord of the church in the midst of His people. If that is a valid way to state the issue, then the New Testament points to the church as a whole rather than to a special person or group of persons as the locus of that authority. The nature of the church yields that conclusion in that each member is endowed with the Spirit to express the living presence of Christ and to participate in His ministry with His authority. The practice of the church corresponds to that reality in that the New Testament, through various examples and instructions, places the final responsibility for doctrine and practice on the church collectively. Although leadership has an important role to play with its own particular authority, in the ultimate sense one must concur with McKenzie that "authority in the Church belongs to the whole Church and not to particular officers."[21]

LEADERSHIP AND AUTHORITY

An extensive discussion of the authority of leadership is beyond the scope of this study, which sought to focus on the fundamental issue of final authority in the church. Nevertheless, a brief word concerning the nature of the authority of those charged with leadership in the church is necessary to complement what has already been discovered relative to the authority of the whole church.

That the ministry of an elder or bishop was one carrying authority is plain in the New Testament. According to the apostle Paul, elders "rule" in the church (1 Tim. 5:17; cf. 3:5). It is probable that Paul also had the elders in mind when he wrote of "those who diligently labor among you, and have charge over you in the Lord and give you instruction" (1 Thess. 5:12). The writer of Hebrews likewise refers to "leaders" who "keep watch over your souls" (13:17; cf. vv. 7, 24). The very name *overseer* or *bishop* implies a ministry with authority. Corresponding to those descriptions of the authority of church leaders are the exhortations to the congregation to value their leaders highly (1 Thess. 5:12-13; 1 Tim. 5:17) and to respond to them with obedience and submission (Heb. 13:17).

The relationship between the authority of leadership and that of the congregation requires a proper understanding of the true nature of all authority in the church. Jesus Himself explained that it would bear no relationship to that authority exercised in the world (Matt. 20:25-28). This should put believers on guard against patterning the church structure after any organization in secular society. Christ's teaching is borne out by the rather surprising avoidance of the wealth of Greek terms for "office" in any New Testament description of the church.[22] Küng points out the reason for that exclusion by noting that those words all have one thing in common: "all express a relationship of rulers and ruled." He goes on to explain that the ministry in the church demanded the development of a new word.

> The word that was chosen was an unbiblical one, current neither in the Jewish nor the Hellenistic environment in this sense—indeed a fundamentally unreligious word. The particular place and function of the individual in the community was comprehensively described with a word which carried no overtones of authority, officialdom, rule, dignity or power: the word *diakonia*, service.[23]

What are often viewed as church "offices" are in reality church "services." Rather than being terms for offices, the words *bishop, pastor, deacon,* and even *apostle* and *prophet* simply describe different functions of service.

This leads to the fundamental basis of authority in the church: authority is always based on ministry and not on office or position. There is no office in the church based on law or power that corresponds to the office of a secular potentate. Likewise, there is no office based on knowledge and dignity that corresponds to the office of the scribes. Church authority is based only on service. This is illustrated with the "household of Stephanas" at Corinth who "devoted themselves for ministry to the saints." With no indication that they held any official position, the apostle charges the church to be in subjection to them and "to everyone who helps in the work and labors" (1 Cor. 16:15-16). Such leaders are to be respected and obeyed because they "diligently labor among you" (1 Thess. 5:12), and "keep watch over your souls" (Heb. 13:17). In the rare instances where the apostle specifically refers to his authority, he testifies that it was given to him "for building . . . up" (2 Cor. 10:8; 13:10). In other words, his authority was given for ministry, which centered in his commission to preach the gospel.[24]

It is the biblical authority associated with a ministry of service to which the church is called to submit. As Schweizer explains, such an explanation does not negate authority or its corresponding responsibility of obedience.

> Ministry and authority are certainly not mutually exclusive opposites, either in the teaching of Jesus himself or in his Church. But it is not an obedience that is demanded on the ground of position or dignity, but an obedience that is given because a person is overcome by the ministry that is performed, and in particular by the word that is preached.[25]

The application of these concepts of authority and submission to the practical functioning of elders within the congregation yields the conclusion that the elders do have a valid, authoritative leadership. This resides in the *charismata* by which they have been equipped by the Lord of the church to guide His people. It is not, however, an ultimate authority for the Lord has given the final authority and responsibility to recognize and test all of the *charismata* to the community as a whole. Having recognized and acknowledged the genuine *charismata* of leadership, the only proper and fitting response of the congregation must be submission.

CONCLUSION

If the biblical record provides a fundamental norm for the structure of church leadership, then the resurgence of a so-called "elder rule" being witnessed in many areas today has validity. If the Lord of the church has equipped some with the gifts of leadership, then the church will prosper most if those gifted leaders are recognized and permitted to lead. On the other hand, care must be taken not to isolate those gifts from their proper relationship to the entire body. All ministries, including those of leadership, are finally subject to the church as a whole as Christ manifests Himself through each member.

NOTES

1. O. Linton, "Church Office in the New Testament," in *This Is the Church*, ed. A. Nygren (Philadelphia: Muhlenburg, 1952), pp. 100-35; R. P. Martin, "Authority in the Light of the Apostolate, Tradition and the Canon," *Evangelical Quarterly* 40 (1968):66-82.
2. T. W. Manson, *The Church's Ministry* (London: Hodder & Stoughton, 1948), p. 52.
3. Ibid., pp. 54-55.
4. Hans Küng, *The Church* (New York: Sheed and Ward, 1967), pp. 379-80.
5. For a good discussion of the priesthood of all believers and the implications for authority see Eduard Schweizer, *Church Order in the New Testament* (London: SCM, 1961), pp. 188-93.
6. I. Howard Marshall, *The Epistles of John*, The New International Commentary on the New Testament (Grand Rapids: Eerdmans, 1978), p. 155.
7. B. F. Westcott, *The Epistles of St. John* (Grand Rapids: Eerdmans, 1966), p. 73.
8. Küng, p. 401.
9. John L. McKenzie, *Authority in the Church* (New York: Doubleday, Image Books, 1971), pp. 59-60.
10. James D. G. Dunn, *Jesus and the Spirit* (Philadelphia: Westminster, 1975), p. 292.
11. Ibid., p. 299.
12. Ernst Käsemann, "Ministry and Community in the New Testament," in *Essays on New Testament Themes* (London: SCM, 1964), pp. 63-94.
13. Hans van Campenhausen, *Ecclesiastical Authority and Spiritual Power in the Church of the First Three Centuries* (Stanford, Calif.: Stanford U., 1969), p. 80.
14. Quotes by Robert Banks in *Paul's Idea of Community* (Grand Rapids: Eerdmans, 1980), p. 185.
15. Maurice Goguel, *The Primitive Church* (London: George Allen & Unwin, 1964), pp. 233-34.
16. Schweizer, p. 192.
17. A. A. W. Meyer, *Critical and Exegetical Handbook to the Acts of the Apostles* (New York: Funk & Wagnalls, 1883), p. 282; cf. J. A.

Alexander, *Commentary on the Acts of the Apostles*, reprint (Grand Rapids: Zondervan, 1956), pp. 550-51.

18. *The Didache* 15.
19. Clement *1 Clement* 44. 3.
20. *Theological Dictionary of the New Testament*, s.v. "presbus," by Günther Bornkamm, 6:673.
21. McKenzie, p. 77.
22. Schweizer, pp. 171-78.
23. Küng, p. 389.
24. John Howard Schütz, *Paul and the Anatomy of Apostolic Authority* (Cambridge: Cambridge U., 1975), p. 224.
25. Schweizer, pp. 177-78.

15

Hermeneutics and Dispensationalism

Elliott E. Johnson

Many students have benefited from the dispensational system of interpretation. Dr. John F. Walvoord has contributed to that heritage for which his students are grateful. Yet in recent years this system of interpretation has been challenged on the basis of its hermeneutical implications.[1] Within the context of those new questions, it seems appropriate to address selected matters concerning hermeneutics and dispensationalism. Three questions are to be addressed: (1) What is the exegetical basis of a dispensational view of progressive revelation? (2) What is a summary statement of the system of theology developed from this base? and (3) What are the hermeneutical implications of this system for interpretation and application?

This article will attempt to answer those questions by proposing that a dispensational view of biblical revelation is a Pauline concept[2] expressed with particular fullness in the book of Ephesians. Within that epistle Paul refers to two dispensa-

ELLIOTT E. JOHNSON (B.S., Northwestern University; Th.M., Th.D., Dallas Theological Seminary) is associate professor of Bible exposition at Dallas Theological Seminary, Dallas, Texas.

tions explicitly and one implicitly.[3] Those references provide
the direction for a theological system of progressive revelation.
That system in turn influences subsequent biblical interpretation in terms of the unity of biblical revelation and of the individual identity of particular revelations.

THE EXEGETICAL BASIS OF DISPENSATIONALISM

The exegetical basis of a dispensational system of interpretation is the first question that must be addressed. The term *dispensation* or *administration* (Greek, *oikonomia*) is used in the
New Testament with various shades of meaning.[4] In Ephesians
Paul uses the term consistently in his discussion of God's progressive revelation and his own apostolic ministry among the
Gentiles. The exegetical basis for dispensationalism is derived
partially from Paul's three references to the term *oikonomia*
within the book of Ephesians (1:10; 3:2, 9).

In Ephesians 1 Paul praises God who has blessed the believers with every spiritual blessing in Christ. Paul's use of the
term *dispensation* (1:10) is included in his discussion of the
outworking of God's purpose in history which is "the summing
up of all things in Christ." Paul's use of *eis oikonomian* ("with
a view to an administration") points toward a climactic stewardship in human history. Ellicott recognizes that the preposi-
tion *eis* does not have a temporal meaning ("until") "but [is]
simply indicative of the *purpose* [or] *intention* of the *prothesis*
[i.e., 'purpose'].''[5] Moule comments, "The Son is the great
'steward' of the Father's house; the keys of all its life and history are in His hands. And His 'management' will at length
conduct the whole operation to a goal, placed and dated by
God's own prescient wisdom."[6]

God's "management" or "stewardship," however, does find
expression in history and includes the realm of heaven and of
earth. Westcott comments on God's management of human and
earthly history when he notes that "the fullness of time" in 1:10
refers to "the close of a series of critical periods, each of which
had its peculiar character and was naturally connected in some
way with the final issue."[7] It is clear that Paul did not perceive
his own age as the ultimate climax of history, for he anticipated

another age yet to come (Eph. 1:21). It is that future age or season that will be the climax of history. That final season will combine the purposes of each preceding season and will bring them to full realization in history.

The goal of the final dispensation in history is "the summing up of all things in Christ" (Eph. 1:10). Hendriksen finds this rendering "somewhat obscure" and so suggests the paraphrase "to bring all things under one head in Christ."[8] Westcott, however, accurately perceives the sense in which the phrase refers to the gathering together in one of all creation. "The word here expresses the typical union of all things in the Messiah, a final harmony answering to the idea of creation. . . ."[9] All of the apparently disparate events and experiences of the created world in history will be gathered together in such a way that Christ will be seen at the center of and in control of all. Whereas Hodge relates the "all things" to the church in heaven and earth,[10] Hendriksen sees it as a reference to Jesus "actually ruling the entire universe from his heavenly abode."[11] Yet today many see the "all things" in 1:10 as referring to something broader than just the church alone. They would view the administration as a more direct, effective expression of rule rather than just sovereign control.[12] Eadie describes the rule and the realm well.

> The idea seems then to be that heaven and earth are now united under one government. Christ as Creator was rightfully the Governor of all things, and till the introduction of sin, that government was one and undivided. But rebellion produced disorder, the unity of the kingdom was broken. Earth was morally severed from heaven. . . . But Jesus has effected a blessed change, for an amnesty has been proclaimed to earth. . . . Not only has harmony been restored to the universe, and the rupture occasioned by sin repaired, but beings still in rebellion are placed under Christ's control. . . . Jesus is universal Regent.[13]

In addition, Westcott observes that the effective expression goes beyond Christ's rule in the church. "This consummation lies beyond the unity of the Church, the Body of Christ, which contributes towards its realisation."[14] This final consummation restores all things in the created world to the immediate rule of Christ.

Thus Paul's first use of the term *dispensation* or *administration* refers to a future stewardship in the coming age in which all creation is restored to the rule of Christ. The stewardship of Christ's rule brings to full realization all of the purposes of God in world history.

Two other uses of the term *oikonomia* occur in the book of Ephesians (3:2, 9). In both passages Paul is referring to his own ministry to the Gentiles. Thus that stewardship was present in Paul's age and has certain purposes of God being effected by Paul. His use of "dispensation" in 3:2, 9 is to be distinguished from the earlier use in 1:10 and needs to be examined in light of Paul's conception of his ministry.

THE NATURE OF PAUL'S MINISTRY

Paul considered his ministry to be a "stewardship of God's grace" (Eph. 3:2). Paul relates this stewardship to the privileged new position of the Gentiles in grace (2:11-22). This stewardship for the Gentiles had resulted in his imprisonment (3:1).

> He thinks of his imprisonment as having been incurred in Christ's service, and more particularly of its having been incurred as a direct consequence of his activity as the apostle to the Gentiles. For it was his faithfulness to the special stewardship entrusted to him by Christ that called forth the peculiarly bitter hostility of his Jewish opponents, as a result of which he was attacked in Jerusalem and put on trial before the Roman courts.[15]

It was the administration of God's grace for the Gentiles accomplished in Christ that characterized Paul's ministry. "St. Paul does not say simply 'of the grace of God which was given to me' but 'of the noble responsibility which was laid upon me of administering the grace which was given to me in a new and unexpected way.' "[16]

THE CONTENT OF PAUL'S MESSAGE

Paul identifies the content of the message which he preaches as *to mystērion* ("the mystery") (Eph. 3:3) and *to mystēriō toi Christoi* ("the mystery of Christ") (3:4). Bruce identifies the content of this mystery. "A mystery in the New Testament sense of the word is something hitherto concealed which has now been disclosed. . . . What this special mystery was is stated expressly in verse 6."[17] Fuller adds further clarification concerning the content of the mystery. "In verse 3 Paul remarks that he had already been speaking about this mystery just a few sentences before, and this indicates that Ephesians 2:11-22 is an elaboration upon the summary statement of the mystery found in Ephesians 3:6."[18]

The essence of Paul's message is that Gentiles have equal privileges with Jews in the formation of God's new spiritual work—the church. Paul develops three basic concepts.

1. Gentiles who were once "separate from Christ, excluded from the commonwealth of Israel, and strangers to the covenants of promise, having no hope and without God in the world" have now been "brought near by the blood of Christ" (2:11-13).

2. Christ has made "the two into one new man" and has removed the wall that the tabernacle and the Law had erected (2:14-17).

3. This "new man" with its equal spiritual privileges is "a dwelling of God in the Spirit" (2:18-22).

THE TIME AND EXTENT OF THE MYSTERY REVEALED

The time of the incarnation marks a sharp distinction between those generations to which the mystery was not made known and the present generation to which Paul was ministering. "The use of *heterais* suggests the thought of two series of generations, one before and one after the Incarnation."[19]

The determination of the extent of the mystery revealed in the Old Testament rests on the interpretation of the phrase *hōs nun* ("as now") in 3:5. Does that phrase indicate that the revelation of equal status between Jew and Gentile had been revealed to some extent in the Old Testament? Eadie, representing many, writes, "The apostle speaks of general intimation which the ancient world had of the mystery, and compares it with those full and exact conceptions of it which these recent revelations by the Spirit had imparted."[20] Fuller adopts the same view and argues that James's quotation of Amos 9:11-12 represents such an Old Testament intimation of equality between Jew and Gentile.[21] However, the point at issue in James's argument is not equality between Gentiles and Jews. Rather, he is arguing that if Gentiles remain distinct as Gentiles in the climax of Jewish history (i.e., the kingdom) then Gentiles can remain distinct and need not become Jewish proselytes in the proclamation of the Gospel.[22] Thus James's quotation of Amos 9:11-12 has no bearing on the proper interpretation of Ephesians 3:5.

An equally valid interpretation of *hōs* in Ephesians 3:5 is that the Old Testament was silent on the question of the equal status of Gentiles and Jews. Contextually, that is supported in 3:9 when Paul speaks of "the administration of the mystery which for ages has been hidden in God. . . ." Walvoord rightly contends that the point of *hōs* is not comparative but rather a denial that there was any revelation of the mystery in that former time.[23] Westcott properly concludes, "The prophets looked for the incorporation of the nations in Israel, but not for their equality with 'the people' in the new church."[24]

THE WISDOM OF GOD DISPLAYED IN THE DISPENSATION OF GRACE

The hidden nature of the dispensation of grace is based on God's eternal purpose (Eph. 3:11). God purposely delayed any revelation of equal privilege for Gentiles until He had completed the provision of Christ. Now, in the church, God provides a redeemed people for Himself taken equally from Jew and Gentile. That equal provision displays the wisdom of God's purpose and ways in history.

Thus Paul's second use of "dispensation" refers to his own present stewardship. As a steward he is responsible to proclaim the truth of equal spiritual access for Gentile and Jew alike. The import of that message was so significant that Paul was willing to suffer at the hands of the Jews for this truth. The dispensation or administration of the mystery (Eph. 3:9), which allows Gentiles to share a position of equal privilege with the Jews, is an essential aspect of the unfolding of the mystery of His will (Eph. 1:9). When the dispensation of the fullness of times is reached, Christ will rule all things, including a host of redeemed Gentiles.

Paul refers to two stewardships directly: the *present* stewardship of God's grace toward Gentiles and the *future* stewardship of Christ's rule over all things in heaven and on earth. Clearly a third stewardship is implied—a *past* stewardship under which the nation of Israel enjoyed spiritual privileges including the promise of the birth of Christ. Those are clear, exegetical conclusions concerning Paul's concept of God's progressive outworking of His purpose and revelation. With this basic design in mind, the interpreter is encouraged to complete the structure by filling in details from the total biblical context. What follows is an attempt to construct a summary statement of a system of theology reflecting the Pauline concept of dispensationalism.

The Dispensational System of Theology

Ryrie proposes the following theological definition of a dispensation. "A dispensation is a distinguishable economy in the outworking of God's purpose."[25] Whereas most of the literature on dispensationalism focuses only on the tests of each economy or dispensation, that definition recognizes the directional importance of God's purpose. Paul also recognizes that in his numerous expressions of the normative control of God's will (Eph. 1:5, "according to the kind intention of His will"; and 3:11, "in accordance with the eternal purpose"). Thus any discussion of the progressive nature of dispensations must be seen in the context of God's expressed will as it is worked out in history.

GOD'S PURPOSE IN HISTORY

Paul does not express directly what that will of God involves. However, in applying Ryrie's suggested definition of a dispensation to human history, one is directed to the first expression of God's will for history in Genesis 3:15. "And I will put enmity between you and the woman, and between your seed and her seed; he shall bruise you on the head, and you shall bruise him on the heel." Kidner recognizes the central thrust of God's statement. "There is good New Testament authority for seeing here the protevangelium, the first glimmer of the gospel. Remarkably, it makes its debut as a sentence passed on the enemy (cf. Col. 2:15), not a promise to man, for redemption is about

God's rule as much as about man's need."[26] Thus as God directs the outcome of human history, He asserts that "man" will be restored to rule through his conquest of the evil one. That is the first controlling statement of God's purpose in His sovereign direction of human history.

Although God decisively asserts His will for fallen man, the accomplishment of that restoration is by no means immediate or direct. In fact, in Genesis 4-6 the evil one continues to exercise his evil authority over Cain and Lamech and ultimately exerts his control over all mankind. God responds in a righteous manner through the selection of a God-fearing remnant (Gen. 5; 11) and through the judgment of the evil world (Gen. 6-8). In grace Noah is delivered into a new world in which God ordains human government to limit the onslaught of the evil one (Gen. 7-10). Thus the first eleven chapters of Genesis set the stage for the effective accomplishment of God's purpose to restore man to his position of authority through his conquest over evil in the remainder of the Bible.

PROMISE

Each distinguishable economy or dispensation is the outworking of a progressive phase of God's purpose as already stated in Genesis 3:15. Each stage is also characterized by additional revelation. The next phase could be labeled "Promise." God promises Abraham and his seed that they will rule creation apart from the evil one. God's original promise (Gen. 12:1-3) focuses specificially on blessing rather than ruling creation. Yet, implied in such a free expression of physical and spiritual blessing is the promise that God's rule would extend throughout an earth that was at that time under the dominion of the evil one. That which is implied in the promise spoken to Abraham is amplified in the promise spoken to David (2 Sam. 7). That promise, bearing the same mark of divine blessing, specifies that God's rule would be expressed through the seed of David.

Whereas God's promise to Abraham fit the immediate historical needs, it anticipated the ultimate divine restoration. That, then, became God's means of separating men from the evil one to Himself. That separation from evil involves both justification (Gen. 15:6) and the righteous obedience of faithfulness (Gen.

22:1-19). But the effective separation from evil is only an un-realized ideal in the experience of Abraham and the other pa-triarchs. An added revelation of God and His purpose is needed to accomplish that separation from and conquest over evil. In addition, added revelation is needed to identify the one man who is to come to rule and to accomplish God's goal in history.

THE LAW

The need for added revelation gave rise to a new phase in God's purpose known as the "Law." It is clear that the stew-ardship of Promise had not yet been fulfilled in any final sense, so this new revelation of God's purpose was added alongside as a means of bringing Promise to its own realization (Gal. 3:19-25). Thus even after the Law was given, the Promise was re-peated for each new generation at circumcision (Gen. 17) and was repeated in the celebration of Passover (Ex. 12—13). In addition, the Promise was amplified and clarified both in the Davidic covenant and in the New covenant. The promise re-mained as the basis for justification by faith. The Law was given to a redeemed nation who, under Moses, had believed God's Promise and been redeemed from Egypt (Ex. 15:13).

A careful reading of the Law indicates that God's purpose in giving it was to express His rule within the redeemed people and thus to establish a nation set in direct conflict with evil. The Law was corporate in both its scope and its form.[27] It con-stituted Israel as a nation under God. In content the Law is a revelation of God's own righteous character, and it reveals how a righteous God will deal with His covenant people under Promise. The Law also imposes demands on those to whom it is given. It demands righteous behavior before God and men. Obedience is established as the means to blessing. Obedience would bring blessing but disobedience would bring cursing. But it is important to remember that whereas the blessing came through obedience, it did not come because of obedience.

Unfortunately, Israel's experience under the Law brought only condemnation. The historical result of condemnation was to bring Israel to a self-realization of her sin and its conse-quences, which included conquest by the evil one. Cursed and conquered, Israel was cast on the mercy of God and His promise of blessing. Under the Mosaic order such mercy was available to the repentant and humble through the sacrificial system. Those sacrifices also anticipated an ultimate and effective provision of mercy.

Although God's broader purpose under the law was to express His rule, the Law also served to help identify the one who was qualified to rule. In the progress of history king after king was shown to be disqualified to mediate divine rule because of his disobedience. Within the hope of Promise there remained the expectation that one would come who would be qualified. He would fulfill all of the Law's demands and would obediently stand in opposition to the evil one.

The revelation of the Law had another purpose. In demanding a righteous standard for man, a direct conflict between man and the evil one was erected. From this conflict, the conquest over the evil one emerged. The Righteous One, who was obedient in life under the Law, remained obedient in His conflict with evil even unto death. Living and dying in faithful obedience He was resurrected from death and exalted by God (Phil. 2:8-9). Thus the Law served to distinguish and to identify the One separated in righteousness.

In Christ the Promise was fulfilled in an inceptive fashion. In His resurrection Christ conquered death and the evil one (1 Cor. 15:12-58), and in His ascension Christ was established in a position of equal authority and glory with God. But the complete results of the promised blessing have not yet extended to all believers. Those results await a future fulfillment. Paul anticipates the redemption of individuals from all nations who will comprise the body of Christ (Eph. 1:22-23), and he expects all creation to one day find its fulfillment in Christ (Eph. 1:10). Those aspects of expectation introduce the final two phases of the outworking of God's purpose in history.

THE GOSPEL

The next phase in the outworking of God's purpose is "Gospel." In this phase, God purposes to restore a gracious rule in man enabling him to stand firm in his conflict with the evil one. That restoration is clearly a limited, but real, fulfillment of God's purpose stated in Genesis 3:15. It is limited only in the sense that Christ has not yet begun to exercise all of His authority. Although He has been elevated to the *position* of supreme authority in the heavens and earth, He has not yet claimed the title of *king*. He was raised from the dead (Eph. 1:20), seated in the heavenlies above all authorities in this age or in the age to come (Eph. 1:20-21), and all things are subject to Him (Eph. 1:22). He is Christ (i.e., the "anointed One"), but He is not yet occupying David's earthly throne. He has been declared to be Lord by God, but He is still challenged by both the evil one and by a world of evil men (Eph. 2:13; 4:17-19; 6:10-20). He is now functioning as head, but only within the defined scope of the church (Eph. 1:22). No Scripture presently identifies Him as the "King" of either the church or the world.

Closely connected with Christ's limited expression of authority is His activity in grace. Paul identifies at least three aspects of Christ's authoritative action in grace. First, He graciously brought to life those dead in trespasses and sins (Eph. 2:1, 4, 5) who were worthy of wrath (Eph. 2:3). Instead of abiding under the wrath of God's judgment, those individuals now share an equal, heavenly position with Christ (Eph. 2:6). That display of grace will make known the immeasurable wealth of His grace for ages to come (Eph. 2:7). Second, Christ graciously provided equal access for Gentiles to the promise and the inheritance (Eph. 3:2-6). Third, He graciously made available for His body the plunder and spoils of His conquest over the evil one (Eph. 4:7-16).

Christ now rules in grace in the lives and activities of those who have trusted in Him. He expresses His authority in the demands that He places on those believers. He expects His own to walk worthy of their calling (Eph. 4:1). His authority expressed in grace does demand obedience. But there is an important change in order from Law to Gospel. Under the Law the demand for obedience *preceded* the promise of blessing. Under the Gospel, the demand for obedience *follows* the promise of blessing. Paul first explains the exalted position in which each believer has already been placed (Eph. 1—3), and then he appeals to those believers for obedience worthy of such a calling (Eph. 4—6). That is the order of the New covenant in contrast to the old covenant. Christ exercises authority through the power made by the Holy Spirit in which the believer may walk. Paul prays that the believers may perceive "what is the surpassing greatness of His power toward us who believe" (Eph. 1:19), and he asks the Father "that He would grant you, according to the riches of His glory, to be strengthened with power through His Spirit in the inner man" (Eph. 3:16). The Holy Spirit now empowers the believers in their stand against the evil one (Eph. 6:10-20).

In this limited sense Christ fulfills God's purpose for human history. He is in the position of supreme authority before God though He is still being challenged by the evil one. He exercises His authority in a manner characterized by grace. In an evil world deserving of wrath, Christ graciously works through the message of truth and the Spirit of promise (Eph. 1:13) to redeem a possession for praise of His glory (Eph. 1:14). In that way Christ's work today enjoys a degree of fulfillment (Eph. 1:13). But there still remains a future hope (Eph. 1:18).

THE KINGDOM

Paul envisions that future hope being exercised in a final phase of fulfillment known as the "Kingdom." In that final age, God purposes to fully restore rule to man, enabling him to triumph over the evil one and to accomplish God's purposes in creation. The final age is a fulfillment of all the previous times or seasons (Eph. 1:10). In the age of Promise blessings were expected but not yet fully experienced. Rulership on David's throne was anticipated but not restored after the Babylonian captivity. New covenant spiritual enablement was announced but constantly challenged by evil. Those blessings will find full display in this final age.[28] In the age of Law conflict with the evil one was precipitated. The ultimate victory was experienced at the cross but still awaits a full implementation in time. That implementation will be finally achieved during the Kingdom age. In the age of the gospel redemption was realized in the forgiveness of transgressions (Eph. 1:7), but believers still await full redemption (Eph. 1:14). A downpayment of the believer's inheritance has been received (Eph. 1:14), but he had yet to experience the full measure of his inheritance (Eph. 1:18).

These aspects of God's purpose will be fully realized in the coming age.

The future age will sum up all things in Christ. Christ is the effective means to fulfill the purpose of God in its entirety (Gen. 3:15). Christ will also fulfill the various aspects of that overall purpose that have been stated progressively in history. In that age all the strands of history will be woven together so that the purpose of God is completely achieved, satisfying each part and filling the unified whole.

THE HERMENEUTICAL IMPLICATIONS

INTERPRETATION

The exegetical base of Paul's epistle to the Ephesians provides sufficient direction to construct a summary statement of a dispensational theology. All who recognize the role of the hermeneutical spiral[29] will acknowledge the interpretive value of such a theological construct. Although the system no doubt needs further clarification or revision, it provides a biblical perspective for subsequent interpretation.

It is the conclusion of this article that the unity and diversity of a dispensational system provides basic answers to traditional hermeneutical issues. At the level of purpose, an overall Christological unity is clearly evident.[30] This clarifies the issue raised by Kaiser on the need to restate the amount of continuity and discontinuity between the Old Testament and the New Testament.[31] The continuity rests in the purpose of God that anticipated Christ and will be accomplished in Christ. At the same time the discontinuity rests at the level of textual revelation. Each individual passage must be interpreted in a literal or normal fashion within its own context. Fuller acknowledges that traditional value in dispensationalism.

> Charles Ryrie was correct in taking me to task for espousing a "theological" hermeneutic in my unpublished doctoral dissertation of 1957 (*Dispensationalism Today*, 93-95). In these pages he strongly argues for a hermeneutic that admits only a "literal" or "normal" interpretation of a given passage, and which never allows a passage from later revelation to invalidate the meaning of a passage in earlier revelation. In the intervening years I have

come to agree with him. But now to my dismay I find that today's dispensationalism has reverted to the hermeneutic of covenant theology.[32]

When a distinction is drawn between an overall Christological purpose and progressive phases of revelation developing that purpose, both unity and contextual integrity can be maintained in interpretation.

APPLICATION

Another aspect of hermeneutics can be clarified through the use of a dispensational approach. Paul affirms without any qualification that all Scripture is profitable and speaks to the Christian's life today (2 Tim. 3:16). But the question of the particular benefit of a specific passage remains open. Since the Old Testament was written to Israel whereas the New Testament was written to the church, it seems clear that the benefits derived from the Old Testament are not the same for the church as they were for Israel. Dispensationalism helps to clarify distinctions needed for authoritative application.

A dispensational system recognizes the theological unity of revelation that leads to a Christological application. Theologically, the content of the Bible focuses on the revelation of Christ. That is profitable as a basis of faith for any age and for any audience.

Contextually, the dispensational system also recognizes the historical nature of revelation that affects the scope of application. The application is related to God's purposes at that point in history when the revelation was given.The scope of direct application is limited to the audience to whom it was first addressed. For instance, the epistles were addressed to specific first-century churches, and the Old Testament prophets spoke to various generations of Israel. The application to each original audience is historically and theologically direct. It is historically direct in that all the particulars of the text apply directly to that audience. It is theologically direct since God speaks directly to that audience.

Those individual books written to specific audiences did not remain in isolation. The Old Testament Scriptures were gathered as a canon for the nation Israel, and later the New

Testament Scriptures were incorporated into a canon for the church. Israel applied her Scriptures in a theologically direct fashion. Similarly the church applied the canon of New Testament Scriptures in a theologically direct fashion. In that sense both groups recognized that God continued to speak directly to later generations in spite of changes in historical circumstances. The reason for that is that the members of each group shared a common relationship with God. In addition, the purpose of God in history for Israel did not change under the Law; nor did God's purpose for the church change after the Gospel for the New covenant had been established. Thus the theologically direct application is defined by and limited to God's purposes in history for specific groups of people.

Whereas the outworking of God's purpose of restoration is historically limited, the moral conflict between God's will and the evil one's schemes have many common elements in human history. The means ordained by God to deal with that conflict are similar throughout history. Faith in the revealed will of God is the requirement for justification throughout history (Rom. 4:1-25). That produces a judicial separation from evil. Similarly, obedience to the standards of a righteous God is the common means of sanctification (Eph. 5:1-8). That produces an experiential separation from evil.

In 1 Corinthians 10:1-13 Paul warns the church in Corinth that God will judge the disobedient in spite of their spiritual privilege. He bases his warning on Israel's example in the wilderness. In this case the Old Testament standards of righteousness are applied to New Testament believers in a morally indirect application. Such moral application rests on the harmony of God's total revelation. It is indirect in that the application is defined in terms of the revelation and relationship of the present dispensation. The Old Testament is used merely as an *example* of common morality. The New Testament provides the theological framework in which the example is worked out. The New Testament commands rest on the finished work of Christ rather than the anticipation of Christ. The spiritual resources for obedience under the New covenant (Eph. 5:9-20) are distinct from the command under the old covenant to place the Law on one's heart (Deut. 6:4-9; 11:18-22).

Within the perspective of progressive revelation another aspect of application needs to be clarified. Although the revelations of God's purposes have primary reference to the historical setting in which they were given, the scope of their application frequently transcends those historical events. As already indicated, they await the final age of Christ's rule to reach their ultimate culmination. As believers in history, a knowledge of such an unfolding of God's purposes is profitable for hope. This historical, progressive application recognizes the sovereign outworking of God's will in history. It is historical in that history is the sphere in which God works. It is progressive in that it gives the believer a perspective of history from its origin to its conclusion. Thus dispensationalism enables one to clarify the distinctions needed to arrive at an accurate application of any given passage of Scripture.

CONCLUSION

The exegetical basis of dispensationalism can be partially derived from a study of Paul's use of *oikonomia* in the book of Ephesians. Paul seems to refer to at least three distinct stewardships in the outworking of God's purpose in history. That basic structure presented by Paul can be expanded by filling in details from the total biblical context as God's will is progressively worked out in history. Such a study leads to the conclusion that there are several different stewardships in the outworking of God's purpose, including the phases of Promise, the Law, the Gospel, and the Kingdom. There are definite hermeneutical implications inherent in this type of dispensational system which aid in both the interpretation and the application of God's Word.

NOTES

1. Daniel P. Fuller, *Gospel and Law: Contrast or Continuum? The Hermeneutics of Dispensationalism and Covenant Theology* (Grand Rapids: Eerdmans, 1980); Walter C. Kaiser, Jr., "The Old Promise and the New Covenant: Jeremiah 31:31-34," *Journal of the Evangelical Theological Society* 15 (1972):11-23.
2. This does not imply that there is a conflict between a Pauline concept and that expressed in the remainder of the Bible.

3. Charles C. Ryrie, "A Basic Idea with a Big Name," *Kindred Spirit* 4 (Fall 1980):9-11.
4. Charles C. Ryrie, *Dispensationalism Today* (Chicago: Moody, 1965), pp. 25-28.
5. Charles J. Ellicott, *Epistle to the Ephesians* (Andover: Warren F. Draper, 1862), p. 24.
6. Handley C. G. Moule, *Ephesians Studies* (London: Hodder and Stoughton, 1920), pp. 32-33.
7. Brooke Foss Westcott, *St. Paul's Epistle to the Ephesians* (Grand Rapids: 1952), p. 13.
8. William Hendriksen, *Exposition of Ephesians*, New Testament Commentary (Grand Rapids: Baker, 1967), p. 86.
9. Westcott, p. 14.
10. John Eadie, *Ephesians*, Classic Commentary Series (Grand Rapids: Zondervan, 1883), p. 56.
11. Hendriksen, p. 87.
12. Ellicott, p. 26; Moule, p. 33.
13. Eadie, p. 56.
14. Westcott, p. 14.
15. F. F. Bruce, *The Epistle to the Ephesians* (London: Pickering and Inglis, 1961), p. 58.
16. Westcott, p. 44.
17. Bruce, p. 60.
18. Fuller, p. 175.
19. Westcott, p. 45.
20. Eadie, p. 217.
21. Fuller, pp. 176-82.
22. J. N. Darby, "The Hopes of the Church of God," in *The Collected Writings of J. N. Darby*, 34 vols., ed. William Kelly (London: G. Morrish, n.d.), 2:555. See also *The New Scofield Reference Bible*, ed. E. Schuyler English (New York: Oxford U., 1967), pp. 1185-86.
23. John F. Walvoord, *Millennial Kingdom* (Findlay, Oh.: Dunham, 1959), pp. 232-37.
24. Westcott, p. 45.
25. Ryrie, *Dispensationalism Today*, p. 29.
26. Derek Kinder, *Genesis*, Tyndale Old Testament Commentaries (London: Inter-Varsity, 1972), p. 70.
27. Meredith Kline, *Treaty of the Great King* (Grand Rapids: Eerdmans, 1963).
28. Willis J. Beecher, *The Prophets and the Promise* (Grand Rapids: Baker, 1963).
29. J. I. Packer, *Jerusalem and Athens*, ed. E. R. Geehan (Philadelphia: Presbyterian and Reformed, 1971).
30. Bernard Ramm, *Protestant Biblical Interpretation* (Boston: W. A. Wilde, 1956), p. 56.
31. Kaiser, p. 11.
32. Fuller, p. 62.

16

The Biblical Covenants and the Birth Narratives

J. Dwight Pentecost

THE UNCONDITIONAL COVENANTS

The eschatological program for Israel is determined by four great, eternal, unconditional covenants that God gave to that people.[1] A proper grasp of those covenants is essential for a correct understanding of the significance of Christ's birth.

THE ABRAHAMIC COVENANT

The first of the covenants was the one confirmed with Abraham in Genesis 15. Prior to the confirmation of the covenant God had appeared to Abraham and had given him a promise. "And I will make you a great nation, and I will bless you, and make your name great; and so you shall be a blessing; and I will bless those who bless you, and the one who curses you will I curse. And in you all the families of the earth shall be blessed" (Gen. 12:2-3). God promised Abraham personal blessings, national blessings, and universal blessings.[2] Whether or not

J. DWIGHT PENTECOST (A.B., Hampden-Sydney College; Th.M., Th.D., Dallas Theological Seminary) is professor of Bible exposition at Dallas Theological Seminary, Dallas, Texas.

Abraham would receive those blessings depended on his obedience to the command to "go forth from your country, and from your relatives and from your father's house" (Gen. 12:1). In obedience to the commands of God and in anticipation of the blessings Abraham believed God would give to him, Abraham left his country. He journeyed as far as Haran where he stayed until his father, Terah, died (Gen. 11:32). Abraham thus had fulfilled two of the conditions, and he proceeded on into the land of Canaan where "the LORD appeared to Abram and said, 'To your descendants I will give this land'" (Gen. 12:7).

The blessings given to Abraham are summarized in the key words *descendants* and *land*. The "descendants" refer to the physical progeny to be born to Abraham, and the "land" refers to the land then occupied by the Canaanites, which land was to become Abraham's inheritance. Abraham responded to that promise by building an altar (Gen. 12:7), which was an act of worship expressing his faith in God's promise. In Genesis 13:5-12 Abraham was separated from Lot. That fulfilled the third part of the command that Abraham had to obey to receive the blessing. It is no accident that the Lord now repeated His promise to Abraham. "And the LORD said to Abram, after Lot had separated from him, 'Now lift up your eyes and look from the place where you are, northward and southward and eastward and westward; for all the land which you see, I will give it to you and to your descendants forever'" (Gen. 13:14-15).

In Genesis 15 Abraham's faith in God was again demonstrated as he believed God's word concerning the descendants from his loins. Because of his faith in the promise that God had given, God "reckoned it to him as righteousness" (Gen. 15:6). God then ratified that promise with a blood covenant which signified an irrevocable, binding agreement.[3] It is significant that when the covenant was ratified Abraham was a recipient—not a participant—in the ceremony. Abraham had fallen asleep (Gen. 15:12), and only the Lord passed through the slaughtered animals (Gen. 15:17). Following the ratification of the blood covenant the text states, "On that day the LORD made a covenant with Abram, saying, 'To your descendants I have given this land . . .'" (Gen. 15:18). Thus from the time of his call in Ur until the ratification of the covenant, Abraham had been

walking by faith in the promise that God would give him physical descendants who would become a nation and that the land
in which he was dwelling would become their inheritance.
The promise that Abraham had claimed by faith was now
ratified by a blood covenant. That is the first great unconditional, eternal covenant that binds God to a course of action.

THE PALESTINIAN COVENANT

God's second great, unconditional covenant is given to Israel
through Moses and is recorded in Deuteronomy 28-30. In
Deuteronomy 28 God states the principle by which He will deal
with His covenant people: Obedience will bring blessing and
disobedience will bring discipline. The blessings are outlined
in Deuteronomy 28:1-14. Those were material blessings the
obedient nation would enjoy in her land. The curses are pronounced in 28:15-68. Those verses indicate that God would
withhold material blessings from His people to bring them to a
place of confession and restoration.

In anticipation of the nation's rejection of God's discipline
and refusal to correct that which brought about the discipline,
God promised that the nation would be delivered into the
hands of Gentile captors who would invade the land, tear down
the walled cities, and either kill or deport the people.
Deuteronomy 30 then outlines the principle on which the nation would be delivered from her discipline and restored to the
blessings that were hers under the Abrahamic covenant.
While in captivity Israel would need to "return to the LORD your
God and obey Him with all your heart and soul according to all
I command you today, you and your sons, then the LORD your
God will restore you from captivity, and have compassion on
you, and will gather you again from all the peoples where the
LORD your God has scattered you. . . . And the LORD your God
will bring you into the land which your fathers possessed, and
you shall possess it. . . . Moreover the LORD your God will cir-
cumcise your heart and the heart of your descendants, to love
the LORD your God with all your heart and all your soul, in order
that you may live" (Deut. 30:2-6).

In the Palestinian Covenant God anticipates the disobedience
of the people. The Palestinian covenant does not abrogate the

unconditional Abrahamic covenant, but it does provide conditions which must be met before the people can enjoy the blessings which are theirs under the Abrahamic covenant.

THE DAVIDIC COVENANT

A third covenant is found in 2 Samuel 7:4-16, which is commonly called the Davidic covenant.[4] It had been David's desire to build a house for the Lord; but because he had been a man of war that house was to be built by Solomon, the prince of peace. God promised David that his descendants would be raised up after him and would reign in his kingdom (2 Sam. 7:12). That was intended as an encouragement to David since God had not set up any of Saul's sons as heirs on the throne. God further promised that He would "establish the throne of his kingdom forever" (2 Sam. 7:13). That again would encourage David because as long as Israel existed as a nation a Davidic descendant would have a right to the throne. Finally in 7:16 God said, "And your house and your kingdom shall endure before Me forever; and your throne shall be established forever."

There are three key words in this promise to David. The word *house* has to do with the descendants in the Davidic dynasty.[5] The word *kingdom* refers to the nation of Israel, and the word *throne* indicates the right to rule, which is derived from divine appointment.[6] While 2 Samuel 7 appears to state that God gave the promise only to David, Psalm 89 indicates that the promise was actually a covenant. "I have made a covenant with My chosen; I have sworn to David My servant, I will establish your seed forever, and build up your throne to all generations" (89:3-4). Thus David, like Abraham, had both a promise and a covenant from God.

THE NEW COVENANT

The fourth of the great eternal, unconditional covenants is found in Jeremiah 31:31-34. Jeremiah gave this promise on the eve of the Babylonian captivity to encourage the people.

> "Behold, days are coming," declares the LORD, "when I will make a new covenant with the house of Israel and with the house of Judah, not like the covenant which I made with their fathers in the day I took them by the hand to bring them out of the land

of Egypt, My covenant which they broke, although I was a husband unto them." declares the LORD. "But this is the covenant which I will make with the house of Israel after those days," declares the LORD, "I will put my law within them, and on their heart I will write it; and I will be their God, and they shall be My people. And they shall not teach again, each man his neighbor and each man his brother, saying, 'Know the Lord,' for they shall all know Me, from the least of them to the greatest of them," declares the LORD, "for I will forgive their iniquity, and their sin I will remember no more."

In that promise a New covenant was to be given which will supercede the Mosaic covenant given to Israel at Sinai during their wilderness experience.[7] The Mosaic covenant provided a temporary covering for sins. It provided God with a basis on which He could deal with a guilty people and dwell among them, and it provided a means for restoration to fellowship for those who sinned. But the Mosaic covenant did not make a final disposition of sin. Jeremiah promises that God will take away the old, temporary arrangement and provide a new arrangement. God will establish a New covenant that will make a final disposition of sin. That covenant contains the glorious promise, "For I will forgive their iniquity, and their sin I will remember no more" (Jer. 31:34).

In these four covenants, then, it can be seen that God has set apart the nation Israel to be His chosen people. He has promised the perpetuity of the nation. He has given continuing national rights to the land originally called Canaan. He has promised the people that they will be ruled over by a Davidic king whose throne rights are established forever. He has warned that a disobedient people will be disciplined, but the disobedience will not cancel their covenants. They cannot enjoy the blessings of the covenants until they acknowledge their sin, turn to the Lord, and walk in obedience. God has promised that someday their iniquity will be removed and they will become an obedient people who will serve God's purpose to be lights to the world.

THE BIRTH NARRATIVES

When one turns to the birth narratives of the New Testament

one finds frequent reference to those four eschatological covenants. The birth narratives need to be examined to see the importance that is placed on the covenants and to see the relationship between the coming of Christ and the fulfillment of those covenants.

Matthew opens his gospel with the words, "The book of the genealogy of Jesus Christ, the son of David, the son of Abraham" (Matt. 1:1). It is significant that although Matthew gives an extended genealogy of Jesus Christ, he singles out David and Abraham for special mention in his introduction. The reason for that seems to be that two of the crucial covenants that determine the program for the nation Israel were made with David and Abraham. Such a notation signifies that Jesus Christ has come as the son of David to rule over Abraham's descendants in that land that God promised to them.[8]

Another reference to the covenant program can be found in Matthew 1:18-25. There the angel told Joseph about the coming birth of Christ. The angel said to Joseph concerning Mary, "And she will bear a Son; and you shall call His name Jesus, for it is He who will save His people from their sins" (Matt. 1:21). The salvation promised through Mary's Son refers to Jeremiah 31:34 where God promised to provide a basis for the total forgiveness of sin.

The chief priests and scribes who identified the birthplace of Christ to Herod (Matt. 2:1-8) also make reference to the fulfillment of God's covenant program by quoting Micah's prophecy. "And you, Bethlehem, land of Judah; are by no means least among the leaders of Judah; for out of you shall come forth a Ruler, who will shepherd My people Israel" (Matt. 2:6). Bethlehem was David's city, and from David's line was to come a king. That Davidic descendant was to be a ruler over the nation Israel. Thus inadvertently the chief priests gave testimony to the fulfillment of the Davidic covenant that promised a king and to the Abrahamic covenant, which promised the perpetuity of Abraham's descendants until they should be gathered into Messiah's kingdom.

The first reference to the covenants in Luke's account of the birth narrative is found in Luke 1:13-17. Joyous news was brought to Zacharias that he and Elizabeth were to have a son who would be given the name *John*. The angel who made that announcement then said, "And you will have joy and gladness, and many will rejoice at his birth. For he will be great in the sight of the Lord, and he will drink no wine or liquor; and he will be filled with the Holy Spirit, while yet in his mother's womb. And he will turn back many of the sons of Israel to the Lord their God. And it is he who will go as a forerunner before Him in the spirit and power of Elijah, to turn the hearts of the fathers back to the children, and the disobedient to the attitude of the righteous; so as to make ready a people prepared for the Lord" (Luke 1:14-17).

The angel announced that John was to be set apart to the Lord's service from infancy in a manner similar to one in the Old Testament who had taken a Nazirite vow.[9] John's ministry was unique in that as he fulfilled the prophetic office he was to be filled with the Holy Spirit so that everything he said and did was under the Spirit's control. The angel emphasized the fact that John's ministry was to be a ministry of turning a disobedient people back to the Lord. His ministry was limited to the nation Israel, and he was to do in his generation what Elijah had done before. Elijah appeared in a time of national apostasy to warn the nation of imminent judgment unless the people would confess their sin and repent. Elijah's ministry was in keeping with the covenant of Deuteronomy 30 where such repentance, confession, and restoration was stated to be a prerequisite to blessing.

The angel announced that John was to have a ministry of turning a disobedient people back to the Lord their God in order to "make ready a people prepared for the Lord" (1:17). Thus John's ministry was directly related to the promised blessings Israel would enjoy under the Abrahamic covenant. The enjoyment of those blessings was conditioned on obedience. Since the nation was disobedient John called the people to confession and restoration so that the blessings might be theirs.

Another clear reference to the covenants is found in the angel's announcement to Mary in Luke 1:26-38. "And behold you will conceive in your womb, and bear a son, and you shall name Him Jesus. He will be great, and will be called the Son of the Most High; and the Lord God will give Him the throne of His father David; and He will reign over the house of Jacob forever; and His kingdom will have no end" (Luke 1:31-33). As a result of the Holy Spirit's ministry, Mary was to conceive a Son who, when born, would be given the name *Jesus*. The Greek word *Iēsous* (Jesus) is the counterpart of the Hebrew word *Yᵉhôshûaʻ* (Joshua).[10] Joshua was the one who delivered Israel out of their wilderness experience and brought the nation into the land and life of blessing as had been promised and covenanted through Abraham. Thus when the name *Jesus* was given to Mary's Son it suggested the future fulfillment of the Abrahamic covenant in which Israel will enjoy blessings in the land that God had given to Abraham's descendants. Further, there is a specific reference to the Davidic covenant in the angel's message. He said, "the Lord God will give Him the *throne* of His father David; and He will reign over the *house* of Jacob forever; and His *kingdom* will have no end" (Luke 1:32-33, italics added). The angel employed the three significant words found in the Davidic covenant in 2 Samuel 7:16—throne, house, and kingdom. It could not have been made clearer that Mary's Son had come to fulfill the covenants that God had made with Abraham and with David.

Elizabeth's response to Mary's visit to their home (Luke 1:39-45) gives another reference to the covenants. "And it came about that when Elizabeth heard Mary's greeting, the baby leaped in her womb; and Elizabeth was filled with the Holy Spirit. And she cried out with a loud voice, and said, 'Blessed among women are you, and blessed is the fruit of your womb! And how has it happened to me, that the mother of my Lord should come to me?' " (Luke 1:41-43). The phrase *my Lord* is a Messianic phrase.[11] It is found in Psalm 110:1-2. "The LORD says to my Lord: 'Sit at My right hand, until I make Thine enemies a footstool for Thy feet.' The LORD will stretch forth Thy strong scepter from Zion, saying, 'Rule in the midst of Thine enemies.' " In this passage the Father is addressing the Son, whom He has appointed to rule by the title "my Lord." When Elizabeth addressed Mary as "the mother of my Lord," she was referring to her as the mother of the one who, in keeping with the Davidic covenant, has the God-given right to rule. That address, then, is a reference to the Davidic covenant.

The response of Mary to Elizabeth's salutation contains many references to the covenant program (Luke 1:46-55). Mary acknowledged that God was her Savior (1:47) and that "the Mighty One has done great things for me" (1:49). Among the "great things" that God had done was to set in motion His plan to bring a king to rule over her people. "He has brought down rulers from their thrones" (1:52). Mary also equated the advent of her Son with God's promises to Abraham. "He has given help to Israel His servant, in remembrance of His mercy, as He spoke to our fathers, to Abraham and his offspring forever" (1:54-55). The Abrahamic covenant has promised blessings not only to Israel but also to all the earth through Abraham's descendants. In keeping with that covenant God was now sending one in Abraham's line to bring blessings to Israel. It had been promised that one of David's sons would triumph over Israel's enemies and rule in peace and righteousness (cf. Isa. 9:6-7; Mic. 5:2-5). Mary anticipated the rule of her Son in fulfillment of the Davidic covenant, and she eagerly awaited the blessings God had promised to her forebearers.

The prophecy of Zacharias, given under inspiration of the Holy Spirit (Luke 1:67-79), is filled with references to the covenants. Zacharias prophesied that God had "accomplished redemption for His people" (Luke 1:68). That "redemption" refers principally to Israel's "being delivered from the hand of our enemies" (1:74). The promised redemption will occur because God has remembered His covenant with David. He "has raised up a horn of salvation for us in the house of David His servant" (1:69). God's deliverance is also in keeping with "the oath which He swore to Abraham our father" (1:73).

Zacharias was anticipating the fulfillment of the Abrahamic and the Davidic covenant promises. But further, he was anticipating deliverance from sin. He said that his child will "give to His people the knowledge of salvation by the forgiveness of their sins, because of the tender mercy of our God, with which the Sunrise from on high shall visit us" (1:77-78). That is a reference to the New covenant of Jeremiah 31:31-34 where God had promised that He would provide for forgiveness of sins. That forgiveness was to be through the one whom John would introduce to the nation Israel. Thus Zacharias was conscious of the covenant program when he spoke of the blessings that would be introduced through the coming Messiah.

Christ's birth did not go unannounced. Angels were dispatched to shepherds near Bethlehem with a glorious message. "I bring you good news of a great joy which shall be for all the people; for today in the city of David there has been born for you a Savior, who is Christ the Lord" (Luke 2:10-11). Once again there is a clear reference to the New covenant. The one who was born in Bethlehem was a Savior, and that Savior was none other than Christ the Lord. According to the Old Testament the Messiah was to have two principle responsibilities: to redeem and to reign.[12] He was to be Savior and Sovereign. In their announcement to the shepherds, the angels were referring to the first of those two great works when they presented Christ as "a Savior" (2:11). They were referring to the second of those works when they describe Christ as "the Lord" (2:11). His work as both Savior and Sovereign is based on the covenants made in 2 Samuel 7:16 and Jeremiah 31:34. Once again angels bore testimony to the importance of those covenants in their announcement of the coming of Christ.

The words of Simeon at the time of the presentation of Christ in the temple forty days after His birth have reference to the covenants (Luke 2:22-35). Simeon, controlled by the Holy Spirit, said, "Now Lord, Thou dost let Thy bondservant depart in peace, according to Thy word; for mine eyes have seen Thy salvation, which Thou hast prepared in the presence of all peoples, a light of revelation to the Gentiles, and the glory of Thy people Israel" (Luke 2:29-32). In praising God for "Thy salvation," Simeon is referring to Isaiah 52:6-10 where the reign of the appointed king is announced (v. 7) and salvation or redemption is provided for Jerusalem (v. 10). In giving that Messianic prediction, Isaiah anticipated the fulfillment of the Davidic covenant in the reign of Christ. He also looked forward to the redemption of Israel, which was further amplified a century later in the New covenant of Jeremiah 31.

When Simeon spoke of Jesus as a light of revelation to the Gentiles, he was probably referring to Isaiah 42:6 where Isaiah said of Christ, "I will appoint you as a covenant to the people, a light to the nations." Simeon's reference to "the glory of Thy people Israel" could look back to Isaiah 49:6-7 where Isaiah wrote, "He says, 'It is too small a thing that You should be My servant to raise up the tribes of Jacob, and to restore the preserved ones of Israel; I will also make You a light of the nations so that My salvation may reach to the end of the earth.' Thus says the LORD, the Redeemer of Israel, and its Holy One, to the despised One, to the One abhorred by the nation, to the Servant of rulers, 'Kings shall see and arise, princes shall also bow down; because of the Lord who is faithful, the Holy One of Israel who has chosen you.' " In that passage God speaks to His Son, the Messiah, and promises Him a throne from which He will rule and before which the nations will bow. Thus, in quoting Isaiah's Messianic prophecies, Simeon was referring to the Davidic covenant promises and to the New covenant promises in which Jesus Christ will both redeem and reign.

CONCLUSION

A careful examination of the birth narratives shows that they refer to the four eternal, unconditional covenants that God gave to His covenant people Israel: the Abrahamic covenant, the Palestinian covenant, the Davidic covenant, and the New covenant. The fact that Christ came to fulfill those covenants gives abundant evidence that Israel's disobedience had not abrogated them. As one reads Israel's history in the Old Testament one reads a record of disobedience, lawlessness, and apostasy. The prophets who appeared in those days of despair anticipated the fulfillment of the covenants and called the covenant people to confession and restoration so that the promised blessings could be theirs. If disobedience could abrogate the covenants, Christ would never have come to fulfill them.

Inasmuch as those covenants have not yet been fulfilled in their fullness, it is reasonable to anticipate a second advent of Christ in which the covenants will be completely fulfilled. Before Christ comes the second time to reign, the nation of Israel will undergo a time of severe discipline. The Tribulation period, called the time of Jacob's trouble (Jer. 30:7) or Daniel's seventieth week (Dan. 9:27), is a period in which the wrath of God will be poured out as discipline on His covenant people to bring them to confession and restoration so that the blessings of Messiah's kingdom may be theirs.[13] God will send two witnesses (Rev. 11:3) who will call a guilty nation to repentance.[14] As a result of God's discipline, coupled with the message of the witnesses, a remnant will turn to the Lord. They will look by faith to the one who was pierced, and as a result there will be cleansing for that remnant (Zech. 12:10; 13:1).

When Messiah returns He will regather the dispersed nation. "He will send forth His angels with a great trumpet and they will gather together His elect from the four winds, from one end of the sky to the other" (Matt. 24:31). That is a direct fulfillment of God's covenant promise. "So it shall become when all of these things have come upon you . . . and you call them to mind in all nations where the LORD your God has banished you, and you return to the LORD your God and obey Him with all your heart and soul according to all that I command you today, you and your sons, then the LORD your God will restore you from captivity, and have compassion on you and will gather you again from all the peoples where the LORD your God has scattered you" (Deut. 30:1-3). Thus at the second advent of Christ the Palestinian covenant will be fulfilled. "But when the Son of Man comes in His glory, and all the angels with Him, then He will sit on His glorious throne" (Matt. 25:31). That throne is the Davidic throne, which will be reinstituted at the second advent in fulfillment of the Davidic covenant. At the second advent God will "restore the captivity of My people Israel, and they will rebuild the ruined cities and live in them, they will also plant vineyards and drink their wine, and make gardens and eat their fruit. I will also plant them on their land, and they will not again be rooted out from their land which I have given them, says the LORD your God" (Amos 9:14-15). That will be the fulfillment of the Abrahamic covenant, in which the land was guaranteed to Abraham's descendants. By the death of Jesus Christ God has ratified a New covenant with the nation Israel.

However, because of her rejection of Christ. Israel has never entered into the benefits of that New covenant. At the second advent, when the remnant turns in faith to the Lord, "a fountain will be opened for the house of David and for the inhabitants of Jerusalem, for sin and for impurity" (Zech. 13:1). That signifies the fulfillment of the New covenant.

At the second advent all four of the unconditional, eternal covenants will be fulfilled; and the remnant from Israel will enter into the blessings and benefits provided by those covenants. They will have been preserved as a nation. They will have been redeemed. They will be installed in their own land under the beneficent, righteous reign of their Davidic king. Israel's hope rests on the promises and covenants of God. The fulfillment of those promises and covenants demands a literal, physical, visible return of Jesus Christ to this earth, the enthronement of Christ as king, the subjugation of all Israel's enemies to the authority of her king, and Israel's experience of the benefits of the salvation provided through the New covenant enacted at the cross. As Christ came the first time in fulfillment of the covenants, so He will come the second time to complete all that was covenanted.

NOTES

1. For a discussion of the four covenants see J. Dwight Pentecost, *Things to Come* (Grand Rapids: Zondervan, 1958), pp. 65-128.
2. John F. Walvoord, *Israel in Prophecy* (Grand Rapids: Zondervan, 1962), p. 32.
3. *The Zondervan Pictorial Encyclopedia of the Bible*, s.v. "Covenant (in the Old Testament)," by J. Barton Payne, 1:1002. See also Pentecost, p. 77.
4. For a helpful treatment of the Davidic covenant see John F. Walvoord, "The Fulfillment of the Davidic Covenant," *Bibliotheca Sacra* 102 (April-June 1945):153-66.
5. "If the ancestor after whom the house was named was a king, we should translate the word *bayith* 'dynasty' . . ." *Theological Dictionary of the Old Testament*, s.v. "*Bayith*," by Harry A. Hoffner, 2:114.
6. According to Brown, Driver, and Briggs, the Hebrew word *kissē'* is used in a figurative sense in 2 Samuel 7:16. It refers to "royal dignity, authority, power" especially in regard to "setting up" or "establishing" a kingdom (Francis Brown, S. R. Driver, and

Charles A. Briggs, *A Hebrew and English Lexicon of the Old Testament* [Oxford: Clarendon, 1972], p. 491).

7. John F. Walvoord, "The New Covenant with Israel," *Bibliotheca Sacra* 110 (July-September 1953):193-205. See also Pentecost, pp. 116-28.

8. Homer A. Kent, "The Gospel According to Matthew," in *The Wycliffe Bible Commentary*, ed. Charles F. Pfeiffer and Everett F. Harrison (Chicago: Moody, 1962), p. 931.

9. I. Howard Marshall, *The Gospel of Luke*, The New International Greek Testament Commentary (Grand Rapids: Eerdmans, 1978), p. 57.

10. *The International Standard Bible Encyclopedia*, 1939 ed., s.v. "Jesus," 3:1624.

11. Plummer sees the phrase as a reference to "The Messiah" and cites Psalm 110:1 as the proof (Alfred Plummer, *The Gospel according to St. Luke*, The International Critical Commentary, 4th ed. [Edinburgh: T. & T. Clark, 1901], p. 29).

12. As Reid notes, "The word of Christ in the history of the world has many sides or facets. As the personal Word of God He created, sustains, and governs the universe (Jn. 1:1ff.). Thus He manifests God in His sovereign work. . . . He is, at the same time, the Redeemer of creation. . . ." *The International Standard Bible Encyclopedia*, 1979 ed., s.v. "Christ, Offices of," by W. Stanford Reid, 1:652.

13. J. Dwight Pentecost, *Will Man Survive?: Prophecy You Can Understand* (Chicago: Moody, 1972), pp. 75-77.

14. Pentecost, *Things to Come*, pp. 304-9.

Part III
Ministry and Communication

17

The Pastor as a Theologian

John W. Reed

Some pastors may respond to this title by declaring that they do not consider themselves to be theologians. Yet the pastor's responsibility is to explain and apply the character and ways of God to his people. That is clearly the work of a theologian. The pastor is not a technical theologian but a biblical theologian at the grass roots level. The only theologian that the great mass of Christians will ever know personally is the pastor of their local church.

THEOLOGY AND MINISTRY

It is my opinion that the activities emphasized by a minister are directly related to the theological views that he holds. A pastor's theology will determine the nature of the activities of his ministry. That is in line with the emphasis of many of the New Testament epistles. Doctrine is presented first and then duty is discussed. In Romans 1-11 the apostle Paul outlines the

JOHN W. REED (A.B., Bryan College; M.A., Bowling Green State University; M.Div., Grace Theological Seminary; Ph.D., Ohio State University) is professor of pastoral ministries at Dallas Theological Seminary, Dallas, Texas.

essential nature of Christian doctrine. Then in chapters 12-15 he demonstrates how that doctrine should influence the life of the believer. A similar structure can also be seen in Galatians, Ephesians, Colossians, and 1 Timothy.

Biblically, the pastor has two primary activities: the evangelization of the lost and the edification of the saved. In John 21 those two concerns are seen in Christ's ministry to Peter and the other disciples. John 21:1-14 recounts the post-resurrection appearance of the Lord as He directed the disciples to a successful fishing venture after their long night of failure. Jesus used that incident to reassure the disciples that He had forgiven them and was expecting them to get back to the work of fishing for men. Then in John 21:15-23 Jesus probed the love that Peter had for Him and commanded Peter to shepherd or feed His sheep. The fishing and the feeding make up the major responsibilities of the pastor. Evangelism is the primary source of growth for the church and edification is the strength of the church. Those two activities characterize the work of the apostles in the book of Acts (cf. Acts 2:43-47).

THEOLOGY AND EVANGELISM

The pastor is to do the work of an evangelist (2 Tim. 4:5) even if he does not possess the gift of evangelism. The pastor's theological perspective will have a major influence on his evangelistic fervor. At issue is his definition of the gospel.

Throughout the history of the church the biblical definition of the gospel in 1 Corinthians 15:1-5 has been the accepted view. That definition focuses on the death and resurrection of Christ for the sins of all mankind. Salvation involves the forgiveness of sins and the inauguration of a new life in the believer (2 Cor. 5:17).

In the last century that definition of the gospel has changed radically in the belief and practice of many segments of the church. The social problems in America at the end of the nineteenth century saw a development of what has become known as the social gospel. Some saw it not as an alternative way of finding salvation but rather as a banding together of regenerate men in common causes. Others declared that reformed social institutions were a means of grace, "even the means of grace."[1]

By 1930 the fundamentalist-modernist controversy had divided liberal and conservative views of the gospel even more radically. The social gospel became the expression of a humanistic philosophy. Most liberals had replaced the biblical gospel of personal salvation through faith in Christ's redemptive work with a gospel that involved bringing social betterment to mankind.[2]

The evangelistic efforts of many of the major denominations were blunted by that social gospel emphasis. Because the liberals no longer believed in the holiness of God or the sinfulness of man, they lost concern for man's soul and sought instead to improve his environmental condition. In contrast, Bible-believing Christians accepted the validity of the commission of Christ in Matthew 28:19-20 to preach the gospel to every creature. They saw God as holy and man as sinful, needing a Savior. In each case the groups' theology determined their behavior.

The great social needs of the world continue to grow more desperate. The darkness of sin grips the planet. Each individual has only one life to give. He must choose whether or not he will spend it in improving man's environment or seeking to save man's soul. Those who adopt a biblical theology must have as their top priority the salvation of man's eternal soul. Then they can seek to help him in whatever other ways they can.

A new form of social activism has emerged in recent years. The concern is not for the improvement of man's environment to meet his basic physical needs. Rather that new activism is concerned with man's moral climate. It desires to improve man's moral climate by influencing or controlling state and national legislative bodies. Some go so far as to say that the only hope for America is to remove what they call the humanistic basis of its laws and reconstruct the Christian civilization of the west "on Christian creedal foundations."[3]

Others take a directly opposite position indicating that the fault lies not in the system of laws but in the hearts of the people. To them the real solution lies in a return to old values and the return of the individual to God.[4] The emphasis of a pastor's ministry will directly relate to the stance he takes on those issues. Clearly this country needs a return to a moral climate free of the abuses that have been seen in the last half of this century. But when the center of ministry moves away from a preaching and teaching that leads people to regeneration through personal faith in Jesus Christ, that preaching has aborted its biblical and theological priorities.

It seems safe to predict that where the emphasis is placed on political reform rather than individual spiritual regeneration or renewal there may well be a misdirection of the activities of the pastor. That may result in the same kind of dissipation of spiritual priorities that characterized the social gospel movement. The real problem seems to be that when the social emphasis is brought to a level of priority equal to that of biblical evangelism, the practice of the ministry tends to shift in the direction of this new priority.

Meadors speaks of that tendency in the ministry of John R. W. Stott as seen in Stott's "Cornerstone" articles in *Christianity Today* from September 21, 1979 to May 23, 1980. In pointing out Stott's emphasis on Christians being active in industrial justice, social missions, anti-war and anti-nuclear power movements, political involvement, and universal opportunity for economic equality, Meadors states:

> It is impossible to evade the impression that the present burden of John R. W. Stott is more social than evangelistic. Evangelicals should be saddened by the fact that Stott has decided to emphasize social action even more than evangelism. His vigorous role of leadership in evangelical missions over the past several years has gained him a place of prominence and respect in both Europe and America. If his new message is followed, evangelism in the third world will suffer.[5]

The real tragedy in the movement away from the biblical gospel toward social activism is seen in the emerging evidence that religious revivals and periods of spiritual reformation have been the major causes of desired social reform. McLoughlin links America's five great religious awakenings to America's five great movements of social reform. He has found that awakenings are periods of revitalization born in times of cultural stress that produce drastic social reform. "To understand the functions of American revivalism and revitalization is to understand the power and meaning of America as a civilization."[6] He further states:

> I propose . . . to view the five great awakenings that have shaped and reshaped our culture since 1607 as periods of fundamental ideological transformation necessary to the dynamic growth of the nation in adapting to basic social, ecological, psychological, and economic changes. The conversion of great numbers of people from an old to a new world view (a new ideological or religious understanding of their place in the cosmos) is a natural and necessary aspect of social change.[7]

McLoughlin sees America currently in a period of awakening. He suggests that this period began in the 1960s and may extend to 1990.[8] Some of the present influence has come from Eastern religions, perhaps because so many have abandoned the biblical gospel for a weak social gospel. Certainly this is a time for pastors to strengthen the theological base of their evangelism and to reach out to meet the inner needs of a struggling humanity. Those who come to trust Christ can have their lives changed (2 Cor. 5:17). Such a change has profound social implications.

THEOLOGY AND EDIFICATION

The pastor must concern himself with the evangelism of the lost. Of equal importance, however, is the edification of the saints. The pastor's theology will regulate the diet that he feeds his people. The source of his teaching is always the Word of God as mandated in 2 Timothy 3:16-17. "All Scripture is inspired by God and profitable for teaching, for reproof, for correction, for training in righteousness; that the man of God may be adequate, equipped for every good work."

The pastor must be a master of the Bible. The sermons that he preaches and the lessons that he teaches must be clear, biblically-based, theological statements that handle "accurately the word of truth" (2 Tim. 2:15).

The recent publication of the *Lindsell Study Bible* points out the need for the pastor to have his theological views clearly established. Lindsell states in the introduction concerning the footnotes of the study Bible:

> The reader should know that the footnotes present a variety of views on matters about which Christians have differed across the years. Thus, for example, neither infant baptism nor anti-infant baptism views are promoted, although information is available by way of explanation for both views. So also various notes present Calvinistic, Arminian, and Dispensational views. A variety of viewpoints about the millennium and the second advent are also given.[9]

A congregation of believers using those footnotes will be looking to someone to explain to them which of the many views are correct. The pastor will be the person to whom that responsibility will fall most often. The awareness of opposing views will increase the requirements for the pastor to give a clear answer for his theological position.

The way in which the pastor uses the Scriptures in edification will be primarily influenced by his theological stance on the authority of the Bible. If he holds a strong position on biblical inspiration and inerrancy, he will preach an authoritative message. If he is weak on that point the diet he feeds his people will also be weak.

While pursuing a master's degree in communication at Bowling Green State University, I sought to validate the generalization stated in the paragraph above. I studied the sermons of eight American Protestant preachers of national reputation.[10] The list included men from a wide range of theological positions. Each of the men responded to a questionnaire sent to him and clarified his theological position. Each provided the name of a sermon representative of his preaching. A rhetorical and homiletical analysis was made of each representative sermon to determine the use made of the Bible. The sermon was compared to many other sermons by the same preacher to validate the conclusions. It was apparent that the preacher's theology influenced his use of the Bible.

BUTTRICK AND OCKENGA

George Buttrick, then pastor of Harvard University Memorial Church in Cambridge, Massachusetts, and Harold John Ockenga, then pastor of Park Street Church in Boston, provided a clear contrast in their use of the Bible. Ockenga's conservative theology led him to use the Bible in a much more intense way then did Buttrick's neo-orthodox position. Ockenga preached expository sermons based on the biblical text. The supporting arguments to enforce the truth of the text were drawn almost wholly from the Bible. He devoted the major portion of his ministry to a verse-by-verse study of individual books of the Bible. He had preached in that fashion through the entire New Testament while at the Park Street Church in Boston.[11] Ockenga made the following theological statement of his view of biblical authority. "The historical view of the Bible as the Word of God has three parts: first, God has spoken; second, the spoken word is inscripturated in the Bible by inspiration; third, the recorded word is authoritative for faith and life."[12]

Buttrick's neo-orthodox theology led him to a liberal view of biblical inspiration. "But can we know the very words of Jesus? No, any honest New Testament scholar is aware of the barriers that beset that task. Yet we can know the *Word* of Jesus within the record of his words, for his silent Spirit is given to those who would follow him."[13]

Buttrick's preaching was textual and biblical but lacked the authoritative ring of clear theological statements. The biblical gospel of 1 Corinthians 15:1-5 became simply "God's love." In a sermon that he considered characteristic of his preaching, he said of Christ:

> At the Cross all the self-hate of men whose pride made human life inferior was spewed on him, and he exposed his heart to it—soldiers loathing their job, the dispossessed mob bitter because they were dispossessed. Temple leaders despising themselves because they knew the Temple asked of them better loyalty. All this he accepted and, there in the alchemy of his own spirit, changed it into revelation and love. That selfsame love, known by faith to be God's love for us is our redemption.[14]

MCCRACKEN AND LEE

Robert J. McCracken was then pastor of the Riverside Church, New York City, which was the church made famous by Harry Emerson Fosdick. His liberal theology gave him a weak view of Scripture. Although he sometimes used the Bible extensively, he preached sermons that at times contained no reference to the Bible. By contrast, Robert G. Lee, then pastor of Bellevue

Baptist Church in Memphis, Tennessee, who stated that he was a conservative-fundamentalist, preached sermons that were saturated with Scripture.

McCracken chose not to give a brief statement of his theological position to this author. He stated that he owed much to his Scottish Presbyterian teachers and had found "in the thinking of men like H. R. Mackintosh and John Baillie guidance and direction."[15] Although the writings of both Mackintosh and Baillie revealed great respect for the Bible, Baillie made the following statement on the nature of biblical revelation.

> We must remind ourselves again that revelation has place only within the relationship between the Holy Spirit of God and the individual human soul. Nothing is the vehicle of revelation for me unless I hear God speaking to me through it. But there is no Christian who hears God speaking to him through every passage in the Bible, so that for each of us there are some passages that are not revelatory at all.[16]

Baillie was willing to admit that the problem was often not with the Bible but with the individual reader's unwillingness to listen.[17] He stated what he considered to be the key issue concerning the nature of inspiration.

> What is denied is the inerrancy of Scripture, which is the same as to say its plenary inspiration. . . . Nothing could be more artificial than to suppose that these writers were endowed with infallibility in all that they had in mind to say, while the Holy Spirit left them to their own devices as to how they should say it. Hence on the other hand we should have no hesitation in affirming that inspiration extended not only to the thought of the writers, but to the very words they employed in the expression of these thoughts: though in neither case can we say that the inspiration was plenary. If then inspiration is not regarded as plenary there is no reason why we should not believe in verbal inspiration.[18]

It is interesting to note at this point that what was a common liberal view twenty years ago is now being openly supported by many evangelicals. Lindsell warns of the danger of that defection.

> No matter how sincere a man may be, and however carefully he guards against further theological concessions, they are inevitable once inerrancy is given up. . . . I am saying that whether

it takes five or fifty years any denomination or parachurch group that forsakes inerrancy will end up shipwrecked. It is impossible to prevent the surrender of other important doctrinal teachings of the Word of God when inerrancy is gone.[19]

McCracken used the Bible in his preaching. It formed the logical base for most of his assertions. However, he would at times preach entire sermons with no mention of the Bible. Such a sermon was his "Wanted: A New Moral Sense." It was included in *Best Sermons.*[20] A similar sermon was found in the 1955 edition of *Best Sermons.*[21] Its title was "Where Does the Sense of Moral Obligation Come From?" It contained seventeen references to other sources and only one to the Bible.

Robert G. Lee stands in sharp contrast to McCracken in both his use of the Bible and in his concept of inspiration. Lee expressed his view of biblical inspiration clearly.

> I go to study with no doubts about the Bible being the inspired Word of God. I believe and preach that "all scripture is given by inspiration of God" (II Tim. 3:16)—I believe that the whole Bible is supernatural in origin, divine in authorship, infallible in authority, infinite in scope, universal in interest, eternal in duration, inestimable in value, unequaled in simplicity of expression, regenerative in power, inspired in totality—the miracle Book of diversity in unity, of harmony in infinite complexity.[22]

Lee insisted that he never tried to substitute a "Thus saith the mind of man" for a "Thus saith the Lord."[23]

The sermon that Lee considered characteristic was "Great Is the Lord."[24] The sermon contained over ten thousand words. By contrast, the average number of words in the characteristic sermons of the other preachers noted in this study was about two or three thousand words. Lee's sermon was textual and was based on Psalm 48:1: "Great is the Lord, and greatly to be praised." There were eighty-six references to various biblical texts in the sermon and forty-four references to nonbiblical sources. Characteristically, Lee laced all his sermons with an extensive use of Scripture.

SOCKMAN AND BARNHOUSE

Ralph W. Sockman, then pastor of Christ Church in New York City, and Donald Grey Barnhouse, then pastor of Tenth Presbyterian Church in Philadephia, were both highly effective in radio and television preaching. Although both men used the Bible consistently, it was apparent that the conservative views held by Barnhouse gave him a greater confidence in the Bible and resulted in his expository method of Bible preaching. Sockman, who held a liberal view of Scripture, used the Bible to a lesser degree.

Sockman indicated that he was on the liberal side and "in the trend of Fosdick, Buttrick, Harold Phillips, only further down the ladder."[25] He was known as a preacher of the social gospel. "He places his influence on the side of those social developments which are generally classified as 'liberal': i.e., the right of labor to organize, the participation of the United States in the United Nations, the extension of the benefits of education to larger groups, the end of racial discrimination."[26] Sockman's view of biblical inspiration was the liberal position that the Bible was a human book rather than the inspired Word of God. Its authority was great, but not in the sense that a conservative theologian understood biblical authority.[27]

Sockman's preaching reflected his theological position. A study of thirty of his published sermons revealed a homiletical procedure that was a combination of the standard textual and topical forms of sermon construction. In those sermons Sockman chose a text and based his sermon on an idea that he found in the text. The number of references to the Bible averaged fifteen, and the average number of references to other sources was nineteen. Sockman preached many topical sermons in which his use of the Bible was slight as compared to references to or quotations from important persons, life situation experiences, literature, poetry, historical characters, history, current events, and science.[28]

In contrast to Sockman, Barnhouse held a conservative theological position with a high view of biblical inspiration. He was an expository preacher. "The prime factor in expository preaching is the belief that the Bible is the Word of God. I can speak of this only as I know it. When I take the Bible into my hands I think of it as originating from God, given by Him to man in the very order, terms, phrases, and words in which He wanted us to have it."[29]

The sermon "Living from the Word of God,"[30] was characteristic of Barnhouse's expository method. The sermon was an exposition of Ephesians 6:17-18. It included fourteen references to the Bible in addition to his extensive references to the chosen text. The word *Bible* was used twenty-five times in the sermon and the phrase *Word of God* was used nine times. The only references to other sources were six illustrations or anecdotes that were used to illustrate the idea of the text.

PEALE AND GRAHAM

Billy Graham's conservative theology led him to Bible-saturated sermons. By contrast, Norman Vincent Peale used the Bible the least of any of the preachers studied. This seemed to validate the general conclusion that a preacher's theology influences his use of the Bible, for Peale's self-stated theology was more obscure and difficult to define than any of the preachers studied. Peale stated that the exact nature of his theology was not the important aspect of his ministry. He wished to be evaluated on the basis of help that he had given to people. In response to my questionnaire he replied, "I tend to the conservative point of view." But he then added, "I would suggest that you perhaps get another subject as to theology, as I do not feel in a position to give you enough information as to be helpful."[32]

Peale's view of inspiration was virtually impossible to deduce. It was obvious that he held the Bible in high regard particularly when it spoke to life related issues. He said of the Bible, "If you want the truth about life, here is where to find it,"[33] and, "the Bible is the greatest of all textbooks on the science of human behavior."[34] He advocated the use of biblical "Thought Conditioners" and recommended a thorough system of Scripture reading and memorization.[35]

Peale stated that he did not regard his sermons as sermons in the usual sense of the word since he delivered them extemporaneously.[36] In seeking to understand Peale's use of the Bible in his preaching, one hundred and seventy-seven sermons preached at Marble Collegiate Church over a period of several years were carefully examined. In every sermon Peale stated a text. He usually made a quick remark about the text or drew a topic idea from it and then began to illustrate profusely with examples of individuals who had applied the idea to themselves. The sermons were all topical.

Peale's sermons contained an average of five references to the Bible and an average of sixteen references to other sources. Of those other sources those used most were anecdotes drawn from Peale's personal contact with people and testimonial letters written by individuals. He also made repeated reference to his philosophy of positive thinking and drew ideas from it for application to the sermons. No sermons were found that had more than eight or less than two references to the Bible. There were usually no attempts to point out the meaning of the biblical references in their context or to indicate the theological significance of the texts.

By contrast, Graham's phrase, "the Bible says," has become famous all over the world. He preaches topical sermons on the new birth based on the Bible. His view of the inspiration of Scripture follows the pattern of his conservative theology. "Some people do not believe with me theologically. In England they say that I am taking preaching back fifty years. I must plead guilty. I believe in the verbal inspiration of the Bible, the Virgin Birth, the vicarious atonement, and in the bodily resurrection of our Lord."[37]

Graham has clearly expressed his view of the Bible and his position on the matter of the Bible's authority.

> Christianity finds all its doctrines stated in the Bible, and the true Christian denies no part, nor attempts to add anything to the Word of God. While the Constitution of the United States may be amended from time to time, no amendment is ever necessary for the Bible. We truly believe that the men who wrote the Bible were guided by the Holy Spirit, both in the thoughts they expressed and in their choice of words.[38]

The study of these eight preachers illustrates again that a pastor's theology does greatly influence the diet that he feeds his people. That is expressed clearly by Haddon W. Robinson.

> The man in the pulpit faces the pressing temptation to deliver some message other than that of the Scriptures—a political system (either right-wing or left-wing), a theory of economics, a new religious philosophy, old religious slogans, a trend in

psychology. A preacher can proclaim anything in a stained-glass voice, at 11:30 on Sunday morning, following the singing of hymns. Yet when a preacher fails to preach the Scriptures, he abandons his authority. He confronts his hearers no longer with a word from God but only with another word from men.[39]

There can be no question that Christians need to be more active in reaching out to those who are in need. But mankind's greatest needs are spiritual. A balanced ministry requires that that be the highest priority. The pastor must set as his goal the task of winning souls to Christ and helping them grow into His image. As he does that he may also minister to those individuals to help meet some of their physical and emotional needs. He can do so with the assurance that he has not left their greatest need untouched.

THEOLOGY AND THE FUTURE

The present theological scene is filled with great confusion. Many pastors who faithfully preach the Bible are finding themselves facing decisions that were little known to previous generations. Members of the congregation are expecting balanced, biblically-based responses to such issues as gay rights and the feminist movement. They want to know what their individual responsibility should be in political affairs. They demand answers on the right-to-life issues and the question of abortion.

Only those who have a firm theological base will be able to cope with the emerging issues of medical ethics such as genetic engineering, artificial insemination, and euthanasia. A biblically-based social ethic will be a requirement for pastors in the future. The pastor will need to minister to people who are having or have had charismatic experiences. America's rising divorce rate also seems to indicate that a ministry to those who are divorced and remarried will characterize the future service of the church.

The pastor who has not laid a firm personal foundation of theological commitment may find his future ministry tottering on an uncertain base. He may be tempted to place too much emphasis on current issues and thus slight the essential matters of biblical evangelism and edification. Those who have taken the time to develop a clearly integrated biblical theology may find the going difficult, but they will have a solid base on which to build an effective ministry. They will maintain the biblical priorities of evangelizing the lost and building up the saved. From that sound theological base they will reach out to a dying world with a message of hope and with actions that are truly life-changing.

NOTES

1. DeWitte Holland, ed., *Preaching in American History* (Nashville: Abingdon, 1969), p. 226.
2. DeWitte Holland, ed., *America in Controversy* (Dubuque: Brown, 1973), p. 195.
3. Rousas John Rushdoony, *The Foundations of Social Order* (Philadelphia: Presbyterian and Reformed, 1968), p. 226.
4. Ralph W. Hood and Rene Noorbergen, *The Death Cry of an Eagle* (Grand Rapids: Zondervan, 1980), p. 184.
5. Gary T. Meadors, "John R. W. Stott on Social Action," *Grace Theological Journal* 1 (Fall 1980):147.
6. William G. McLouglin, *Revivals, Awakenings, and Reform* (Chicago: U. of Chicago, 1978), pp. 1-216.
7. Ibid., p. 8.
8. Ibid., pp. 179-216.
9. Harold Lindsell, ed., in foreword to the *Lindsell Study Bible* (Wheaton, Ill.: Tyndale, 1980).
10. John W. Reed, "The Use of the Bible in the Preaching of Eight Representative American Preachers" (Master's thesis, Bowling Green State University, 1961).
11. Clarence Stonelynn Roddy, ed., *We Prepare and Preach* (Chicago: Moody, 1959), p. 115.
12. Harold J. Ockenga, *The Church in God* (Westwood, N.J.: Revell, 1956), p. 85.
13. George Arthur Buttrick, *Sermons Preached in a University Church* (New York: Abingdon, 1959), p. 86.
14. Ibid., p. 50.
15. Thesis questionnaire received from Dr. Robert J. McCracken in answer to request by John W. Reed, 27 September 1960.
16. John Baillie, *The Idea of Revelation in Recent Thought* (New York: Columbia U., 1956), p. 119.
17. Ibid.
18. Ibid., p. 115.
19. Harold Lindsell, *The Battle for the Bible* (Grand Rapids: Zondervan, 1976), pp. 142-43.

20. G. Paul Butler, ed., *Best Sermons*, 1949-50 ed. (New York: Harper, 1949), pp. 16-22.
21. G. Paul Butler, ed., *Best Sermons*, 1955 ed. (New York, McGraw-Hill, 1955), pp. 89-91.
22. Roddy, p. 81.
23. Ibid., pp. 81-82.
24. Robert G. Lee, *Great Is the Lord* (Westwood, N.J.: Revell, 1955), pp. 109-31.
25. Personal letters received by John W. Reed from Ralph W. Sockman, 4 October 1960.
26. Everett C. Parker, David W. Barry, and Dallas W. Smythe, *The Television-Radio Audience and Religion* (New York: Harper, 1955), p. 133.
27. Ralph W. Sockman, *Recoveries in Religion* (Nashville: Cokesbury, 1938), pp. 61-62; and Ralph W. Sockman, *Now to Live* (New York: Abingdon-Cokesbury, 1946), p. 59.
28. Reed, pp. 74-77.
29. Roddy, pp. 29-30.
30. Ibid., pp. 37-44.
31. Arthur Gordon, *Norman Vincent Peale, Minister to Millions* (Englewood Cliffs, N.J.: Prentice-Hall, 1958), p. 254.
32. Personal letter from Norman Vincent Peale to John W. Reed, 12 October 1960.
33. Norman Vincent Peale, *Life Can Always Be Yours* (Pawling, N.Y.: Foundation for Christian Living, 1960), p. 3.
34. Gordon, p. 179.
35. Norman Vincent Peale, *Inspired Messages for Daily Living* (Englewood Cliffs, N.J.: Prentice-Hall, 1955), pp. 3-4.
36. Personal letter from Peale to Reed, 12 October 1960.
37. Curtis Mitchell, *God in the Garden* (Garden City, N.Y.: Doubleday, 1957), pp. 21-22.
38. Billy Graham, *Peace with God* (Garden City, N.Y.: Doubleday, 1953), p. 27.
39. Haddon W. Robinson, *Biblical Preaching* (Grand Rapids: Baker, 1980), p. 18.

18

The Preacher As Persuader

Donald R. Sunukjian

When the preacher stands to speak, is he an expositor or a persuader? Should the preacher view himself as an expositor—one who makes the message plain but leaves the results to God? Is his task simply to unfold the Scriptures, to make the Word clear, to explain the biblical content? Is the goal of preaching simply to be instruction and understanding? Or, should the preacher view himself as a persuader—one who consciously does his best to move his hearers in a certain direction?[1] Is it his responsibility to skillfully influence his audience toward some specific course of action? Is the goal of preaching to seek to change the attitudes or behavior of the listener?

Some, perhaps, would answer affirmatively to the first set of questions. Their thinking might be as follows: "It is the preacher's job to declare truth, not to persuade men. His responsibility is to make the Word clear; only God can make it

DONALD R. SUNUKJIAN (A.B., University of Southern California; Th.M., Th.D., Dallas Theological Seminary; Ph.D., University of California at Los Angeles) is associate professor of pastoral ministries at Dallas Theological Seminary, Dallas, Texas.

effective." That group believes that the goal in preaching is to proclaim God's Word. Any attempt to shape or induce a response would be fleshly activity, and the results would be of men and not of God. Whatever effect is achieved from preaching should not be due to the preacher's skill or to the attractiveness of his presentation. Any results should be attributed solely to the fact that the Word is alive and that the Spirit's power has made it accomplish God's purpose. Furthermore, those individuals argue, the Scriptures themselves reject any focus on persuasion. The Scriptures teach that God's work is "not by might, nor by power, but by [His] Spirit" (Zech. 4:6). The Scriptures warn that "unless the LORD builds the house, they labor in vain who build it" (Psalm 127:1). And, in the words of Paul, the Scriptures commend a type of preaching that rests on the power of God and not on the persuasion of men. "And when I came to you, brethren, I did not come with superiority of speech or of wisdom, proclaiming to you the testimony of God. For I determined to know nothing among you except Jesus Christ, and Him crucified. And I was with you in weakness and in fear and in much trembling. And my message and my preaching were not in persuasive words of wisdom, but in demonstration of the Spirit and of power, that your faith should not rest on the wisdom of men, but on the power of God" (1 Cor. 2:1-5).

Such a view initially commends itself because of its readiness to be content with a simple proclamation as opposed to anything that might hint of coercion or manipulation. At its best it represents a genuine desire to turn from the abuses, the psychological excesses, and the unethical pressures that sometimes occur under the name of "persuasion." But to maintain that "our goal is to make the message clear and to leave the results to God" is to neglect some clear teaching of Scripture and to miss the excitement of a partnership with God.

The purpose of this article is to suggest that every preacher intuitively acts as a persuader, that the Scriptures teach persuasion as the goal of preaching, and that God has sovereignly chosen to accomplish His purposes through the combination of human skill and divine power.

AN INTUITIVE ACT

Though a preacher might not consciously view himself as a persuader, his choices in preaching indicate that he intuitively believes that his goal is to change men and that what he says or does on a human level will largely determine whether or not that happens.

In the first place, the very decision to stand and preach has at its heart a persuasive intent. It indicates a desire to cause growth, to produce a difference, to influence a change in either salvation or spiritual maturity. The intuitive reason for speaking is to achieve some change in the listener's behavior.

Second, any "expositional elaboration" of the biblical content is also a tacit acknowledgment that the preacher is a persuasive agent in the process. If the power of the Word and the activity of the Spirit are all that really matter in preaching, then even an expositional amplification is superfluous. A simple reading of the Scriptures, in the original Hebrew and Greek languages, should be sufficient to elicit a response from the hearers. If that reduction ad absurdum is rejected, however, the argument quickly moves to the opposite extreme. Once it is acknowledged that the supernatural requires the least bit of human assistance, then it is difficult to object to the maximum amount. If reading the Scriptures from an English translation and discoursing on them in sermonic form is not a contradiction of divine power, then neither is persuading from them according to the best of the speaker's ability.

Third, whenever the preacher "applies" the content, he reveals most clearly that his intent is to move the listener in a desired direction. As soon as the sermon moves to answer the question, "What does this mean to me?" the preacher has moved beyond a simple understanding of what the Bible says, and has begun to concern himself with the response he wants the listener to make.

Thus, the very fact that a man decides to preach at all, the fact that he enlarges on the biblical sentences, and the fact that he applies the content all indicate a persuasive desire to move men and an intuitive assumption that what he is saying will somehow make a difference in whether it will happen or not.

A Scriptural Pattern

That intuitive behavior is openly articulated in the New Testament. The Scriptures teach that the preacher is to aim at persuasion; he is to speak for the purpose of moving men to a desired response. The persuasive focus in preaching is confirmed by an examination of Paul's comments in 1 Corinthians 2:1-5 and by an understanding of his preaching in general.

First Corinthians 2:1-5

Paul's remarks in 1 Corinthians 2:1-5 need to be understood not as a rejection of persuasion but as a comment on his oratorical style and an explanation of his speaking vocabulary.

The apostle is reminding the Corinthians that when he spoke among them his oratorical style did not follow the fashion of the day. When he came to Corinth, he did not employ the "superiority of speech or of wisdom" (1 Cor. 2:1) that were so common among contemporary orators. He did not imitate the current inflated style by using "persuasive words of wisdom" (1 Cor. 2:4), but instead he used a simple, straightforward style and relied on the Spirit and power of God.

To fully understand Paul's comments, it is necessary to know that by the middle of the first century A.D. Greek oratory had focused almost exclusively on the matter of style. The rhetoric of Paul's day was almost totally preoccupied with the ornamental aspects of public speaking. This preoccupation can best be seen by considering: (1) the treatises that were being written, (2) the Asiatic-Atticist controversy that was raging, and (3) the Second Sophistic movement that was emerging.

For several centuries prior to Paul the subject of speech style had been receiving more and more attention in the rhetorical treatises being written. In the fourth century B.C. Aristotle dealt only briefly with the matter in the third book of his *"Art" of Rhetoric*. But from that modest beginning the element of style soon came to dominate the theoretical works of classical authors. Half of the *Rhetorica ad Herenium* (86 B.C.) is devoted to the kinds and qualities of style. Most of Cicero's attention in his *De Oratore* (58 B.C.), *De Optimo Genere Oratorum* (46 B.C.), *Brutus* (46 B.C.), and *Orator* (46 B.C.) is directed to stylistic matters. And at the turn of the first century, that one aspect of speaking is the total concern of Dionysius's *On Literary Composition*, Longinus's *On the Sublime*, and Demetrius's *On Style*. In other words, the matter of speech style, initially only a limited segment of the literature, became the dominating feature of classical theory by the time of Paul.

Certain historical and political factors accounted for that concentration on stylistic theories. As Greek democracy faded and power became concentrated in the hands of the imperial authorities, popular assemblies became both infrequent and perfunctory since their decisions could be altered at any moment. Pleading in the courts was simultaneously restricted. As a result, the voice of the orator no longer had any force in legislative or judicial matters, and his only remaining outlet as a public speaker was the ceremonial oratory of special occasions. Baldwin describes that narrowing of public address.

> Of the three fields of oratory distinguished by Aristotle, deliberative, forensic, and occasional, the first was restricted by political changes. It faded with democracy. So later it faded at Rome, and still later in other realms. Deliberative oratory presupposes free discussion and audiences that vote. The steady increase of government from above administered by an appointed official class hastened also the tendency of the second kind of oratory, forensic, to become technical, the special art of legal pleading. Thus the only field left free was the third, occasional oratory, encomium, or panegyric, the commemoration of persons and days, the address of welcome, the public lecture.[2]

The narrowing of the field of oratory had a concomitant effect on the focus of rhetorical theory. Since only the innocuous and utterly predictable inanities of ceremonial occasions were open to the orator and since his success on such occasions would depend more on *how* he spoke than on *what* he said, it was only natural that the theorists would turn their attention to that which had the most immediate and utilitarian value—the treatment of speech style.

As the subject of style became of paramount theoretical interest, there arose a dispute known as the Asiatic-Atticist controversy. The quarrel between the Asiatics and Atticists was largely over the relative merits of the plain and grand styles of speech. The rhetorical theory of the day recognized three different oratorical styles—the plain, the middle, and the grand. According to Cicero, the plain style orator is "to the point, explaining everything and making every point clear rather than impressive, using a refined, concise style stripped of ornament."[3] He follows the "ordinary usage," uses "plain and simple" words, and avoids "the charm and richness of figurative ornament."[4] He is free from "the bonds of rhythm," "modest" in metaphor, and not "bold in coining words."[5] "His delivery is not that of tragedy nor of the stage; he will employ only slight movements of the body, but will trust a great deal to his expression."[6] His speech, however, is "sprinkled with the salt of pleasantry," i.e., with humor and wit.[7]

"The second style is fuller and somewhat more robust than the simple style just described."[8] This middle style contains "a minimum of vigour, and a maximum of charm. For it is richer than the unadorned style, but plainer than the ornate and opulent style."[9] It uses neither the intellectual appeal of the former, nor the fiery force of the latter.

> Akin to both, excelling in neither, sharing in both, or to tell the truth, sharing in neither, this style keeps the proverbial 'even tenor of its way,' bringing nothing except ease and uniformity, or at most adding a few posies as in a garland, and diversifying the whole speech with simple ornaments of thought and diction.[10]

"The orator of the third style is magnificent, opulent, stately and ornate."[11] His eloquence "rushes along with the roar of a mighty stream," and "has power to sway men's minds and move them in every possible way."[12] The grand orator shows "splendid power of thought and majesty of diction;" he is "forceful, versatile, copious and grave, trained and equipped to arouse and sway the emotions."[13]

The orators of Asia Minor preferred the florid, luxuriant, and bombastic rhetoric of the grand style. The Atticists favored the plain style, which was characterized by clearness, simplicity, and restraint. The heat of the controversy belongs to the latter half of the first century B.C. and is reflected in the works of Cicero and Quintilian.[14] The important point to note here is that by the time of Paul the Greek world had been split into two camps—those who favored the elegant and pure style associated with Athens and Corinth, and those who preferred the flowery and redundant prose that came out of Ephesus and the cities of Asia.

Those two phenomena—the theoretical preoccupation with style, and the Asiatic-Atticist controversy—eventually culminated in an era of Greek oratory known as the Second Sophistic. The Second Sophistic can best be described as the triumph of the Asiatic school.[15] The oratory of that period was committed to the extravagances of the grand style. Whereas Aristotle had conceived of rhetoric as the art of giving effectiveness to the truth, the Second Sophistics saw it only as a means of giving effectiveness to the speaker.

> The sophist was over-expressive lest for a moment he should cease to be impressive. The audience need not be held to any course of thought; it must not be held too long by any one device of style; but it must unflaggingly admire. It must be spell-bound. The constant implication of Philostratus probably echoes the idea of orator and audience alike: behold a great speaker![16]

During that era it mattered little whether the speaker had a purpose in speaking. The glory of the speech was an end in itself.

> For the composition of the whole speech sophistic generally had little care. That planned sequence, that leading on of the mind from point to point, which is the habit of great orators and the chief means of cogency, presupposes urgency toward a goal. Sophistic often had no goal. The audience need be won only to admiration, not to decision.[17]

The mark of the Second Sophistic is that it "reduced rhetoric to style"[18] and made the speaker more important than the speech.

That, then, was the state of oratory in the middle of the first century A.D. The theorists had been focusing on the single element of style, the orators had been polarized into two stylistic factions, and the Asiatic devotees of the grand style were beginning to carry the day. It is against the backdrop of those trends that Paul writes to the Corinthians. "And when I come to you, brethren, I did not come with superiority of speech or of wisdom, proclaiming to you the testimony of God. For I determined to know nothing among you except Jesus Christ, and Him crucified. And I was with you in weakness and in fear and in much trembling. And my message and my preaching were not in persuasive words of wisdom, but in demonstration of the Spirit and of power, that your faith should not rest on the wisdom of men, but on the power of God" (1 Cor. 2:1-5).

Paul had not come to Corinth with the flowery words and elaborate style of an Asiatic orator. Rather, he had spoken in reliance on the power of the Spirit and had used the straightforward speech that was associated with their own Attic region. Nor had he been, as a Sophistic orator, more concerned about his own image than about the substance of his speech. On the contrary, his presence among them had been nothing and the substance of his speech had been everything. He had been with them "in weakness and in fear and in much trembling," and his unfailing theme had been "Jesus Christ, and Him crucified." Whenever he preached, the style and substance of his message was such that men's faith "should not rest on the wisdom of men, but on the power of God."[19]

In 1 Corinthians 2:1-5, therefore, Paul is not rejecting persuasion. Instead, he is recalling his continual determination to preach in a clear and cogent style, and to emphasize the message rather than the speaker.

PAUL'S PREACHING

Paul's own preaching reveals a strong persuasive intent. Throughout his sermons in Acts his purpose is not simply to inform, or expound, or teach, or instruct. An analysis of his message to Jewish, Gentile, and Christian audiences reveals instead a continuous attempt to persuade.[20] All of his efforts are deliberately directed toward moving his listeners to a specific response.

The biblical pattern of persuasion is not only seen in Paul's individual sermons, but also in the general description of all his preaching. The book of Acts repeatedly uses the Greek word peithō ("to persuade") to describe the nature and results of Paul's preaching activity. After the apostle's sermon to the Jews of Pisidian Antioch, the follow-up activity is recorded. "Now when the meeting of the synagogue had broken up, many of the Jews and of the God-fearing proselytes followed Paul and Barnabas, who, speaking to them, were urging [peithō] them to continue in the grace of God" (Acts 13:43).

When Paul was in Thessalonica, he went into the synagogue, "and for three Sabbaths reasoned with them from the Scriptures, explaining and giving evidence that the Christ had to suffer and rise again from the dead, and saying, 'This Jesus whom I am proclaiming to you is the Christ.' And some of them were persuaded [peithō] and joined Paul and Silas, along with a great multitude of the God-fearing Greeks and a number of the leading women" (Acts 17:2-4).

The same pattern of persuasion appeared in Corinth as Paul "was reasoning in the synagogue every Sabbath and trying to persuade [peithō] Jews and Greeks" (Acts 18:4). In Ephesus he "entered the synagogue and continued speaking out boldly for three months, reasoning and persuading [peithō] them about the kingdom of God" (Acts 19:8). The objection of the silversmiths to his preaching in Ephesus was that he had "persuaded [peithō] and turned away a considerable number of people" (Acts 19:26). Even King Agrippa sensed the impelling thrust of Paul's words and remarked, "In a short time you will persuade [peithō] me to become a Christian" (Acts 26:28).

Finally, the book of Acts closes with the apostle in Rome, seeking to persuade the Jews. "And when they had set a day for him, they came to him at his lodging in large numbers; and he was explaining to them by solemnly testifying about the kingdom of God, and trying to persuade [peithō] them concerning Jesus, both from the Law of Moses and from the Prophets, from morning until evening. And some were being persuaded [piethō] by the things spoken, but others would not believe" (Acts 28:23-24).

Throughout all of Paul's ministry, therefore, the goal of his preaching was not simply to expound, but also to persuade. He himself declared that the primary and consistent purpose of all of his preaching was to "persuade men" (2 Cor. 5:11).

The preacher's intuitive inclination, therefore, is the apostle's open pattern. God's man is to preach with an aim toward persuasion; he is to speak for the purpose of moving men to action. And as he does, he discovers that God has chosen to accomplish His purposes through the combination of human skill and divine power.

A Sovereign Choice

The wonder of God's working is that He chooses to use human instruments. He could send angels to clean the house of an invalid, but he chooses to scrub through the strong arms of church women. He could supernaturally prevent static in a public address system, but He chooses to correct it through the skills of an electrician. He could communicate His truth with fiery letters across the sky, but He chooses to use the imperfect eloquence of human messengers.

To those who preach, God promises the assistance of His Spirit. As a result, His spokesmen will find their memories sharpened (John 14:26), their abilities heightened (Acts 4:8-13; 6:8-10), and their boldness overflowing (Acts 4:31; 13:9-12). Difficult and reluctant audiences will strangely and unaccountably yield (John 16:7-11).

But that supernatural assistance is to be coupled with human excellence (Col. 3:23). The chosen instrument is to expend every effort, utilize every skill, and exhaust every ability. And then, in God's hands, he will be part of the outworking of God's sovereign will.

Notes

1. Persuasion is "a conscious attempt by one individual to change the attitudes, beliefs, or behavior of another individual or group of individuals through the transmission of a message" (Edwin P. Bettinghaus, *Persuasive Communication*, 3d ed. [New York: Holt, Reinhart & Winston, 1980], p. 4).
2. Charles Sears Baldwin, *Medieval Rhetoric and Poetic (to 1400), Interpreted from Representative Works* (Gloucester, Mass.: Peter Smith, 1959), p. 5.
3. Cicero *Orator* 6. 20.
4. Ibid., 23. 76, 79.
5. Ibid., 23. 77; 24. 81.
6. Ibid., 25. 86.
7. Ibid., 26. 87.
8. Ibid., 26. 91.
9. Ibid.
10. Ibid., 6. 21.
11. Ibid., 28. 97.
12. Ibid.

13. Ibid., 5. 20.
14. Cicero *Brutus* 82. 284-84. 291; *De Optimo Genere Oratorum* 3. 7-4. 10; *Orator* 7. 23-9. 32. Quintilian *Institutio Oratoria* 21. 10. 12-26. For an analysis of the Asiatic-Atticist dispute, consult M. L. Clarke, *Rhetoric at Rome; A Historical Survey* (London: Cohen & West, 1953), pp. 80-83; G. M. A. Grube, *The Greek and Roman Critics* (London: Methuen & Co., 1965), pp. 122-23, 181-84; George Kennedy, *The Art of Persuasion in Greece* (Princeton: Princeton U., 1963), pp. 302-3, 330-36; and Lester Thonssen and A. Craig Baird, *Speech Criticism; the Development of Standards for Rhetorical Appraisal* (New York: Ronald, 1948). pp. 40, 152-57, 187-90.
15. Grube, p. 325.
16. Baldwin, pp. 16-17.
17. Ibid., p. 20.
18. Ibid., p. 39.
19. It is instructive to compare Paul's rejection of "superiority of speech" [*huperochēn logoy*] and inconsequential substance with Eunapius's description of the Sophistic orator Maximus: "Maximus is one of the older and more learned students, who, because of his lofty genius and superabundant eloquence [*logōn huperochēn*] scorned all logical proof" (Eunapius *Lives of the Philosophers and Sophists* 475).
20. Donald Robert Sunukjian, "Patterns for Preaching — A Rhetorical Analysis of the Sermons of Paul in Acts 13, 17, and 20." (Th.D. dissertation, Dallas Theological Seminary, 1972).

19

Counseling and the Nature of Man

Frank B. Minirth and Paul D. Meier

The nature of man is complex, and how one views that nature has a profound impact on how one approaches the
counseling process. Various views have been proposed including the naturalistic, biological, cultural, humanistic, and existential.[1] If the counselor views man from a humanistic perspective, then, as with Rogers, he will desire to let the counselee
"self-actualize" and all will be well. The model is built on the
assumption that man is basically good, constructive, and
forward-moving. If the counselor views man from a strictly
biological perspective, he will desire to find the right drug or
physical manipulation and all will be well. But worst of all, if

PAUL D. MEIER (A.B., Bob Jones University; M.S., Michigan State University;
M.D., University of Arkansas Medical Center; residency in psychiatry, Duke
University and University of Arkansas Medical Center; graduate study toward
M.A.B.S., Dallas Theological Seminary) is assistant professor of pastoral minis-
tries at Dallas Theological Seminary, Dallas, Texas.

FRANK B. MINIRTH (B.S., Arkansas State University; M.D., University of Ar-
kansas Medical Center; internship and residency in psychiatry, University of
Arkansas Medical Center; graduate study toward M.A.B.S., Dallas Theological
Seminary) is assistant professor of pastoral ministries at Dallas Theological
Seminary, Dallas, Texas.

the counselor views man from an existential perspective he will conclude that all is hopeless anyway, so why even try!

In contrast to those perspectives, the Christian counselor views the nature of man from the perspective of the Bible. But what does the Bible say about the nature of man? The following section will examine some aspects of man's nature found in the Bible that should influence the Christian counselor.

MAN'S NATURE

MAN IS LOST

Basic to the understanding of counseling and the nature of man is the realization that apart from the saving grace of Christ man is lost in his sin. To help someone solve his present problem while ignoring his eternal destiny seems poor logic at best. Without Christ a man is lost (John 14:6) and eternally doomed to a literal hell (Matt. 10:28; 2 Thess. 1:9). That belief must affect the counseling process. It should be the counselor's desire to see the counselee come to salvation by simply trusting in Christ's substitutionary death for his sin (John 1:12; Rom. 3:23; 6:23). No single act has solved more problems or provided the potential for resolving more conflicts than freely accepting what Christ has done (John 6:37; Eph. 2:8-9).

MAN IS INCOMPLETE

Not only is man lost, he is also incomplete. He faces an "existential" loneliness and is plagued by his inability to solve many conflicts with his own meager resources. He is lacking the deepest comfort and most powerful resource in the universe for solving problems—Jesus Christ. When one trusts Christ as Savior the Holy Spirit comes to indwell (2 Cor. 3:16), empower (Eph. 3:16), guide (Rom. 8:14), teach (John 14:26), and free (Rom. 8:2) the believer. The individual who has received Christ as Savior literally has the resources of God Himself available for living life (John 15:4-7) and coping with problems (1 Pet. 5:7).

It is interesting to note that psychiatric research has shown that for a child to be healthy he must feel that his parents are present to meet his dependency needs and that they will never reject him.[2] Certainly the same holds true for a child in the family of God. Understanding this concept regarding the nature of man has to affect the counseling process.

MAN IS DEPRAVED

Man is not basically good, he is depraved. Although he may have some consciousness of right and wrong (Rom. 2:14-15), may not be as sinful as he could be (2 Tim. 3:13), and may have some "good works" (Isa. 64:6) he is still depraved. He has sin in every area of his person (Rom. 3), has a tendency to evil (Rom. 7), and, of course, is incapable of satisfying God (Rom. 10). Even after he accepts Christ he is still depraved. Although he now has a new nature, he still has a dangerous old nature with its pull toward sin (Rom. 7:20; 8:13; Gal. 5:17; Eph. 4:22-24).

If the counselor views the nature of man as being depraved, then he knows that "self-actualization" is not adequate. He must agree with Jeremiah the prophet who wrote, "The heart is more deceitful than all else and is desperately sick; who can understand it?" (Jer. 17:9). The mind is deceitful and tricky. That has extensive implications which will be dealt with later in the discussion of defense mechanisms.

MAN IS UNDER ATTACK

Man is under attack by a most powerful enemy — Satan. He is more powerful, clever, and shrewd than most people ever realize. Satan desires that nonbelievers stay in spiritual darkness (2 Cor. 4:3-4). He oppresses people mentally (Luke 8), and he can cause insanity (compare John 13:2 with Matt. 27:3-5). He deceives people (1 Tim. 4:1-3) and influences their thinking (Matt. 16:21-23). He can hinder (1 Thess. 2:18), and he can tempt (1 Cor. 7:5). In short, Satan desires to destroy the mental health of Christians (Eph. 6:10-17; 1 Pet. 5:8-9).

Demon possession is also a way in which Satan works (Mark 9:14-29), but usually he operates in a more subtle manner. Satan often attacks the believer by tempting him in his areas of weakness (materialism, pride, lust, depressive mood).

Recognizing that man is under attack does make a difference in counseling. Unlike Skinner, the Christian counselor must wrestle with more than just the stimuli in the counselee's environment; unlike Freud, he must deal with more than just the counselee's inner conflicts. "For our struggle is not against flesh and blood, but against the rulers, against the powers, against the world forces of this darkness, against the spiritual forces of wickedness in the heavenly places" (Eph. 6:12).

MAN IS PHYSICAL

It has been said that man begins to die at birth. After the age of forty literally thousands of brains cells die daily. Man is constantly struggling against physical disease, and sometimes these physical problems can appear to be spiritual or psychological. Also, since man is an organic whole, a physical problem can affect one's psychological or spiritual well-being (and vice versa). For example, certain physical problems can produce symptoms of depression,[3] psychotic symptoms (a loss of touch with reality),[4] symptoms of anxiety,[5] and changes in personality.[6]

Physical problems can produce emotional difficulties, but emotional problems can also produce physical difficulties. For example, stress seems to predispose to illness in general. Speed of recovery from infectious diseases and surgery correlates with a person's life-style and exposure to stress. Stress can result in various psychophysiologic diseases (ulcers, colitis, high blood pressure). Bereavement studies show that first-degree relatives of the deceased have a sevenfold increase in the mortality rate during the first year when compared with a control group. Individuals that are stress-oriented with a sense of time urgency are more prone to coronary artery disease. Loneliness may also be an important factor in the development of both coronary artery disease and in the susceptibility to certain forms of cancer. In addition, stress can alter neuro-transmitters within the brain (norepenephrine, serotonin, dopamine) and produce depression or psychosis.

Certain emotional or physical problems can also appear to be spiritual. An individual with an impending psychotic break may be intensely preoccupied with religion. An individual with an obsessive-compulsive neurosis may be paralyzed with the fear of having committed the unpardonable sin or the fear that he did not really trust Christ. Individuals with temporal lobe epilepsy may have renewed religious interests and moral piety. Individuals with a manic-depressive psychosis may talk in a religious jargon. Also, individuals with schizophrenia, obsessive-compulsive ego-alien thought, and multiple personalities may be thought to be demon-possessed when they actually are not. For example, demon voices would not respond to antipsychotic medication as do schizophrenics' "voices," which are actually merely auditory hallucinations.

Man is physical and he does inherit a certain physical (genetic) makeup that may make him more predisposed to certain psychological problems.[7] For example, schizophrenia occurs in only 1 percent of the general population. However, if one parent is schizophrenic then the risk rises to 10 percent. If both parents are schizophrenic the risk is 50 percent. In dizygotic (fraternal) twins the risk is 10 percent that if one becomes schizophrenic the other will also. By contrast, in monozygotic (identical) twins the risk is about 50 percent whether the twins are reared together or separated at birth. Studies of those treated for manic-depressive psychosis and for depression reveal similar patterns. The data is overwhelming. Although in general people do not inherit mental disorders, they can inherit the potential weakness, and that weakness can be manifested under stress.

Man is physical. And yet, man is an organic whole. Physical disease can produce psychological symptoms, and psychological stress can produce physical disease. But, either directly or indirectly, spiritual issues lie at the core of both.

MAN IS PSYCHOLOGICAL

Man is psychological. In fact, the English word *psychology* is derived from the Greek word *psychikos* which means, "pertaining to the soul" or "life."[8] Its Hebrew equivalent is the word *nephesh*. It hardly seems necessary to document the various functions of the soul (Intellect—Psalm 139:14; Prov. 19:2; Emotions—2 Sam. 5:8; Song of Sol. 1:7; and Will—Job 6:7; 7:15). Because man's psychological nature is composed of the interrelated components of intellect, emotion, and will, it is sometimes difficult to discern the relationship between those three distinct facets and a man's overall personality. Various symptoms can be manifested, and various etiologies should be considered.

The description of psychological problems can range from

symptoms so bizarre that anyone could recognize them to those that are so subtle that the most trained observer may miss them. The counselor needs to ask such questions as: Is the counselee an introvert or an extrovert, aggressive or shy, sensitive or not sensitive, active or passive, tense or calm, euphoric or sad, intense or bland, warm or cold, disciplined or impulsive, hostile or tolerant, suspicious or not suspicious, dominant or submissive, in reality or not in reality. The counselor also needs to observe the counselee's dress, activity, behavior, gestures, facial expression, speech, mood, judgment, insight, and attitude.

Not only should various symptoms be considered, but possible causes should also be considered.[9] Incidentally, considering the psychological causes for an individual's behavior in no way should discount the spiritual aspect. Man is a whole. All aspects complete each other—they do not negate each other.

In exploring possible causes for the counselee's present difficulties, the counselor must consider early childhood. If the parents were absent and the child's dependency needs were not met, then the individual is more prone to depression or sociopathy, depending on how he handles the conflict. If the parents would not allow the child to be an individual but were symbiotic with him, then he is more prone to schizophrenia. If the parents were harsh, then the individual may be a guilty compulsive, a critical paranoid or an acting-out sociopath, depending on how he handles the conflict. If the parents were seductive or rewarded overly dramatic behavior, then the individual is more likely to have hysterical problems. If both parents were in constant conflict, the individual is more prone to deep-seated insecurity and anxiety or neurosis. Thus man can have unresolved conflicts from childhood, and those conflicts can intensify his present problems. Man does have conflicts. Man is psychological.

THE COUNSELOR'S TASK

DEVELOP A HOLISTIC STYLE OF COUNSELING

As can be seen by the preceding pages, the nature of man is complex and thus demands a holistic approach to counseling. Spiritual needs or problems are most important. Physical difficulties may be involved. And, finally, psychological problems must also be considered. All of those are integrally related and affect one another. The counselor can do several things to help provide a holistic approach to counseling.

Remember spiritual needs. The counselor's most basic concerns must center on the spiritual. In fact, the word *healthy* originated from the Old English root word, "holy."[10] Ministering to a person's spiritual needs and producing a holy person can produce a healthy person. Thus the counselor must seek to determine the spiritual condition of the counselee. Does the counselee need to know Christ? Is the counselee immature and in need of growing in Christ? Is he in bondage to some sin? Those are the types of questions the counselor must ask.

Because of the nature of man, the counselor must be sensitive to the use of the Word of God in counseling. He must have a thorough grasp of the written counsel of God so he can share God's solutions to the individual's problems. He must enjoy the Word, and that enjoyment must be evident to the counselee. The counselor may need to teach the counselee how to study the Word of God.

Select the proper approach. The counselor must be sensitive in selecting a counseling approach that is appropriate for the particular counselee. The counselee may need advice (Prov. 19:20), encouragement (Rom. 1:11-12), support (Gal. 6:2), correction (Gal. 6:1), comfort (2 Cor. 1:3-4), insight (1 Tim. 4:6), or confession (James 5:16). There are times to be direct (Prov. 27:6) and times to be indirect (2 Sam. 12:1-7). There are times to confront (Gal. 2:14); and there are times to encourage (1 Thess. 5:14). There are times to speak and times to listen (Ecc. 3:1, 7). Some individuals need to focus on the past (1 John 1:9), others need to concentrate on the present (Matt. 6:34), and still others must be reminded of the future (John 14:1-3). The Scriptures show the necessity of using many approaches. That is logical since everyone does not have the same problem or need. Even Christ used a number of different approaches as He ministered on earth. Sometimes He was very matter-of-fact (Mark 10:14); at other times He was very gentle (Mark 10:16).

Be a model of Christ. It is imperative that the counselor be a model of a Christlike individual. The nature of man demands that since a counselee will identify with his counselor. The counselor should be kind and gentle (2 Cor. 1:3-4; 10:1; Gal. 6:1; 1 Thess. 2:7, 11; 2 Tim. 2:24; Titus 3:2). Surely, the modeling of a Christlike approach is essential. Successful counselors are ones that demonstrate warmth, empathy, and genuineness. The counselor needs to be able to say as Paul did, "Be imitators of me, just as I also am of Christ" (1 Cor. 11:1).

Know when to refer. The counselor who realizes the complex nature of man must be sensitive to those counselees that may have physical or biochemical problems (psychotics, endogenous depressions, etc.). Those individuals need to be referred to another professional. The counselor must also be sensitive to those individuals that are in danger of suicide and need referral for hospitalization. It is tragic when a person who needs physical or psychiatric help does not receive it because his "counselor" feels that seeking other professional help is not spiritual.

UNDERSTAND PSYCHOLOGICAL DEFENSE MECHANISMS

Perhaps the best example of both man's complexity and his depravity can be seen in a study of his psychological *defense mechanisms.* Psychological defense mechanisms are defined as "the ways people react to frustration and conflict by deceiving themselves about their real desires and goals in an effort to maintain their self-esteem and avoid anxiety."[11] There are several factors that the serious student of Christian psychology should remember about defense mechanisms.

1. Defense mechanisms are automatic reactions to frustration and conflict.

2. They are often unconscious, or out of the awareness of the person using them, since they are "deceiving themselves about their real desires and goals."

3. They are sinful, since all forms of deceit, even self-deceit, are evil.

4. Their purpose is to keep the real conflict from being known to the conscious mind because the real conflict seems overwhelming. They maintain a false sense of self-esteem and avoid anxiety.

5. They are common to all of mankind.

Since individuals must habitually and continually deceive themselves in order to maintain a false sense of self-esteem and alleviate emotional pain (anxiety), then the truth must be that human thoughts, desires, goals, and motives, on a deep inner level of consciousness, must be desperately wicked. That is borne out in the Scriptures. The key to understanding Christian psychology is found in Jeremiah 17:9. "The heart is more deceitful than all else and is desperately sick; who can understand it?" The human heart (mind, emotions, and will) is more deceitful than anything else in God's universe, and is so desperately sick that man cannot even understand the depths of human depravity. It is man's depraved nature that forces him to adopt these means of self-deception to enable him to cope with life.

Through years of scientific research and personal experience involving an in-depth analysis of thousands of patients, psychiatrists and psychologists have come up with scores of defense mechanisms that humans commonly use. No human probably uses all of them, but every human uses many of them daily. In humans of different personality types, certain defense mechanisms frequently appear to predominate. For example, the primary defense mechanism of paranoid personalities is *projection*. Nearly all humans use projection commonly, but paranoid individuals use it as their chief method of self-deceit and use it more often than persons with other personality traits. Nearly all of the known defense mechanisms are described in Scripture. Projection, for example, is described in Matthew 7:1-5 more simply than in any psychiatric or psychology textbook. Projection is also described in Romans 2:1-3 and James 1:13-17.[12]

It is beyond the purpose of this article to discuss the forty-one different psychological defense mechanisms described most often in scientific literature. However, the Christian should strive to become aware of and gradually do away with unconscious defense mechanisms as he grows toward Christlike maturity. He will thus replace his self-deceiving defense mechanisms with healthy coping mechanisms. There are at least fifteen healthy, scripturally acceptable mechanisms for coping with emotional pain.

Forgiving. Forgiving is the primary scriptural/psychological defense against unhappiness and depression. Holding grudges is the basic cause of nearly all human depression. Christians are encouraged in Scripture to get angry without sinning, but to *never* have a grudge-holding, vengeful spirit (Lev. 19:17-18; Eph. 4:26).

Confession. The primary conscious defense against the emotional pain that comes from true guilt is confession (agreeing with God that the sin committed was wrong). Confession to God should then be followed by an attitude of forgiveness toward oneself (1 John 1:9). James also encourages Christians to confess their sins to each other, and promises that this will result in physical/spiritual healing (James 5:16).

Patience. Patience is an excellent conscious defense against the frequent minor frustrations of life. Selfish, immature individuals give themselves too many rights and then are constantly plagued with anger when so many of their "rights" are violated. Giving up those "rights" to God and expecting fewer things in life to go perfectly will result in patience, greater humility, less anger, and greater joy.

Love. Love is a conscious choice. A mature person loves another person because he *chooses* to love that other person. The feeling of love follows the action, and the action follows the conscious choice. The giving and accepting of genuine Christian love is the primary conscious defense against inferiority feelings and loneliness. The "Great Commandment," given in Luke 10:25-27, involves loving God, others, and self (genuine, godly self-worth).

Faith. Anxiety is basically a lack of faith. If an individual does not have faith in what he and God can do together as a team, then that individual will be troubled with much anxiety. Faith is the primary spiritual/psychological defense against anxiety.

Healthy compensation. If an individual is aware of personal deficiencies which are correctable, he can obtain God's help to overcome them (Phil. 4:13). This will not only increase that individual's self worth, but will also make him a more efficient tool to be used for furthering the cause of Christ.

Altruism. Altruism is basically doing good deeds for others in order to please the Lord. Altruism has the following benefits: (a) It furthers the cause of Christ and is an act of obedience to God; (b) it will increase the altruistic person's self-worth since it is easier for a person to like himself when he is worthwhile to others; (c) it will enable the altruistic person to get his mind off himself and to worry less about minor personal frustrations; and (d) it will build friendships, which are essential for mental health.

Anticipation. Anticipating God's help through a difficult situation with a prayerful, trusting attitude can reduce anxiety. As Paul reminded the believers at Corinth, "No temptation has overtaken you but such as is common to man; and *God is faithful,* who will not allow you to be tempted beyond what you are able, *but with the temptation will provide the way of escape also,* that you may be able to endure it" (1 Cor. 10:13, italics added).

Conscious control. Most individuals are too passive. They go through life passively letting conflicts arise and passively waiting for their conflicts to "go away." Unfortunately, very few conflicts "go away" by merely waiting them out. Taking conscious control means becoming responsible and making conscious choices for resolving conflicts. Conscious control enables individuals to overcome many of their unconscious defense mechanisms, which would control their behavior if they remained passive.

Healthy identification. Healthy identification means making conscious choices to develop some godly personality characteristics seen in other Christians. God does not expect any Christian to try to become someone else, but the apostle Paul encouraged his converts to mimic some of his own godly behavior (1 Cor. 11:1). The Christian's primary identification should be with Jesus Christ (Rom. 8:29).

Humor. The ability to have fun and enjoy life, and the ability to laugh at oneself, is a definite sign of mental and spiritual health. Laughing at one's own minor mistakes (like forgetting something, etc.) is much better than self-condemnation for not being perfect.

Redirection. Redirection is the conscious, healthy counterpart of the unconscious defense mechanism of sublimation.

The difference is that with redirection a mature individual can become aware of some unwanted psychological/spiritual conflict, such as repressed hostility. He is then able to redirect his energy (e.g., take up jogging or contact sports) to help dissipate some of that hostile energy while he is in the process of getting rid of any repressed hostility through prayer, forgiveness, counseling, etc.

Restitution. When a mature individual offends someone, he should show genuine humility and concern for the offended individual by making restitution. The restitution can be a verbal apology or may involve financial payment for damages done to someone else's possessions.

Healthy suppression. Suppressing the truth without first dealing with the problem is a sin. However, constantly dwelling on a past failure without forgiving oneself is equally sinful. A mature individual will confess past errors to God, then forgive himself, and then suppress the past error so he can concentrate on present or future concerns. The apostle Paul stated, "Forgetting what lies behind and reaching forward to what lies ahead, I press on toward the goal for the prize of the upward call of God in Christ Jesus" (Phil. 3:13-14).

Dreaming. Adults dream twenty minutes out of every ninety that they are asleep. Most people do not realize that they dream so much because they never remember their dreams unless they wake up during one. Dreams are mediated biochemically by serotonin and norepinephrine, the same brain amines that result in clinical depression when depleted. Holding grudges, for example, depletes those essential brain amines. Many research studies have shown that normal, mature individuals, when deprived of dream time (even though they get enough nondream sleep), begin to develop depressive and even psychotic symptoms within three nights of dream deprivation. God somehow uses dreams each night to resolve unconscious conflicts, or at least to dissipate some of the emotional pain tied to unconscious conflicts. Thus the Christian should not deprive himself of sleep. Sleeping and dreams are gifts of God to maintain sanity.

Defense mechanisms are a very complex subject.[13] The Christian counselor must be aware of those unconscious means of self-deception used by all individuals. One of the goals in counseling is to help an individual recognize and do away with unconscious defense mechanisms and to replace them with scripturally acceptable methods of coping with emotional pain.

Conclusion

The nature of man is complex, and how one views that nature has a profound impact on how one approaches the counseling process. Man, by his very nature, is spiritually lost, incomplete, depraved, under attack, physical, and psychological. His complex nature demands a holistic approach to counseling. The counselor must place a priority on his spiritual needs, seek a proper approach to his problems, be a model of Christ, and know when to refer the counselee to others for additional help. Both the complexity and the depravity of man's essential nature are well illustrated by his defense mechanisms. It is the task of the counselor to help the individual recognize his unconscious means of self-deception and to replace them with scripturally acceptable methods of coping with problems.

Notes

1. Ramesh P. Richard, "Toward a Premillennial Social Ethic: An Anthropological Model" (Paper presented to the faculty of Dallas Theological Seminary, Dallas, Texas, August 26, 1980).
2. Robert F. Shannon and Joe T. Backus, "The Psychodynamics of Depression." *The Journal of the Arkansas Medical Society,* 1 (December 1973); Frank B. Minirth, and Paul D. Meier, *Happiness Is a Choice* (Grand Rapids: Baker, 1978).
3. Those physical problems that can produce symptoms of depression include viral illnesses like mononucleosis or viral pneumonia; an endocrine disorder like hypothyroid; the effects of drugs such as high blood pressure medication, minor tranquilizers, major tranquilizers, birth control pills, diet pills, or alcohol; and other medical diseases like cancer of the pancreas or multiple sclerosis.
4. Psychotic symptoms can be produced by endocrine disorders like hyperthyroid; tumors of the temporal lobe of the brain; the effects of illegal drugs such as amphetamines, cocaine, LSD, PCP, and marijuana; the effects of prescription drugs such as antiseizure medication, antituberculosis medication, antidepressive medica-

tion, and antiparkinsonian medication; the effects of over-the-counter medications such as sleeping preparations, nasal sprays, and bromide-containing compounds for anxiety; alcohol; and various medical diseases such as porphyria, Wilson's disease, or Huntington's chorea.

5. Symptoms of anxiety can be produced by endocrine disorders such as hyperthyroid and hypoglycemia; tumors like pheochromocytoma; and drugs such as caffeine, marijuana, LSD, PCP, and amphetamines.

6. Perhaps the best known physical problem that can produce personality changes is senility.

7. John M. Davis, *Depression: A Practical Approach* (New York: Medcom, 1974); Ronald L. Green, "Genetics of Affective Disorders," Weekly Psychiatry Update Series No. 35 (New York: Biomedia, 1977); Alfred M. Freedman, et al. *Modern Synopsis of Psychiatry* (Baltimore: Williams and Wilkins, 1972); Phillip Solomon and Vernon D. Patch, *Handbook of Psychiatry*, 3d ed. (Los Altos: Lange Medical Publications, 1974).

8. William F. Arndt and F. Wilbur Gingrich, *A Greek English Lexicon of the New Testament and Other Early Christian Literature* (Chicago: U. of Chicago, 1957), p. 902.

9. Harold Kaplan, Alfred M. Freedman, and Benjamin J. Sadock, *Comprehensive Textbook of Psychiatry*, 3d ed. (Baltimore: Williams & Wilkins, 1980); Freedman, *Modern Synopsis of Psychiatry;* Solomon & Patch, *Handbook of Psychiatry;* Merrill T. Eaton, Jr., and Margaret H. Peterson, *Psychiatry* (New York: Medical Examination Publishing Co., 1969); Silvano Arieti, et al, eds., *American Handbook of Psychiatry*, 2d ed. (New York: Basic Books, 1974); and Lawrence C. Kolb, *Modern Clinical Psychiatry* (Philadelphia: W. B. Saunders, 1973).

10. Haddon W. Robinson, "Whole-Person Medicine," *The Christian Medical Society Journal* 9 (1980):5.

11. Charles Morris, *Psychology, An Introduction* (New York: Appleton-Century-Crofts, 1973), pp. 439-40.

12. For a thorough description of projection and other defense mechanisms described in the book of James, see Melvin R. Nelson, "The Psychology of Spiritual Conflict," *Journal of Psychology and Theology* 1 (Winter 1976):34-41.

13. Eaton and Peterson, *Psychiatry;* Freedman, *Modern Synopsis of Psychiatry;* Kolb, *Modern Clinical Psychiatry;* Minirth and Meier, *Happiness Is a Choice;* and Solomon and Patch, *Handbook of Psychiatry.*

20

The Missionary as a Theologian

J. Ronald Blue

Theology! Why in the world does a missionary need theology? All he needs is a good blade and the Good Book! If he has enough stamina to chop his way through the jungle with a sharp machete and enough sense to share the gospel with those poor lost pagans, he will be a great success.

It would be a terrible waste to send out a missionary who has been well trained in theology. In fact, theology would only confuse him. How can a missionary benefit from knowing the ontological arguments for the existence of God or the eschatological significance of the pretribulation rapture?

Unfortunately, many people share that view of the missionary task. To those individuals "missionary" is synonymous with "mediocrity" in relation to theological training. They feel that a little biblical knowledge and a lot of brawn is all a missionary needs! But nothing could be further from the truth. Of all people engaged in the Lord's work, the missionary is proba-

J. RONALD BLUE (A.B., University of Nebraska; Th.M., Dallas Theological Seminary; Ph.D. candidate, University of Texas at Arlington; graduate study, University of Madrid) is chairman and associate professor of world missions at Dallas Theological Seminary, Dallas, Texas.

bly the one who is in greatest need of sound, thorough theological training.

The "chop-the-grass-and-chatter-the-gospel" view of missions is wrong on two counts. First, there is a false concept of the missionary's *territory*. Although there is still much to be done in primitive areas of the world, the vast majority of mission work today is accomplished in the arena of sophisticated societies and progressive peoples. Of the more than two billion "unreached" people who have not yet heard a clear presentation of the gospel, most are not primitive pagans. They are more than likely enlightened individuals who are quite religious. They are people who are wrapped up in complex counterfeit religious systems. The God-given vacuum in their souls has been stuffed full with a virtual smorgasbord of religions that supposedly give meaning to life. Islam claims over 750 million adherents, Hinduism boasts nearly 570 million followers, and Buddhism embraces about 350 million people.[1]

The modern missionary is called on to penetrate those complicated religious systems, which seem to grow like weeds from strange theological substructures. The roots may be hopelessly entangled, but they all claim to draw from some mysterious revelation declared by some strange divinity or god.

Non-Christian religions are only a part of the challenge. Divergent theologies are found as well in the broad spectrum of the world's largest religion—Christianity. Almost 30 percent of the world's population profess to be Christian. Kane rightfully questions, "Are those 1.2 billion Christians all genuine, practicing Christians?"[2] How many of the world's "Christians" are recorded in the only accurate record book, the Lamb's book of life? Much missionary endeavor is rightfully directed to the areas of the world where "Christianity" has become as garbled and confused as the non-Christian religions.

In addition to the missionary challenge among all those who claim some kind of religious affiliation, it is estimated that as many as one-fourth of the world's population is enmeshed in what might be termed "secularism." There are over one billion secularists—men and women who have fallen prey to the gods of humanism, Marxism, existentialism, hedonism, and materialism. That too is mission territory.

The mission field is hardly some unblemished plot of enriched soil waiting to receive the good seed. The territory in which today's missionary must work is infested with an unending variety of devastating weeds and parasitic plants that mat the soil of men's souls like an impenetrable shield. The modern missionary is called on to move into that "jungle" of diverse ideologies and divergent theologies.

Second, the "chop-the-grass-and-chatter-the-gospel" view of missions fails to correctly account for the missionary's *task*. There is more to the missionary endeavor than gospel proclamation. For many people evangelism has been reduced merely to sharing a standardized presentation of the gospel or spouting a few key verses to the unfortunate and unsuspecting pagans of the world.

Missionary evangelism, of course, is considered more glamorous. Colorful tracts in strange languages are dropped like quaint bombs over jungle villages. The fallout is amazing. Sound trucks race through dusty streets in far-off hamlets with recordings of John 3:16 playing at full volume. The noise is astounding. Powerful transmitters hum with delight on remote islands as they fire salvos of soundwaves into the air to isolated souls who huddle around their radios to hear the good news. The outreach is alluring. But mission work is glamorous only to the gullible! The task is exceedingly more complex.

It is the missionary's task to acquire a new language, adapt to a new culture, appropriate a new world view, analyze a new religious system, appreciate new values, avoid new dangers, attain new habits, account for new emotions, ascend to new expectations, ascribe to new regulations, abstain from new taboos, address new problems, anticipate new opposition, answer new conflicts, apply new criteria, advocate new solutions, advance new goals, affect new changes, admit new defeats, acknowledge new limitations—and proclaim the gospel message. And, of course, that is but the beginning. Once the missionary has adequately penetrated the target culture and has effectively proclaimed the good news of life in Jesus Christ, he must then work diligently with those who have responded to bring them to productive spiritual maturity. That task demands the best theological training available.

The *territory* in which a missionary works is as big as the world, and the *task* he must perform is as wide as God's diverse work in that world. Neither the arena nor the assignment is for theological neophytes. This article will try to substantiate the pressing need for missionary theologians in today's world and suggest some modest proposals for meeting that need.

THE NEED FOR MISSIONARY THEOLOGIANS

Never in the history of the church has there been a greater demand for missionaries well trained in the Bible and theology. The day of a simplistic approach to missions, if there ever was one, is over. Unfortunately it is all too easy for Christians in the United States to view missions as a "foreign endeavor" that is unrelated to life in America.

The United States is like a huge mission compound that has fenced out the rest of the world. It is difficult to sense the needs of the world while living in a self-sufficient state. A nation that has but 6 percent of the world's population and yet consumes 50 percent of the world's goods tends to be provincial and complacent.[3] The well-painted, tall-spired church that dominates the landscape of the "USA compound" tends to be rather provincial as well. It boasts of a multiple staff of well-trained leaders even when membership or attendance hardly warrants it.

When one steps outside the borders of the United States, one is suddenly engulfed in a crowded, convulsing, and chaotic world—a world that is in desperate need of sensitive, alert theologians who desire to serve others and obey God. Why is the need so acute? At least three factors may be cited: demographic explosion, ecclesiastical expansion, and theological erosion.

DEMOGRAPHIC EXPLOSION

According to the mid-1980 "World Population Data Sheet," there are 4.4 billion people living on the earth, and the number keeps rising. Every day there are an additional 203 thousand mouths to feed. If the present trend continues, by the year 2000 the globe will be laboring under the weight of over 6 billion inhabitants![4]

The vast majority of the world's people live in Asia. China alone is rapidly approaching 1 billion inhabitants, India claims 676 million, Indonesia 144 million, and Japan 117 million. That is not the area of the world, however, that boasts the greatest rate of population growth. While the world population is increasing at a sizeable 1.7 percent per year, Mexico and other Central American republics are experiencing a skyrocketing 3.4 percent increase each year.[56]

The astounding growth of the global village can best be seen by tracing the progress historically. Scientists estimate that mankind did not reach the one billion mark in population until the early nineteenth century. Then it took only the next 120 years to add a second billion. In the short span of 32 years a third billion was added. In but 15 years the fourth billion joined the world crowd. If the population explosion continues at the present rate, the next billion should push their way into the teeming masses of humanity in about a decade.[6]

What does all this have to do with missions and theology? Not a thing, except that missions means *reaching people* and theology involves *teaching people*. God's work is "people work." More people means more work, and that is the plight facing the church today. It must be emphasized that every day there are 203 thousand more people to be evangelized and edified.

With the fast-paced population increase, the whole world scene has changed. This is an age of acceleration in every area of life. The world is on a racetrack or, better yet, a dragstrip. For centuries change took place over a reasonable period of time, but now it surges forward with a deafening roar. As the world explodes numerically, the missionary's task takes on a new sense of urgency. This is no day for a relaxing journey to the field on a slow-moving steamship. It is time to board an airplane and take off for that globe-encircling endeavor called "world missions." That does not mean, however, that men and women should depart without being prepared theologically. On the contrary, the whole enterprise will produce nothing of any lasting value if the preparation is defective. To board that airplane without the benefit of adequate training is nothing short of suicide. The increased complexity and urgency of missions today demands more, not less, preparation. Theological proficiency is no longer an option, it is a prerequisite.

ECCLESIASTICAL EXPANSION

Not only is the world growing at an astounding rate, but the church is also increasing with rapidity. Often the church in America is unaware of that worldwide growth. "Throughout the Third World, and particularly in Africa, Christianity is undergoing the largest numerical expansion in church history. David Barrett, a Nairobi-based researcher who is completing a major multi-volume work on world religious trends, estimates that more than six million Africans are added to Christianity every year, at an astonishing rate of 16,600 believers a day."[7]

Similar spectacular church growth may be noted in some areas of Asia. In South Korea, for example, the Protestant church is growing five times faster than the population. One-third of all government leaders are Christian and at least one-fourth to one-half of the 600 thousand men in the armed forces of South Korea are Christians.[8] It is estimated that six new churches are established every day and that every 45 seconds a new Christian is added to the church.[9]

Similar advances for the Christian church have been evidenced in Indonesia, the world's fifth largest nation. Of the twenty million Christians in Indonesia today, ten million have turned to the Christian faith in the past ten years, the largest increase in Christians ever recorded in a Muslim country.[10] In India one pastor baptized seven hundred new believers during the first two months of 1980. His group of churches has grown from two thousand members in 1972 to twenty thousand in 1980.[11]

Latin America is also experiencing unbelievable growth among evangelicals. Orr reports that in 1900 there were only fifty thousand Protestants in all of Latin America, but in 1970 there were twenty million.[12] Some recent breakthroughs in ethnic sub-groups in Latin America demonstrate the spurts of growth that can occur. Read, Monterroso, and Johnson in their momentous volume, *Latin American Church Growth*, reported in 1969, "The thin end of the wedge of Christianity has barely entered among the Quechua Indians. Perhaps five per cent of this population has been won to Christ. . . ."[13] Today the vast majority of the Quechuas have come to Christ.

In Central America, although the population growth is soaring, the church growth is skyrocketing. A few examples may be cited from one mission's report. Whereas the annual rate of population growth in Honduras stands at a record-breaking 3.5 percent per annum, the 88 churches associated with CAM International reported an astronomical 16.5 percent rate of growth in one year. Costa Rica's rate of population growth is a more modest 2.5 percent, yet the churches there reported a 20.4 percent increase in baptized believers during the year.[14]

It is important to note in this discussion that the growth of the church in the Third World countries is not like that in the United States. Most of the American churches that boast any growth are usually doing so at the expense of neighboring churches. The growth is almost entirely transfer growth. By contrast, almost all of those joining the church overseas are new Christians. They are not weathered veterans of the faith who have decided to sip sermons from a more scintillating fountain. These are babes in Christ who, in many cases, have never peeked inside a Bible before.

The pressing need for theologically-trained teachers is obvious. With so great an influx of new believers, biblical training becomes crucial. The Third World church is at a point of crisis. If adequate teaching is not soon forthcoming in the exploding churches of Africa, Asia, and Latin America, a warped, ill-contrived, self-wrought theology will develop that may be so far removed from the Bible it will hardly be recognized as Christian.

When new Christians are not adequately taught in the Word of God, they naturally devise their own standards, their own regulations, and their own systems of religious experience. Rampant legalism and complex religiosity are but symptoms of a more severe disease—Bible anemia. Crippled saints will manufacture crooked canes on which to lean while they hobble through life. God-starved believers will sacrifice their prized possessions to forge some golden calf that they can see and worship. Blinded Christian neophytes will grope for a leader and will embrace whoever might come along.

If some care is not taken to better store the grain of one of the greatest harvests in the history of the church, there may be nothing left but piles of rotting seed so stricken with blight and mildew that future plantings will be impossible. One bumper crop is not enough. The Lord of the harvest *demands* reproduction. A key to that process is proper care of the seed and prudent cultivation of each tender new shoot in God's garden.

The marvelous growth of the church overseas brings to every true believer great joy and thanksgiving. At the same time, the growth should bring deep concern to thinking Christians. All too few seem to sense the world crisis. While the theologically trained stand behind church pulpits in the United States to deliver sermonic masterpieces to sleepy audiences, masses of new Christians in the rest of the world are crying to receive some biblical answers to burning questions hurled at them in a hostile environment. They plead for training from God's Word. They look for guidance in their new-found faith. The need for well-trained theologians is acute.

THEOLOGICAL EROSION

The world is exploding, the church is expanding, and in the midst of all the growth, theology is dissipating in an increasing variety of confusing and contradictory directions. Where the Bible is not faithfully taught, insipid substitutes are concocted by intellectually brilliant but spiritually destitute pseudo-Christians. Entire volumes could be written about some of the already popular theological fashions that are presently being shown on the market. It is sad enough that self-made designers have conceived those bizarre models. Worse by far is the open reception given them and the rage of unsuspecting buyers for those wild wares. Two examples should suffice to demonstrate the pressing need for biblically-trained theologians both to correct the damage done and to prevent further erosion.

Liberation Theology. Claimed by Latin Americans as their own unique contribution to the church today, the "theology of liberation" is one of the most talked-about innovations on the theological spectrum. Actually this system should not be labeled "theology" since its dominant themes are economic, social, and political. One of the best-known spokesmen and designers of the popular movement, Gutierrez, states, "Indeed, *liberation* is a term which expresses a new posture of Latin Americans. They believe that there can be authentic development for Latin America only if there is liberation from the domination exercised by the great capitalist countries, and especially by the most powerful, the United States of America. This liberation also implies a confrontation. . . , a social revolution"[15]

The thrust of liberation theology is clearly toward a social, political, and economic liberation of people oppressed by sins that are seen as collective rather than individual. It is amazing how old tunes are slightly arranged with unique new chords and the world thinks it is a new song. Liberationists are dancing to antiquated themes: their theology proper is but discordant pantheism, their soteriology smacks of universalism, their ecclesiology is ecumenical, and their eschatology is an echo of More's utopianism.[16] Perhaps the most devastating aspect of liberation theology is that it is admittedly Marxist.[17] Millions are not only deceived but may soon be devoured.

Where are the biblical theologians in Latin America and elsewhere who can effectively answer the counterfeit theologies of "praxis"? Where are the theologians who can demonstrate what God has already done for those who would "do" their theology? Where are the theologians who can show that the central issue of individual sin and Christ's personal redemption can transform corrupt societies through multiplied changed lives? Where are the spokesmen for the true revolutionary forces of moral righteousness and biblical justice?

African Theology. Someone has called the dark continent of Africa a large question mark sprawled out below Europe. Africa today is no question mark; it is one gigantic exclamation point poised at the center of the globe. A continent that was so recently controlled by foreign masters has suddenly issued eviction orders and seized her own destiny. Hesitancy or delay has not been tolerated. Many of the former title holders have been thrown out with violent force. Colonialism has essentially ended. A new breeze is blowing across the continent, and with that breeze has come some incredible new church growth, especially in the sub-Sahara regions.

With the increased political independence and rapid church

growth has come a rather volatile theological movement. Whereas Latin Americans are crying for a surging revolution forward to a newly liberated society, the Africans are suggesting a sentimental return backward to old traditional practices.

African theology is a label that defies precise definition. The label has been indiscriminately attached to far too many concepts. Mbiti, probably the greatest exponent of the so-called African theology, admits this dilemma. "It is all too easy to use the phrase 'African theology,' but to state what that means, or even to show its real nature, is an entirely different issue."[18]

Though the specific forms may vary, African theology is primarily a reactionary theology that resulted from the battles for independence. The leaders in the movement equate Christianity with colonialism. "It is the imposition of western culture in the garb of the Gospel that people react against. It is the interpretation of the Bible by the standard of the western social and cultural yardstick, without reference to the indigenous African spiritual heritage and social norms, that stings some African politicians, Christians and theologians."[19]

The "African spiritual heritage and social norms" are apparently key ingredients within that theological movement. Turner suggests that African theology implies an attempt to amalgamate elements of Christianity and elements of traditional belief.[20] That being so, Kato has rightfully surmised that that theology poses a threat to biblical Christianity through the poisonous influence of syncretism and universalism.[21]

Where are the biblical scholars in Africa who can present God's truth to the searching believers of today? Where are the theologians who can provide a refreshing, but intellecutally alert, flow of spiritual nourishment to the thousands of new babes in Christ across the African continent? Where are the missionaries who can expound the Word to a scripturally starved African leadership?

Many other cases of Third World theologies could be cited. In every case it is apparent that the leaders of the most dynamic churches of the world, those of Latin America, Africa, and Asia, are not sitting in their studies waiting for the latest shipment of theological treatises from Europe or the most recent package of well-bound commentaries printed in the United States. They are writing their own versions of theology, which all too often bear little relationship to the Bible.

Well-trained biblical scholars and adept, sensitive theologians are desperately needed to establish—not *for* the Third World church, but *with* the Third World church—a sound foundation grounded in the bedrock of God's unchanging Word. The missionary theologian may then assist in the structure that rises from that foundation—a structure that will reflect the beauty and unique tastes of the culture in which it is built, but at the same time will be true to God's plumbline. National architects will give the edifice an appearance that is aesthetic to all who pass by, and yet a divine building code will insure that every beam will be level and every corner square. The missionary theologian is needed not as a building inspector but as an invited consultant, a colaborer in the gigantic, history-making project.

The influence of aberrant theologies is not just limited to the distant countries in which they are developed. Few conservative evangelicals are aware that the whole ecumenical movement finds its roots in a missionary conference held in Edinburgh in 1910. Hoekstra has traced what he calls the "demise of evangelism" from that important missions conference.[22] A strong warning is sounded by Johnston lest the same trend away from evangelistic outreach occur in the world congresses and missions' consultations that are occurring with greater frequency among evangelicals. Is he right when he contends, "Evangelicalism by its very nature is ecumenical"?[23] Bassham contends that the ecumenical, evangelical, and Roman Catholic traditions "have developed a significant convergence on the main issues in mission theology."[24] If he is correct, then there is good cause to heed the alarm sounded by Johnston. Could Pinnock be right when he suggests, "Today's evangelicals may be tomorrow's liberals"?[25]

A missionary today needs to know more than just simplistic slogans. The winds of theology blow hot and hard on the mission field, and in no way may they be confined to one locality. More well-trained, biblically-sound theologians are desperately needed to give direction to those winds before they turn into destructive cyclones.

THE PROVISION OF MISSIONARY THEOLOGIANS

Throughout most of the world the church is reeling under the tension of an exploding population, a rapidly growing membership, and an increasingly divergent array of theologies. At the same time the Western church has become increasingly provincial and complacent. It is time for the materially enriched and spiritually blessed Western church to review her responsibility and renew her commitment to share with her brothers abroad, especially in providing more well-trained theologians.

Three suggestions may be given that could help alleviate the severe shortage of trained theologians. First, individual Christians need to resolve to make theological education in the non-Western church a priority in their own commitment to prayer and financial support. Second, churches need to reassess their missionary outreach and develop a new emphasis in the area of theological training. Third, mission boards need to recruit more actively candidates with biblical and theological proficiency and to encourage the present missionary force to upgrade its training in those areas.

INDIVIDUAL RESOLUTION

Christians are like yeast. The influence of an individual can act as a catalyst to change the group. If individual Christians could sense the urgency of theological training in missions and resolve to make that a priority, their commitment would affect others in the church and soon the entire body would be dedicating more prominence to this pressing issue. One by one, individuals and families in the church can "adopt" Third World countries and start praying daily for God's work within that area. Country profiles prepared by the conveners of the International Congress on World Evangelism in Lausanne,[26] Johnstone's *Operation World,* or the information-packed cards on fifty-two spiritually needy nations compiled by Operation Mobilization,[27] can serve as a start in assembling vital information about the country of adoption. A small card with a silhouette of the country and a few continuing prayer requests can be placed in some strategic location in the home as a constant reminder for daily prayer. An appropriately labeled clock may be set at the time of the adopted nation to more adequately relate to their schedule. The concern for the people of that nation will grow with increased information. Above all, there will be an increased concern for the theological welfare of the country. Perhaps the family, or several families together, could see to it that a well-deserving student from the adopted country receives three or four years of theological training in his own country, a nearby country, or in a reputable institution in the United States. Information yields more involvement and that involvement could spell new hope for a theologically needy nation.

CHURCH REASSESSMENT

Church leaders need to assign new importance to the responsibility of their congregation for world outreach. Some of the myths about missions already outlined in this paper need to be exploded. Missions is a vibrant activity filled with life and adventure. Never in the history of mankind have there been greater opportunities or greater challenges in world missions.

Because of the pressing need for theological training in the growing church abroad, every church in the West needs to re-evaluate its present emphasis. In far too many churches missions has been relegated to an annual pep rally. It is more than a conference. Missions for other churches is calculated only in dollars and cents. It is more than a budget. Missions for some churches has been dressed entirely in skirts. It is more than a women's guild. Missions for still others has been confined to a bulletin board in the church foyer. It is more than a map.

Missions must come alive as a part of the regular church services through occasional long distance telephone calls to missionary members overseas or through crisp and penetrating interviews with visiting missionaries followed by a special emphasis in prayer for current activities and challenges overseas. Continuing education and missions exposure is needed in *all* levels of the Sunday school curriculum with a special thrust on career opportunities at the junior high school and high school levels.

Above all, a new commitment should be evidenced toward

training theological leaders and supporting those leaders in overseas assignments. A truly missionary church is one providing personnel for the needs of the world. To the extent that a church is able financially, it should support fully those emerging from that church for missionary service. In addition to sending missionary personnel, the church can "adopt" international students during their years of theological training. A scholarship accompanied by loving, personal concern is an investment with both immediate rewards for the church and long-term benefits in God's work. If the church could provide just one well-trained theologian totally committed to invest his life for the benefit of a Third World country, it would do more toward justifying its existence than all the self-perpetuating services and self-centered promotional programs combined. Far too much attention is given in most churches to increased attendance and budgets and not enough to what God is doing through those added numbers to reach the world for His glory.

MISSION RECRUITMENT

It is imperative that mission leaders give new priority to recruitment at the seminary level. That emphasis should not be at the expense of the Bible college and Bible institute training, which has produced many capable missionaries. It is becoming increasingly evident, however, that the needs of the growing church overseas are such that the highest theological training available will be demanded.

Capable students at reputable seminaries need to be personally challenged with specific opportunities for service. The broadside approach from chapel pulpits seeking volunteers is increasingly counterproductive. How many churches send an elder or deacon to tell about their church in a chapel service and then ask that all those who would like to serve as pastor to sign up at some literature table? Field surveys carefully conducted by mission leaders will yield more specific challenges to which talented and well-trained individuals may respond.

Opportunities for theologians on the mission field need not be confined to classroom teaching. Pastoral retreats, leadership seminars, theological education by extension, camp and conference ministries, and untold other areas of service also demand the best in theological training.

Missionary organizations need to take a new interest in recruiting key national leaders for advanced theological training as well. In some cases adequate institutions are available overseas. In all too many instances that is not a viable option. For example, the United States has over eight hundred Christian colleges and a number of excellent theological seminaries. Africa, however, with over three times the land area and over one and a half times the population of the United States, has only a handful of Christian schools.[28]

Not only is there a pressing need to establish new top-level theological institutions in most of the Third World countries, there is a demand to provide scholarships to proved leaders of those countries for study abroad. There could be no greater investment. Sudan Interior Mission's Byang Kato, who received his doctorate from Dallas Theological Seminary, gave leadership to the Association of Evangelicals of Africa and Madagascar at a time when such high caliber leadership was desperately needed. Wakatama pleads, "Africa urgently needs fifty Byang Katos."[29] Since Kato's untimely death, another doctoral graduate, Tokunboh Adeyemo, is giving that quality leadership while acquiring an added doctor of philosophy degree from the University of Aberdeen.

Another recent example of the value of investing in the education of key nationals can be seen in Dr. Chris Marantika, said to be the first Indonesian evangelical to hold a doctoral degree in theology. During his years in the United States he gathered a team of several Western couples to assist in founding the Evangelical Theological School of Indonesia. The well-trained faculty team felt that if the initial class would number thirty it would be a good beginning. They launched the seminary in late 1979 with over seventy students! As a part of their training, those seminary students must plant a new church. In the first six months of 1979, twenty-seven new congregations have been formed. In one location seventy converts — primarily from Islam — were baptized after the required preparation, including three months of study and an oral examination.[30] It behooves mission leaders and church leaders alike to become more actively engaged in this vital answer to the pressing need for theological leaders overseas.

CONCLUSION

Theological training for today's missionary is no longer an optional luxury, it is a vital necessity. The modern missionary endeavor is one centered in sophisticated societies of highly religious peoples. It includes both evangelism and edification. The missionary's territory and his task are as immense and complex as the twentieth-century world.

The need for competent biblical theologians in missions is acute. Demographic explosion, ecclesiastical expansion, and theological erosion all contribute to the need. World population is increasing at astronomical rates. Much of the Third World church is growing at an even greater rate. In the midst of the growth, diverse nonbiblical theologies are proliferating. Trained biblical expositors and theologians are needed to serve in that exploding and eroding climate.

It is often easier to identify needs than it is to provide solutions. The provision of biblical theologians demands the concentrated attention and sacrificial efforts of every Christian, every church leader, and every mission leader. Church members can "adopt" a country or group of people and work and pray toward the theological welfare of that area or group. Church leaders can give priority in their mission outreach to theological training and to the development of competent workers. Mission leaders can more actively recruit theologically equipped candidates and can provide more opportunities for their present missionaries to upgrade their training in theology.

Mediocrity in missions theology must cease. God's growing church demands biblical strength and theological precision. Failure today will spell defeat tomorrow. Without healthy roots in the Word, the flowering Third World Church will be laid low by "every wind of doctrine." Without a strong theological anchor, the world-encircling church will be split open on some rocky shoal by the violent "waves" of false teaching.

"Speaking the truth in love, we are to grow up in all aspects into Him, who is the head, even Christ" (Eph. 4:15). Every member is responsible for the biblical health and theological well-being of the "whole body," the church around the world.

NOTES

1. Patrick J. Johnstone, *Operation World: A Handbook for World Intercession* (Bromley, England: Send the Light Publications, 1978), pp. 23-24.
2. J. Herbert Kane, *Life and Work on the Mission Field* (Grand Rapids: Baker, 1980), p. 255.
3. Ronald J. Sider, *Rich Christians in an Age of Hunger* (Downers Grove, Ill.: Inter-Varsity, 1978), pp. 45-46.
4. *World Population Data Sheet* (Washington, D.C.: Population Reference Bureau, 1980).
5. Ibid.
6. Ross S. Bennett, ed., *Our World* (Washington, D.C.: National Geographic Society, 1979), pp. 20-22.
7. "Faith in Africa," *Time*, 21 January 1980, p. 50.
8. Johnstone, pp. 117-18.
9. Joon Gon Kim, "New Life in Korea," *Asia Theological News* 5 (November 1979): 19.
10. Lorry Lutz, "A Church-Planting Seminary in Indonesia," *Asia Pulse* 13 (April 1980): 2.
11. C. Peter Wagner, "The Current Scene," *School of World Mission Newsletter* 3 (May 1980): 3.
12. J. Edwin Orr, *Evangelical Awakenings in Latin America* (Minneapolis: Bethany Fellowship, 1978), p. 216.
13. William R. Read, Victor M. Monterroso, and Harmon A. Johnson, *Latin American Church Growth* (Grand Rapids: Eerdmans, 1969), p. 219.
14. CAM International, "Annual Report," 1978.
15. Gustavo Gutierrez, *A Theology of Liberation* (Maryknoll, N.Y.: Orbis Books, 1973), p. 88.
16. Thomas More, *Utopia*, 1516, reprint (New York: Simon and Schuster, 1965).
17. Gutierrez, *Theology of Liberation*, pp. 9-10.
18. John S. Mbiti, *New Testament Eschatology in an African Background* (London: Oxford U., 1971), p. 185.
19. J. K. Agbeti, "African Theology: What It Is," *Presence* 5 (October 1972): 3.
20. Philip Turner, "The Wisdom of the Fathers and the Gospel of Christ: Some Notes on Christian Adaptation in Africa," *Journal of Religion in Africa* 4 (June 1971): 55.
21. Byang H. Kato, *Theological Pitfalls in Africa* (Kisumu, Kenya: Evangel, 1975), p. 55.

22. Harvey T. Hoekstra, *The World Council of Churches and the Demise of Evangelism* (Wheaton, Ill.: Tyndale, 1978), p. 19.
23. Arthur P. Johnston, *The Battle for World Evangelism* (Wheaton, Ill.: Tyndale, 1978), p. 358.
24. Roger C. Bassham, *Mission Theology: 1948-1975, Years of Worldwide Creative Tension Ecumenical, Evangelical, and Roman Catholic* (Pasadena, Calif.: William Carey Library, 1979), p. 331.
25. Clark H. Pinnock, "Hope for Theology and the Church in the Eighties," *Vanguard* (January-February 1980):27.
26. For information on how to obtain Lausanne "Country Profiles," write: MARC, 919 West Huntington Drive, Monrovia, Calif. 91016.
27. Both the book *Operation World* and the set of cards *Pray for 52 Spiritually Needy Nations* are available from Send the Light, Inc., Box 148, Midland Park, N.J. 07432.
28. Wakatama goes so far as to limit the number of schools to one (Pius Wakatama, *Independence for the Third World Church: An African's Perspective on Missionary Work* [Downers Grove, Ill.: Inter-Varsity, 1976], p. 64).
29. Ibid., p. 80.
30. Lutz, p. 2.

21

Theological Issues in Contemporary Feminism

A. Duane Litfin

One of life's persistent dilemmas for contemporary Christians is how to respond to feminism. To be sure, modern Christians are not the first to face that dilemma. The recent phase of the feminist movement, which is usually dated from the emergence of Betty Friedan's *The Feminine Mystique* in 1964, is but the current wave of a tide that has been encroaching on male dominion for over two centuries. Yet that current wave is broader and more powerful than any of its precursors, and it seems to be part of a worldwide trend that may now be inexorable. It will no doubt ebb and flow with political currents, but the overall result seems assured in the decades to come: the dismantling of distinctions between male and female that are as old as the race. So the dilemma for modern Christians may be deeper and more difficult than ever before.

The problem Christians face stems from a profound ambivalence toward feminism. On the one hand, Christians sense that

A. DUANE LITFIN (B.S., Philadelphia College of Bible; Th.M., Dallas Theological Seminary; Ph.D., Purdue University; doctoral study, Oxford University) is associate professor of pastoral ministries at Dallas Theological Seminary, Dallas, Texas.

there is much there to be embraced. What student of history, for example, could deny that females have often been abused and oppressed at the hands of males? What follower of Jesus could ignore the fundamental injustice of laws that work to the disadvantage of women as women? Who could fail to be outraged at the prospect of a woman being paid a fraction of what a man earns for doing the same work? What fair-minded person is not dismayed when reminded that it has only been within the life spans of many living Americans that women have been thought worthy of the vote? And what believer has not discovered blind spots within his own perspective that, on closer inspection, caused embarrassment and repentance? Any who are willing to see can find much in the feminist movement to be praised and supported.

But therein lies the proverbial rub, for the worthy goals of the movement do not stand alone. They occur as part of a structure of thought that Thomas Howard has labeled "the most bitterly ruinous and the most grievously mendatious set of notions to appear on the public scene in a long time."[1] That structure of ideas, says Howard, is contrary to the Bible and "repugnant to the ancient wisdom of the Church, and ages less flaccid than our own would have named it heresy."[2] Just here lies the Christian's dilemma, then. To put a fine point on it, should a Christian embrace the movement with its heresy, or reject it with its truth?

The issue is not really so clear cut, of course, as one realizes when one examines how various Christians have responded to the movement. Some have simply capitulated and embraced the feminist cause entirely. Their Christian brothers and sisters look on in awe, as if watching a reptile devour its prey whole, marveling at those Christians' ability both to avoid gagging and to assimilate seemingly anything into their system; but in the end the sight is not a very attractive one and they turn away. At the other end of the spectrum are those who are so incensed at the heresies of the feminist movement that they are blinded to its worthier aspects. They tar both good and bad with a single brush, marching vice and virtue out of town on the same rail. But the unlovely spectacle of Christians' responding to the feminists in an unchristian way proves equally repugnant.

That leaves most Christians in the middle, struggling in their debate with one another to find the *via media* between the two extremes. Some lean to one pole, others to the opposite pole, but most seem to be searching to find that point of balance where they can embrace the good aspects of feminism while eschewing the bad.

That search is especially difficult because of the sheer number and complexity of the issues and because of the emotional overtones of the debate. The temptation is sometimes overwhelming to boil off the many theological and philosophical issues as so much excess in order to get down immediately to the really crusty issues of practical behavior. But such an approach condemns the discussants to a constant haranguing of each other, which never reaches or even recognizes the real differences. Practical matters of male/female relationships are important, but they are only the most visible part of a deeper structure of ideas. That submerged substructure is the underlying state of disease or health that shows itself to the eye in good or bad symptoms. So the answering of the deeper questions must come first; the practical implications will then follow.

That approach assumes, of course, that the participants in the debate understand what theological issues are up for grabs. But that is by no means a valid assumption. Because of the complexity of the questions, many Christians are unaware of (or have avoided facing up to) the theological choices they must make. They have attempted to grapple with the practical issues on the basis of "what seems fair," or "good old American common sense," never realizing that in embracing seemingly harmless proposals they may have purchased a piece of condemned territory at the price of God's truth. They simply have not grasped the theological issues at stake.

This essay will attempt to identify some of the key theological issues in the contemporary debate over feminism. But in order to do so it is necessary to define the terms that will be used. The term *feminist* will be used to denote those who wish to eliminate all gender-based roles in society, up to and often including roles that are purely biological in nature. ("Anatomy is not destiny," goes the slogan.) Though that proposal takes many forms and has many faces, it is at the heart of what it means to be a feminist today. A *traditionalist,* on the other hand, is one who wishes to maintain gender-based roles in society. The traditionalist argues that gender is a valid basis for defining social (not to mention biological) roles, that males and females are not "equal" in the sense of being interchangeable, and that society can and must observe gender differences.

Three major subgroups must be distinguished among the feminists.[3] First, there are the *secular feminists* who come to their feminism via a straightforward humanism that disallows any voice in the matter to God, revelation, or religion. Feminism represents a crucial aspect of their humanistic vision of what the world should be, and they advocate it with great enthusiasm. Second, there are the *liberal religious feminists* who maintain various ties with the Judeo-Christian religious establishment and who view themselves as moving somehow within that tradition. Although their feminist agenda is virtually indistinguishable from that of their secular counterparts, it is usually set forth within a liberal Jewish or Christian theological framework. Finally there are *evangelical feminists* who hold to conservative views of the Bible and theology but who nevertheless embrace the feminist proposals to abolish gender-based roles in society, church, and home. Evangelical feminists believe that the Bible, which they consider authoritative, is congenial to feminist ideas when rightly understood, and they use it constantly to buttress their feminist proposals.[4]

With that taxonomy of groups in mind, it is time to turn to three important areas of theological debate: the doctrine of Scripture, the doctrine of God, and the doctrine of man. Other areas of theology will enter the discussion periodically, but these three areas are most seriously at stake.

THE DOCTRINE OF SCRIPTURE

Evangelical Christians must surely agree with Ramm that the doctrine of Scripture is not the essence of Christianity.[5] On the other hand, one's view of the Bible is crucial in determining how one approaches the feminist debate. Hence no other realm of theology has received more attention than bibliology, especially toward the conservative end of the theological spectrum.

Secular feminists, of course, have no time for the Bible at all and are irritated at the very mention of it. They consider the Bible to be a relic of antiquity that is useful only in providing more examples of how men have oppressed women through the years. They rule out all attempts to appeal to the Bible.

Liberal religious feminists, by contrast, vary widely in their approach to the Bible. Some, like their secular counterparts, reject it altogether as an oppressive, patriarchal burden that must be cast off before any real progress can be achieved.[6] Others of a less radical bent seek to retain for the Bible some semblance of the role it has played in the church throughout the centuries, yet seemingly from motives more historical than theological. From such feminists the Bible often receives much attention but with feminist conclusions assured from the outset. Moreover, liberal religious feminists harbor little hesitation to dismiss large portions of Scripture as inauthentic, unhistorical, mythological, sexist, or simply erroneous.

The freedom with which the liberal feminists revise or reject the Bible's teachings stems from their view of the very nature of the Bible. Modern concepts of biblical revelation lend themselves to a "pick and choose" approach that allows the interpreter to accept what is congenial and leave whatever seems deficient. Hence the liberal case for or against some point in the feminism debate, although often couched in biblical terms or concepts, is seldom dependent on biblical authority, since such an argument from authority requires precisely the kind of Bible liberal views disallow.

In the view of most modern liberal theologians revelation must not be equated with the Bible. Rather, revelation is viewed as the product of personal encounter with God's acts in history, preeminently in the act of God in Christ. The Bible may therefore be a fallible human witness to God's revelation in history, but it is not itself revelation. It cannot be because revelation is not propositional. All past Christian ideas, including those in the Bible, are open to evaluation, reformulation, or even rejection in the light of fresh encounters with God's redemptive acts. Consequently, revelation is never finished and complete; it is always continuous, unfolding, building out of the process of culture and experience.

With such a view of the Bible it should come as no surprise that liberal Christian feminists show little patience with attempts to establish biblical precepts or patterns as normative for contemporary Christians. The Bible is merely a human witness to God's dealings with His people in the past, not a handbook for the church today. To view the teachings of the Scriptures as God's will for all times and places is, according to that view, absurd and represents a misunderstanding of the nature of the Bible. Therefore liberal Christian feminists, although not ruling biblical arguments out of court, nevertheless set them aside as irrelevant whenever they contradict established societal insights.

Another important feature of a liberal view of the Bible is its strong attachment to the various methods of higher criticism. That bears directly on how the Bible is used by liberals in the debate over feminism. For example, Robin Scroggs, a respected professor of New Testament at Chicago Theological Seminary, wrote a widely quoted article entitled "Paul and the Eschatological Woman" in which he attempted to establish the apostle Paul as "the only certain and consistent spokesman for the liberation and equality of women in the New Testament."[7] How Scroggs accomplishes that goal is instructive. He begins by dismissing as inauthentic most of the passages in the epistles that contradict his view. "Ephesians, Colossians, and the Pastorals are . . . immediately discarded and, for our purposes, hopefully forgotten. Also to be discarded as a post-Pauline gloss is 1 Corinthians 14:33b-36, which prohibits women from speaking in the Christian assemblies."[8] Thus Scroggs is left with only 1 Corinthians 11:2-16 standing in the way of Paul's full rehabilitation as a feminist. Of that passage he says, "In its present form this is hardly one of Paul's happier compositions. The logic is obscure at best and contradictory at worst. The word choice is peculiar; the tone, peevish. All these difficulties point to some hidden agenda, hidden probably to the Apostle himself as well as his readers."[9] Paul's "hidden agenda," Scroggs believes, was a fear of homosexuality. Nonetheless, Scroggs proceeds in an adroit bit of revisionist exegesis to show that no subordination of the woman is suggested in 1 Corinthians 11. So, considering that the only other "authentically

Pauline" comment on the subject is Galatians 3:28 ("There is neither male nor female; for you are all one in Christ Jesus."), Paul was actually a strong spokesman for the liberation and equality of women.[10]

Two of the responses to Scrogg's article show the variety of liberal feminist approaches to the Bible. On the one hand, Scroggs was rebuked by Mary Daly for even attempting to portray Paul as a feminist. Said she, "It is rather obscene to be more concerned with justifying an author long dead and with berating women for an alleged lack of scholarship than with the deep injustice itself that is being perpetrated by religion."[11] On the other hand, Scroggs's approach to the New Testament passages did not go far enough for William Walker, who agrees with Scroggs that the pastorals, Ephesians, and Colossians are non-Pauline, and that 1 Corinthians 14:33b-36 is a post-Pauline gloss. Walker takes Scroggs's argument one step further to argue that 1 Corinthians 11:2-16 is also unreliable.

> My conclusion, then, is that 1 Cor. 11:2-16 is an interpolation, that it consists of three originally separate and distinct pericopae, each dealing with a somewhat different though related topic, and that none of the three pericopae is authentically Pauline. This means, of course, that the passage cannot be used as a source for determining Paul's attitude toward the proper status and role of women. If the authenticity of 1 Tim. 2:8-15; Tit. 2:3-5; Eph. 5:22-23; Col. 3:18-19; and 1 Cor. 14:33b-36 (or 34-35) is similarly rejected on critical grounds, as I am inclined to do, then the genuine Pauline corpus contains none of the passages which advocate male supremacy and female subordination in any form. On the contrary, the only direct Pauline statement on the subject is Gal. 3:28, which insists on absolute equality in Christ.[12]

Evangelical feminists typically take a much less critical approach to the Bible. Admittedly, some are willing to question the Pauline genuineness of the Pastorals and the historicity of Genesis 2. For example, Paul Jewett raises doubts about the Pauline authorship of 1 Timothy and distinguishes those epistles "that are directly from the apostle's pen" from "those that are indirectly so."[13]

Both Jewett and Virginia Mollenkott speak of the "story of

Adam's rib" being "poetic narrative," "myth," or "saga" rather than history.[14] Yet judged against the theological spectrum as a whole, even Jewett and Mollenkott, not to mention their more conservative feminist companions, must be placed in the conservative camp.

But the question remains: How do evangelical feminists square their feminism with a commitment to the authority of the Bible? Since the traditionalists, the secular feminists, and most liberal religious feminists alike believe the Bible teaches the subordination of women, how is it that the evangelical feminists alone find their authoritative Bible upholding feminism?

The evangelical feminists have worked valiantly to solve that dilemma, and in doing so have proposed a variety of complicated solutions.[15] Each of the solutions has raised massive questions about how evangelicals are to understand the Bible and its relevance to modern readers. At the simplest level some evangelical feminists have attempted to solve the problem exegetically, arguing that both ancient and modern readers have been reading the subordination of women into the text rather than deriving it from the text. Other evangelicals have suggested that the problems must be seen as largely hermeneutical, having to do with the relevance of key biblical passages to a modern audience. According to that argument, the cultural baggage of the Bible must be discarded rather than set up as normative for today.[16] In recent years a third approach has gained momentum among evangelicals. This position argues that even though the Bible does affirm the subordination of women, that aspect of biblical teaching is simply in error.[17] It should be noted that the third approach begins to blur any clear distinction between the evangelical and liberal feminists by requiring a "canon within a canon" view of inspiration. The Bible is no longer viewed in its entirety as God's Word. Rather it is God's Word mingled with elements of error contributed by the human authors, and the two must be sorted out by the interpreter. Traditionally evangelicals have rejected such a view of the Bible, but evangelical feminists who resort to that means of squaring their feminism with conservative biblical commitments usually insist on retaining their evangelical credentials.[18]

It is interesting to observe that the evangelical feminist position, which attempts to straddle a difficult fence, is found wanting by opponents from both sides. Traditionalists, of course, although granting some worthy arguments and correctives in their position, reject its egalitarian conclusions out of hand. They believe the evangelical feminists have unwittingly allowed the secular culture to set the social/political agenda and are now trying to cut the Bible to fit.[19] Significantly, observers at the other end of the spectrum tend to read the situation in a similar way, agreeing that the attempt to straddle the fence is unacceptable, albeit for different reasons. Thus, referring to the evangelical feminists as "young evangelicals" or "activist evangelicals," Robert Price observes, "Most conservative evangelicals have been taught that personal opinions and cultural views are worthless unless they can make direct appeal to a biblical warrant of some sort."[20] He then continues:

> The young evangelical approaches the problem like this: "Feminism (for example) is true; the Bible teaches the truth; therefore the Bible *must* teach feminism." Now it is far from obvious that the Bible explicitly *teaches* feminism, yet the young evangelical will feel that he or she has no right to be a feminist unless "the Bible tells me so." Thus the primary task of the reform-minded evangelical is to make the Bible teach feminism in the most plausible way.[21]

After discussing the differences among evangelical feminists, Price states, "The agreed-upon goal is that the Bible is to support feminism. The debate is over the best way to arrive at this predetermined goal exegetically! The Bible *must* support the desired social position; otherwise how can the young evangelical believe it, much less persuade fellow evangelicals?"[22] In that way, says Price, evangelical feminists "think to espouse positions because of the Bible, but do so actually because of unsuspected political/cultural factors."[23]

The questions raised by the feminist issue in the realm of bibliology are far-reaching. They sprawl across the broad reaches of arguments over the nature of revelation, higher criticism, hermeneutics, and inerrancy. They cut through the entire width of the theological spectrum, left to right. Yet at the heart of the discussion are these recurring questions: What is the Bible? How does it speak to believers if, in fact, it does at all?

The answers are inextricably bound up in the debate over feminism, sometimes shaping and sometimes being shaped by the social commitments of the participants. And the debate shows no sign of letting up.

THE DOCTRINE OF GOD

As important as the discussion of the Bible may be, it is arguable that even this should be viewed as symptomatic of still deeper philosophical and theological issues. Those deeper issues have to do with questions about the fundamental nature of physical and metaphysical reality. At the core of those issues lies the realm of theology proper.

One thing is certain. For most feminists the God of the ancient Christian creeds will not do. As feminists Elizabeth Clark and Herbert Richardson put it, "The emancipation of women, we are sure, will demand a new understanding of God."[24] Traditional Christian concepts of deity are too "patriarchal" to support a feminist ideology, Clark and Richardson argue, so those concepts must be replaced with views more amenable to egalitarianism, which is the unquestioned first principle to which all else must be accommodated.[25]

To secular feminists, of course, that first principle requires the elimination of God altogether.

> Traditional theism, especially faith in the prayer-hearing God, assumed to love and care for persons, to hear and understand their prayers and to be able to do something about them, is an unproved and outmoded faith. Salvationism, based on mere affirmation, still appears as harmful, diverting people with false hopes of heaven hereafter. Reasonable minds look to other means for survival.[26]

That should not be interpreted to mean that secular humanists are without faith. They have simply transferred their faith from God to man (cf. Rom. 1:23, 25). Thus "views that merely reject theism are not equivalent to humanism" because "they lack commitment to the positive belief in the possibilities of human progress and to the values central to it."[27] Secular humanists believe man must be his own God. Hence the theology of the humanist is anthropocentric.

> We find insufficient evidence for belief in the existence of a
> supernatural. It is either meaningless or irrelevant to the ques-
> tion of the survival and fulfillment of the human race. As
> nontheists, we begin with humans not God, nature not deity. . . .
> We can discover no divine purpose or providence for the human
> species. While there is much that we do not know, humans are
> responsible for what we are or will become. No deity will save
> us, we must save ourselves.[28]

With man thus ensconced as creator and savior, feminism is
free to flourish. There exists no blueprint to follow, no purpose
or pattern to act out. Humans are now creating themselves and
can be whatever they will be.

Liberal religious feminists, by contrast, are more interested in
redefining God than in eliminating Him.[29] Indeed, God is not a
"Him" at all. The overwhelming masculinity of the biblical
references to God is merely another evidence of male-
dominated patriarchal thinking throughout the centuries.
Quite literally, the feminists believe, men have made God in
their own image.[30] Conceptions of God as Father, Master, Lord,
and King are resisted by feminists; they are, to put it bluntly,
sexist. A more balanced approach that draws on the insights of
women will see God to be something quite different from traditional portraits.

The revised picture of God that emerges from liberal thought
usually moves away from a sovereign, transcendent, immutable, personal Being toward more fluid, evolutionary, process-
oriented visions. Traditional or (especially) Barthian views are
rejected in favor of more limited and impersonal conceptions
based on notions such as Tillich's Ground of Being, or the
philosophies of Whitehead, James, Jaspers, or Heidigger.[31]

Such modern definitions of God are infinitely more congenial to feminism. With those open-ended views of deity the
remaking of society becomes a constant priority. There is no
primordial divine pattern or design for the creature to discover
or fulfill. The world is a kaleidoscope, ever evolving and unfolding the divine call to freedom and liberation in Christ. Thus
the transcending of the old and the redefining of the new is
always on the human agenda. God's love is ever on the side of
liberation from structures and stereotypes, moving men and

women toward freedom from all forms of oppression, overt or covert. Hence the feminist movement becomes one of God's most noble causes. To press for the complete liberation of one half of the human population is nothing less than working for the establishment of God's Kingdom on earth.

That freedom to redefine God at will is a direct result of liberal views of revelation. Most liberal thinkers would acknowledge that the biblical writers seemed to view God along the lines of traditional thought, but they would then argue that the writers of the Bible were simply men of their times and limited in their perspectives. Their word cannot be final or definitive. But how do evangelical feminists, who claim a finished and authoritative revelation in the Bible, manage the conflict between the biblical picture and their egalitarian views?

The answer is that although evangelical feminists sometimes find their conservative view of God to be heavy baggage, their commitments to the inspiration of the Bible prevent them from casting it aside. Liberal feminists find oppresssive the biblical notion of a sovereign, immutable, personal God whose design and will is to be obeyed by His creatures, and they dismiss it as a typical projection of the long-dominant male imagination.[32] A conservative view of Scripture, however, prevents such an easy dismissal, leaving evangelical feminists the precarious task of balancing an ancient, biblical view of the Creator with a modern, egalitarian view of the creature. Since the two do not mix easily, both the ancient writers and today's liberals appear more consistent in their divergent visions than the evangelical feminists who attempt to synthesize the two. Nonetheless, the difficulties have not dissuaded the evangelical feminists from trying; and the result has been a vast outpouring of literature over the past twenty years.

A perusal of that literature shows that some of the less agreeable (to egalitarianism) doctrines of theology proper are soft-pedaled or ignored (e.g., sovereignty, authority, immutability), and some of the more strident egalitarian demands are avoided or repudiated (e.g., the elimination of all authority-submission roles in society).[33] In this way the problems are minimized. But the main approach of the evangelical feminists is to argue that in Christ a new order was instituted in which all sex roles were swept away (Gal. 3:28). Egalitarianism is thus a direct and necessary deduction from Christ's redemptive work, a deduction that transcends or supercedes whatever social patterns may have existed before. Needless to say, how such a sweeping deduction could have been lost on Christ's apostles — for it is nowhere taught and often contradicted in the New Testament[34] — requires and receives a great deal of attention.

THE DOCTRINE OF MAN

The most obvious theological differences among those debating feminism fall in the realm of anthropology. Here the psalmist's question "What is man?" reverberates, seeking some definitive answer.[35]

Secular feminists have little difficulty in responding to the question, but they can claim no authority but their own for the worth of their answer. Man, they believe, can be whatever he wants to be. But they insist that mankind be measured against no other yardstick but that of his own potential. There can be no design for man apart from the one he creates for himself in his own power to be and to become.

Liberal religious feminists, on the other hand, often speak of man as God's creature, man made in the image of God, and even of God's work in history to bring man to his full potential as typified in Jesus Christ. Yet beyond such God-language the scenarios of the secular and religious feminists sound much the same. What they share is a commitment to an egalitarian society that emphasizes unity rather than polarity, sameness rather than distinctiveness, wholeness rather than dichotomy.

For both groups the goal is the transcendence of maleness and femaleness in the quest for an androgynous ideal. All strictures and stereotypes in society that emphasize sexual differentiation are viewed as pernicious and are to be resisted. According to the feminists, the healthiest people — the ones most adaptable and capable of handling the fullest range of human experience — are those who can manifest both female and male responses.[36] That is what it means to be androgynous.

The androgynous ideal is very old, reaching back at least to the *Symposium of Plato.* According to Aristophanes, human beings were originally of three types—male, female, and the Androgyne, which incorporated the characteristics of both sexes. The androgynous beings, who possessed enormous strength and vitality, arrogantly attacked the gods. Consequently Zeus split them in half, rendering them, like the others, weakened and incomplete. Thus the road to recovery of strength and vitality lies along the path to androgyny, minimizing male and female distinctions by emphasizing the androgynous possibilities in all.

Many modern feminists take that androgynous myth seriously in the sense that they find here a kernel of truth.[37] The way to harmony leads through synthesis. Dualities represent estrangement; they are unnatural and exist only to be overcome. Such crippling polarities as object-subject, reason-emotion, male-female, each so indicative of the alienation of the human situation in general and of Western culture in particular, must be integrated and correlated to find the deeper wholeness and unity that undergirds them. Hence the feminists' emphasis in the social realm on egalitarianism, interchangeability, and freedom from set roles, and their strident attacks against traditional concepts of hierarchy, authority, and obedience.[38]

What must be grasped here is that the secular or liberal feminists' social views are merely the visible manifestation of their deeper philosophical or theological commitments. That can be seen by contrasting Barth with Tillich. As Romero points out, the more traditional view of God espoused by Barth is inimical to feminism,[39] whereas the views of Tillich are more "sympathetic."[40] "The basic theme of Tillich's theology is the notion of God as Being. . . . This was the basis for a nonhierarchical view of reality. In coming to grips with historical existence and culture he attempted to overcome the many dualities that he found."[41]

For Tillich, Being was "the wholeness of reality, grasped in a unifying experience."[42] What is more, says Romero, according to Tillich, "At the end of time all the partial realizations of being will be taken up into Being itself, and all the ambiguities of existence will be overcome. This is the return movement to unity and fulfillment, which Tillich describes as the return to essentialization."[43] Thus, for feminist Romero:

> Tillich's theology of Being as creative Ground avoids the whole problem that we found so intimidating in Barth's theology—the basic authoritarianism that related man to God as slave to master, or as child to a Father who retained the characteristics of the master. Tillich's understanding of God is nonauthoritarian, and he is able to allow the human person real power by participation in the power of Being.[44]

Clearly, Tillich's notions about God and reality (along with those of other modern philosophers and theologians like him) lead naturally and easily to feminist conclusions. Both are concerned with transcending perceived dichotomies of the human situation. By contrast, the feminists believe, traditional views of God as sovereign Father and Lord lead to alienation, polarity, and hierarchy, and are responsible for much of the oppression history has known.[45] Such views must therefore be uprooted without mercy.

Perhaps nowhere in liberal feminist thought is that emphasis on moving beyond polarity toward the androgynous ideal more explicit than in their views of sin and salvation.

> Feminist theology does not hypostatize sin as an event that *happened* or as something that people *do*. Rather, it defines sin as a basic alienation within the psyche—a failure to lay claim to that part of one's humanity that one then projects onto an "other." The male's failure to claim his own emotionality, his insecurities or creatureliness, his capacity for nurturance and his need to be creative, as well as the female's failure to recognize her own aggressiveness, power, competence and intellectuality are examples of such psychic alienation. . . .
>
> Sin, then, is not so much a falling away from God or a deliberate transgression of a divine being's orders as it is a failure to recognize the God within us and our fellow creatures. Feminists are therefore more likely to stress immanence rather than transcendence. They hold that sin is institutionalized wherever hierarchies are established; for hierarchies inescapably separate persons from one another or from part of themselves. . . .
>
> For the feminists, salvation is that discovery and celebration of the 'other' in ourselves. When men discover the femininity and women their masculinity, then perhaps we can form a truly liberating and mutually enriching partnership. . . . The new hu-

manity is a humanity which is becoming, impelled by a revelation that is not located in the distant past but is only now becoming manifest in the clamor for dignity and liberation on the part of underdeveloped peoples.

Feminist theology calls for a repudiation of the old male-oriented hierarchical symbols—God as Lord, King, Master and Almighty Father—in favor of something like Tillich's notion of the "ground and power of being" or Whitehead and Hartshorne's conception of a feeling, responding, relational God.[46]

Here liberal ideas on God, revelation, humanity, sin, and salvation coalesce into a unified theology that informs and feeds the feminist social agenda.

But once again the question arises, if the feminist social vision is so deeply rooted in liberal ideas of God and reality, how can evangelicals, holding as they do to traditional views of God, espouse an unreserved feminism? The answer is, not without gaping inconsistency. Yet most of the evangelical feminists show little or no awareness of the philosophical roots of their pleas for the elimination of gender-based roles. As Price pointed out above, they seem to have appropriated their culture's political and social goals uncritically and are striving now to overcome the resulting inconsistencies.

Not all evangelical feminists have opted for their feminism naively, of course. One who has not is Jewett. Jewett is a respected evangelical theologian and as such has attempted to avoid major inconsistencies by rejecting some of the more radical feminist ideas on the one hand, and by fudging on his evangelical views on the other. For example, in a passage that Mollenkott calls "the most troubling segment of the book" to other feminists,[47] Jewett strongly rejects as unbiblical the concept of the androgyny.[48] On the other hand, Jewett also hedges on a traditional evangelical view of Scripture by holding that some of the apostle Paul's teachings in the Bible are in error.[49]

Jewett claims as the theological underpinning for his feminist position a view of the *imago dei* whose finest exponent was Barth.[50] Without rejecting "the classical view of the image,"[51] Jewett sees the image of God in Man as referring primarily to human sexuality. Basing his argument on the "simultaneous" creation of Genesis 1, rather than the "story" of Genesis 2,

Jewett argues (as did Barth) that the complementary partnership of male/female mirrors the "being in relationship" of the Trinity.[52] Then Jewett argues (as Barth did not) from that partnership to the elimination of gender-based roles. Building on the concept of the image of God and Galatians 3:28, Jewett thus attempts to bridge the incongruities of being both a feminist and an evangelical. Though Jewett's effort is better than most, his basic approach is quite typical of what most evangelical feminists hold.

The greatest difficulty for the evangelical feminists is that in the end the Bible does teach sex roles, hierarchy, male authority, and female submission. To be sure, the biblical versions of those concepts must be distinguished from both their sinful abuses throughout history and their caricatures as found in feminist rhetoric. And they should probably be distinguished further from the well-intended efforts of some of their friends to expound them. (For example, some of C. S. Lewis's ideas on hierarchy may owe more to Plato than Paul.)[53] Yet when the fog clears, objective readers of both liberal and traditional stripes find the Bible to be teaching those concepts. Furthermore, they see those concepts fitting hand in glove with an orthodox view of God and the world.[54] Liberals largely reject that biblical world view and traditionalists largely embrace it; but both agree that it comes from the Bible. Only the evangelical feminists attempt to have it both ways, pleading at once for a traditional theology and a feminist society. In the eyes of many observers, such a position seems to be a house divided against itself, and they are watching to see how long it can stand.

NOTES

1. Thomas Howard, "A Traditionalist View," *Post American* 4 (May 1975):10.
2. Ibid., p. 15.
3. Defining theological categories is a slippery business, especially where the issues are complex and the thinkers numerous. Those "subgroups," therefore, should not be viewed as clearly defined entities so much as clusters along the philosophical-theological

continuum. Moreover, any specific individual may fall between the clusters, thereby sharing some of the characteristics of two or more groups.

4. Foh distinguishes between "biblical feminists" and "Christian feminists." (Susan T. Foh, *Women and the Word of God* [Phillipsburg, N.J.: Presbyterian and Reformed, 1980], p. 3). Those categories correspond to "evangelical feminists" and "liberal religious feminists," respectively. This writer has chosen to use the latter set of categories so as to be able to include Jewish feminists in the discussion, of whom there are a growing number.

5. "Is 'Scripture Alone' The Essence of Christianity?" in *Biblical Authority*, ed. Jack Rogers (Waco, Tex.: Word, 1977), pp. 107-23.

6. "As in many other areas of religious concern, so also in the understanding of the role of women, the biblical message has been, and continues to be, regarded as both bane and blessing. From the perspective of feminist theologians the Bible has served in the past primarily as burden, and so some will argue that what has been so long a millstone should be thrown off from around our necks" (Katharine D. Sakenfeld, "The Bible and Women: Bane or Blessing," *Theology Today* 32 [October 1975]:222). See also Mary Daly, *Beyond God the Father: Toward a Philosophy of Women's Liberation* (Boston: Beacon, 1973), p. 7.

7. *Journal of the American Academy of Religion* 49 (1972):283.

8. Ibid., p. 284.

9. Ibid., p. 297.

10. See also Robin Scroggs, "Paul and the Eschatological Woman Revisited," *Journal of the American Academy of Religion* 42 (1974):532-37.

11. Daly, p. 5.

12. William O. Walker, "1 Corinthians 11:2-16 and Paul's Views Regarding Women," *Journal of Biblical Literature* 94 (March 1975):109. For the continuation of this discussion see Jerome Murphy-O'Connor, "The Non-Pauline Character of 1 Corinthians 11:2-16" *Journal of Biblical Literature* 97 (September 1978):435-36; and Jerome Murphy-O'Connor, "Sex and Logic in 1 Corinthians 11:2-16," *Catholic Biblical Quarterly* 42 (October 1980): 482-500.

13. Paul King Jewett, *Man as Male and Female* (Grand Rapids: Eerdmans, 1975), pp. 116, 119.

14. Ibid., pp. 120-28; Virginia Mollenkott, *Women, Men and the Bible* (Nashville: Abingdon, 1977), p. 101.

15. See Jack Buckley, "Paul, Women, and the Church: How Fifteen Modern Interpreters Understand Five Key Passages," *Eternity* 31 (December 1980):30-35.

16. "The most crucial question the biblical feminists have raised is how to interpret the Bible" (Foh, p. 2). For two helpful discussions

of "cultural hermeneutics," see Grant R. Osborne, "Hermeneutics and Women in the Church," *Journal of the Evangelical Theological Society* 20 (December 1977):337-52; and J. Robertson McQuilkin, "Limits of Cultural Interpretation," *Journal of the Evangelical Theological Society* 23 (June 1980):113-24.

17. See Mollenkott, pp. 90-106; and Jewett, pp. 111-49.
18. For a fuller discussion of the above three approaches to the Bible see A. Duane Litfin, "Evangelical Feminism: Why Traditionalists Reject It," *Bibliotheca Sacra* 136 (July-September 1979):260-63.
19. For example, see Foh, p. 3.
20. Robert M. Price, "A Fundamentalist Social Gospel," *Christian Century*, 28 November 1979, p. 1184.
21. Ibid.
22. Ibid.
23. Ibid., p. 1185.
24. Elizabeth Clark and Herbert Richardson, *Women and Religion: A Feminist Sourcebook of Christian Thought* (New York: Harper & Row, 1977), p. vii.
25. Many feminists are explicit about their methodological priorities. Their feminism comes first and all else is measured against that standard. For example, see Daly, p. 21; and Rosemary Radford Ruether, "The Call of Women in the Church Today," *Listening* 15 (Fall 1980): 248.
26. *Humanist Manifestos I and II* (Buffalo: Prometheus, 1973), p. 13.
27. Ibid., p. 15.
28. Ibid., p. 16.
29. Carole P. Christ quotes Susan Rennie and Kirsten Grimstad's *The New Women's Survival Sourcebook* (New York: Knopf, 1975), p. 191, as follows, "We found that wherever there are feminist communities, women are exploring psychic and nonmaterial phenomena: reinterpreting astrology; creating and celebrating feminist rituals around birth, death, menstruation; reading the Tarot; studying pre-patriarchal forms of religion; reviving and exploring esoteric goddess-centered belief systems such as wicce; developing and cultivating dream analysis, ESP, astral projection, precognition; learning psychic and homeopathic healing; rescuing the wholistic perspective of the right hemisphere of the brain from the contempt of left-brain linear mindedness. . . ." Then Christ comments, "Out (sic) of the key motifs of this spirituality movement is a new naming of ultimate power or powers. Many women are rediscovering that one of the oldest names for the fundamental energy — the energy of natural processes, the energy of life and death, the energy of sexual attraction and repulsion, the energy concentrated in meditation and ritual, the energy felt vibrating in a room when people are really speaking to one another, the energy of psychic healing — is goddess" (Carol P. Christ,

"Heretics and Outsiders: The Struggle Over Female Power in Western Religion," *Soundings* 61 [Fall 1978]:274).

30. See Dorothee Soelle, "The Emancipation That Never Happened," in *Women in a Strange Land: Search for a New Image*, ed. Clare Benedicks Fisher, Betsy Brenneman, and Anne McGrew Bunnett (Philadelphia: Fortress, 1975), pp. 84-85.

31. Joan Arnold Romero, "The Protestant Principle: A Woman's Eye View of Barth and Tillich," in *Religion and Sexism: Images of Women in the Jewish and Christian Traditions*, ed. Rosemary Radford Ruether (New York: Simon and Schuster, 1974), pp. 319-40.

32. Says Daly, "The entire conceptual apparatus of theology, developed under the conditions of patriarchy, has been the product of males and serves the interests of a sexist society" (Mary Daly, "The Women's Movement: An Exodus Community," *Religious Education* 67 [September-October 1972]:331). For a still more radical statement of this point, see Daly's latest book, *Gyn/Ecology: The Metaethics of Radical Feminism* (Boston: Beacon, 1978), a work that gives new meaning to the term *ad absurdum*.

33. See Jewett, pp. 130-31.

34. Foh, pp. 37-44.

35. According to latest reports, the new edition of the *Revised Standard Version* due out in 1990 will read in Psalm 8:4, "What is a human being that you are mindful of him, and a mortal that you care for him?" ("Unmanning the Holy Bible," *Time*, 8 December 1980, p. 128).

36. See Sandra L. Bem, "Androgyny vs. the Tight Little Lives of Fluffy Women and Chesty Men," *Psychology Today* 9 (September 1975):58-72. The term *androgyny* is from the combination of the greek terms *andros*, man, and *gyne*, woman.

37. Virginia E. O'Leary and Charlene E. Depner, "Alternative Gender Roles Among Women: Masculine, Feminine, Androgenous," *Intellect* 104 (January 1976):313-15.

38. See Sheila D. Collins, "The Familial Economy of God," *Radical Religion* 4 (1979):46-55, for a denunciation of these and other concepts (especially capitalism) as evils stemming from patriarchalism. See also Sally Gearhart, "The Lesbian and God-The Father," *Radical Religion* 1 (Spring 1974):21.

39. Romero, in *Religion and Sexism*, p. 326. As Clark and Richardson put it, "Feminists, as one would expect, find Barth's views either infuriating or laughable" (*Women and Religion*, p. 243).

40. Ibid., p. 336.

41. Ibid., p. 329.

42. Ibid., p. 332.

43. Ibid., p. 335.

44. Ibid.

45. For example, see Rosemary Radford Ruether, *New Woman/New Earth: Sexist Ideologies and Human Liberation* (New York: Seabury, 1975), p. 65; "The Call of Women in the Church Today," *Listening* 15 (Fall 1980): 246-49.

46. Sheila Collins, "Toward a Feminist Theology," *The Christian Cen-*

tury, 2 August 1972, pp. 798-99. (Copyright 1972, Christian Century Foundation. Reprinted by permission from the August 2, 1972 issue of *The Christian Century.*)

47. Mollenkott, p. 10.

48. Ibid., pp. 24-28.

49. Ibid., pp. 111-49.

50. See Karl Barth, *Church Dogmatics,* Part 3: *The Doctrine of Creation,* ed. G. W. Bromiley and T. F. Torrance (Edinburgh: T. & T. Clark, 1961), 1:42-94; 2:285-324; 4:116-240.

51. Jewett, p. 13.

52. Ibid., pp. 33-40, 43-48. For three other helpful discussions of Barth's views on male/female relationships, see A. J. McKelway, "The Concept of Subordination in Barth's Special Ethics," *Scottish Journal of Theology* 32 (1979):345-57; Clifford Green, "Liberation Theology? Karl Barth on Men and Women," *Union Seminary Quarterly Review* 29 (Spring & Summer 1974):221-31; and Clark and Richardson, pp. 239-44.

53. C. S. Lewis *A Preface to Paradise Lost* (London: Oxford U. 1942), pp. 72-80. But for a more restrained (and more biblical) view, see C. S. Lewis, "Membership," in *The Weight of Glory and Other Addresses* (Grand Rapids: Eerdmans, 1949), pp. 30-42; or Howard, pp. 8-15. For a critique of hierarchicalism, see Letha Scanzoni, "The Great Chain of Being and the Chain of Command," *The Reformed Journal* 26 (October 1976):14-18.

54. Mary Daly, *The Church and the Second Sex* (New York: Harper & Row, 1968), pp. 138-49.